Richard Baxter

The Gospel Truth

Alan C. Clifford

CHARENTON REFORMED PUBLISHING

2016

Text © The Publisher 2016

Layout © Quinta Press 2016

First published in Great Britain 2016

by Charenton Reformed Publishing

www.christiancharenton.co.uk

ISBN 978–0–9929465–0–0 (pbk)

ISBN 978–0–9929465–3–1 (hbk)

Typeset in Bembo MT Pro 12 on 14 point

by Quinta Press, Weston Rhyn, Oswestry, Shropshire

Printed and bound in Great Britain by Lightning Source

British Library Cataloguing in Publication Data.

A catalogue record for this book is available from the British Library.

Cover concept: A. C. Clifford, formatting by Barkers Print & Design,
Attleborough, Norfolk

Cover picture: the author's 1970s photograph of the Kidderminster statue.

DEDICATION

The heroes covered in this story were blest with wonderful wives.
Without them, their contributions might possibly have been less worthy
of our attention and regard. To cite but three examples, Baxter had his
Margaret, Doddridge had his Mercy and John Jones, Talsarn had his
Fanny. This unworthy author is blest with wonderful

MARIAN

to whom I gratefully dedicate this book.

SOLI DEO GLORIA

The Love of God to the World was the first womb where the work
of Redemption was conceived, John 3: 16.
Richard Baxter's first book (*Aphorismes of Justification*, 1649)

CONTENTS

ILLUSTRATIONS

PREFACE

For my own part, I admire the gifts of God in our first reformers, Luther, Melanchthon, Calvin, &c. And I know no man, since the apostles' days, whom I value and honour more than Calvin, ... (*The Saints' Everlasting Rest*, 1650).

A Christian man who, in the estimate of others, was ranked with the Prophets, the Apostles and the Church Fathers, must be extraordinary by any standard. Such was Richard Baxter. More widely read than Shakespeare in his day, he is one of England's greatest Christian preachers. His extraordinary seventeenth-century ministry at Kidderminster, Worcestershire is celebrated by an appropriate local statue. A more significant monument, Baxter's nationwide influence was diffused by such still-gripping 'page turners' as *The Saints' Everlasting Rest* and *Call to the Unconverted*. His lovely hymn 'Ye holy angels bright' is still enjoyed by modern worshippers. Neither must we ignore his colourful and dramatic life as recorded in his autobiography with its exotic Latin title *Reliquiae Baxterianae*. Baxter also made a mark on English history by his courageous stand before the infamous Judge Jeffreys in 1685.

Richard Baxter is arguably the greatest of all the Puritans—a giant among giants! As a saintly, energetic, dedicated, brilliant and large-hearted servant of Christ, he is probably the most effective pastor-evangelist this country has ever known. Certainly, what C. H. Spurgeon was to the 19th, and George Whitefield (together with the Wesley brothers) was to the 18th, Baxter was to 17th century England. A. B. Grosart wrote that Baxter is said 'to have drawn more hearts to the great bleeding heart than any other Englishman of his age'.

Furthermore, his pen-productions proved just as famous as his pulpit ministry at Kidderminster. The sheer scale and variety of his contribution over a forty-two year period is breathtaking, including his late massive scholarly Latin treatise *Methodus theologiae christianae* (1681) and the earlier popular persuasive to holiness *A Saint or a Brute* (1662). Remarkably, many of Baxter's writings are still being published 300 years on. His style remains surprisingly lucid and lively when most of his contemporaries are obviously dated. Baxter's books still retain their power to inform, arouse and edify the modern reader.

This book has an unusually-critical as well as celebratory character. Besides revisiting the eulogies of those who knew, heard and loved Richard Baxter in Part I, the author offers challenging critiques of Baxter's numerous critics. It is an attempt to vindicate the man. Part II provides the complete texts of two of Baxter's shorter publications, probably the first (1656) and last (1692) of his evangelistic works. Consisting of a selection of my articles dating from 1982 to 2014, Part III explores the contributions of those whose lives and ministries inspired, reflected and perpetuated his wonderful legacy.

Commissioned by Oxford University Press, I am thus delighted to acknowledge current projects to publish scholarly editions of Baxter's Autobiography (5 vols.) and Correspondence (9 vols.), under the direction of Professor John Coffey of Leicester University and Professor Neil Keeble of Stirling University, in conjunction with Dr Williams's Library, London.

ACKNOWLEDGEMENTS

For the type-setting, layout and production of this book I am grateful for the personal interest and professional expertise of Dr Digby James of Quinta Press. Barkers Print & Design are thanked for help with formatting the cover and the facilities provided by Lightning Source are much appreciated. The engraving of Baxter comes from my 1701 copy of his *Paraphrase on the New Testament*. That of his trial before Judge Jeffreys is found in Wylie's *History of Protestantism* (London, Paris & New York: Cassel, n.d.), Volume 3. Dr Edmund Calamy's portrait is taken from A. H. Drysdale's *Short Biographies for the People* (London: Religious Tract Society, 1890) and that of William Bates is found in his *Whole Works* (London: 1815), Volume 1. I am grateful also to John Smith of Chingford for supplying a picture of Richard Baxter's house at Eaton Constantine, Shropshire. Thanks are also due to a sizeable circle of Christian friends. Their constant encouragement and interest in this project has been invaluable. Due to the controversial nature of the book and the expected negative reaction to it, I refrain from naming them lest I incriminate them! Suffice to say that they share the theological and pastoral implications of this book.

Biographical Introduction[1]

A brief outline

Birth and Education

Who then was Richard Baxter? He was born at Rowton, Shropshire on 12 November 1615, returning at the age of ten to his parents' home at Eaton Constantine, 'a mile from the Wrekin Hill, and above half a mile from Severn River and five miles from Shrewsbury'.[2] His parents were godly folk yet lacking the means to educate an obviously gifted son. Young Richard was deeply influenced by the writings of puritan authors like William Perkins and Richard Sibbes. Following an early conversion, he had an immense thirst for knowledge. Although he never attended university, he probably mastered more information through the years than many a college professor!

Ordination

A private education led to ordination by the Bishop of Worcester in 1638 and a brief curacy at Bridgenorth. For all his zeal, his parishioners were a 'hard-hearted' people. A loyal son of the Church of England with nonconformist sympathies, Baxter's attachment to Puritanism was heightened by the 'Romanising' measures of Archbishop Laud. Baxter accepted an invitation to a living at Kidderminster where he was to exercise an extraordinary ministry for around sixteen years (over two periods).

Parliamentary Chaplain

With the advent of the Civil War, he supported the Parliamentary cause. His life being threatened by the Royalists of Worcestershire, he withdrew to Coventry where he became a chaplain. After the decisive Battle of Naseby

---

1 For overall factual usefulness, see Geoffrey F. Nuttall, *Richard Baxter* (London: Nelson, 1965).

2 Richard Baxter, *The Autobiography of Richard Baxter*, ed. J. M. Lloyd Thomas (London: J. M. Dent, 1931), 3. Hereinafter *Autobiography*.

(1645), Baxter served in Colonel Whalley's regiment. Unlike John Owen, he had first-hand experience of the war, being present at several battles.[1] However, he remained an observer, and was never a combatant: 'I never struck with a sword in war or peace'.[2] Yet, as a contender for Christian truth, he was to become embroiled in battles of another kind. Indeed, his experience of religious sectarianism during these years disturbed him deeply. He considered that the war had been a disaster for the Gospel. His special dread was the alarming growth of antinomianism—a stress on the doctrines of grace at the expense of practical godliness. These developments profoundly influenced Baxter's conception of the Christian life. In fact, he acknowledges he had shared some of these errors himself:

> I had ... engaged myself as a disputer against Universal Redemption ... but [when] new notions called me to new thoughts ... I went to the Scripture, where its whole current, but especially Matth. 25 did quickly satisfy me in the doctrine of Justification: and I remembered two or three things in Dr Twisse (whom I most esteemed) ... [who] ... every where professeth, that Christ so far died for all, as to purchase them Justification and Salvation, if they believe.[3]

The Kidderminster Ministry

On leaving the army in 1647, Baxter was seriously ill. While convalescing at the home of Sir Thomas Rouse at Worcester, he conceived his first two books—*Aphorismes of Justification* and the *Saints Everlasting Rest*. They were published in 1649 soon after resuming his parish ministry. Baxter never enjoyed robust health. He says "In my labours at Kidderminster after my return I did all under languishing weakness, being seldom an hour free from pain ..."[4] But how God blessed the prayers and preaching of Richard Baxter! Although the parish church was large, five galleries were added before long. Dr D. Martyn Lloyd-Jones had no hesitation in saying of 'Baxter at Kidderminster' that 'we are entitled to speak of revival'.[5]

---

1   Tim Cooper, *John Owen, Richard Baxter and the Formation of Nonconformity* (Farnham, Surrey: Ashgate, 2011); also 'Why Did Richard Baxter and John Owen Diverge? The Impact of The First Civil War' in *The Journal of Ecclesiastical History*, 61.3 (Cambridge: CUP, 2010).

2   *Richard Baxter's Penitent Confession* (London: 1691), 49.

3   *Richard Baxter's Catholick Theologie* (London: 1675), Preface.

4   *Autobiography*, 76.

5   'Revival: An Historical and Theological Survey' (Puritan Conference Report, 1959) in *The*

He published numerous books during the Kidderminster years, including the famous *Gildas Salvianus: The Reformed Pastor* (1656) and *A Call to the Unconverted* (1658). Of the *Call*, Baxter declared, "… I published this little book, which God hath blessed with unexpected success beyond all the rest that I have written (except *The Saints Rest*)."[1]

The town witnessed an astonishing spiritual and moral reformation. In Baxter's words, "On the Lord's Days there was no disorder to be seen in the streets, but you might hear an hundred families singing psalms and repeating sermons as you passed through the streets. In a word, when I came thither at first there was about one family in a street that worshipped God, and when I came away, there were some streets where there was not passed one family … that did not so …"[2]

Passionate Preacher

There was a heavenly unction and fervour about Baxter's preaching. None could hear him without being deeply affected. Burdened for souls while gripped with persistent pain and weakness, he tells us that he preached 'as a dying man to dying men, never sure to preach again'.[3] When Baxter preached of Christ, faith, repentance, holiness, heaven and hell, his vivid and impassioned eloquence left none doubting their reality. Not surprisingly, Baxter deplored lifeless preaching: 'Nothing is more indecent than a dead preacher, speaking to dead hearers the living truths of the living God!'[4]

Protestant Unity

Baxter was not only famous for his evangelistic and pastoral work. His view of Roman Catholicism was uncompromising, yet, grieved at the sectarianism of the times, he is also remembered for his attempts to unite Protestants. Believers of all denominations regularly worshipped at Kidderminster parish church and his 'Worcestershire Association' successfully united ministers on essential gospel truths. It became a model for similar gatherings in other counties.

What then was Richard Baxter's churchmanship? As a conservative Puritan,

---

Puritans: Their Origins and Successors (Edinburgh: The Banner of Truth Trust, 1987), 3.

1   *Autobiography*, 96.

2   Ibid. 79.

3   Ibid. 79 and 281.

4   Cited in *Lectures on Preaching* in *The Works of the Rev. P. Doddridge, D. D.* ed. E. Williams and E. Parsons (Leeds: 1804), v. 461.

he believed the Church of England needed further reformation. Believing that the 'old diocesan frame'[1] was 'intolerable',[2] he welcomed Parliament's reform agenda[3] and spoke warmly of the Westminster Assembly of Divines. However, he thought some of the Presbyterians—with whom he had most sympathy—too hierarchical. Independents and Baptists he thought too 'ultra' in many things. They encouraged fragmentation and pride. However, Baxter loved all true godly men, whatever their views about church order and baptism. Disgusted by 'party spirit', Baxter the 'mere Nonconformist' liked to call himself a 'Catholic Christian'[4] and a 'mere Christian"[5] who would as soon be a 'martyr for love as any article of the creed.'[6] His guiding principle was *'unity in things necessary and liberty in things unnecessary, and charity in all'*.[7] It was this that justified his policy of 'occasional conformity' after 1662: his rejection of imposed Anglicanism did not imply that he thought everything Anglican was wrong. Imperfect Christians ought not to deny some degree of fellowship with other imperfect Christians, especially when the 'fundamentals' were sincerely believed and faithfully preached.[8] Nonetheless, besides irritating the puritan sects, such ideals placed Baxter on a collision course with the eventually-restored and inflexible Anglican establishment.

Authentic Calvinist

Richard Baxter also proposed a solution to the major theological division of the day, the Calvinist-Arminian debate. Published in later years, his monumental folio *Richard Baxter's Catholic Theologie* (1675) is testimony to his enduring efforts in this regard. While he believed Arminians were in error at many points, Baxter believed that *High* Calvinists like John Owen (whose antipathy to universal atonement he once shared) were guilty of an 'ultra-orthodox' over-reaction. As we have seen, the Civil War conflict

---

1   *Autobiography*, 155.

2   Ibid. 98.

3   See *The Constitutional Documents of the Puritan Revolution 1625–1660*, ed. S. R. Gardiner (Oxford: Clarendon Press, 1906), 137ff.

4   Nuttall, *Richard Baxter*, 84.

5   *Autobiography*, 293.

6   Ibid. 170; also William Bates, *A Funeral Sermon* William Bates, *A Funeral Sermon for the Reverend, Holy and Excellent Divine, Mr Richard Baxter* (London: 1692), 120; also W. Bates, *The Whole Works of the Rev. W. Bates, DD*, ed. W. Farmer (London: 1815), iv. 297ff.

7   *Autobiography*, 91.

8   See *Autobiography*, ed. N. H. Keeble (London: Dent, 1974), pp. xxff.

and the consequent war of words had led him to a fresh examination of the Bible. So, as the Huguenot theologian Amyraut had argued in France, Baxter—aided by the views of Dr William Twisse—argued in England that, notwithstanding the truth of sovereign divine election, the Scriptures taught a designed sufficiency in the death of Christ for all mankind. This double emphasis was rooted in the paradox of God's hidden purposes and his revealed promises. Besides being rigorously scriptural, he believed that his position possessed vital evangelistic and pastoral advantages. Fully endorsing the Canons of Dort, Baxter pointed out that John Calvin and several members of the Westminster Assembly also taught universal atonement. Above all, he argued his case from plain texts of the Bible:

> When God saith so expressly that Christ died for all [2 Cor. 5: 14–15], and tasted death for every man [Heb. 2: 9], and is the ransom for all [1 Tim. 2: 6], and the propitiation for the sins of the whole world [1 Jn. 2: 2], it beseems every Christian rather to explain in what sense Christ died for all, than flatly to deny it.[1]

Against Antinomianism

Baxter's response to antinomianism proved troublesome. Rightly stressing that the sinner's justification before God involves a trusting, loving and obedient faith in Christ as Prophet, Priest *and* King (thus the gospel covenant involves grace *and* law), his doctrine of justification—involving a proper understanding of faith and works—was misunderstood. Yet his apparent deviations from orthodoxy were more verbal than real. His view being sounder than Owen's, his valid emphasis on the necessity of holiness for salvation never detracted from the Reformation doctrine of salvation by grace alone through faith in Christ alone:

> I abhor the opinion of any works necessary to justification or salvation, or to any common blessings in the sense of Paul; such as make the reward to be of debt, and not of grace. I think few men living, are less tempted to magnify or trust to any worth of their own, than I am. I look not for a bit of bread, or an hour's ease, or life, or the pardon, or acceptance of one duty, or of my holiest affections (so faulty are they by their great imperfection) but merely from the free grace of God, and the merits

---

1 See Richard Baxter, *The Universal Redemption of Mankind* (London: 1694), Joseph Read, 'To the Reader' and 286.

and intercession of Christ. ... The faith by which we are justified, is that true Christianity which includeth our believing consent to God the Father, Son, and Holy Ghost; our belief of Christ, and our thankful acceptance of him to be our Teacher, Intercessor or Priest, and King, with his offered Grace; and that this acceptance is with desire, love, and hope, expressed in a holy contract or covenant. This is the soul's marriage with Christ, and allegiance to him, and it includeth the renouncing our trust in all creatures, or in any righteousness of our own, so far as they would usurp the least part of Christ's office, works, or honour. None of all this is justification by works.[1]

Nonconformist Leader

While Baxter was sympathetic with the Parliamentary cause, he was unhappy with many features of Oliver Cromwell's Protectorate. Believing –surely not without *some* qualification—'our ancient monarchy to be a blessing and not an evil',[2] Baxter considered the Lord Protector's 'design' was 'to do good in the main, and to promote the Gospel and the interest of godliness more than any had done before him'.[3] Indeed, the preacher's ministry had flourished more under Cromwell's rule than under the Stuarts. However, in his view, the excessive religious liberty of the new order was no just alternative to the tyranny of the old. Following Oliver's death, Baxter's concern to resolve differences and promote concord continued. He dedicated his *Five Disputations of Church Government and Worship* (1659) and *A Key for Catholics* (1659) to Richard Cromwell who, much to the chagrin of John Owen, favoured the Presbyterians and government by political consensus.

In 1660, Baxter left Kidderminster for London. He was involved in plans to restore Charles II to the throne, and he preached before Parliament at St Margaret's, Westminster. Baxter became a chaplain to the King who offered him the bishopric of Hereford. Preferring to return to his people at Kidderminster—a move which was thwarted—Baxter refused the King's offer on conscientious grounds.

Anxious to secure a just church settlement, he took a prominent part in the Savoy Conference of 1661 where he stood shoulder to shoulder with moderate Episcopalians and Presbyterians. Still uncomfortable with several

---

1   Richard Baxter, *A Defence of Christ and Free Grace* (London: 1690), 'To the Reader' and 24.
2   *Autobiography*, 140.
3   Ibid. 70.

unbiblical features of the *Book of Common Prayer*, Baxter contributed to the liturgical discussion by producing his *Reformed Liturgy*, written in the space of fourteen days.

The Great Ejection

However, Baxter's essential conservatism blinded him to the scheming duplicity of Charles II. Although the restored King had promised to grant religious liberty, many, including Baxter, were utterly deceived. Once it became clear that the Church of England was to be restored with all its strictness, Baxter soon realised his duty. A few months before the infamous Act of Uniformity came into effect on 24 August 1662—which led to the ejection of around 2,000 sound, godly, evangelical ministers—Baxter bid farewell to the Church of England in a sermon at Blackfriars. The inflexible and intolerant terms of the Act—deliberately framed to secure this objective—made it impossible for conscientious Bible-believing pastors to conform.[1] Re-ordination by an unbiblical episcopate and strict imposition of an anti-Puritan liturgy and lectionary were too much to stomach. Strict conformity to the Word of God was all that mattered to the courageous Nonconformists. Becoming the leading figure among the ejected clergy, Baxter's account of the 'Great Ejection' vividly portrays the pain of his brethren and their families:

> When Bartholomew Day came, about one thousand eight hundred or two thousand ministers were silenced and cast out. ... And now came in the great inundation of calamities, which in many streams overwhelmed thousands of godly Christians, together with their pastors ... Hundreds of able ministers, with their wives and children, had neither house nor bread ... The people's poverty was so great that they were not able much to relieve their ministers ...[2]

Marriage

In September 1662 Baxter married Margaret Charlton, a young woman whom he had led to Christ at Kidderminster. He was 47 and she only 23. Many tongues wagged and eyebrows were raised, for Baxter had favoured celibate self-denial in the interests of pastoral dedication. That said, he

---

1 See A. H. Drysdale, *History of the Presbyterians in England* (London: Pubication Committee of the Presbyterian Church of England, 1889), 383ff; also G. F. Nuttall, 'The First Nonconformists' in *From Uniformity to Unity*, ed. G. F. Nuttall and O. Chadwick (London: SPCK, 1962), 149ff.

2 *Autobiography*, 175.

amusingly reports: 'And I think the king's marriage was scarce more talked of than mine'.[1] However, it was indeed a marriage made in heaven. The couple were ideally suited, and Margaret was to prove a great comfort and encouragement to Richard until her early death in 1681.

Published soon after his wife's death, grief-stricken Baxter's *Poetical Fragments* reveal the mystical side to his nature. Besides including the two still-popular hymns 'Ye holy angels bright' and 'Lord, it belongs not to my care', the work contains some pretty impressive poetry, bordering on the Miltonic. In the 'Epistle to the Reader', we discover his love of music:

> For myself, I confess that harmony and melody are the pleasure and elevation of my soul and have made a Psalm of Praise in the Holy Assembly the chief delightful exercise of my religion and my life; and hath helped to bear down all the objections which I have heard against church music, and against the 149, 150 Psalms. It was not the least comfort that I had in the converse of my late dear wife, that our first in the morning, and last in bed at night, was a Psalm of Praise, (till the hearing of others interrupted it).[2]

Evidently, the Baxters sang lustily and fervently! One also imagines how glorious the singing must have been at Kidderminster when the five added galleries were full! While we may assume the music was confined to the tunes of the metrical psalms, one wonders what Baxter might have thought in later years of the church music of Henry Purcell (1658–95). If the pompous Anglican service might have been not quite to his puritanical liking, it is difficult to imagine—had it been technically possible—he wouldn't have relished the 'pietistic' music of his near-contemporary, the German Lutheran composer Dietrich Buxtehude (1637–1707). After all, several of Baxter's works were translated into German, widely distributed and warmly appreciated.

The Plague Year

Baxter was living with his wife and mother-in-law at Acton in Middlesex when the terrible plague sent many to an early grave during the hot summer of 1665. Most of the conforming Anglicans left the city while the nonconformist pastors gloriously adorned their ordination vows, a fact Baxter justly observed:

---

1   Ibid. 174.

2   Richard Baxter, *Poetical Fragments: Heart Employment with God and Itself* (London: 1681), 'Preface to the Reader'.

And when the plague grew hot most of the conformable ministers fled, and left their flocks in the time of their extremity, whereupon divers Nonconformists, pitying the dying and distressed people that had none to call the impenitent to repentance, nor to help men to prepare for another world, nor to comfort them in their terrors, when about ten thousand died in a week, resolved that no obedience to the laws of any mortal men whosoever could justify them for neglecting of men's souls and bodies in such extremities, ...[1]

Baxter and his family were preserved. The great fire of London occurred the following year, 'one judgement on the back of another' as one historian wrote. The widespread devastation included old St Paul's cathedral where, twelve years earlier (17 December 1654), Baxter had preached to the largest congregation he ever witnessed.[2] That said, he lamented the destruction of books more than buildings:

And among the rest, the loss of books was an exceeding great detriment to the interest of piety and learning. Almost all the booksellers in St Paul's churchyard brought their books into vaults under St Paul's church, where it was thought almost impossible that fire should come. But the church itself being on fire, the exceeding weight of the stones falling down did break into the vault and let in the fire, and they could not come near to save the books.[3]

Christian Apologist

Notwithstanding these events, Baxter preached and pastored when he could. He was also busy with his books. *The Divine Life* was published in 1664, *Reasons for the Christian Religion* appeared in 1667 followed in 1670 by *A Cure of Church Divisions*. Then *More Reasons for the Christian Religion* appeared in 1672. Powicke is right to highlight Baxter's magnificent accomplishment in demonstrating the intellectual integrity of the Christian Faith. *The Reasons of the Christian Religion* 'still stands as a monument of convincing apologetic. It was one of the first of its kind in the language, and in respect of its method, one of the best ... It presents Baxter intellectually on his highest level; and

---

1 *Autobiography*, 196.
2 See Nuttall, 79. It was 'the greatest congregation that ever I saw', *Sermon on Judgement* (London, 1658), Epistle dedicatory, ii.
3 *Autobiography*, 198f.

is not the less impressive because of the intense emotion which, here and there, breaks through the hard crust of his argument'.[1] One may add that Baxter provided a solid foundation for Christian convictions, secure even against the subsequent pseudo-scientific assaults inspired by David Hume and Charles Darwin.

Global visionary

Baxter was not only concerned with reforming the Church, preaching the Gospel and contending for the Faith at home. His obedience to 'the Great Commission' possessed a remarkable global dimension. In view of the merciful victory against the Turks at the gates of Vienna in 1683, he was evidently aware of the implications of the Islamic threat.[2] With strikingly-prophetic significance, he expressed himself thus:

> I was wont to look but little further than England in my prayers, as not considering the state of the rest of the world. Or if I prayed for the conversion of the Jews, that was almost all. But now, as I better understood the case of the world and the method of the Lord's Prayer, so there is nothing in the world that lieth so heavy upon my heart as the thought of the miserable nations of the earth. It is the most astonishing part of all God's providence to me, that he so far forsaketh almost all the world, and confineth his special favour to so few; that so small a part of the world hath the profession of Christianity in comparison of heathens, Mahometans and other infidels ... No part of my prayers are so deeply serious as that for the conversion of the infidel and ungodly world, that God's name may be sanctified and his kingdom come, and his will be done on earth as it is in heaven.[3]

Driven by his view of the Gospel, such was the thinking that led to Baxter's enthusiastic support for the work of John Eliot amongst the Indians of Massachusetts, more than a century before William Carey and Andrew Fuller commenced the era of modern missions proper.

Suffering for Christ

Baxter shared in the cruel persecution and sufferings of the Nonconformists.

---

1   F. J. Powicke, *Richard Baxter Under the Cross* (London: Jonathan Cape Ltd, 1927), 66.
2   See *The Reasons of the Christian Religion* (London: 1667), 202–4.
3   *Autobiography*, 117.

He was imprisoned for a week at Clerkenwell in 1669, and for nearly two years at Southwark in 1684–6, aged 70. This second term of imprisonment is associated with his trial at the hands of the notorious Judge Jeffreys, occasioned by the publication of Baxter's *Paraphrase on the New Testament* (1685). Because of certain textual comments, the author was accused of libelling the Church of England. However, at the deepest level, the real clash between Jeffreys and his puritan prey was over spirituality rather than legality. Piety was savaged by impiety. Baxter's preface probably challenged and irritated the ungodly Judge:

> Reader, I beg of you, as from Christ, for his sake, for your soul's sake, for your children's sake, for the sake of Church and Kingdom, that you will conscionably and seriously set up family religion, calling upon God, singing his praises, and instructing your children and servants in the Scripture and Catechism, and in a wise and diligent education of youth. Hear me, as if I beg'd it of you with tears on my knees. Alas, what doth the world suffer by the neglect of this! It is out of ungodly families that the world hath ungodly rulers, ungodly ministers, and a swarm of serpentine enemies of holiness and peace, and their own salvation. What country groaneth not under the confusions, miseries and horrid wickedness, which are all the fruits of family neglects, and the careless and ill education of youth.[1]

The trial—immortalized by Lord Macaulay[2]—was a forgone conclusion. The Lord Chief Justice wasn't very interested in truth or justice. The sick and aged Baxter was repeatedly shouted down when attempting to speak. Scurrility knew no bounds when Jeffreys abused the saintly Baxter. "This is an old rogue" cried the judge, "and hath poisoned the world with his Kidderminster doctrine!" Baxter was reviled as "an old schismatical knave, a hypocritical villain!" When further attempting to explain his views, the Lord Chief Justice burst forth, "Richard, Richard, dost thou think we'll hear thee poison the court? Richard, thou art an old fellow, an old knave; thou hast written books enough to load a cart, every one as full of sedition, I might say treason, as an egg is full of meat. Hadst thou been whipped out of thy

---

1   Preface to *A Paraphrase on the New Testament* (London: 1685).

2   See Lord Macaulay, *History of England,* intr. A. G. Dickens (London: Heron Books, 1967), i. 381–5.

writing trade forty years ago, it had been happy ..."[1] Such is how Christ's
enemies treat his faithful servants!

Liberty to Preach

Baxter was released from prison on 24 November 1686. The Lord's aged
warrior still had plenty of fight left in him, so he moved to Charterhouse Yard
to assist the ministry of his friend Matthew Sylvester. More theological and
devotional books flowed from his pen. Indeed, Baxter had written enough
books 'to load a cart'—141 in all.[2] His final offering was *The Certainty of
the World of Spirits*, a work typical of the other-worldliness of one who lived
and laboured that others might enjoy 'everlasting rest.'

Last Years and Death

Baxter lived to see better days. With the 'Glorious Revolution' of
1688, Protestant William and Mary ascended the throne. His hopes for
'comprehension' within the national Church being dashed, Baxter had
to be content with the 'toleration' provided by the Act of 1689. Thus he
continued preaching until the end. After his last sermon, he crept home to
his bed, utterly exhausted. There was a glory about Baxter's last hours. To
his friends Matthew Sylvester and William Bates he declared in a whisper,
"I bless God I have a well grounded assurance of my eternal happiness, and
great peace and comfort within."[3] When reminded of the good his books
had done, the dying saint replied, "I was but a pen in the hand of God; and
what praise is due to a pen?"[4] As his agonies intensified, he admitted, "I
have pain, there is no arguing against sense, but I have peace, I have peace."[5]
Baxter's final words were spoken to Matthew Sylvester: "The Lord teach
you to die."[6] And so, on 8 December 1691, Richard Baxter entered that rest
which remains for the people of God.

I close this brief outline with the slightly-edited 'eulogy' of J. M. Lloyd
Thomas:

He towered above most of even the leaders of his contemporaries, ...

---

1   *Autobiography*, 262.

2   See the Baxter bibliography in Nuttall, 132ff.

3   William Bates, *A Funeral Sermon*, 126.

4   Ibid. 125.

5   Ibid. 129.

6   Matthew Sylvester, *Elisha's Cry after Elijah's God* (London, 1696), 17.

His physical and moral courage matched the bravest valour of his times. Earth had little to bestow on him wherewith to comfort his diseased body or console his longing soul. He looked up wistfully to the Saints' Everlasting Rest and groaned in spirit for release from his pains and the contentions of the world.[1]

---

1   *Autobiography*, p. xviii.

Theological Introduction

The writings of Richard Baxter, whose quatercentenary was—at best—inadequately celebrated, have been a dominant influence in my developing understanding of the Christian Faith. Since the publication of my *Atonement and Justification*,[1] I have explored the careers and contributions of others who, in their day, felt the influence of Baxter. I speak of 'Baxterian' pastors and preachers rather than academic historians and theologians whose personal—and often dubious—agendas (not obvious to the undiscerning reader) are usually hidden in the midst of documentary discussion and comment. While I am grateful for the latter's contributions, the mere historian is incapable of doing full justice to Baxter's testimony without sharing his passionately-held biblical, spiritual and protestant theological values. Indeed, the 'result' is more important than the 'game' (to invoke a soccer analogy). We are to answer the question: what is Truth? Indeed, the book's subtitle indicates a double purpose: to tell the truth about Baxter and the Gospel he preached. In this respect, theology takes precedence over history. For instance, for all that is useful and informative in Dr Geoffrey Nuttall's Baxter biography (and other numerous related contributions), he admitted to me in a personal letter (notwithstanding his DD): 'I am a historian, not a theologian'.[2] That said, while his book avoids any discussion of the big theological issues at the heart of Baxter's ministry, at least he had enough theological awareness to note that Baxter was 'no Arminian'.[3] As if to illustrate the danger of evaluating Baxter without accurate knowledge of his theology, William Lamont's 1994 edition of Baxter's *A Holy Commonwealth* sets forth the Puritan as an 'Arminian' three times in the space of a dozen pages.[4]

---

1   See Alan C. Clifford, *Atonement and Justification: English Evangelical Theology 1640–1790—An Evaluation* (Oxford: Clarendon Press, 1990).

2   Letter dated: 9 February 2002.

3   Geoffrey F. Nuttall, *Richard Baxter* (London: Nelson, 1965), 121.

4   See Richard Baxter, *A Holy Commonwealth*, ed. William Lamont (Cambridge: CUP, 1994),

Besides countering Lamont's obvious mistake, the theological direction of this primarily-theological book may be summed up in Hugh Martin's largely-correct assessment from 1954:

> Baxter was not happy with the extremes of Calvinism, though probably he could not have endured to be regarded as anything else but a Calvinist. 'When Calvinism was a living faith it had a great deal of beauty in it and had the strength of the granite rocks.' But Calvin's great and wholesome insistence on the sovereignty of God and the sinfulness of sin became embedded in a rigid and soul-less system of exact definitions, as cold and precise as a volume of mathematical tables.[1]

However, Baxter studies were to be thrown off course when, in the same year, Dr J. I. Packer expressed an acute ambivalence towards the subject of his highly-acclaimed DPhil thesis.[2] This established a perspective embraced too readily and uncritically by others, notably Iain H. Murray[3] and—following Murray—Philip H. Eveson.[4] While I remain grateful for Dr Packer's early books,[5] I regret having to say that, in his 1969 Puritan Conference paper[6] and his 'Introduction' to the 1974 Banner of Truth Trust edition of *The Reformed Pastor*,[7] he effectively 'prosecutes' Baxter before he 'praises him'. More recently, in his 'Foreword' to the 2004 Regent College edition of Baxter's *Saints' Everlasting Rest*,[8] Packer fails to avoid a 'dig' at Baxter's alleged doctrinal defects. While commending his personal and pastoral accomplishments, he

---

pp. xviii, xxii, xxx.

1   Hugh Martin, *Puritanism and Richard Baxter* (London: SCM Press, 1954), 132.

2   See J. I. Packer, 'The Redemption and Restoration of Man in the Thought of Richard Baxter', D. Phil. thesis (Oxford, 1954); pub. *The Redemption and Restoration of Man in the Thought of Richard Baxter* (Vancouver, BC: Regent College Publishing, 2003), 262, 398.

3   See Iain H. Murray, 'Richard Baxter—the Reluctant Puritan?' (Thornton Heath, Surrey: Westminster Conference report, 1991).

4   See Philip H. Eveson, *The Great Exchange: Justification by faith alone in the light of recent discussion* (Bromley, Kent: Day One Publications, 1996).

5   See J. I. Packer, *'Fundamentalism' and the Word of God* (London: Inter-Varsity Fellowship, 1958) and *Evangelism and the Sovereignty of God* (London: Inter-Varsity Fellowship, 1961).

6   See J. I. Packer, 'The Doctrine of Justification in Development and Decline among the Puritans' in *By Schisms Rent Asunder* (Puritan and Reformed Studies Conference, 1969).

7   See Richard Baxter, *The Reformed Pastor* (Edinburgh: The Banner of Truth Trust, 1974).

8   See Richard Baxter, *The Saints' Everlasting Rest*, ed. John T. Wilkinson (Vancouver, BC: Regent College Publishing, 2004).

judged that Baxter's theology of atonement and justification was 'something of a disaster'.[1] As I demonstrated in *Atonement and Justification*, it is strangely incoherent that Packer can lament Baxter's theological activity, yet praise his pastoral accomplishments. After all, many of the ideas objected to in the theological treatises can be found (albeit with reduced intensity) in the very devotional and practical writings Packer praises so highly. Baxter's theological and pastoral activities were all of a piece: the conclusions of his 'polemical' works drove the teaching evident in his 'practical' works. He was a thoroughly integrated 'pastor-theologian'. In short, there is no valid basis for Packer's dichotomy.

What was needed was a proper historical awareness of the dubious developments in Calvinistic thought from the sixteenth to the eighteenth centuries. Indeed, there were four discernible periods, set out as follows:

First, the Reformation era itself, as expressed in the early reformed confessions and the writings of the first reformers. While divine predestination was affirmed according to God's *secret* will, His *revealed* will concerning the all-sufficient and universally-available death of Christ was given Gospel priority. The biblical balance of Deuteronomy 29: 29 was carefully maintained, especially by Calvin.

Second, in response to the Arminian threat, the Canons drawn up at the Synod of Dort represent a transitional balanced orthodoxy emphasising the atonement's universal sufficiency as well as its efficacy for the elect. As we will see, compared with the exaggerations of later Calvinism, the Canons are more in line with Calvin than is often realised.

Third, the era of high-orthodoxy which found expression in the *Westminster Confession of Faith* and its derivatives. The Westminster divines and John Owen effectively deleted the dimension of a universal sufficiency, a conviction that was important to earlier generations of Reformed theologians. Thus, 'Calvinism' really became 'Owenism'.

Fourth and last, the development process terminated with the dead-end of hypercalvinism. Limited atonement and an unhealthy if not fatalistic preoccupation with divine sovereignty ruled out any idea of 'free offers

---

1 'The Doctrine of Justification', *By Schisms Rent Asunder*, 27.

of grace'. In short, undeniable changes occurred between the time of John Calvin and the time of John Gill.

At the risk of over-simplifying a highly-complex set of soteriological issues, this book demonstrates Baxter's concern to perpetuate the emphases of the Reformation period and the correctly-assessed proceedings of Dort. Consistent with Baxter's acknowledged personal indebtedness to Calvin, my agenda differs profoundly from Peter Toon's 1971 case for John Owen.[1]

Having no reason to amend my academic evaluation of Baxter since the publication of *Atonement and Justification*, I—as a Christian and a pastor—now offer a personal tribute to Richard Baxter, for whom I feel immense and increasing admiration. Like F. J. Powicke and G. F. Nuttall, I too find Baxter fascinatingly attractive. However, I am chiefly drawn by his love for Christ and mankind, and his full grasp of the biblical Gospel. I state this in the face of ongoing criticism of him. Indeed, no scholar who is familiar with the broadly-sympathetic contributions of E. Calamy,[2] P. Doddridge,[3] S. Johnson,[4] A. Fuller,[5] W. Orme,[6] T. W. Jenkyn,[7] J. C. Ryle,[8] A. B. Grosart,[9] G. P.

---

1   'The term Calvinism is not used in this book to describe the theology of Calvin himself but rather that of the Reformed Churches as expressed by such divines as Beza, Zanchius, Perkins, Ames, etc. and systematised in the *Westminster Confession of Faith* of 1648' (Peter Toon, *God's Statesman: The Life and Work of John Owen* (Exeter: Paternoster Press, 1971), 15).

2   See Edmund Calamy, 'Preface' to *The Practical Works of the Late Reverend and Pious Mr Richard Baxter* (London: 1707).

3   See *Lectures on Preaching* in *The Works of the Rev. P. Doddridge, D. D.* ed. E. Williams and E. Parsons (Leeds: 1804), v. 431; *Calendar of the Correspondence of Philip Doddridge, DD (1702–1751),* ed. G. F. Nuttall (London: HMSO, 1979), Letters 149–150 and 155.

4   See J. Boswell, *Boswell's Life of Johnson* (2 vols., 1791; London: Heron Books, 1960), i. 120; ii. 445, 471–2, 480, 496.

5   See Andrew Fuller, *Works,* ed. Andrew Gunton Fuller (1841, rep. Edinburgh: The Banner of Truth Trust, 2007), 324.

6   See William Orme, *The Practical Works of the Rev. Richard Baxter* (London: James Duncan, 1830), i. 763ff.

7   See Thomas W. Jenkyn, 'Essay on His Life, Ministry and Theology' in Richard Baxter, *Making Light of Christ,* etc. (New York: Wiley & Putnam, 1846).

8   See J. C. Ryle, 'Richard Baxter' in *Light from Old Times* (London: Chas. J. Thynne, 1902), 303–42.

9   See A. B. Grosart, 'Baxter, Richard' in *The Dictionary of National Biography* (Oxford: Clarendon Press, 1885–1900), iii; also *Annotated List of the Writings of Richard Baxter* (Liverpool: 1868).

Fisher,[1] F. J. Powicke,[2] J. M. Lloyd Thomas,[3] A. R. Ladell,[4] H. Martin,[5] J. I. Packer,[6] G. F. Nuttall,[7] C. F. Allison,[8] O. C. Watkins,[9] E. Donnelly,[10] N. H. Keeble,[11] D. M. Lloyd-Jones,[12] M. Roberts,[13] I. H. Murray,[14] H. Boersma,[15] P. H. Eveson,[16] M. A. Capill,[17] E. Evans,[18] T. Cooper,[19] R. Strivens,[20] P. T. Nimmo

1   See G. P. Fisher, *The History of the Christian Church* (London: Hodder and Stoughton, 1904); also 'The Writings of Richard Baxter' in *Bibliotheca sacra*, 9 (London, 1851), 135–69; 301–29.

2   See F. J. Powicke, *Richard Baxter Under the Cross* (London: Jonathan Cape Ltd, 1927).

3   See J. M. Lloyd Thomas, *The Autobiography of Richard Baxter, Being the Reliquiae Baxterianae*, *Edited with Introduction and Notes* (London: J. M. Dent, 1931).

4   See A. R. Ladell, *Richard Baxter: Puritan and Mystic* (London: SPCK, 1925).

5   See H. Martin, *Puritanism and Richard Baxter* (London: SCM, 1954).

6   See J. I. Packer, 'The Redemption and Restoration of Man in the Thought of Richard Baxter', D. Phil. thesis (Oxford, 1954); pub. *The Redemption and Restoration of Man in the Thought of Richard Baxter* (Vancouver, BC: Regent College Publishing, 2003); also 'The Doctrine of Justification in Development and Decline among the Puritans' in *By Schisms Rent Asunder* (Puritan and Reformed Studies Conference, 1969).

7   See Geoffrey F. Nuttall, *Richard Baxter* (London: Nelson, 1965).

8   See C. F. Allison, *The Rise of Moralism: The Proclamation of the Gospel from Hooker to Baxter* (London: SPCK, 1966).

9   See Owen C. Watkins, *The Puritan Experience* (London: Routledge & Kegan Paul, 1972).

10   See Edward Donnelly, 'Richard Baxter—A Corrective for Reformed Preachers' in *The Banner of Truth Magazine*, 166–7 (July–August 1977).

11   See Neil H. Keeble, *Richard Baxter: Puritan Man of Letters* (Oxford: Clarendon Press, 1982); also, *The Autobiography of Richard Baxter*, ed. N. H. Keeble (London: J. M. Dent, 1985).

12   See D. M. Lloyd-Jones, *The Puritans: Their Origins and Successors* (Edinburgh: The Banner of Truth Trust, 1987).

13   See Maurice Roberts, 'Richard Baxter and His Gospel' in *The Banner of Truth Magazine*, 339 (December 1991).

14   Iain H. Murray, '*Richard Baxter—the Reluctant Puritan?*' (Thornton Heath, Surrey: Westminster Conference report, 1991).

15   See Hans Boersma, *A Hot Pepper Corn: Richard Baxter's Doctrine of Justification in Its Seventeenth-Century Context of Controversy* (Zoetermeer: Uitgeverij Boekencentrum, 1993).

16   See Philip H. Eveson, *The Great Exchange: Justification by faith alone in the light of recent discussion* (Bromley, Kent: Day One Publications, 1996).

17   See Murray A. Capill, *Preaching With Spiritual Vigour, Including Lessons from the Life and Practice of Richard Baxter* (Fearn, Ross-shire: Mentor, Christian focus Publications, 2003).

18   See Eifion Evans, 'Richard Baxter's Influence in Wales' in *The National Library of Wales Journal/Cylchgrawn Llyfrgell Genedlaethol Cymru*, XXXIII. 2 (2003).

19   See Tim Cooper, *John Owen, Richard Baxter and the Formation of Nonconformity* (Farnham, Surrey: Ashgate, 2011); also 'Why Did Richard Baxter and John Owen Diverge? The Impact of The First Civil War' in *The Journal of Ecclesiastical History*, 61.3 (Cambridge: CUP, 2010).

20   See Robert Strivens, 'Richard Baxter and his Legacy' in *Authentic Calvinism?* (Dewsbury:

& D. A. S. Ferguson,[1] D. James[2] (and others) can escape considering the 'odium' associated with Richard Baxter. Heated hostility towards 'Baxterianism' dates from his lifetime and shows no sign of cooling. For instance, in late 2015, American 'pro-Owen' scholar R. Scott Clark decried Baxter's doctrine of justification as 'theological arsenic'.[3] We are told that Baxter 'effectively scuttled the Reformation doctrine of justification'. The question for such critics is simply stated: from a strictly Christian perspective, how could Baxter be so successful if he was so unsound? One wonders whether the vituperation simply reflects the inability of his frustrated critics to deal with Baxter's views. In short, go for the 'man' rather than the 'ball'!

Considering the stances and careers of many of Richard Baxter's critics, it is difficult not to accuse them of sheer impertinence. More than three centuries on, what have any of us achieved in the light of Baxter's magnificent and wonderful accomplishments, not to speak of his courageous sufferings for Christ? In the spirit of a public defence of Baxter I made at the Westminster Conference in December 2014, and despite all that has been said, I intend in my unashamedly-hagiographical tribute to align myself with men who knew, heard and loved Richard Baxter—his colleague at Charterhouse Yard, Finsbury, Matthew Sylvester (1637–1708);[4] his close friend and supporter, Dr William Bates (1625–99);[5] and Dr Edmund Calamy (1671–1732),[6] whose dedicated labours ensured that Baxter's wonderful legacy would endure. With reference to these able and godly men, I intend—to the glory of God—to celebrate, then vindicate, the life and testimony of Richard Baxter. My stance is that of William Bates, who declared: 'His name will shine longer than his enemies shall bark'.[7]

I close this introduction with a personal expression of regret. Had the 'Reformed revival' of the late 1950s (associated with the Banner of Truth

---

Westminster Conference Report, 2014).

1   See Paul T. Nimmo & David A. S. Ferguson, *Reformed Theology* (Cambridge: CUP, 2016).

2   'Richard Baxter 1615–1691', The Evangelical Library Lecture 2015 in *IN WRITING*, The Evangelical Library (London: 2016).

3   See R. Scott Clark, *Burying The Lead On Baxter: Baxter's doctrine of justification* http://theaquilareport.com/burying-the-lead-on-baxter/#.Vknkzb6LqnE.facebook

4   See *Oxford DNB* (http://www.oxforddnb.com/view/article/26874).

5   See *Oxford DNB* (http://www.oxforddnb.com/view/article/1682?docPos=1).

6   See *Oxford DNB* (http://www.oxforddnb.com/view/article/4357?docPos=3).

7   William Bates, Epistle Dedicatory, *A Funeral Sermon for the Reverend, Holy and Excellent Divine, Mr Richard Baxter* (London: 1692).

Trust and other publishers) given 'iconic' status to Richard Baxter instead of John Owen, I believe—on many levels—that evangelical witness would have been generally more effective and fruitful. Evangelism would have been warmer and less-inhibited, holiness more evidently fruitful, and biblical church unity more fervently pursued. In view of J. I. Packer's ambivalence towards Baxter, is one surprised that the latter's works have been so under-promoted? Young ministers were not likely to devour the practical works commended so highly by Packer if Baxter's theology was 'so disastrous'.[1] As we shall see, there is a precedent for my criticism in one of Baxter's fervent but little-known admirers, one Samuel Clifford (d. 1726), son of the ejected Rector of East Knoyle in Wiltshire, also Samuel (d. 1699).[2] After surveying the sadly-neglected positive assessments of his friends, Sylvester, Bates and Calamy, a consideration of Clifford's brief but significant contribution *plus* an extensive theological vindication of Baxter, will hopefully serve at least to quieten if not totally silence Baxter's critics.

---

1   See J. I. Packer, The Doctrine of Justification in Development and Decline among the Puritans' in *By Schisms Rent Asunder* (Puritan and Reformed Studies Conference, 1969), 27.

2   See *Calamy Revised* (Oxford: Clarendon Press, 1934), 122.

PART I
BAXTER'S FRIENDS

1. Sylvester on Baxter

Beginning with Sylvester's funeral sermon for Baxter, preached on 18 December, 1691, I cite a paragraph which will significantly bear on his eventual 'vindication'. This passage includes a highly-relevant testimony from Baxter not cited by Orme, Powicke, Nuttall or Keeble. In the case of Powicke, who (unlike Nuttall) does show considerable interest in Baxter's theology, he lamented: 'Is there no light on Baxter for the last five years of his life?'[1] Doing his best to remedy the sad deficiency by quoting two pages of Sylvester's sermon,[2] he stops short of what is surely vital for our appreciation of 'Baxterianism':

> On Tuesday morning about four of the clock, December 8, 1691, he expired; though he expected and desired his dissolution to have been on the Lord's Day before, which with joy, to me, he called an High Day, because of his desired change expected then by him. *He had frequently before his death, owned to me, his continuance in the same sentiments that he had discovered to the world before, in his polemical discourses, especially about Justification, and the Covenants of Works and Grace, etc.* And being asked at my request, whether he had changed his former thoughts about those things; his answer was *That he had told the world sufficiently his judgement concerning them by words and writing, and thither he referred men.* And then lifting up his eyes to heaven, he uttered these words, "Lord, pity, pity, pity the ignorance of this poor city."[3]

Clearly, in a vehement and not-unpoetic statement, Baxter confirmed and sealed his long-held views.

Before we sample Sylvester's admiration of his hero, we must respond to the oft-repeated objections to these 'polemical discourses'. Of course, Baxter

---

1   F. J. Powicke, *Richard Baxter Under the Cross* (London: Jonathan Cape Ltd, 1927), 166.
2   Appendix 10: Sylvester's Description of Baxter, ibid. 288–90.
3   Matthew Sylvester, *Elisha's Cry After Elijah's God* (London: 1696), 16 (emphasis mine).

expressed his thoughts copiously and repeatedly in numerous publications. He even admitted that 'fewer well studied and polished had been better' than the plethora of his hasty publications. 'I wrote them', he says, 'in the crowd of all my other employments, which would allow me no great leisure for polishing and exactness, or any ornament; so that I scarce ever wrote one sheet twice over, nor stayed to make any blots or interlinings, but was fain to let it go as it was first conceived'.[1]

Indeed, to be fair to his critics, when Baxter's somewhat tedious analytical method—in the polemical works—is added to his self-confessed indiscipline, he is clearly open to the charge he frequently levelled at others, that of 'over doing'. Powicke, who lists this as a fault which impaired Baxter's influence, admits that he simply shared 'the common Puritan abuse of the inherited scholastic way' but that in Baxter's case, 'it was carried to a singular length'.[2] Keeble disagrees, on the grounds that Baxter refused 'to pass over difficulties or to spare the reader, eschewing all over-simple solutions, neglecting nothing'.[3]

There are precedents for Keeble's support. Among the very early champions of Baxter after his death is the famous Wrexham-born Welsh Presbyterian Dr Daniel Williams[4] who effectively became the 'Baxterian' leader until his death in 1716. While the world had to wait until 1696 for Sylvester's publication of the *Reliquiae Baxterianae* with his appended funeral sermon, Williams teamed up with Sylvester in an apologetic introduction to Baxter's (probably second) posthumous work, *The Protestant Religion Truely Stated and Justified* (1692). The Baxterian duo wasted no time in answering their master's critics:

> It is not to be concealed, that some complain of the multitude of his distinctions; but such may consider, that the comprehensiveness of his mind accommodated things to the most subtle, as well as the less intelligent reader; and provided against future errors, as well as the mistakes he attends to in the particular point before him.[5]

---

1   *Reliquiae Baxterianae*, i. 124.

2   F. J. Powicke, *Richard Baxter Under the Cross,* 253.

3   N. H. Keeble, *Richard Baxter: Puritan Man of Letters* (Oxford: Clarendon Press, 1982), 67.

4   See *Oxford DNB* (http://www.oxforddnb.com/view/article/29491?docPos=1); also Roger Thomas, 'Presbyterians in Transition' in Bolam, Goring, Short and Thomas, *The English Presbyterians: From Elizabethan Puritanism to Modern Unitarianism* (London: G. Allen and Unwin, 1968), 113ff.

5   *The Protestant Religion*, 'To the Reader'.

Apart from this particular exoneration of Baxter, Williams evidently shared Sylvester's intense and glowing admiration of him:

The Author of the following tract is the Reverend Mr Richard Baxter, now enjoying that glory he so conversed with in his mortal state. Among his many excellencies, his love to God, to peace, and truth, was not the least eminent. The last rendered him averse to logomachies and confusion; well knowing, how vain all [critical] debates be, if the question be not truly and plainly stated. This book will give thee a specimen of that particular accuracy in this kind, as even determineth the controversy before an argument be produced.[1]

Proceeding to defend Baxter's teaching on such subjects as Freewill, Election, Good Works and the Merits of Christ, the authors quoted Baxter's 'triple pity' utterance, later to appear in Sylvester's funeral sermon. They concluded by stating that they were 'assured' that Baxter's *Protestant Religion* 'will give more light than some greater volumes on this subject'.[2] This was important in view of a detail to do with the 'pity' utterance not found in the funeral sermon. Having laboured in numerous books to establish a proper understanding of the place of 'good works' in salvation, Baxter seemed to dismiss his lifelong concerns when he said, "No works, I will leave out works, if He grant me the other."[3] This was the immediate context which produced the 'pity' statement. Hence Sylvester carefully clarified Baxter's stance:

And truly, in health none spake more humbly of his own works than he used to do. But ... some confident weak persons have inferred from that passage, that he changed his principles when he came to die ...[4]

In short, while Baxter never flinched from insisting that 'good works' were the necessary evidence of a genuine faith—'the fruit from the root'—he never questioned that the saving work of Christ was the sole meritorious basis of salvation. Indeed, from the *Aphorismes of Justification* (1649) to *A Defence of Christ and Free Grace* (1690) this was his consistent view, as the latter response to Crisp's antinomianism made clear:

---

1 Ibid.
2 Ibid.
3 Ibid.
4 Ibid.

I abhor the opinion of any works necessary to justification or salvation, or to any common blessings in the sense of Paul; such as make the reward to be of debt, and not of grace. I think few men living, are less tempted to magnify or trust to any worth of their own, than I am. I look not for a bit of bread, or an hour's ease, or life, or the pardon, or acceptance of one duty, or of my holiest affections (so faulty are they by their great imperfection) but merely from the free grace of God, and the merits and intercession of Christ.[1]

Daniel Williams staked his claim to be Baxter's successor by publishing in the same year his own critique of 'Dr Crisp's Opinions' entitled *Gospel-Truth Stated and Vindicated* (1692). The list of nearly fifty subscribers (in two editions)—including Dr William Bates, John Howe, John Quick (historian of the Huguenots) and Edmund Calamy (Williams' eventual 'successor')—indicates the scale of Baxter's posthumous influence.

We return to Nottinghamshire-born Sylvester, a graduate of St John's College, Cambridge, the ejected vicar of Great Gonerby, Lincs and, after moving to London, devoted friend and admirer of Baxter. His self-confessed inabilities and defects as an editor of Baxter's papers are acknowledged in the literature. While Calamy's more-coherent third-person *Abridgement* (1702) of the *Reliquiae* (1696) made Baxter's legacy more accessible, Sylvester's somewhat 'superstitious' attachment to Baxter's papers nonetheless guaranteed the reader's direct exposure to Baxter's soul. As a man, J. M. Lloyd Thomas' 1925 verdict seems just: 'Sylvester was a meek and lovable man, of considerable learning and of great ministerial ability and piety, but not very popular. His personal devotion to Baxter was profound'.[2]

More significantly, Baxter himself thought very highly of Sylvester: indeed, 'no Man ever valued him more'.[3] Baxter described Sylvester as 'a Man of excellent meekness ... peaceable principles, godly Life, and great ability in the ministerial Work'.[4] He also recommended Sylvester's sermon, *Being For Ever with the Lord, The Great Hope, End and Comfort of Believers* (1688). His six reasons for doing so include the author's 'concise, and naturally elegant'

---

1   *A Defence of Christ and Free Grace* (1690), To the Reader [p. 7].

2   J. M. Lloyd Thomas, *The Autobiography of Richard Baxter, Being the Reliquiae Baxterianae Edited with Introduction and Notes* (London: J. M. Dent, 1931), p. xxxi.

3   Calamy, *Abridgement*, 2.449.

4   *Reliquiae Baxterianae*, 3.96.

style, and the importance of the subject.[1] In passing, one notes in Baxter's recommendation a striking example of his thoughts on the advantages of the printed over the spoken word (a point discussed at length by Keeble[2]):

> If the Devil knew what printing was like to do against his kingdom, I wonder that he did no more to hinder the inventing of it ... You printers and booksellers look well to yourselves, for next to Magistrates and Ministers, there are few that devils have more malignant designs upon than you ... To many thousands you either preach wholesome saving truth, or vend flagitious and pernicious evil.[3]

In an earlier letter, Baxter also admired Sylvester for his patient sufferings as an ejected pastor:

> And I pity Mr Matthew Sylvester most of all; he hath a wife and children & nothing of his own; pursued by informers, & hath lately bled so much as hath left him convulsive & much discouraged; & is so modest that he tells none of his want: ... I know not a more sincere & worthy man in London.[4]

An autobiographical glimpse of Sylvester chimes with Baxter's opinion of him:

> My congregation is but small: but they are worthy of a far better pastor than myself. And they are kind to me, rather beyond, than at the rate of their ability. And I have found God's blessing on what they have allowed me. And I find my labour not in vain amongst them.[5]

Evidence for Baxter's regard is clear in Sylvester's funeral sermon for Baxter. Usually mentioned in passing yet little discussed, *Elisha's Cry after Elijah's God* is—for preachers if not historians—an impressive, instructive and moving discourse. While he resists the temptation to compare himself with Elisha—and, in respect of leadership qualities at least, the parallel is more applicable to Daniel Williams—Sylvester has no doubts that Richard

---

1   N. H. Keeble and Geoffrey F. Nuttall, *Calendar of the Correspondence of Richard Baxter* (Oxford: Clarendon Press, 1991), ii. 296 (Letter 1190).

2   *Richard Baxter: Puritan Man of Letters* (Oxford: Clarendon Press, 1982), 33ff.

3   Ibid.

4   *Calendar*, ii. 264 (Letter 1137A).

5   *Reliquiae Baxterianae*, Preface.

Baxter was 'England's Elijah'. His description of Israel's prophet fits his hero perfectly. Indeed, Baxter served God

> ... whose interest and glory he designed, and pursued, in his whole prophetic course (1 Kings 18: 36–7). He neither baulked nor flattered any. He did not fear the frowns or rage either of armed or enrobed dust: nor did he court the smiles, protections, gifts, or honours of the enemies of God upon dishonourable and mean terms. He did not talk, nor act deceitfully for God. He did not seek himself in what he appeared, and professed to do for God. God was the Lord his God; as being most entirely minded, most highly valued, most thoroughly served, most intimately trusted, most closely followed, and most absolutely delighted in by him. And his whole care, purpose and work was this; that all he was, and did, in spirit, speech, and practice, might reach and witness his devotedness and faithfulness to God. His whole self was a daily offering to God; and to the concernments of God's government and name, he most entirely and faithfully sacrificed his all: as if he had known before, the urgency, and import of that charge and counsel, given long after, in Romans 12: 1–2. He knew the narrowness and meanness; the insignificancy, emptiness, contemptibleness, and danger of that soul that is not more for God than for itself; and that it was not worth his while, to live and act, were not his all devoted, and directed to that end, which is infinitely better than its self. He thought God's glory needful; but not his own interest, or being; save to this end.[1]

Doubtless Sylvester had in mind Baxter's longevity in the face of his constant and debilitating ill-heath when he said 'God preserved his life and person most miraculously; and indeed, faithful prophets, under divine protection, are immortal till their work be done'.[2]

Resisting the temptation to be 'too copious',[3] the preacher makes one feel the heavy emotional impact of Baxter's passing on all concerned:

> ... this is a providential day for funeral thoughts and sorrows, because of God's heavy hand upon the world and church, myself and you, by

---

1   *Elisha's Cry*, 6.
2   Ibid.
3   Ibid. 15.

the removal of Elijah's lively image, the Reverend and excellent Mr Richard Baxter.[1]

The preacher brings Baxter to life for us:

Mr Baxter was a person deservedly of great fame and character in his day ... a Gospel prophet ... And extraordinary in the evident acceptance and successes of his ministerial labours. A man of clear, deep, fixed thoughts; a man of copious and well-digested reading; a man of ready, free, and very proper elocution; ... He had a moving *pathos*, and useful acrimony in his words; ... And when he spoke of weighty soul-concerns, you might find his very spirit drenched therein ... He was sparingly facetious; but never light or frothy. His heart was warm, plain fixed; his life was blameless, exemplary, uniform.[2]

We are not denied a glimpse of Baxter's appearance:

His person was tall and slender, and stooped much: his countenance composed and grave, somewhat inclining to smile. He had a piercing eye, a very articulate speech, and his deportment rather plain than complemental.[3]

While Sylvester emphatically states 'I am not Elisha',[4] he was deeply conscious of the privileges he enjoyed in having Baxter as his 'curate' (the latter's joke![5]):

Thus were we yoked together in our ministerial work and trust, to our great mutual satisfaction: and because his respects to me living and dying were very great; I cannot but the more resent the loss. ... So ready was he to communicate his thoughts to me, and so clearly would he represent them, as that I may truly say, it was greatly my own fault, if he left me not wiser than he found me at all times.[6]

Sylvester reveals a significant anecdote concerning Baxter's preaching:

---

1   Ibid. 14.
2   Ibid.
3   Ibid. 16.
4   Ibid. 17.
5   See *Reliquiae Baxterianae*, Preface.
6   *Elisha's Cry*, 16.

He had a great command over his thoughts. He had that happy faculty, so as to answer the character that was given to him by a learned man dissenting from him, after discourse with him; which was, that, *He could say what he would, and he could prove what he said.* He was most intent upon the necessary things. Rational learning he most valued, and was an extraordinary master of: and as to his expressive faculty, he spake properly, plainly, pertinently, and pathetically. He could speak suitably, both to men's capacities, and to the things insisted on. He was a person wonderful at extempore preaching; for having once left his notes behind him, he was surprized into extemporate thoughts upon (as I remember) Heb. 4: 15. *For we have not an High priest*—Whereupon he preached to very great satisfaction unto all that heard him: and when he came down from the pulpit, he asked me, *If I was not tired?* I said, *With what?* He said, *With his extemporate discourse.* I told him, *That had he not declared it, I believe none could have discovered it.* His reply to me was, *That he thought it very needful for a minister to have a body of divinity in his head.*[1]

Mourning Sylvester relates some of the oft-quoted personal details of Baxter's death, including the well-known final words: 'And indeed, the last words that he spake to me (being informed that I was come to see him) were these, "O I thank Him, I thank Him;" and turning his eye to me, he said, "The Lord teach you to die."'[2] We also learn some of Baxter's honest and realistic reflections on a believer's assurance from his own personal experience:

As to himself, even to the last, I never could perceive his peace and heavenly hopes assaulted or disturbed. I have often heard him greatly lament himself, in that he felt no greater liveliness in what appeared so great and clear to him, and so very much desired by him. As to the influence thereof upon his spirit, in order to the sensible refreshments of it, he clearly saw what ground he had to rejoice in God; he doubted not of his right to heaven: he told me, he knew it should be well with him when he was gone. He wondered to hear others speak of their so sensible passionately strong desires to die, and of their transports of spirit when sensible of their approaching death: when as he himself thought he knew as much as they; and had as rational satisfaction as they

1   Ibid. 16–17.
2   Ibid.

could have, that his soul was safe: and yet could never feel their sensible consolations. And when I asked him, whether much of this was not to be resolved into bodily constitution? He did indeed tell me, that he thought it might be so. But I have often thought, that God wisely made him herein (as in many other things) conformable to his great Master Jesus Christ; whose joys we find commonly the fruit of deep and close thought. Christ argued himself into his own comforts. Which thing is evident from Scriptures not a few; take for a taste, Ps. 16: 8–11; Heb. 12: 2. The testimony of his conscience was ever his rejoicing: like that in 2 Cor. 1: 12. He ever kept that tender; and gave such diligence to run his race, fulfil his ministry, and so to make his calling and election firm and clear, as that I cannot but conclude an entrance was ministered abundantly to his departed spirit into the everlasting kingdom of (Elijah's and) his God and Saviour; and that it will be more abundant to his raised person when the Lord appears.[1]

Whatever Baxter's physical and emotional state near the end, he certainly testified to having felt God's gracious consolations at other times:

Of all the personal mercies that I ever received, next to the love of God in Christ to my own soul, I must most joyfully bless Him for the plentiful success of my endeavours upon others. O what fruits then might I have seen, if I had been more faithful![2]

We conclude with some of Sylvester's 'application', lessons which possess an ongoing challenge from his day to ours, to those who at least have access to Baxter's books and who seek to identify themselves with all that he stood for:

Have we been mindful of him? Have we been thankful for him? Have we been faithful to, and fruitful under, the advantages of his ministerial Day? Should you not bemoan your ignorance, heedlessness, and barrenness? Should you not take up new resolutions and improve the mantle which he hath left behind him; and to prepare yourselves to meet Elijah and his God; Mr Baxter, and his returning Lord in peace (2 Pet. 3: 1–14)? ... You have had in him, whilst with you (who was longer a preacher unto

---

1 Ibid. 15.
2 *Saints' Everlasting Rest* (London: Religious Tract Society, 1833), 193.

you, than Christ was to the Jews), one of the best of casuists, preachers, patterns, supplicants, and companions in the world.[1]

For all his grief at Baxter's passing, Sylvester—with great humility—focused his attention on Baxter's God:

> Our great concern and cry this day should be about, and after the Lord God of Elijah: the God whom Mr Baxter owned, loved, feared, served and preached. Nor must Elijah's mantle be forgotten. As to me, the Prophet's mantle is far more valued, and desired, than expected … And as to you and me, the special presence of Elijah's God is greatly needful with, and for us. Elisha in several things out-went his master; (so must not I) but he was not translated as Elijah was: for he afterward fell sick and died, 2 Kings 13: 14. But yet with very ample testimony of God's peculiar respects to him. But I am not Elisha. And may I stand amongst the meanest of God's faithful prophets, I shall account it great. And though I cannot look to be Elijah, Elisha, or like to him that's lately gone: yet all that unction, countenance, and special presence which my soul-work, and ministry doth require, let it this day (and ever, whilst we live) become your joint concern and cry with me, to God, that I may have it, and that you may reap great benefit thereby. As to us all: O how desirable is the presence of the Lord God of Elijah with us! That so the Prophet's prayers and labours be not lost upon us, nor his God set against us, nor his heaven be denied us, nor himself at last called out to testify against us when Christ sits in solemn judgement upon us.

Taking thus Matthew Sylvester's impressive message to heart, we surely should continue to celebrate and thank God for Richard Baxter—without forgetting his devoted friend.

POSTSCRIPT

Two months after Baxter's death in December 1691, Dr John Tillotson wrote to Matthew Sylvester. Concerned to encourage and advise him in publishing the deceased's *Autobiography*, Tillotson spoke glowingly of the character, labours, books and sufferings of his friend of 40 years:

---

1   Ibid. 17.

Nothing more honourable than when the Reverend Baxter stood at bay, berogued, abused, despised—Never more great than then. Draw this well ... This is the noblest part of his life, & not that he might have been a bishop. The Apostle when he would glory, mentions his labours & stripes & bonds & imprisonments; his troubles, weariness, dangers, reproaches; not his riches & coaches, & honours, & advantages ...'[1]

He was glad to hear of Sylvester's project 'to write our Reverend & beloved Mr Baxter's life'. Among other personal things, Tillotson urged Sylvester to

... clearly & briefly lay down his judgment concerning Justification (which few do clearly & fully understand) which some in the city have so opposed, & show he really magnifies Christ & faith & grace, & doth not really differ from honest true Protestants ...[2]

---

1   N. H. Keeble and Geoffrey F. Nuttall, *Calendar of the Correspondence of Richard Baxter* (Oxford: Clarendon Press, 1991), ii. 330 (Letter 1260); also *Autobiography*, 298.

2   Ibid. 328–31 (Letter 1260).

2. BATES ON BAXTER

Born in Bermondsey, Surrey, William Bates (1625–99) was a graduate of Queen's College, Cambridge and later DD of that university. Vicar first at Tottenham, then of St Dunstan's-in-the-West, he was one of the leading Presbyterians in London during the Commonwealth period. If ever a minister may be called 'graciously aristocratic', it was William Bates. Much loved and respected, he maintained a faithful and spiritual pastoral ministry. The diarist Samuel Pepys wrote warmly of him:

> Walked to St Dunstans, the church being now finished and is a very fine church; and here I heard Dr Bates, who made a most eloquent sermon. And I am sorry I have hitherto had so low an opinion of the man.[1]

Though supportive of the Restoration of Charles II, Bates would not bow to the unbiblical terms of Anglican conformity. Yet, faithful as he was, there was no trace of bitterness in his nonconformity. In his farewell sermon, he remarked:

> I know you expect I should say something as to my non-conformity. I shall only say thus much. It is neither fancy, faction nor humour that makes me not to comply, but merely for fear of offending God. And … if it be my unhappiness to be in an error, surely men will have no reason to be angry with me in this world, and I hope God will pardon me in the next.[2]

The noble Bates was to distinguish himself by standing at Baxter's elbow during the latter's infamous trial by Judge Jeffreys in 1685. However, he early came to love the future hero. A letter from 1659 indicates Bates' warm admiration for Baxter. Through another, he had thanked him for '… those

---

[1]   See *DNB* (Bates).
[2]   See *DNB* (Bates).

excellent books you were pleased to send me'. His further warm reply speaks well of both these servants of Christ:

> ... 'tis a singularity of your own to excel in every subject: none so movingly speaks to the affections or with greater clearness and power convinces the understanding: and that which puts a lustre upon all your productions is a spirit of holiness and zeal ... I assure you without a complement I know not what I value most, either that I love you or am loved by you ...[1]

Despite being 'out in the cold' for his nonconformity after 1662, and suffering occasional persecution, Bates ministered courageously as opportunity allowed. His latter years were spent in Hackney where he was living at the time of Baxter's death. He felt honoured that his deceased brother had asked him to preach the funeral sermon, published as *A Funeral Sermon for the Reverend, Holy and Excellent Divine, Mr Richard Baxter* (1692).[2] It was published at the specific request of one of Baxter's fervent admirers, Sir Henry Ashurst, first Baronet (1645–1711), the eminent businessman and politician.[3]

As Bates indicates in his 'epistle dedicatory', young Sir Henry was one of many who traced their conversion to the reading of Baxter's *Saints' Everlasting Rest*. Besides having absorbed the presbyterian heritage of his family, he befriended Baxter and other prominent dissenting clergy. He also provided Baxter with legal counsel during his trial in 1685, and Baxter dedicated his Treatise of *Knowledge and Love Compared* (1689) to him. Sir Henry was also an executor of Baxter's will.

The text for Bates' sermon are the words of Jesus: 'Father, into thy hands I commend my spirit' (Luke 23: 46). The sermon is valuable in two respects. *First*, it exhibits the kind of theological and pastoral impact Baxter had on many 'moderate' puritan pastors. *Second*, it reveals the depth of affection men like Bates had for their inspiring mentor. Regarding the first, Bates' homiletical elegance is permeated with the kind of Calvinism often lamented as 'moderate Calvinism', but—as I have argued—more accurately known as 'authentic Calvinism'. Less vivid than Baxter's gripping and dynamic style,

---

1   N. H. Keeble and Geoffrey F. Nuttall, *Calendar of the Correspondence of Richard Baxter* (Oxford: Clarendon Press, 1991), i. 400 (Letter 586).

2   The original sermon is cited in this chapter. See also W. Bates, *The Whole Works of the Rev. W. Bates, DD*, ed. W. Farmer (London: 1815), iv. 297ff.

3   See DNB (http://www.oxforddnb.com/view/article/74440?docPos=2).

Bates' smooth eloquence does full justice to the biblically-balanced Gospel truths espoused by such men. Avoiding the overstrained orthodoxy of the 'Owenite' ultra-Calvinists, Bates does not suppress election in the midst of providing pastoral encouragement:

> [God the Father's] sovereign free love was the principle of His electing any to the dignity of being His children: this love is as unchangeable as free; and election that proceeds from it, is as unchangeable as His love. What can induce Him to alter His affection towards them? ... He foresaw all the sins of His people, with their provoking aggravations. Now if the foresight of them did not hinder His electing love in its rise, can they frustrate its end, the bringing of them to glory?[1]

In his 'Application', Bates was every bit as concerned as Baxter had been to insist, like the Apostle Paul, that the elect are chosen 'to be holy and without blame before' God (Ephesians 1: 3). Thus any antinomian interpretation of election is nipped in the bud:

> [The] Scripture account distinguishes between that substantial faith that is proper to the elect children of God, and the shadow of it in the unregenerate; the one is the intimate and active principle of obedience, the other is a dead assent without efficacy, a mere carcass and counterfeit faith .... 'Tis strange to astonishment, that men who have reason and understanding, should presume in a high degree of the present favour of God, and their future happiness, as if they were His dear children, when their enmity against His holy name and will is evident in their lives.[2]

Like Baxter, Calvin and numerous other 'authentic Calvinists', Bates does not cramp the Gospel offer with the Owenite 'limited atonement' dogma:

> The Lord Jesus is the only peace-maker of the righteous and holy God to sinners ... Our reconciliation only is by *redemption in His blood* [Col. 1: 20] ... *God was in Christ reconciling the world to Himself* [2 Cor. 5: 19]. There is now an act of oblivion offered in the Gospel to all that come to God by Him. We have sure salvation in His name: But we must with consenting wills, close with Him as our Lord and life.[3]

---

1 Bates, *Funeral Sermon,* 19–20.
2 Ibid. 69–70.
3 Ibid. 80–1.

In line with Baxter's view of saving faith, Bates is careful to avoid any semblance of what is now known as 'easy-believism':

> We must not separate between Christ the Saviour, and Christ the Lord; between His salvation and His dominion. God indispensably requires we should resign ourselves to His Son as our King, and rely upon Him as our priest to atone His displeasure.[1]

Before Dr Bates directed his hearers to the legacy of Richard Baxter, he concluded with a beautiful and appropriate example of pastoral encouragement, too good to ignore:

> Old Simeon is a leading example to believers: after he had embraced Christ in his arms, how earnestly did he desire his dissolution? *Lord, now lettest thou thy servant depart in peace, for mine eyes have seen thy salvation.* St Stephen in the midst of a shower of stones, with a blessed tranquillity, makes his dying prayer, *Lord Jesus receive my spirit.* If the fears of humble souls arise in that hour, because they have not the conspicuous marks of God's children, the graces of the Spirit in that degree of eminency, as some saints have had: Let them consider, there are different ages among the children of God: some are in a state of infancy and infirmity; others are more confirmed: but the relation is the same in all, and gives an interest in His promised mercy. The weakness of their faith cannot frustrate God's faithfulness. 'Tis the sincerity, not the strength of grace, that is requisite to salvation. If faith be shaking *as a bruised reed*, and but kindling as *the smoking flax*, it shall be victorious. O that these powerful comforts may encourage dying Christians to commend their souls with ardency and assurance to God, their Father, and felicity.[2]

The eloquence of the preacher then gave way to the eloquence of the admirer. While two-thirds of Bates' sermon consisted of exposition and application, the final third was devoted to eulogy and biography. It is abundantly clear that Bates saw Baxter not as an idolized 'celebrity' but as a trophy of Grace in the purposes of Grace:

> I have now finished my discourse upon the text, and shall apply myself to speak of the other subject, the Reverend Mr Richard Baxter, that

---

1   Ibid. 81.
2   Ibid. 84–5

excellent instrument of Divine Grace, to recover and restore so many revolted souls to God, out of the empire of his enemy: ...[1]

Dr Bates was concerned to make the right impression. Indeed, he was aware of a double problem:

For those who perfectly knew him, will be apt to think my account of him to be short and defective, an imperfect shadow of his resplendent virtues: others who were unacquainted with his extraordinary worth, will from ignorance or envy be inclined to think his just praises to be undue and excessive.[2]

Yet, Bates was undaunted:

Indeed if love could make me eloquent, I should use all the most lively and graceful colours of language to adorn his memory: but this consideration relieves me in the consciousness of my disability, that a plain narrative of what Mr Baxter was, and did, will be a most noble eulogy: and that his substantial piety no more needs artificial oratory to set it off, than refined gold wants paint to add lustre and value to it.[3]

Thus far, my own handling of the material might be seen—like Bates' own enthusiasm—somewhat 'over the top', at least to cool academics and those theologically prejudiced. I too remain undaunted, as I proceed to cover, not the biographical facts easily available elsewhere, but a selection of details from Bates' eulogy.

We are reminded that at Kidderminster, Baxter's 'ministry by the divine influence, was of admirable efficacy'.[4] Determined as he was 'to glorify [God] in the saving of souls, this was the reigning affection in his heart'. His prayers melted the hearts of the worshippers. 'His soul took wing for heaven, and rapt up the souls of others with him. Never did I see or hear a holy minister address himself to God with more reverence and humility'.[5] As Baxter prayed, so he preached:

In his sermons there was a rare union of arguments and motives to

---

1   Ibid. 85.
2   Ibid. 86.
3   Ibid.
4   Ibid. 88.
5   Ibid. 89.

convince the mind and gain the heart: All the fountains of reason and persuasion were open to his discerning eye. There was no resisting the force of his discourses without denying reason and divine revelation. He had a marvellous felicity and copiousness in speaking. There was a noble negligence in his style: for his great mind could not stoop to the affected eloquence of words: he despised flashy oratory: but his expressions were clear and powerful, so convincing the understanding, so entering into the soul, so engaging the affections, that those were as deaf as adders, who were not charmed by so wise a charmer. He was animated with the Holy Spirit, and breathed celestial fire, to inspire heat and life into dead sinners, and to melt the obdurate in their frozen tombs.[1]

Baxter's ministry was as effective out of the pulpit as in it. His insistence on catechising, both in families and one-to-one, is well known. He published 'that accomplished model of an evangelical minister, styled *Gildas Salvianus, or the Reformed Pastor*' in which he shows that 'the duty of ministers is not confined to their study and the pulpit'.[2] By this means he was fruitful in establishing souls in the faith. Often those instructed and exhorted would leave his presence in tears. As surely as love begets love, Baxter's Kidderminster congregation loved their loving pastor. 'His unwearied industry to do good to his flock, was answered by a correspondent love and thankfulness. He was an angel in their esteem'.[3]

Sadly, Baxter's pastoral success had too-little an impact upon the whole ecclesiastical establishment. The traditional Anglican mind-set was incapable of considering the kind of reforms Baxter believed both Scripture and antiquity demanded. As we have seen, the Savoy Conference was a disaster. He was equally grieved at the sectarian tendencies of Puritanism. All things considered, while he rejoiced in fellowship with godly souls whatever their churchmanship, Baxter's zeal for saving sinners was matched by his zeal to unite saints. His paraphrase on Christ's prayer for unity (John 17: 21) perfectly sums up his numerous treatises on the subject:

May all speak the same thing which they have heard from Thee by me, and may love what we love, and do our work and not their own:

---

1   Ibid. 90–1.
2   Ibid. 92–3.
3   Ibid.

That by their concord in faith, love and practice the world may be won
to Christianity, and not scandalized by their discord and fractions, or by
forsaking the true unity, and combining for worldly interest on worldly
terms.[1]

Too few shared Baxter's vision, with all its tragic consequences. Yet, as Dr
Bates reminded his hearers, Baxter's ideals and hopes had found expression
in Worcestershire Association:

> While he remained at Kidderminster, his illustrious worth was not
> shaded in a corner, but dispersed its beams and influence around the
> country. By his counsel and excitation, the ministers in Worcestershire,
> Episcopal, Presbyterian and Congregational were united, that by their
> studies, labours, and advice, the doctrine and practise of religion, the
> truths and holiness of the Gospel might be preserved in all the churches
> committed to their charge. This Association was of excellent use, the
> ends of church-government were obtained by it: and it was a leading
> example to the ministers of other counties. Mr Baxter was not above
> his brethren ministers, by a superior title, or any secular advantage, but
> by his divine endowments and separate excellencies, his extraordinary
> wisdom, zeal, and fidelity: he was the soul of that happy society.[2]

That said, for Baxter, evangelism took priority over ecumenism, as Bates
made clear: 'Mr Baxter, after his coming to London [in April 1660], during
the time of liberty, did not neglect that which was the principal exercise
of his life, the preaching of the Gospel, being always sensible of his duty of
saving souls'.[3] As with his first preaching in London in 1654 (when old St
Paul's cathedral was packed out![4]), so now, Baxter always drew large crowds,
sometimes with more than a touch of the dramatic:

> He preached at St Dunstans on the Lord's-days in the afternoon. I
> remember one instance of his firm faith in the divine providence, and
> his fortitude when he was engaged in his ministry there. The church
> was old, and the people were apprehensive of some danger in meeting

---

1   *A Paraphrase on the New Testament*, John 17: 21.

2   Bates, *Funeral Sermon*, 94–5.

3   Ibid. 99.

4   'the greatest congregation that ever I saw', *Sermon on Judgement* (London: 1658), Epistle
dedicatory, ii.

in it: and while Mr Baxter was preaching, something in the steeple fell down, and the noise struck such a terror into the people, they presently, in a wild disorder, run out of the church: their eagerness to haste away, put all into a tumult: Mr Baxter, without any visible disturbance, sat down in the pulpit: after the hurry was over, he resumed his discourse, and said, to compose their minds; *We are in the service of God to prepare ourselves, that we may be fearless at the great noise of the dissolving world, when the heavens shall pass away, and the elements melt in fervent heat; the earth also, and the works therein shall be burnt up.*[1]

With the events of the Restoration (1660), and despite every endeavour to return to his beloved people at Kidderminster (1661), Baxter's hopes for a comprehensive and reformed English church were dashed by the Act of Uniformity (1662). Along with other brethren, Baxter—'who was their brightest ornament'[2]—had done his best to avert the calamity, being 'of Calvin's mind',[3] not over-hastily to expect too much by human means. That said, it was a monstrous crime against God to deprive the people of England of so many fit, able and godly pastors. Baxter spoke thus of the Episcopal misdeeds: 'For ought I see, the Bishops will own the turning of us out, at the tribunal of Christ, and thither we appeal'.[4] So, his public ministry was virtually over. He actually preached his farewell sermon a few months before the 'fateful day' of the Great Ejection—'black Bartholomew', 24 August— when near two-thousand ministers lost their livings and ministries.

While there were occasional opportunities to preach thereafter, Baxter proceeded to pour his energies into his books—although he'd published many up until then. Understandably, William Bates drew his hero's remarkable literary labours to the attention of his hearers:

His books, for their number and variety of matter in them, make a library. They contain a treasure of controversial, casuistical, positive and practical divinity. Of them I shall relate the words of one, whose exact judgement, joined with his moderation, will give a great value to his testimony; they are of the Very Reverend Dr Wilkins, afterwards Bishop of Chester: he said that "Mr Baxter had cultivated every subject

---

1   Bates, *Funeral Sermon.* 99–100.
2   Ibid. 103.
3   Ibid. 97–8.
4   Ibid.

he handled; and if he had lived in the primitive times, he had been one of the Fathers of the Church." I shall add what he said with admiration of him another time, "That it was enough for one age to produce such a person as Mr Baxter."[1]

Bates' assessment is strikingly free from any trace of the negativity of contemporary and later critics. Not simply concerned to say nice things in a funeral sermon, he states the biblical basis of Baxter's books: 'He adhered to the Scriptures as the perfect Rule of Faith, and searched whether the doctrines received were consonant to it'.[2] Bates then alludes to Baxter's 'several books against the Papists' written 'with that clearness and strength as will confound if not convince them'.[3] Baxter also 'wrote several excellent books against the impudent atheism of this loose age'[4] as well as 'some warm discourses, to apologize for the preaching of Dissenting ministers'.[5]

Dr Bates then turned his attention to Baxter's stance on the 'modern controversy' over Calvinism and Arminianism, Baxter having 'advised young divines' to follow the 'middle way'.[6] As I have argued elsewhere, this expression, repeatedly used by historians, is as misleading as the label 'moderate Calvinist'. In view of Baxter's confessed concurrence with the 'authentic Calvinism' of John Calvin, his was a 'middle way' between Arminianism and *Owenism*, the 'over-orthodoxy' of John Owen being an exaggerated form of Calvin's teaching, especially regarding the atonement. In other words, Baxter was not moderating *true* Calvinism. Doubtless Bates was aware of this, while unhelpfully using the standard categories of contemporary discussion. Certainly, his summary of Baxter's theology is 'consonant' with 'the Scriptures as the perfect Rule of Faith' and all that Calvin *actually* taught about the Gospel. Unless one is to say from an *ultra*-Calvinist perspective that 'proto-Arminian' elements are discernable in Calvin's teaching (which is true!), only in this sense may one admit that Baxter had some sympathy with Arminianism. Bates speaks thus for Baxter:

He was 'a clear asserter of the sovereign freeness, and infallible efficacy

---

1 Ibid. 105–6.
2 Ibid. 106.
3 Ibid. 106–7.
4 Ibid. 108.
5 Ibid. 109.
6 Ibid. 110.

of divine grace in the conversion of souls' and that 'Divine grace makes
the rebellious will obedient, but does not make the will to be no will
… He preached that the death of Christ was certainly effectual for all
the elect to make them partakers of grace and glory, and that it was so
far beneficial to all men, that they are not left in the same desperate state
with the fallen angels, but are made capable of salvation by the grace
of the Gospel: not capable of efficience to convert themselves, but as
subjects to receive saving grace. He did so honour the sincerity of God, as
entirely to believe His will declared in His Word: he would not interpret
the promises of the Gospel in a less gracious sense than God intended
them: therefore if men finally perish, 'tis not for want of mercy in God,
nor the merits in Christ, but for their wilful refusing salvation.[1]

It is interesting that Bates doesn't mention Baxter's much-controverted
views on Justification. From his own teaching in the funeral sermon on
the believer's obedience to the Lordship of Christ,[2] he obviously found
no problems with it. Consequently, unlike those who question Baxter's
'soundness' yet applaud his 'success', Bates is happy to see a consistency
between his teaching and his preaching. 'His books of practical divinity have
been effectual for more numerous conversions of sinners to God, than any
printed in our time'. What an astonishing claim! Bates then adds that 'there
is a vigorous pulse in them that keeps the reader awake and attentive'.[3] Not
surprisingly, the preacher—with his own eloquence—highlighted the two
most popular works of Baxter:

His book of the *Saints' Everlasting Rest*, was written by him when
languishing in the suspense of life and death, but has the signatures of his
holy and vigorous mind. To allure our desires, he unveils the sanctuary
above, and discovers the glory and joys of the blessed in the divine
presence, by a light so strong and lively, that all the glittering vanities of
this world vanish in that comparison, and a sincere believer will despise
them, as one of mature age does the toys and baubles of children. To
excite our fear he removes the screen, and makes the everlasting fire of
hell so visible, and represents the tormenting passions of the damned in

---

1   Ibid. 110–11.
2   Ibid. 69–70, 80–1.
3   Ibid. 111–12.

those dreadful colours, that if duly considered, would check and control the unbridled licentious appetites of the most sensual wretches.[1]

Of the *Call to the Unconverted*, we are reminded by a snippet of evidence of its fame:

He told some friends, that six brothers were converted by reading that Call; and that every week he received letters of some converted by his books. This he spake with most humble thankfulness, that God was so pleased to use him as an instrument for the salvation of souls.[2]

Indeed, it is remarkable that such success did not go to his head, as a statement already quoted (but worth repeating) from the *Saints' Rest* indicates:

Of all the personal mercies that I ever received, next to the love of God in Christ to my own soul, I must most joyfully bless Him for the plentiful success of my endeavours upon others. O what fruits then might I have seen, if I had been more faithful![3]

Consistent with this reflection, Dr Bates then proceeded to speak of Baxter's character as a Christian:

In him the virtues of the contemplative and active life were eminently united. His time was spent in communion with God, and in charity to men. He lived above the sensible world, and in solitude and silence conversed with God ... His life was a practical sermon, a drawing example. There was an air of humility and sanctity in his mortified countenance; and his deportment was becoming a stranger upon earth, and a citizen of heaven.[4]

Bates supplies a striking example of Baxter's genuine humility. When most men would be flattered to be thought well of by godly souls, Baxter's reply to a letter from a well-meaning admirer is revealing:

You do admire one you do not know; knowledge will cure your error. The more we know God, the more reason we see to admire Him; but our knowledge of the creature discovers its imperfections, and lessens our esteem. To the

---

1   Ibid. 112–13.
2   Ibid. 113.
3   *Saints' Everlasting Rest* (London: Religious Tract Society, 1833), 193.
4   Bates, *Funeral Sermon*, 114.

same person expressing his veneration of him for his excellent gifts and graces, he replied with heat, *I have the remainders of pride in me, how dare you blow up the sparks of it?*[1]

Bates further reminded his hearers that 'the offer of a bishoprick was no temptation' to Baxter, and 'he valued not an empty title upon his tomb'.[2] Furthermore, probably no Christian pastor in England had to put up with more fierce and unjust aspersions than Richard Baxter. The cruel indignity he suffered at the hands of Judge Jeffreys is well known. Accused, convicted and imprisoned for alleged 'non-PC' aspersions against Church and State in his *Paraphrase on the New Testament* (1685), we are reminded of Baxter's humble and heroic spirit: '*What could I desire more of God, than after having served Him to [the utmost of] my power, I should now be called to suffer for Him*'.[3]

Criticism and persecution were not Baxter's only sufferings. His life-long battle with ill-health is also well known, especially the frequent and acute agonies of a kidney-stone. Bates' narrative includes a pertinent point: 'But his patience was more eminently tried by his continual pains and languishing. Martyrdom is a more easy way of dying, when the combat and the victory are finished at once, than to die by degrees every day'.[4] One may therefore forgive Baxter's occasional outbursts of irritability when every hour is punctuated by sharp pain. It is thus all the more remarkable—if not miraculous—that his dominant characteristic was 'love', not least when relations between too many Christians were defective in this respect:

> Love to the souls of men was the peculiar character of Mr Baxter's spirit. In this he imitated and honoured our Saviour, who prayed, died, and lives for the salvation of souls ... He said to a friend, *I can as willingly be a martyr for love, as for any article of the Creed.*[5]

We have noted Baxter's last days and dying moments in Sylvester's sermon. Bates' narrative reminds us that the full account of his last words are compiled from the testimonies of separate visitors including Bates and Cotton Mather of New England. Perhaps the most memorable Baxter statement is his reply

---

1   Ibid. 115–16.
2   Ibid. 117.
3   Ibid. 118.
4   Ibid. 119.
5   Ibid. 121, 120.

to one who commended our hero for his preaching and books: "I was but a pen in God's hand, and what praise is due to a pen?"[1] Of course, fuller if less-memorable things were said. Indeed, never was Baxter's soul more visible at such a time, as Bates makes clear:

> Not long after his last sermon, he felt the approaches of death, and was confined to his sick bed. Death reveals the secrets of the heart, then words are spoken with most feeling and least affectation. This excellent saint was the same in his life and death: his last hours were spent in preparing others and himself to appear before God. he said to his friends that visited him, *You come hither to learn to die, I am not the only person that must go this way, I can assure you, that your whole life be it never so long is little enough to prepare for death. Have a care of this vain deceitful world, and the lust of the flesh: be sure you choose God for your portion, heaven for your home, God's glory for your end, His Word for your rule, and then you need never fear but we shall meet with comfort.*[2]

To the last, Baxter's testimony is astonishing. His eloquence challenges, instructs and inspires us, not least in the face of those who dismiss Christianity on account of suffering:

> Being in great anguish, he said, O how unsearchable are His ways and His paths past finding out! The reaches of His providence we cannot fathom: and to his friends, Do not think the worse of religion for what you see me suffer. Being often asked by his friends, how it was with his inward man, he replied, I bless God I have a well-grounded assurance of my eternal happiness, and great peace and comfort within; but it was his trouble he could not triumphantly express it, by reason of his extreme pains ...[3]

When asked if he experienced 'joy from his believing apprehension of the invisible state', Baxter replied:

> What else think you Christianity serves for? The consideration of the Deity in His glory and greatness was too high for our thoughts, but the consideration of the Son of God in our nature, and of the saints in

---

1   Ibid. 125.
2   Ibid. 123–4.
3   Ibid. 126.

heaven, whom he knew and loved, did much to sweeten and familiarize heaven to him.[1]

The former 'Apostle of Kidderminster' was an evangelist to the last:

At other times he gave excellent advice to young ministers that visited him, *and earnestly prayed to God to bless their labours, and make them very successful in converting many souls to Christ.*[2]

The day before he died, Bates and Cotton Mather visited him:

I went to him with a very worthy friend, Mr Mather of New England, the day before he died, and speaking some comforting words to him, he replied, *I have pain, there is no arguing against sense, but I have peace, I have peace.*[3]

Bates finally adds:

When asked how he did, his reply was, *almost well.* His joy was most remarkable, when in his own apprehensions death was nearest: and his spiritual joy at length was consumate in eternal joy.[4]

Dr Bates was doubtless on the edge of tears as his discharged duty drew to a close:

Thus lived and died that blessed saint. I have without any artificial fiction of words, given a sincere short account of him. All our tears are below the just grief for such an unvaluable loss. It is the comfort of his friends, that he enjoys a blessed reward in heaven, and has left a precious remembrance on the earth. Now blessed be the gracious God, that He was pleased to prolong the life of His servant, so useful and beneficial to the world to a full age: that he has brought him slowly and safely to heaven.[5]

In his concluding paragraph, we get a glimpse of the gentle preacher, so

---

1   Ibid. 126–7.
2   Ibid. 128.
3   Ibid. 129.
4   Ibid. 130.
5   Ibid. 131.

obviously and deeply moved by the life, labours and passing of a brother beloved:

> I shall conclude this account with my own deliberate wish: may I live the short remainder of my life, as entirely to the glory of God, as he lived; and when I shall come to the period of my life, may I die in the same blessed peace wherein he died; may I be with him in the kingdom of light and love forever.[1]

William Bates continued to serve the cause of Christ for another seven years. Dying on 14 July 1699, his funeral sermon was preached by another Baxter admirer, John Howe (1630–1705).[2]

---

1 Ibid.
2 See *The Whole Works of the Rev. W. Bates, D.D.*, ed. W. Farmer (London: 1815), iv. 418ff.

3. CALAMY ON BAXTER

Apart from modest attention from nonconformist scholars, Dr Calamy is a largely unsung hero of a depressing period in English church history. While he never had the impact of his hero Richard Baxter (and how many could claim that until George Whitefield appeared in 1735?), admiring Calamy shared most of Baxter's convictions, a good deal of his piety and an equally-strong pastoral and evangelistic commitment. In addition, besides documenting the sacrifice of the ejected ministers of 1662, he perhaps more than any other preacher and theologian transmitted Baxter's wonderful legacy to the eighteenth century and beyond. At a time when frequently-persecuted Protestant Dissent struggled to justify its existence within late Stuart and early Hanoverian society, Dr David Wykes points out that Calamy emerged as the 'Champion of Nonconformity'.[1] His own fascinating autobiography illuminates the period in which he lived. For these reasons, we do well to explore the life and labours of Dr Edmund Calamy.

To start with, Edmund Calamy had a remarkable ancestry. He was the third Edmund in a line beginning with his grandfather (1600–66) whose own Norman French Huguenot father came to England via Guernsey following the St Bartholomew persecution of 1572. A graduate of Pembroke Hall, Cambridge and an eminent preacher among the Puritans, Edmund I played a prominent part in the Westminster Assembly (1643–9). Our Edmund's father—Edmund II (1634–85)—was born in Bury St Edmunds, Suffolk, his father having previously ministered in Swaffham, Norfolk. Edmund II became Rector of Moreton in Essex, losing his living—as did his father in London—at the time of the Great Ejection (1662). In these momentous times—the Plague of 1665 followed by the Great Fire of London in 1666—Edmund I died. The sight of the devastated city soon brought him to his grave. Our Edmund was born in London in 1671. Then Edmund III's son Edmund IV

---

1 *DNB*: David. L. Wykes, 'Calamy, Edmund (1671–1732)', *Oxford Dictionary of National Biography* (Oxford University Press, 2004), (http://www.oxforddnb.com/view/article/4357?docPos=3).

(1697–1755) also became a minister of the Gospel. Not forgetting Calamy's significant Huguenot origins, he was conscious of his godly pedigree: 'I count it my honour to be descended on ye side both of Father & Mother from the Old Puritans'.[1] Accordingly, his early published sermons indicated that the author was 'E. F. & N.'—Edmundus Filius et Nepos (i.e. Edmund, son and grandson).

Knowing the grace of God early in his life, Edmund's education prepared him for future pastoral service. Robert Tatnal's school in Westminster, then Thomas Doolittle's Academy at Islington led via Thomas Walton's School in Bethnal Green to Merchant Taylors' School after his father's death in 1685. A year later he entered Samuel Cradock's Academy at Wickhambrook near Newmarket, Suffolk. Professing personal conversion at this time, he then 'went to the Lord's Table'. In every respect, he declared: 'I must freely own I can look back on the time spent at Mr Cradock's academy with comfort and pleasure, blessing God for the benefit I there received ... it was no small encouragement to me, to have this good old gentleman, upon his hearing me preach, a good many years after, come and embrace me in his arms, thanking God for the hand he had in my education'.[2]

In 1688, on the advice of the eminent Puritan John Howe (1630–1705), Edmund travelled to the Netherlands with other ministerial students to study at Utrecht. Studying in foreign Reformed institutions was the only way to obtain a higher education, entry to Oxford and Cambridge then being only open to Anglicans. This was a critical year for the future of European Protestantism. In October, Calamy saw William of Orange embark on his enterprise to liberate England from the Catholic designs of James II.

As much as Calamy and his generation valued the rigours of academic training, they were aware of the danger of unsanctified intelligence. Just as Baxter, Howe and others were careful to promote piety as well as sound learning, young Calamy shared their concerns. Besides escaping from a near-fatal accident on Dutch ice, he was aware of the threat of frozen orthodoxy. On leaving Holland for home in 1691, he expressed regret that though there were many English ministerial students at Utrecht,

---

1   Ibid.

2   *An Historical Account of My Own Life* (London: Henry Colburn and Richard Bentley, 1830), i. 145 (cited in A. H. Drysdale, 'Dr Edmund Calamy' in *Short Biographies for the People by Various Writers* (London: Religious Tract society, 1890), vii. No. 77, 6).

... we had no meetings among ourselves for prayer and Christian converse. Had I not been provided with many good practical books of English divinity, which I read frequently with profit and pleasure, I doubt it would have been worse with me than it was. From my own experience I can heartily recommend all students of theology, while laying in a stock of divinity in speculative way, to read pious and devotional works, so as to have a warmer sense of the things of God on their minds and hearts.[1]

Calamy's concern probably explains why he appreciated worshipping among the Huguenot refugees:

In the French Church at Utrecht ... there was ... M. Saurin ... a very grave man, and one of great depth of thought; who was for going to the bottom of a subject, and when he had doctrinally opened it, had a marvellous way of touching the passions.[2]

Returning to London, Edmund met the aged Richard Baxter. This was an important event in his life, as he makes clear:

I particularly waited on Mr Baxter, who talked freely with me about my good old grandfather, for whom he declared a particular esteem.

Part of this esteem would have related to the 'Amyraldian' (or Davenantian!) convictions articulated by Edmund Calamy I during the sessions of the Westminster Assembly.[3] Edmund continued:

I several times heard [Mr Baxter] preach, which I remembered not to have done before. He talked in the pulpit with great freedom about another world, like one that had been there, and was come as a sort of an express from thence to make a report concerning it. He was well advanced in years, but delivered himself in public, as well as in private, with great vivacity and freedom, and his thoughts had a peculiar edge. I told him of my design of going to Oxford, and staying sometime there, in which he encouraged me: and towards the end of the year, (Dec. 8) when I was actually there, he died; so that I should never have had an

---

1   Ibid. 188 (Drysdale, 7).

2   *Account of My Own Life,* i. 145.

3   See Alan C. Clifford, *Atonement and Justification: English Evangelical Theology 1640–1790—An Evaluation* (Oxford: Clarendon Press, 1990/2002), 75.

opportunity of seeing, hearing, or conversing with him, had I not done it now.[1]

The chief purpose of Calamy's studies at this time was to settle the question: was he to serve in the Church of England or among the Protestant Dissenters? So, aided by a letter of recommendation from one of his Dutch professors, he availed himself of the facilities of the Bodleian Library, Oxford. Among other works, he read Richard Hooker's *The Laws of Ecclesiastical Polity* (1590). However, as his detailed and comprehensive critique makes clear, Calamy remained totally unimpressed by the author's case for classical Anglicanism.[2] Carefully studying his Bible, 'and particularly the New Testament', he concluded that 'the plain worship of the Dissenters' was 'more agreeable to that, than the pompous way of the Church of England'.[3] William Chillingworth's *The Religion of Protestants* (1638) persuaded him that the Bible alone, rather than man-made confessions of faith (however sound), must be the basis of faith and concord among Christians.[4] Lodging with the Oxford Presbyterian minister Joshua Oldfield, Calamy was encouraged to preach his first sermon. As yet unordained, he felt somewhat intimidated by the event. His hearers included a 'greater number of scholars than usual'. However, our young preacher says "I bless God, however, I was not dashed, but came off pretty well. I discoursed both parts of the day from Heb.2: 3, 'How shall we escape if we neglect so great salvation?' "" Speaking of 'the great salvation of the Gospel', he expounded 'the necessity' of 'the satisfaction that our blessed Saviour made for sin by offering up himself as a sacrifice ... according to the common way of our Protestant writers'.[5]

Returning to London in 1692, Calamy accepted a call from Matthew Sylvester's congregation at Meeting-House Court, Blackfriars. He and five other candidates were eventually ordained at Dr Samuel Annesley's Meeting House on 22 June 1694, Dr Daniel Williams—the eminent Presbyterian leader—and five ejected ministers officiating. This was the first public ordination of the Dissenters since the Act of Uniformity (1662). Calamy's first published sermon appeared around this time: *A Practical Discourse concerning*

---

1 Calamy, *An Historical Account*, i. 220–1.
2 Ibid. 235–46.
3 Ibid. 224–5.
4 Ibid. 227–34.
5 Ibid. 268.

Vows: with a special reference to Baptism and the Lord's Supper (1694). This work, indicates Drysdale, 'proved' a blessing to 'more than his hearers. "If ever any saving impressions have been made upon my soul," writes one, "the reading of your treatise on vows was the great instrument. May I never forget the strong and lively influence it had on me."'[1]

The following year, Edmund Calamy became assistant to Dr Daniel Williams at Hand Alley, Bishopsgate Street. In the same year (1695) he married Mary Watts, a marriage that proved happy and fruitful until Mary died in 1713. Their eldest son, Edmund IV (d. 1755) was born in 1698.

Having recently commenced a regular and dedicated pastoral ministry in London lasting thirty-eight years, Calamy also embarked on his career as an historian. So, in 1696, he aided Matthew Sylvester in publishing Richard Baxter's *Autobiography: the Reliquiae Baxterianae*. Thereafter, he amazingly found time to preserve and promote the memory of Baxter and the ejected ministers. Believing that Sylvester's devoted yet defective work would be more effective in an edited form, Calamy published *An Abridgement of Mr Baxter's History of His Life and Times with An account of the Ministers ... who were Ejected after the Restoration of King Charles II* (1702). Integral with his ministry, Calamy clearly felt called of God to transmit the heroic faith of Baxter and his brethren: "To let the Memory of these Men Dye is injurious to Posterity".[2] His *Abridgement* involved great courage, and it provoked a storm. At a time of continuing Anglican-inspired hostility to the heirs of the Puritans, this inspiring material marked out Edmund Calamy as 'the Champion of Nonconformity'.[3]

In 1702, Calamy was chosen as one of the Tuesday lecturers at Salters' Hall. Dating from earlier times, these public merchants lectures played a vital role in promoting Christian edification. Calamy's first and highly-impressive contribution was *Divine Mercy Exalted: or Free Grace in its Glory* (1703), 'Published at the Request of Many Encouragers of the Lecture'.[4]

That same year, Calamy became the minister of Tothill Street, Westminster. As his influence in the public affairs of the Dissenters began to increase, he was concerned clearly to define the Dissenting Presbyterian position *vis-à-vis* the Anglican Establishment, but without rancour and extremism. Thus, in

---

1 Drysdale, 11.
2 Wykes, *Oxford DNB*.
3 Ibid.
4 *Divine Mercy Exalted*, title page.

the manner of Calvin, the Westminster divines and Baxter, and to vindicate the ejected clergy, this English churchman preached and published his *Defence of Moderate Nonconformity* (in three parts, 1703–5). For all his 'moderation', he—as did Baxter before him—presents a cogent and comprehensive biblical demonstration 'that presbyters are by Divine Right the same as Bishops'[1] and that the apostolic meaning of 'bishop' is *not* 'the sense the Church of England gives that word'.[2]

Far from ignoring—in some doctrinaire fashion—that biblical pastoral order is designed to promote practical piety in the lives of God's people, Calamy published Richard Baxter's *Practical Works* in 1707.[3] This was a major publishing event where Calamy was concerned. In his preface, after highlighting the 'valuable treatises of practical divinity published in this country', Calamy states that

> there are no writings of that kind among us, that have more of a true Christian spirit, a greater mixture of judgement and affection, or a greater tendency to revive pure and undefiled religion that have been more esteemed abroad, or more blessed at home for the awakening the secure, instructing the ignorant, confirming the wavering, comforting the dejected, recovering the profane, or improving such as are truly serious, than the Practical Works of this author'.[4]

Adept at citing 'opposition' support, Calamy says 'That great man Bishop Wilkins was used to say of Mr Baxter, that if he had lived in the Primitive times he had been One of the Fathers of the Church: what then more fit than a collection of his works, that posterity may be taught to do him justice?[5]

Before we explore Calamy's edition of Baxter's *Practical Works*, a look at his own theology is appropriate. The best source for this is his little-known and generally-neglected publication, *Divine Mercy Exalted*. Indeed, in a thoroughly dismissive manner, the Unitarian historian Alexander Gordon declared that 'no one reads Calamy's sermons'.[6] Neither does he bother to

---

1 *Defence of Moderate Nonconformity* (London: Thomas Parkhurst, 1703), 71.

2 Ibid. 72.

3 *The Practical Works of the Late Reverend and Pious Mr Richard Baxter*, in Four Volumes (London: Thomas Parkhurst, 1707).

4 Ibid. p. iii.

5 Ibid.

6 See the article on Calamy in the *DNB* (Oxford: OUP, 1885–1900).

mention *Divine Mercy Exalted*. Even Dr David Wykes (also a Unitarian), while stating that 'Calamy was Baxterian in theology',[1] fails to mention this most important testimony to Calamy's Baxterian soteriology. The 'sermonic lecture' was clearly intended not only to edify his hearers but to advertise the young minister's commitment to 'Baxterian Calvinism' *vis-à-vis* the prevailing extremes of Arminianism and Owenism. Judging by the title page, it met a widespread need for clarity over many of the most controversial issues of recent history. Indeed, this work is a well-structured, biblically-based and luminously-insightful exposition of the Gospel which repays careful study.

In the preface to *Divine Mercy Exalted*, Calamy reveals his perspective on the subject in hand. In order to express his position, he appeals not to the over-refined orthodoxy of the Westminster Assembly (1643–9) but to the unexaggerated theology of the Synod of Dort (1618). While he often made respectful references to the WCF in later years, Calamy was evidently happier with the more moderate stances of Dort and of Bishop John Davenant who was one of the British delegates at the Synod:

> I have considered Divine grace as actually discovering itself to sinners, rather than as purposed in the Decree: but he that would see that discussed, and the doctrine of particular election maintained, consistently with a general love of God to the world, would do well to consult the learned and peaceable Bishop Davenant's *Animadversions upon Hoard's Treatise of God's Love to Mankind*; a book which is not valued according to its worth: though one would think it were therefore the more to be regarded in these points, because the worthy author was so considerable a member of the forementioned Synod, in which the controversy about grace and free-will was so distinctly debated.[2]

Perhaps surprisingly, without even a single reference to Richard Baxter, Calamy does what his hero also did—appeal to John Davenant's 'middle way' between 'free will' Arminianism and what became 'limited atonement' Owenism. In the context of these debates, Davenant's *Dissertation on the Death of Christ* (originally in Latin[3]) is well known (even though the Banner of Truth Trust deleted it from their 2005 edition of Davenant's *Exposition of*

---

1   David L. Wykes, 'Calamy, Edmund (1671–1732)', *Oxford DNB*.

2   *Divine Mercy Exalted: or Free Grace in its Glory* (London: Thomas Parkhurst, 1703), pp. iii-iv.

3   *Dissertationes Duae; prima, de Morte Christi; altera, De Praedestinatione et Electione, &c* (Cambridge, 1650). Later published as *An Exposition of the Epistle of St Paul to the Colossians* by The Right Revd

Colossians, an omission remedied by Dr Digby James of the Quinta Press).[1] However, Calamy's citation of Davenant's lesser-known-work[2] against the Arminian Anglican Samuel Hoard is important in dealing with the predestinarian background to the atoning work of Christ. Indeed, Davenant's *Animadversions* is probably the best balanced, albeit brief, biblical exposition of predestination ever written. Besides resolving numerous knotty issues, it provides practical guidance to preachers on how and how not to preach on the subject. In the process of rescuing the Bible's teaching on this subject from Hoard's repeated misrepresentations, Davenant also rescues John Calvin from the unjust aspersions cast on him on account of the doctrine.[3] In short, Davenant's teaching was the perfect Bible-based antidote to a later extremism of the kind Baxter and later Calamy sought to oppose. This was a Gospel stance[4] which could not only claim support from Calvin and many other reformers. Above all, Calamy—like Baxter—believed such was the true teaching of the Holy Scriptures.

We now return to Calamy's edition of *The Practical Works of the Late Reverend and Pious Mr Richard Baxter,* In Four Volumes [folio]. With a Preface; Giving some Account of the Author, and of this Edition of his Practical Works (London, 1707).

Fully-conscious of the importance of the publication, Calamy's enthusiasm is evident in the 'proposal', to which is added a list of thirty-four subscribers. The gracious, courageous and attractive grandeur in the text demands a full quotation:

John Davenant, D. D., translated from the original Latin; with a life of the Author by Josiah Allport (two volumes, London, 1831).

1 See my Introduction to John Davenant, *A Dissertation on the Death of Christ* (Weston Rhyn: Quinta Press, 2006).

2 *Animadversions written by the Right Rev. Father in God, John, Lord Bishop of Salisbury, upon a treatise intituled, God's Love to Mankind* (Cambridge, 1641).

3 See *Animadversions,* 26, 39, 42, 64, 96, 99, 135, 139–43, etc.

4 'Christ died for all and every singular person, who by repentance and faith in His blood may, according to the tenor of the Gospel, have eternal life given him through Jesus Christ our Lord. And Christ died thus for all, not only because His death was in regard of the worth a sufficient ransom for all and more than all, but because it is God's settled purpose, by Christ's bloodshed to save any man that shall believe truly in Him, and to save no man that continueth an unbeliever. Christ died not to save any few selected ones without their repentance and faith; and Christ died not with an exception or exclusion of any one man in the world from the benefit of salvation, performing the condition of faith and repentance' (ibid. 472–3).

AMONG all the great and useful projects of this kind that have been set on foot this age, perhaps there have been none so likely to reach all the desirable purposes this may be serviceable for. Here you have not only a few particular heads of Christian Faith and Practice, but Christianity itself, in its full extent and compass, most accurately handled, and at the same time with greatest plainness suited to the meanest capacities, and pressed home upon the consciences of readers with inimitable life and fervour. And how great an advantage must it be to have such an help at hand in families, to which you may have recourse upon all occasions, to clear your judgements in the great Articles of Religion, to ease your minds in the most perplexing cases of conscience, to engage and direct you in the several most important exercises of godliness! You need not fear any danger from hence of being influenced for or against any party of Christians as such: For in all his writings you will find the evidences of a large and truly Christian spirit, too great to be confined to the narrow limits of one or other party; and that noble catholic temper is what he everywhere labours to infuse into his readers: A temper not only most pleasant to the persons themselves in whom it has place, but which at last must heal all the unhappy differences in the Christian world, if ever God have so much mercy for us.[1]

Boosted by Bishop Wilkins' commendation (as noted earlier), and affirming that Baxter's works are 'a treasure of practical divinity as no other part of the Christian Church can furnish [us] with', Calamy uses the Preface to inform the reader about the author. Although Sylvester's edition of the *Reliquiae Baxterianae* (1696) and Calamy's *Abridgement* (1702) had already appeared, Calamy is aware that many might not have access to those publications. What is, in effect, Calamy's second abridgement of Baxter's life, his preface provides a useful overview, not least on account of its brevity. My intention is to select some quotations that highlight Calamy's admiring sense of Richard Baxter's uniqueness as a faithful servant of our Lord Jesus Christ.

After announcing the birth on 12 November 1615 of Puritanism's 'Shropshire lad', Calamy briefly sketched Baxter's family connections. Doubtless partly because he was denied access to the English Universities on account of his Dissenting persuasions, Calamy was quick to highlight his hero's largely self-taught academic accomplishments. Encouraged by others, Baxter

---

1   *Practical Works*, p. xviii.

followed his studies with indefatigable earnestness; and soon made such improvements as amazed those that knew, how slender his helps were, and how difficult it is for a man to beat out his way himself. Though he never led an academical life (which he much desired), yet by the divine blessing upon his rare dexterity and diligence, his sacred knowledge (as Dr Bates expressed it in his funeral sermon) was in that degree of eminence, as few in the university ever arrive to'.[1]

More important than Baxter's cerebral brilliance was his spiritual progress:

His early seriousness was remarkable. Dr Bates tells us, that his father said with tears of joy to a friend, my son Richard I hope was sanctified from the womb: for when he was a little boy in coats, if he heard other children in play speak profane words, he would reprove them, to the wonder of them that heard him. As he grew up, he listened to the instructions of his father, and abhorred those profane sports which were common on the Lord's Days, in the places where he lived, and while the rest were dancing he was employed in religious exercises. He betimes loved his Bible, and was afraid of sinning. He loathed the company of scoffers, and loved religion the better for their reproaches.[2]

Reinforced by health concerns, Baxter's spiritual progress was aided by books of practical piety, notably 'Parson's of *Resolution*, as corrected by Bunny'.[3] Because his precarious health forbad any expectation of a long-life, and desiring 'to do some good to ignorant and careless sinners before he died', he entered the ministry, being 'examined and ordained by the Bishop of Worcester'. Baxter commenced his ministry (one might say) as 'a conventional Anglican'. However, after his settlement at Dudley, a book by William Ames persuaded him that Puritanism had a strong case against 'Anglicanism'. Accordingly, after moving to Bridgnorth, 'he neither baptized with the sign of the cross, nor wore the surplice'. Furthermore, he became convinced that diocesan Episcopacy—'the English frame of Church Government'[4]—was of doubtful validity.

---

1   Ibid. p. iv.
2   Ibid.
3   Ibid.
4   Ibid. p. v.

Calamy introduces Baxter's famous ministry at Kidderminster with a sense of rhapsody:

> He spent two years at Kederminster [sic] before the Civil War broke out [1642], and above 14 years after, ... He found the place like a piece of dry and barren earth; ignorance and profaneness as natives of the soil were rife among them: But by the blessing of heaven upon his labour and cultivating, the face of paradise appeared there in all the fruits of righteousness. At first rage and malice created him much opposition: but it was soon over, and a special Divine blessing gave his unwearied pains among that people an unexpected success.[1]

At this point, instead of Calamy's paraphrase, I quote Baxter's own gripping account of the town's transformation:

> The congregation was usually full, so that we were fain to build five galleries after my coming thither, the church itself being very capacious, and the most commodious and convenient that ever I was in. Our private meetings also were full. On the Lord's Days there was no disorder in the streets, but you might hear an hundred families singing psalms and repeating sermons as you passed through the streets. In a word, when I came thither first there was about one family in a street that worshipped God and called on His name, and when I came away there were some streets where there was not passed one family in the side of a street that did not so, and that did not, by professing serious godliness, give us hopes of their sincerity. And those families which were the worst, being inns and alehouses, usually *some persons* in each house did seem to be religious ...[2]

Continuing with Calamy, Baxter 'had 600 communicants; and there were not above 12 of them, of whose sincerity in religion he had not hopes. There were few families in the whole town that refused to submit to his private catechizing, and personal conferences; and few went away, without some tears, or seemingly serious promises of a godly life'.[3]

The figure of '600 communicants' is worth pausing for. In a town of around 3–4,000 souls and 1800 adults (including the surrounding villages),[4]

---

1   Ibid.
2   *Reliquiae Baxterianae*, I, i. §136; Nuttall, 49, 47.
3   *Practical Works*, p. vi.
4   Nuttall, 46.

the scale of the impact of Baxter's ministry becomes clearer. In short, about a third of the population of seventeenth-century Kidderminster made a sincere profession of faith. In terms of the 2011 census which recorded a population of 55,530 in the town,[1] it is virtually impossible to imagine a church building large enough for Baxter's congregation had he lived in our time. Perhaps even the facilities of Kidderminster Town's soccer stadium would struggle to accommodate it!

No less remarkable is the bond of love between Baxter and his congregation. 'In short, so much of the presence of God did Mr Baxter find accompanying him in his work, and so affectionate was his regard to the loving people of that place, that he would not willingly have changed his relation to them for any preferment in the Kingdom, nor could he without force have been separated from them.[2]

Proceeding beyond the period of the Civil War (which Calamy briefly narrates), neither will I re-visit Baxter's enormous influence on other ministers and churches via the Worcestersire Association (as already touched on by Dr Bates) except to add some remarks on Baxter's view of church order. On this issue, Calamy says:

> In the controversy about church government, which was then so hotly agitated, Mr Baxter was all along against extremes. He neither fell in with the Erastian, nor Episcopal, nor Presbyterian, nor Independent party entirely; but thought that all of them had so much truth in common among them, as would have made these Kingdoms happy, had it been unanimously and soberly reduced to practice, by prudent and charitable men.[3]

Calamy's 'entirely' is important. Baxter thought that each party 'had some truths in peculiar … and each one had their proper mistakes'.[4] Towards the end of his life, he declared, 'You could not (except a Catholic Christian) have trulier called me than an Episcopal-Presbyterian-Independent'.[5]

Such a potentially-confusing 'triple label' needs clarification! Looking at the first, Baxter embraced Archbishop Ussher's reduced Episcopacy—

---

1   https://en.wikipedia.org/wiki/Kidderminster
2   *Practical Works*. p. vii.
3   Ibid. p. viii.
4   *Reliquiae Baxterianae*, I, ii, §1.
5   *A Third Defence of the Cause of Peace* (1681), i. 110; see Nuttall, 84.

with Calvin and Beza's support![1] This meant a rejection of the traditional diocesan scheme in favour of a local, 'hands-on' parochial bishop or pastor, a preaching bishop, not a 'remote' church administrator or prelate out of direct touch with parish reality. Baxter believed this was the New Testament idea of a 'bishop'.[2]

Looking at the second 'label', it was not for nothing that Baxter was viewed as the English Presbyterian leader. He affirmed the biblical Presbyterian idea that 'presbyter' and 'bishop' were one and the same office.[3] Such pastors were 'presbyter-bishops' or 'elder-overseers'. Hence Judge Jeffreys' jibe that Baxter's concept of a parochial bishop was 'presbyterian cant'.[4] Yet Baxter rejected the idea of 'lay elders'.[5] At Kidderminster, aided by deacons, he and his assistant were the only church elders. He held that synods had a place, not as authoritative courts but as assemblies for fellowship and encouragement.[6] Such 'Presbyterian' ideas found expression in the Worcestershire Association. Regarding the third 'label', he considered that the local church had all rights and privileges under Christ, and that neither diocesan nor synodical power provide validity for the congregation's functions.[7] Thus, from week-to-week, the church at Kidderminster worshipped as a self-functioning congregational community.[8]

Yet to discuss and defend Baxter's contribution at the conference over 'Fundamentals' (1654), I cite Calamy's justly positive assessment:

> Mr Baxter was for offering to the Parliament the Creed, the Lord's Prayer, and the Ten Commandments, as the Fundamentals of Christianity: But the rest were not for so large a bottom, but were for having a greater number of Fundamentals. If he did no other service among them, he at least prevented the running many things so high as might otherwise have been expected.[9]

---

1 Baxter, *Five Disputations of Church Government* (London, 1659), 344ff.

2 Baxter, *Paraphrase on the New Testament* (London, 1685), note on Acts 20: 17.

3 Ibid. note on Titus 1: 7.

4 *Autobiography of Richard Baxter,* ed. J. M. Lloyd Thomas (London: J. M. Dent, 1931), 262. Hereinafter, *Autobiography.*

5 Baxter, *Five Disputations,* 5.

6 Baxter, *Five Disputations,* 348; Baxter, *Paraphrase,* note on Ephesians 4: 16.

7 Baxter, *Five Disputations,* 348; Nuttall, 54.

8 Nuttall, 61.

9 *Practical Works,* p. viii.

That said, while Owen was responsible for wording the proposed sixteen articles, this 'minimalist' approach did not prevent him from later producing for the Independents a 'maximal', *ultra*-biblical statement (derived from the *Westminster Confession*) in the *Savoy Declaration* (1658). Baxter obviously lamented Owen's 'over-orthodox' view of imputation.[1]

Calamy also commends Baxter's proposal to reform worship at the Savoy Conference (1661). His *Reformed Liturgy*—a document of sacred, Bible-based eloquence—was an attempt to provide a more biblical alternative to the *Book of Common Prayer* for those who dare not subscribe the latter as in all respects agreeable to Holy Scripture. Even today, for those who dare not imagine Cranmer could be supplanted by anyone, let alone Baxter, Calamy's narrative retains its cogency:

> For the design of [Baxter's] liturgy was not to justle out the old one as it was, where persons were satisfied with it, but to relieve those that durst not use the old one as it was, by helping them to forms taken out of the Word of God. Or suppose we, that the old Liturgy had in the esteem of many fallen short of this new one; others are at a loss to discover why this should appear so preposterous, unless it be unaccountable for persons to prefer a liturgy entirely Scriptural, to one that is made up of human phrases, and some of them justly enough exceptionable.[2]

Calamy makes it clear that Baxter's alternative was not driven by disrespect for Cranmer's *magnum opus*. The 'old liturgy' was an honourable replacement for pre-Reformation forms of worship, drawn up in an era of persecution and martyrdom. It was simply Baxter's desire to build on their legacy. Surely, would not Cranmer *et al* have approved of Baxter's endeavours? Yes, says Calamy:

> Had they risen from the dead, there's good reason to believe they would generally have approved of it; and been so far from looking upon it as detracting from them, that they would have applauded it as a good superstructure upon their foundations.[3]

Needless to say, the 'Anglican élite' sought to discredit Baxter's work on grounds of his lack of university education. Apart from Baxter himself not

---

1   See Baxter, *Catholick Communion Defended* (1684), II. 8 and *An End of Doctrinal Controversies* (London: 1691), 266.

2   *Practical Works*, p. ix.

3   Ibid.

being in the least intimidated by the bishops,[1] Calamy makes the point that the author's brethren at the Savoy Conference had full confidence in his abilities:

They approving it when they perused it, and joining in the presenting it, made it their own, as sufficiently appears from the Preface prefixed; and some of them [notably Dr Bates and Dr Manton] had academical education, and great applause in the world too, and yet thought not Mr Baxter at all their inferior.[2]

Calamy mentions Baxter's refusal of the 'Bishoprick of Hereford'[3] and his frustration at being denied a return to his beloved people at Kidderminster. Continuing to preach 'up and down occasionally' in London, 'he was fix'd a lecturer with Dr Bates at St Dunstan in Fleet Street ... Here he had a crowded auditory'.[4] Following the Great Ejection (24 August, 1662), including persecution and imprisonment, the authorities did everything to silence Baxter. His ever-popular preaching was considered a dangerous threat to the Restoration order. Although Calamy doesn't mention it, the sadness Baxter must have felt was dispelled by his happy marriage to Margaret Charlton in September 1662.[5] At the time of the Plague (1665), living and preaching at Acton was likely to produce another Kidderminster! 'He had so many came to hear him, that he wanted room'.[6] After a six months prison sentence, he moved to Totteridge near Barnet. Legally free to preach during the King's Indulgence (1672), 'He returned to his preaching in the City'.[7] In response to growing public demand for Baxter's preaching, enthusiastic friends built a meeting house in Oxenden Street. He only preached there once, and, providentially being out of town soon after, narrowly escaped arrest. Undaunted, Baxter 'afterwards built another meeting house in St Martin's

---

1   '... our frequent crossing of their expectations ... had made some of the bishops angry; above all Bishop Morley, who overruled the whole business, ... But that which displeased them most was the freedom of my speeches to them; that is, that I spoke to them as on terms of equality as to the cause, yet with all honourable titles to their persons' (*Autobiography*, 165).

2   *Practical Works*, p. ix.

3   Ibid.

4   Ibid. p. x.

5   See *Autobiography*, Appendix 2; 'Richard Baxter's Love-story and Marriage', 267ff; also Nuttall, 93ff.

6   *Practical Works*, p. xi.

7   Ibid.

Parish, but was forcibly kept out of it, by constables and officers'.[1] However, there was some respite from this incessant opposition. A way opened for Baxter to preach when a pastor in Southwark died; 'he upon the invitation of his people preached to them many months in peace'.[2]

When one realises that in all this harassment, Baxter's treatment was accompanied by 'great pain', it is astonishing that he remained unembittered towards the authorities. Yet, this irrepressible servant of Christ received ambiguous treatment, as Calamy makes clear: 'Though he was thus treated all King Charles's reign [1660–85], he yet prayed as heartily for him as any man; and he was often consulted about terms and measures for an union, between the Conformists and the Nonconformists as to which he was ever free to give his sentiments'.[3] In 1674, Baxter (along with his friends Dr William Bates, Dr Thomas Manton and Matthew Poole) was involved in a scheme for comprehension with such 'low church' Latitudinarians as Dr Edward Stillingfleet and Dr John Tillotson. Alas, the 'high church' establishment made sure the scheme would never be approved.

Ever the pastor, in 1685 Baxter published *A Paraphrase on the New Testament with Notes, Doctrinal and Practical.* This was intended for 'the Use of religious families, in their daily reading of the Scriptures'. Calamy narrates the well-known impact of this book thus: 'In the reign of King James II [1685–88], Mr Baxter was committed to the King's Bench prison by warrant from the Lord Chief Justice Jeffreys, for his *Paraphrase on the New Testament*, which was called a scandalous and seditious book against the Government. On May 30, 1685, he was brought to his trial'.[4]

Baxter's comments on several texts relating to bishops and liturgy were cited as evidence by the Prosecution. Despite the endeavours of the Defence, 'Jeffreys interrupted his Counsel in pleading for him, and treated Mr Baxter most scornfully'.[5] Indeed, the story is well known. A fuller account of the proceedings is found in Calamy's *Abridgement of Mr Baxter's History.* The racy narrative makes it clear that the Lord Chief Justice wasn't very interested in truth or justice. The sick and aged Baxter—he was nearly 70—was repeatedly shouted down when attempting to speak. Scurrility knew no bounds when

---

1   Ibid.
2   Ibid.
3   Ibid. p. xii.
4   Ibid.
5   Ibid.

Jeffreys abused the saintly Baxter. "This is an old rogue" cried the judge, "and hath poisoned the world with his Kidderminster doctrine!" Baxter was reviled as "an old schismatical knave, a hypocritical villain!" When further attempting to explain his views, the Lord Chief Justice burst forth:

> Richard, Richard, dost thou think we'll hear thee poison the court? Richard, thou art an old fellow, an old knave; thou hast written books enough to load a cart, every one as full of sedition, I might say treason, as an egg is full of meat. Hadst thou been whipped out of thy writing trade forty years ago, it had been happy ...[1]

Strange as it may seem, a report of Baxter's trial by one 'I. C.' was sent to Matthew Sylvester in 1694 during his work on Baxter's papers. For some reason, he appears to have made no use of it in the *Reliquiae* (1696).[2] However, this was remedied by Calamy who included the information in his *Abridgement* (1702, 2nd ed. 1711). While few details of the trial appear in the *Preface* under review, neither is Tillotson's moving letter (1692) to Sylvester referred to, although Baxter's conformist friend—the future Archbishop of Canterbury—is. It is surely appropriate to include an extract from it here:

> Nothing more honourable than when the Reverend Baxter stood at bay, berogued, abused, despised—Never more great than then. Draw this well ... This is the noblest part of his life, & not that he might have been a bishop. The Apostle when he would glory, mentions his labours & stripes & bonds & imprisonments; his troubles, weariness, dangers, reproaches; not his riches & coaches, & honours, & advantages ...'[3]

Duly convicted, Baxter was in prison from June 1685 to November 1686. Eventually, 'His fine was remitted: and November 24, Sir Samuel Astrey sent his warrant to the keeper of the Kings bench to discharge him'. Being allowed to 'reside in London', in February 1687 he moved 'to a house in Charterhouse Yard'.[4] For the remainder of his life, Richard Baxter served alongside Matthew Sylvester, whose account we have already explored,

---

1   See Calamy, *Abridgement of Mr Baxter's History of His Life and Times*, Second edition (London: 1713), 370–1; also *Autobiography*, 262.

2   *Autobiography*, 258.

3   See N. H. Keeble and Geoffrey F. Nuttall, *Calendar of the Correspondence of Richard Baxter* (Oxford: Clarendon Press, 1991), ii. 330 (Letter 1260); also *Autobiography*, 298.

4   *Practical Works,* p. xii.

together with details supplied by William Bates. With his own personal touches, a few details of Calamy's summary are in order here:

After his settlement [at Charterhouse Yard], he gave Mr Sylvester (whom he particularly valued, and had a special intimacy with) and his flock, his pains, *gratis*, every Lord's Day in the morning; and every other Thursday morning at a weekly lecture. And thus he continued for about 4 years and a half; rejoicing as much as any man in the happy Revolution under the conduct of King William [1688], though he appeared not much in public ... At length his distempers took him off [his ministerial labours], and confined him first to his chamber, and then to his bed. Under sharp pains, he was very submissive to the will of God. And when he was inclined to pray most earnestly for a release, he would check himself and say, *It is not fit for me to prescribe: Lord, when Thou wilt; what Thou wilt; how Thou wilt.* As his end drew near, being often asked by his friends, how it was with his inward man, he replied, *I bless God I have a well-grounded assurance of my eternal happiness, and great peace and comfort within.* He gave excellent counsel to young ministers that visited him, earnestly prayed God to bless their labours, and expressed great hopes that God would do a great deal of good by them, and great joy that they were of moderate and peaceable spirits. Being at last asked how he did, his answer was *almost well.* And at length he expired, Dec. 8, 1691, and was a few days after interred in Christ Church, in London, whither his corpse was attended by a numerous company of persons of different ranks, and especially of ministers; some of them conformists; who paid him the last office of respect. There were two discourses made upon the occasion of his funeral, one by Dr Bates, and the other by Mr Sylvester. which are both in print: the former may be met with in the Doctor's *Works*; and the latter at the end of Mr Baxter's *Life* in folio.[1]

Quoting the preamble from Baxter's final Will, dated 7 July 1689, Calamy felt it to be 'something peculiar'. Indeed, it provides an amazing 'self-portrait', and deserves to be quoted in full:

I Richard Baxter, of London, Clerk, an unworthy servant of Jesus Christ, drawing to the end of this transitory life, having through God's great mercy the free use of my understanding, do make this my last Will

---

1   Ibid.

and Testament, revoking all other Wills formerly made by me. My spirit I commit with trust and hope of the heavenly felicity, into the hands of *Jesus* my glorified Redeemer and Intercessor; and by His Mediation into the hands of God my reconciled Father, the infinite eternal Spirit, Light, Life, and Love, most great and wise and good, the God of Nature, Grace and Glory; of Whom and through Whom, and to Whom are all things; my absolute Owner, Ruler, and Benefactor Whose I am, and Whom I (though imperfectly) serve, seek and trust; to Whom be Glory for ever, Amen. To Him I render most humble thanks, that He hath filled up my life with abundant mercy, and pardoned my sin by the merits of Christ, and vouchsafed by His Spirit to renew me, and seal me as His own; and to moderate and bless to me my long sufferings in the flesh, and at last to sweeten them by His own interest, and comforting approbation, who taketh the cause of Love, and Concord as His own, etc..[1]

Being a 'great observer of providence', Baxter provided vivid examples of God's 'abundant mercy' with which He had 'filled up' his life. Indeed, says Calamy, 'he met with many surprising deliverances'.[2] These include surviving a riding accident, and being 'rescued' from gambling temptations, when he was 17. In later years, 'travelling from London into the country, about Christmas, in very deep snow, he met on the road a loaded waggon, where he could not pass by, but on the side of a bank: passing over which, all his horse's feet slipped from under him, and all the girts broke, so that he was cast before the waggon wheel, which had gone over him, but that it pleased God the horses suddenly stopped, without any discernable cause, till he got out of the way'.[3]

Baxter also recorded remarkable instances of physical healing in the Kidderminster years, in answer to the prayers of his devoted congregation: 'his neighbours set apart a day to fast and pray for him'. In particular, he suffered a tumour in his throat. 'He feared a cancer, and applied such remedies by the advice of the physician as were thought fittest, but without alteration; for it remained hard as at first'.

At the end of a quarter of a year, he was under some concerns, that

---

1   Ibid. p. xiii.
2   Ibid.
3   Ibid.

he had never praised God particularly for any of the deliverances He had formerly afforded him. And thereupon being speaking of God's confirming our belief of His Word, by His fulfilling His promises, and hearing prayers (as it is published in the 2nd Part of his *Saints' Rest*) he annexed some thankful hints as to his own experiences; and suddenly the tumour vanished ...'[1]

Another riding accident occurred at Worcester:

The horse reared up, and both his hinder feet slipped from under him; so that the full weight of the body of the horse fell upon his leg, which yet was only bruised, and not broken: when considering the place, the stones, and the manner of the fall, it was a wonder his leg was not broken in shivers.[2]

Calamy reminds us that Baxter was not necessarily safe from danger at home, not least from his library:

Another time as he sat in his study, the weight of his greatest folio books broke down 3 or 4 of the highest shelves, when he sat close under them; and they fell down on every side of him, and not one of them hit him, except one upon the arm. Whereas the place, the weight, and greatness of the books was such, and his head just under them, that it was a wonder they had not beaten out his brains, or done him an unspeakable mischief. One of the shelves just over his head having Dr Walton's *Polyglot Bible*; all Austin's *Works*; ...[3]

As J. M. Lloyd Thomas notes, this was 'No unreal peril. Gerard J. Vossius was thus killed in his library at Amsterdam (1649)'.[4]

The last of several examples highlighted by Calamy suggests the work of an assassin: 'At another time, viz. March 26, 1665, as he was preaching in a private house, a bullet came in at the window, and passed by him, but did no hurt'. Thankful Calamy thus concludes:

Such things as these, he carefully took notice of, and recorded. And indeed his being carried through so much service and suffering too, under

---

1   Ibid.
2   Ibid.
3   Ibid.
4   *Autobiography*, 282.

so much weakness, was a constant wonder to himself, and all that knew him; and what he used himself often to take notice of, with expressions of great thankfulness'.[1]

Calamy speaks glowingly of Baxter's reputation: 'Living and dying, he was much respected by some, and as much slighted by others as any man of the age'. Besides the thousands who blessed Baxter for his preaching and books, he lists the Lord Broghill, Archbishop Ussher, the Earl of Lauderdale, Sir Matthew Hale and Sir Henry Ashurst among the 'respecters'. We have already noted Dr Bates's account of Sir Henry's admiration for Baxter. Calamy adds that Sir Henry 'was the most exemplary person for sobriety, self-denial, piety and humility that London could glory of'.[2] Notwithstanding the later dubious reputation of King Charles II, it should be noted that His Majesty requested the publication of Baxter's sermon *The Life of Faith* (1670), before whom it was preached. As Calamy notes, Baxter 'added in the title page, By His Majesty's special Command'.[3] Needless to say, Baxter's jealous enemies challenged this claim. He also 'had many letters full of respects from eminent divines in foreign parts'. These include letters from German Lutheran Pietists[4] and such French Reformed divines as Moïse Amyraut,[5] whom Calamy also considered 'a great man'.[6]

Amyraut's letter to Baxter is significant theologically. The French theologian appreciated Baxter's affirmative remarks about him and his theology in many publications. Of course, the writings of the Saumur professor were a major source for the so-called 'middle-way' position taken by Baxter (which is yet to be discussed). From this perspective, Calamy narrates the suspicions entertained by the ultra-Calvinists or Owenites (or worse) towards Baxter:

He was vehemently aspersed by those that were fond of extremes on all hands. When the lecture was set up at Pinners Hall [1672], if he did but preach for unity and against division, or unnecessarily withdrawing from each other, or against unwarrantable narrowing the Church of

---

1   *Practical Works,* p. xiv.

2   Ibid.

3   Ibid. p. xv.

4   See N. H. Keeble and Geoffrey F. Nuttall, *Calendar of the Correspondence of Richard Baxter* (Oxford: Clarendon Press, 1991), ii. 296 (Letter 1189).

5   Ibid. Letter 708.

6   Calamy, *The Inspiration of the Holy Writings of the Old and New Testament* (London: 1710), 201.

Christ, it was presently said he preached against such and such persons. If he did but say that the will of man had a natural liberty, though a moral thraldom to vice, and that men might have Christ and Life if they were but truly willing, though grace must make them willing; and that men have power to do better than they do, he was said to preach up Arminianism and free will.[1]

Three years later, Baxter published his major work on these and related issues—*Richard Baxter's Catholick Theologie* (1675). He persisted in propagating what he believed to be 'the Gospel Truth' to the last year of his life, including his own abridgement of *Catholick Theologie, An End of Doctrinal Controversies* (1691). Of the former work, Calamy wrote in his *Abridgement of Mr Baxter's History*, that avoiding unbiblical and ambiguous words, 'there is no considerable difference between the Arminians and Calvinists, except some very tolerable difference in point of perseverance. For which book he expected to be fallen upon by both sides, but had the happiness to escape: neither has it as I know been answered to this day'.[2]

In the biographical preface to his edition of Baxter's 'practical works', Calamy considers it inappropriate to comment further on the 'polemical works'. Quoting the commendations of Dr Bates and Bishop Wilkins already noted, he says 'I'll touch only upon those of his works that are here collected together in four volumes'.[3] Beginning with the *Christian Directory*, Calamy considers it 'is perhaps the best body of practical divinity that is extant in our own or any other tongue'.[4] We are told that *The Reasons of the Christian Religion* 'hath relieved many when under temptations to infidelity'. The *Unreasonableness of Infidelity* provides a 'clear account' of 'the nature of the witness of the Spirit to the truth of Christianity'. These apologetic works remain an antidote to the secularism which has gone from strength to strength since the seventeenth century. An added 'Discourse … about the *Arrogancy of Reason* in opposition to divine revelation … is very proper for those who being for a freedom of thought would know how to keep it within due bounds, so as to prevent extravagance'. This discourse also refutes the charge that since Baxter stressed the importance of reason in religion, he paved the

---

1   *Practical Works*, p. xv.
2   *Abridgement of Mr Baxter's History*, second ed. (London: 1713), 417.
3   *Practical Works*, p. xvi.
4   Ibid.

way for a later rationalism. Indeed, biblical 'rationality' (Romans 12: 1–2; 1 Peter 3: 15) is not the same thing as 'rational*ism*', a vital distinction many still fail to draw.

Of further relevance to the 21st century, Baxter's *Reasons of the Christian Religion* provides a devastating critique of Islam.[1] Fully informed of the wider events of his day, Baxter was aware of the threat to Europe posed by Islam's happily-defeated assault at the gates of Vienna in 1683. In a posthumous practical work *The Grand Question Resolved: What We Must Do to be Saved* (1692), a tract not known to Calamy (or Orme), Baxter was blunt in his estimation of Islam:

And as you very soon discover that the religion of heathens and Mahometans is so far from shewing the true remedy that they are part of the disease itself: so you may learn that a wonderful Person the Lord Jesus Christ, hath undertaken the office of being the Redeemer and Saviour of the world: ...[2]

Calamy waxes eloquent regarding Baxter's famous *Call to the Unconverted*:

... which has been blessed by God with marvellous success in reclaiming persons from their impiety. Six brothers were once converted by reading it. Twenty thousand of them were printed and dispersed in little more than a year's time. It was translated into French and Dutch, and other European languages: and Mr Eliot translated it into the Indian language; and Mr Cotton Mather gives an account of a certain Indian Prince, who was so affected with this book, that he sat reading it with tears in his eyes till he died, not suffering it to be taken from him.[3]

Predictably, besides remarks on other lesser-known publications, Calamy spoke warmly of *The Saints' Everlasting Rest*: 'a book written in a very languishing condition, when in suspense of life and death: and yet it has the signatures of an holy and vigorous mind. Multitudes will have cause to bless God for ever for this book'.[4] Indeed, the book has a long and wonderful

---

1   See *The Reasons of the Christian Religion* (London: 1667), 202–4; also Volume 2 of Calamy's edition.

2   Baxter, ed. A. B. Grosart, *What We Must Do to be Saved* (Liverpool: 1868), 10.

3   *Practical Works,* p. xvi.

4   Ibid.

history of blessing.[1] According to Dr Grosart, it was the last book read by the Duke of Wellington in 1852, 'and that within a few days of the end'.[2]

As for *Gildas Salvianus, or the Reformed Pastor,* Calamy says it 'perhaps contains the best model of a Gospel minister that ever was published'.[3] He concludes his book comments as follows:

> I shall only add, that if the recommendations of others would have any influence upon the readers, or their characters of the author increase their esteem, few writers would have more advantage than Mr Baxter. For besides that there are none of our practical divines whose works have been translated into more foreign languages, nor are read with more admiration abroad than his; there is no one who by the fittest judges has been more applauded.[4]

Among several 'judges', Calamy quoted the famous chemist Robert Boyle (1627–91) 'who declared Mr Baxter to be the fittest man of the age for a casuist, because he feared no man's displeasure, nor hoped for any man's preferment'.[5]

Calamy's pre-penultimate testimony came from Joseph Glanville (1636–80), a Fellow of the Royal Society and later Rector of Bath. In his opinion, Richard Baxter 'was a person worthy of great respect' and that 'he was the only man that spake sense in an age of nonsense'.[6] In an early letter to Baxter, Glanville had this to say about the eloquent Puritan's books:

> When you deal in practical subjects, I admire your affectionate, piercing, heart-affecting quickness: and that experimental, searching, solid, convictive way of speaking, which are your peculiars; for there is a smartness accompanying your pen that forces what you write into the heart, by a sweet kind of irresistible violence; which is so proper to your serious way, that I never met it equalled in any other writings.[7]

---

1   See 'Introductory Essay' by John T. Wilkinson in *The Saints' Everlasting Rest,* Foreword by J. I. Packer (Vancouver: Regent College Publishing, 2004), 1–23.

2   Ibid. 21.

3   *Practical Works,* p. xvii.

4   Ibid.

5   Ibid.

6   ibid.

7   N. H. Keeble and Geoffrey F. Nuttall, *Calendar of the Correspondence of Richard Baxter* (Oxford: Clarendon Press, 1991), ii. 21 (Letter 683).

So much for Baxter's 'practical works', which many would similarly applaud. What then of the 'polemical works'? Glanvill was no less enthusiastic: 'And when you are engaged in doctrinal and controversial matters ... I find a strength, depth, concinnity [harmony], and coherence in your notions, which are not commonly elsewhere met with'.[1]

Undoubtedly saving the highest accolade for Baxter until the last, it comes from the lips of a fellow Puritan. If for Matthew Sylvester, Baxter was 'England's Elijah', and if (as endorsed by William Bates) Bishop Wilkins thought he stood alongside the early Church Fathers, Dr Thomas Manton 'declared in the hearing of several, that he thought Mr Baxter came nearer the Apostolical inspired writers, than any man in the age'.[2]

I close with quintessential Baxter, words written a few years before his death (being the very final paragraph in Dr Nuttall's biography):

My Lord, I have nothing to do in this world, but to seek and serve Thee; I have nothing to do with my tongue and pen, but to speak to Thee, and for Thee, and to publish Thy Glory, and Thy will.[3]

After being exposed to the life and labours of Richard Baxter, I personally am left almost speechless at the display of the amazing grace of God in one who may be described as the greatest Christian man England has ever produced.

SOLI DEO GLORIA

AN ELEGY

On the Death of that Learned, Pious, and Laborious minister of Jesus Christ

Mr. RICHARD BAXTER

Who departed this Mortal Life on the 8th Day of December, 1691.[4]

HOW hardly we sad doleful Truths believe!

---

1   Ibid.

2   *Practical Works*, p. xvii.

3   *Richard Baxter's Dying Thoughts* (1683), 214; Nuttall, 131.

4   These items are possibly compositions by a relative of Thomas Baldwin, one of Baxter's Kidderminster assistants. The Epitaph probably adorned Baxter's gravestone at Christ Church, Newgate. In 1924 a mural inscription was placed in the church to mark his burial there. Sadly nothing remains. The church was demolished after bomb damage in 1941.

And though prepar'd, unwillingly we grieve.
But here's a Subject calls for Floods of Tears,
For who of *Baxter's* late Departure hears,
But is prepar'd to weep? Yet Tears are vain,
Not us they profit, nor that happy Man
Who from the Vale of Sorrows is remov'd,
Baxter so much Esteem'd, Amir'd, Belov'd;
Whose pious Words which from his Mouth did come,
Distill'd with Sweetness like the Hony-Comb,
Is silent ——Yet that Word I must recall,
Tho' Dead, *his Words yet speak unto us all.*
Who can attempt the Subject of his Praise?
All we alas ! can say, are faint essays.
But still Respect to's pious Worth is due,
We cannot flatter, but we must be true:
Learn'd tho' he was with all that Human Skill,
Which empty Heads with wind too often fill,
Yet humble without Pride——his Learning he,
Still made the Handmaid to Divinity;
Those Parts which other Men so much abuse,
He still improv'd to a Religious use,
Witness his Works in which tho' learning shine,
Yet serv'd as Foils to set off Thoughts Divine.
But who his Heavenly Piety can paint?
He did not seem, but surely was a Saint:
His private Notions, though some men condemn,
Not Envy could his Life and Actions blame;
So much of Heaven in his Talk was known,
Atheists from him have with Convictions gone;
To prove the Truth some men have much time spent,
He was *Religion's Living Argument*:
For whosoe're his pious Actions knew,
He must believe Religion to be true.
If as a private Man his Graces were
So bright; what was he as a Minister?
That Holy Function he his Pleasure made,
Religion was his Business, not his Trade:

With empty Shews his God he did not mock,
He neither car'd to fleece nor starve his Flock;
Painful in Preaching, constant still in Prayer,
The good of Souls was his——his only care.
His Doctrins he so well apply'd, that all
Who came to him for help, did never fail:
To Weak gave Strength, to Scrupulous gave ease,
And Balm apply'd to wounded Consciences;
The kind Physician of the sickly Soul,
How many now in Grief his Loss condole!
Altho' we cannot reach his Graces height,
Yet lawfully we all may imitate.
The Sweets of Sin how quickly are they past!
The Godly Life brings pleasure at the last.
This Truth full well the Reverend *Baxter* knew,
Who when he died, had nothing else to do:
His peace with God was made, how few alas!
Of bright Professors are in such a Case?
If for Degrees of Grace are here attain'd,
Degrees of Glory are in Heaven gain'd.
Sure Pious *Baxter* may be thought to be,
A Star in Glory of the first Degree;
Who after a long Life of Pains and Age,
Death took him from this Frail, this Mortal Stage;
Who now in Heaven undoubtedly is blest,
With what he in his Works so well exprest,
The Saints expected *Everlasting Rest.*

EPITAPH

Consider, Reader, who lies here,
And for thy Loss then Drop a Tear;
'Tis BAXTER, whose unwearied Pen
Strove to Reform the Lives of Men:
Who Godliness and Learning joyn'd

To all the Beauties of his Mind;
Of God and of good Men belov'd;
None e'er their Talents more improv'd;
Heav'n lengthened out his Glass, that we
By him might learn true Piety:
His Soul is gone, true Bliss to find,
His body here is left behind,
And through the World the Product of his Mind.

LONDON, Printed for Richard Baldwin, MDCXCI

4. A Vindication of Richard Baxter

1. The Doctrine of Justification

As all the scholarly literature makes clear, ever since Baxter's *Aphorismes of Justification* (his first book) appeared in 1649, his teaching aroused suspicion and irritation among 'the orthodox'. Repeatedly attacked throughout his life, Baxter was, so to speak, allowed no rest after his death! There was a flurry of activity around the turn of the century, indicating in itself the ongoing impact of Baxter's teaching.

Probably the most severe 'anti-Baxterian' book of the time was Thomas Edwards' *The paraselene dismantled of her cloud, or, Baxterianism barefac'd drawn from a literal transcript of Mr. Baxter's, and the judgment of others, in the most radical doctrines of faith, compar'd with those of the Orthodox, both conformist and nonconformist, and transferr'd over by way of test, unto the Papist and Quaker* (1699).

Nothing that might be said against Baxter is left unsaid in this turgid and abusive book. The author was probably stung by Baxter's masterly refutation of the republished works of the ultra-antinomian Tobias Crisp (who taught the notions of eternal justification before faith and God seeing no sin in his people). Edwards was attempting to refute one of Baxter's last polemical works against lawless Christianity, the full title of which makes clear his utter dread of the abuse of the Gospel of Grace known as antinomianism: *The Scripture Gospel defended, AND Christ, Grace and Free Justification Vindicated Against the Libertines* (1690), the work being bound with *A Defence of Christ and Free Grace: Against the Subverters, Commonly Called Antinomians or Libertines; Who Ignorantly Blaspheme CHRIST on pretence of extolling Him* (1690).

The reason for this important and brilliant work is simply not appreciated by J. I. Packer whose criticisms of Baxter I have cause to challenge in this 'vindication'. To accuse Baxter of having 'effectively wrecked the 'Happy Union' between Presbyterians and Independents [1691] almost before it had been contracted'[1] betrays a complete lack of awareness of the dangerous antinomian distortions of Tobias Crisp—who still has his promoters today.[2] Baxter was correct: if Crisp's Christianity had a part in the 'Happy Union', it was not a marriage made in heaven, as the title-page explains. The book was written

> On the occasion of the reviving of those errors, and the reprinting and reception of Dr. Crisp's writings, and the danger of subverting many thousand and honest souls by the notions of Free Grace and Justification, misunderstood and abused by injudicious, unstudied, prejudiced preachers.

Somewhat less severe but just as critical of 'Baxterianism' is John England's, *Man's sinfulness and misery by nature asserted and opened in several sermons on Ephes. 2, verses 1, 2, 3: designed chiefly for the unconverted: whereunto is added a disputation concerning the headship of Adam and Christ* (1700).

Challenging Baxter in the 'added' disputation, the Gospel minister from Sherborne in Dorset sets out to refute 'Baxterianism, or that new scheme of Divinity, Mr Baxter has presented the world with'.[3]

In a booklet of no more than twenty-two pages, published in 1701, Samuel Clifford of East Knoyle in Wiltshire exposed the fallacies of England's case with clarity, charity and a mild degree of pugnacity! Even the title-page is impressive:

> *An Account of the Judgement of the Late Reverend Mr. Baxter: Concerning the Imputation of Adam's Sin, and Christ's Righteousness: As also what he ascribes and denies to Works of Justification, and of the difference between Faith and Gospel Works, etc.*

> *Collected from his own Writings, as a necessary Vindication of that Excellent Divine, from the false Aspersions cast upon him by Mr. John England, in a late Disputation of Christ's Federal Headship.*

Before we take a brief look at Clifford's reply to England, the admiration

---

1   J. I. Packer, 'The Doctrine of Justification in Development and Decline among the Puritans', *By Schisms Rent Asunder* (Puritan and Reformed Studies Report, 1969), 26.

2   See David N. Samuel, *"Christ Alone Exalted": Themes in the preaching of Tobias Crisp, D.D.* (Ramsgate: The Harrison Trust, 2008) and David H. J. Gay, *Four Antinomians Tried and Vindicated* (Brachus, 2013). Gay voices 'reservations' about Crisp, all of which effectively negate his attempted 'vindication'.

3   *Man's Sinfulness*, p. 383.

of the Foreword's author, one B. Robinson of Hungerford in Berkshire is further evidence of widespread respect and affection for Baxter:

> There seemed to me some kind of necessity, that something of this nature should be published, for the just defence of the late excellent Mr. Baxter. There was no name which God has more highly honoured in this last age, no labours in preaching or writing (practical or polemical) which have been attended with greater or better fruits: upon which account his memory ought to be very dear to every pious mind.

Robinson clearly rates Clifford's work highly, expressing the hope that John England and others 'may be benefited by these papers: they seem well fitted to help on his humiliation, and deep repentance for the wrong he has done to that excellent Name'.

One notices that Robinson sees no inconsistency between Baxter's 'polemical' and 'practical' works. Clifford himself was thoroughly acquainted with Baxter's writings[1] (from his father's library?). He was thus well-qualified to provide a challenging and convincing reply to England's critique. The short specimen of witty pugnacity is not to be ignored either. Not without some relevance to J. I Packer's 'acute ambivalence' two and a half centuries later, Clifford took England to task thus:

> He acknowledgeth himself (p. 424) 'That Mr. B. was a great man, and that the world was much beholden to his useful labours, and that his memory was to him dear and precious'. Considering this, and seeing this great man was gone to his rest; methinks he might have let him alone in his grave, to sleep quietly there without disturbance. Or, if he must annoy him in his grave, it would have looked better if he had tarried till his beard had been more grown, before he had meddled with Mr. B's dust.[2]

What is striking about Clifford's refutation of England is his constant appeal to 'matters of fact'. He charges his opponent with accusing Baxter of denying truths which he affirms, thus totally misrepresenting him in the process.

---

1 In order of appearance, Clifford cites (X3) *Richard Baxter's Confession of His Faith* (1655), (X6) *A Treatise of Justifying Righteousness* (1676), *Two Disputations of Original Sin* (1675), *Methodus Theologiae Christianae* (1681), *Richard Baxter's Catholick Theologie* (1675), *Universal Redemption of Mankind* (1694), *An End of Doctrinal Controversies* (1691), *The Scripture-Gospel Defended* (1690), *The Life of Faith* (1660) and *Aphorismes of Justification* (1649).

2 *A Defence of Mr Baxter*, 2 (hereinafter *Defence*, as per Clifford's main heading).

England's first charge is that Baxter's teaching is at odds with the Westminster *Confession of Faith* and *Catechisms*, and the *Thirty-nine Articles* of the Church of England. Clifford refutes this by quoting from *Richard Baxter's Confession of His Faith* (1655), wherein he generously commends the *Shorter* and *Larger Catechisms* as 'excellent' summaries of 'Divinity'.[1] Of the *Confession of Faith*, Baxter declared it to be 'the most excellent for fulness and exactness, that I have ever read from any Church'.[2]

What then was the problem? While a fuller and more detailed discussion is available in my *Atonement and Justification*, I will now be selectively-brief in handling the issues. Anticipating the charge later repeated by Packer, Clark and others, England and other Anti-Baxterians complained (among other things) that the great Puritan erred in teaching that the believer's obedient faith was his righteousness before God, rather than Christ's righteousness imputed. The charge is absurd, as Baxter makes crystal-clear when he states what is the *true*, as opposed to a *false*, view of imputation:

> But in the just sense of imputation all is imputed to us, that is Christ's habitual, active and passive Righteousness, fulfilling his own part of the Covenant, advanced in dignity by the union of the Divine nature and perfection; this was the true meritorious cause of our justification, and not any one of these alone.[3]

While such teaching is scattered throughout his works, Baxter is also jealous to maintain the clear biblical distinction between 'Christ's part' and 'our part' in salvation:

> Christ's righteousness is not imputed to us instead of our faith and repentance and sincere holiness, which is made by himself the condition of life.[4]

Neither does Baxter suggest that 'our part' is done in our own strength:

> Christ hath done all his part, but he hath appointed us a necessary part which must be done by ourselves; and though without him we can do nothing [Jn. 15: 5], yet by him we must believe and be new creatures,

---

1   *Defence*, 3; Baxter's *Confession*, 14, 18–19 (hereinafter *Confession*).
2   *Defence*, 4–6; *Confession*, 21–22.
3   *The Scripture Gospel Defended* (1690), 24–5.
4   Ibid. 35.

and by him that strengtheneth us we can do something [Phil. 4: 13]; and must work out our salvation, while he worketh in us to will and to do [Phil. 2: 12–13].[1]

What the critics fail to realise is Baxter's explicit biblical teaching that a believer's 'faith is accounted for righteousness' (Rom. 4: 5, 9). But did he mean to exclude Christ's righteousness? Of course not! However, in a display of ultra-Protestant anxiety over the idea of the believer's 'part' in salvation, the relevant texts are played down. Significantly, Clifford quotes Baxter's charitable interpretation of the somewhat dubious *Larger Catechism* statement which, on the face of it, is 'expressly contrary to the Scripture':

> Whereas it is said [*Larger Catechism*, A. 73]: 'Nor as if the grace of faith, or any act thereof were imputed to him for his justification', I understand it thus, and assent to it, that our faith is not imputed to us, as being instead of a perfect righteousness of obedience, to the ends as it was required by the Law of Works; nor is our faith the matter, or the meritorious cause of that remission of our sin, or our right to salvation.[2]

Clifford accuses England, over and over again of 'Baxter abuse'.[3] Packer, Iain H. Murray and Clark are similarly guilty. Indeed, careful students of Baxter's theology know that he always insists that the believer's 'imperfect' faith is only accepted 'through the merits and righteousness of Christ'.[4] But, as well as rightly stating that the phrase 'Christ's righteousness imputed' is 'not in the Scripture' though capable of a 'sound sense',[5] he also refuses 'flatly and simply' to deny that faith is imputed for righteousness 'when God saith it is'.[6]

Clearly, for Baxter, 'biblical correctness' takes precedence over 'confessional correctness'. He was undeniably a 'Bible man', totally governed by the principle of 'Scripture-sufficiency'. For this reason, many allegedly Bible-based critics of Baxter end up frustrated in their failure to refute him. In short, it is very difficult to penalise Baxter when he hurls text after text against his objectors. Unlike Packer's broad theological dismissal, Robert

---

1 Ibid. I have added the Bible references to indicate the biblical basis of Baxter's words.
2 *Defence*, 3; *Confession*, 18–19.
3 *Defence*, 2, 6, 9, etc.
4 *Paraphrase on the New Testament*, Rom. 4: 3.
5 *Defence*, 11; Baxter, *End of Doctrinal Controversies*, 259.
6 *Defence*, 4; *Confession*, 19.

Strivens' more recent study doesn't even attempt a biblical critique. After outlining Baxter's view of justification, the most this generally-positive and warm 'Owenite' portrayal of Baxter offers is: 'I differ significantly from Baxter on his theology of justification'.[1] From this subjective perspective, Strivens confesses sometimes to missing 'the note of joy and confidence in the all-sufficiency of the work of redemption achieved on my behalf by Christ'.[2] Yet such a 'note' peppers Baxter's books. One example from *Making Light of Christ* is surely typical. Here he waxes eloquent on

> ... the wonderful love and mercy that God hath manifested in giving his Son to be the Redeemer of the world, and which the Son hath manifested in redeeming them by his blood; for all his full preparation by being a sufficient sacrifice for the sins of all; for all his personal excellencies, and that full and glorious salvation that he hath procured; and for all his free offers of these, and frequent and earnest invitation of sinners ...[3]

While England's pro-Owen critique covers Baxter's view of the nature of the atonement,[4] rather than its extent (a matter to be addressed later), Clifford cites Baxter's *qualified* approval of the *Confession of Faith*'s rejection of 'universal redemption'. This is important since Baxter is generally accused of holding to mere universalism. While he may fairly be understood to lament the *Confession*'s failure to speak of the universal sufficiency of Christ's death as in the *Canons of Dort*, Baxter agrees with the *Confession* provided it only speaks 'of that *special* redemption proper to the elect, which was accompanied with an intention of actual application of the saving benefits in time'.[5] So, since Baxter has been charged with mere universalism, who can justly quarrel with him on this subject? As his numerous books constantly testify, Baxter never denied the atonement's designed *particularity* in *application* whilst arguing for the equally-designed *universality* of *provision*. It was the latter aspect which John Owen, John England and others couldn't stomach, of which more anon.

Clifford doesn't only respond to England's criticism of Baxter's views of justification and the atonement. Regarding the imputation of Adam's

---

1   Robert Strivens, 'Richard Baxter and his Legacy', *Authentic Calvinism?* (Westminster Conference report, 2014), 99.

2   Ibid.

3   Richard Baxter, *Making Light of Christ* (1656), 4.

4   See *Man's Sinfulness*, 431ff.

5   *Defence*, 4; *Confession*, 21 (emphasis mine).

sin, Clifford defends his hero over false charges regarding 'the Salmurian professors'.[1] Like Amyraut, Baxter actually disagreed (possibly mistakenly) with De la Place whom he was accused of endorsing![2] Typical of his method, at this point, England was quite cavalier with the evidence: 'His abuse of Mr. B. in this particular is so very gross …':

We would only advise him (if we might be his monitor) that before he shall publish the next disputation, to express his zeal against *Baxterianism* (as he terms it) and to inform the world of Mr. B's errors, he would better consider of what he reads in Mr. B's books.[3]

Clifford further defends Baxter over the relationship between faith and obedience,[4] and the conditionality of the covenant of grace.[5] He also dismisses the absurd idea that Baxter directs the believer to his faith rather than to Christ, since 'all know [including Baxter] that Christ as the object is connoted'.[6] Packer *et al* virtually charge Baxter with the same idea, that the believer's 'faith is in faith'. Our Christ-exalting preacher could not be clearer:

[There is] no question but the faith that we talk of, is *faith in Christ*, even the believing receiving of a Saviour and his Grace freely given to us … And there is no doubt but Christ is the soul's riches which faith receiveth.[7]

Clifford also defends Baxter concerning the place of good works in the believer's continuing and final justification[8] (matters yet to be addressed). What chiefly irritated Clifford was England's failure to deal with the Baxter evidence carefully and honestly.

What Clifford evidently highlights is Baxter's rejection of the antinomian view of the Gospel (including false notions of imputation), in which the human aspect of salvation is effectively nullified under the weight of exaggerated,

1 *Defence*, 6.
2 Ibid. 8.
3 Ibid. 9.
4 Ibid. 14–15.
5 Ibid. 16.
6 Ibid. 16. Baxter, *Catholick Theologie*, I. ii. 51.
7 *The Scripture Gospel Defended* (1690), 34.
8 Ibid. 17.

over-orthodox notions of divine grace.[1] In a piece of vintage Baxter, Clifford
reveals the cluster of Gospel truths affirmed by the 'abused' Puritan:

> Christ being truly reputed to have taken the nature of sinful man,
> and become a Head for all true believers, in that undertaken nature and
> office in the person of a Mediator, he fulfilled all the Law imposed on
> him, by perfect holiness and obedience, and offering himself on the
> cross a sacrifice for our sins, voluntarily suffering in our stead, as if he
> had been a sinner (guilty of all our sins). As soon as we believe, we are
> pardoned, justified, adopted, that for the sake and merit of this holiness,
> obedience, and penal satisfaction of Christ with as full demonstration
> of divine justice at least amid more full demonstration of his wisdom
> and mercy, than if we had suffered ourselves what our sins deserved, or
> had never sinned. And so righteousness is imputed to us, that is, we are
> accounted or reputed righteous, (not in relation to the precept, that is
> innocent or sinless, but in relation to the retribution, that is such as have
> right to impunity and life;) because Christ's foresaid perfect holiness,
> obedience, and satisfaction, merited our pardon, and adoption, and
> the Spirit; or merited the New Covenant, by which, as an instrument,
> pardon, justification, and adoption, are given to believers, and the Spirit
> to be given to sanctify them: And when we believe, we are justly reputed
> such as have right to all these purchased gifts.[2]

Clifford ended his case by saying that in no way was Baxter's teaching—
fairly and fully grasped—threatened by the Westminster Standards or the
Anglican Articles.[3] However, his chief anxiety was that England's attempted
'demolition job' on Baxter might diminish the impact of the very godly and
'useful labours' John England admits 'the world was much beholden to Mr.
B. for'.[4]

Speaking personally, Clifford's *Defence* provided a precedent for my own
criticism of Dr Packer. As did John England, Packer repeatedly charged
Baxter with denying things which he actually affirmed.[5] R. Scott Clark

1   Ibid. 10.
2   Ibid. 11; Baxter, *A Treatise of Justifying Righteousness* (1676), 51–2.
3   *Defence*, 18–19.
4   Ibid. 20.
5   See *Atonement and Justification*, 199, n. 37.

is likewise—and outrageously—out of order.[1] Doubtless Samuel Clifford would have been horrified—as I was in the autumn of 2015—to find Baxter's faithful, biblical theology dismissed as 'arsenic'.[2]

Denying that he relished refuting his opponent, Clifford feared the consequence of a devaluation of Baxter's legacy, if only because too many people had admired England's book:

> We had never undertaken such an ungrateful work as this hath been to us; so ungrateful indeed, that we could heartily wish we had never had occasion to be concerned about it. 'Tis but justice to right those which are wronged: we think we may without vanity say, that we have made it manifest beyond all contradiction, that Mr. B. hath been wronged very much, even in matters of fact; For which reason we shall promise ourselves, that what we have done, will (by all impartial considerate readers) be interpreted as a piece of justice to the name and memory of that great man; and the rather, because he is dead, and cannot right himself from the wrongs which are done him.[3]

Baxter himself would have been pleased by Clifford's efforts, not least for the manner with which he put down his quill. Indeed, as famous (or infamous!) as Baxter was for his robust polemics, he also longed to promote love, harmony and peace. This was not lost on Samuel Clifford who sets a standard for theological debate. He said of England, 'by what we hear of him he is a pious man, upon which account we do unfeignedly love him'.[4] While their criticisms arouse considerable annoyance, I say the same of Packer et al! Therefore …

> … notwithstanding his difference from Mr. B. in judgement, and these unhappy mistakes in matters of fact, and the wrong he hath (ignorantly) done to the name of Mr. B. thereby, we cannot but add this in the close of all, that we have such a character of Mr. En. for a pious and religious

---

1 'His 1649 *Aphorismes on Justification* taught quite clearly that faith justifies because it obeys. Where the orthodox (e.g., *Westminster Larger Catechism*, 70–73) had been explicit that only Christ's obedience is the ground and that, in the act of justification, faith's only virtue is Christ's finished work' (*Burying The Lead On Baxter: Baxter's doctrine of justification was theological arsenic*) http://theaquilareport.com/burying-the-lead-on-baxter/#.Vknkzb6LqnE.facebook

2 Ibid.

3 *Defence.* 20.

4 Ibid. 20–1.

man, as gives us good ground to hope, that Mr. Baxter and Mr. England
will live together in heaven, where there will be unity both in judgement
and affection.[1]

Building on Samuel Clifford's defence of Richard Baxter, it is vital to define
accurately the context in which Baxter's theology should be assessed. The
common view is that he occupied the 'middle ground' between Calvinism
and Arminianism, a hybrid or compromise known as 'Moderate Calvinism'.
However, this *via media* between two embattled soteriologies demands a
radical reassessment. As I demonstrated in my *Atonement and Justification*,
Baxter's theology may be justly depicted as an alternative to Arminianism
and *Owenism*. The fact remains that, driven by the unbiblical lust of lop-sided
logicality, 'Calvinism' underwent progressive change from the over-systematised
orthodoxy of Theodore Beza to the hyper-orthodoxy of John Gill. The high-
orthodoxy of the *Westminster Confession* and John Owen was a stage in this
evolutionary process. Accordingly, Baxter rightly styled Owen as the 'over-
orthodox doctor'.[2] Despite the attempt of scholars like Dr Richard Muller
to close down the 'Calvin *versus* Calvinism' debate, the evidence for the shift
away from John Calvin's conspicuous teaching remains too compelling to be
ignored. The mistake is to assume an exact shared identity between Calvin
and John Owen. Historians do this when they write of Baxter's seeming
discomfiture with Calvinism. However, they should be more discerning. The
problem was *Owenism* not properly-defined Calvinism. In short, Baxter was
not *moderating* but largely *re-affirming* Calvin's Calvinism. His was a mission
to return the goalposts to their proper place!

Typical of the lack of clarity are two statements by Neil Keeble:

Although [Baxter] wrote 'I know no man since the Apostles days whom
I value and honour more than *Calvin*',[3] his dread of the antinomian
tendencies latent in Calvinism, and his intense pastoral and evangelical
concern, led him to lay more stress upon man's role in the scheme of
salvation than is usually thought to be compatible with Calvinism.[4]

---

1   Ibid. 21.

2   *Reliquiae Baxterianae*, ii. 199.

3   Keeble cites the first edition (1650) of Baxter's *Saints Everlasting Rest*, 526. The quote appears
in the 1658 edition at page 559.

4   N. H. Keeble (ed), *The Autobiography of Richard Baxter* (London: J. M. Dent, 1985), p. xviii
(emphasis Keeble's).

Though we may wonder that Baxter could say 'I am no Arminian', it is no surprise to find him denying whole-hearted allegiance to Calvin, and undertaking, in *Richard Baxter's Catholick Theology* (1675), 'to reconcile the Arminians and Anti-Arminians' in the belief that 'The middle way which [Cameron ... Amyraut, Davenant, etc] ... is nearest the Truth.'[1]

Several comments are in order:

First, Keeble's half-quote from Baxter in the first extract possibly consists with the alleged 'denial of whole-hearted allegiance to Calvin' in the second, but Baxter's *full* statement creates an entirely contrary impression:

I know no man, since the Apostles' days, whom I value and honour more than Calvin, *and whose judgement in all things, one with another, I more esteem and come nearer to.*[2]

Before we examine the major areas of agreement between Baxter and Calvin, one notes that, in his funeral sermon, Dr William Bates was careful to state that Baxter 'was of Calvin's mind' regarding the intractable problems of church reform.[3] Baxter himself cited Calvin in support of his view of church order[4]—a synthesis of the elements of truth in the episcopal, presbyterian and congregational schemes.

Second, as we shall see shortly, Baxter's anxieties about 'Calvinism' arose from tendencies latent in Owenism (and worse), *not* in Calvin's actual teaching. Indeed, as we shall see in due course, Baxter's evangelical and pastoral concerns find full precedents in Calvin's 'authentic Calvinism'.

Third, as has been demonstrated,[5] Baxter's preferences for the soteriology of John Cameron, Moïse Amyraut and John Davenant are thoroughly consistent with 'the Truth' Baxter found in Calvin, whom he so much admired. Indeed, Baxter rather than John Owen (as his supporters like to claim) may be called 'the Calvin of England'. One may go a little further and say that Baxter was a 'turbo-charged' Calvin!

A. R. Ladell suggested that 'as [Baxter] grew older, he shed considerably

---

1   N. H. Keeble, *Richard Baxter: Puritan Man of Letters* (Oxford: Clarendon Press, 1982), 72.

2   *Saints Everlasting Rest* (1650), 526; (1658), 559.

3   William Bates, *A Funeral Sermon for the Reverend, Holy and Excellent Divine, Mr Richard Baxter* (London, 1692), 97–8. Bates cites Calvin on Matt. 13: 40.

4   Richard Baxter, *Five Disputations of Church Government and Worship* (London, 1659), 347.

5   See my *Amyraut Affirmed* (Norwich: Charenton Reformed Publishing, 2004, rep. 2014).

the Calvinism that is evident in the ... *Saints Everlasting Rest*' and that 'His conception of Predestination, though never extreme, became so moderate as practically to mean nothing'.[1] Apart from the close affinities between Baxter's and Calvin's teaching on the subject,[2] this is simply misleading at best. Published in his final year, Chapters V and VI of *An End of Doctrinal Controversies* (1691) demonstrate that Baxter's teaching was as clear and robust as ever. Regarding so-called 'double predestination', Baxter insists 'That the decree of damnation goeth on the *foresight* of sin, but the decree of salvation containeth a decree to give that grace that shall certainly save us'.[3]

What then of the other half of the acutest of all antinomies, the subject of free will? In another late, posthumously-published work, Baxter's long-held view—and strikingly similar to Calvin's—was confirmed.[4] Indeed, contrary to later ill-informed Arminian and *ultra*-Calvinist discussion, Calvin even denied that the human will—man being a voluntary slave—is divinely coerced. Calvin seems also quite happy to admit the term 'free will,' provided it is carefully defined.[5] The human tragedy is that we sin willingly and freely without the regeneration of the Holy Spirit. When Ladell further claimed that 'Baxter inclined more and more to his own interpretation of Common and Special Grace,' insisting 'upon the possibility of salvation including every man',[6] there was a precedent for such teaching in Calvin—and, surprise, surprise, even in John Owen![7]

Regarding his views as a whole, historian G. F. Nuttall was right to state

---

1 *Richard Baxter: Puritan and Mystic* (London: SPCK, 1924), 132–3.

2 A precedent for Baxter's position, Calvin plainly taught (while affirming an ultimate agnosticism over the advent of sin) that God providentially arranges all the factors behind human choices, *without being the author of sin*. Agreeing with Augustine, Calvin teaches that the 'cause and matter' of reprobation is *foreknown* human guilt rather than a naked supralapsarian decree: 'Man therefore falls, divine providence so ordaining, but he falls by his own fault ... he took the matter of it from himself, not from God, since the only cause of his destruction was his degeneration from the purity of his creation into a state of vice and impurity' (see *Inst.* 3: 23: 7–9). For all that he has been charged with 'double predestination', Calvin requires a more nuanced interpretation. He is clear that, since *external* grace is the cause of undeserved salvation, *internal* sin is the cause of deserved damnation, this being 'the true source' (ibid. 9; see also 3: 23: 10–11). As Baxter was later to argue, the twin decrees of salvation and damnation are not strictly 'parallel'.

3 *An End of Doctrinal Controversies* (London: 1691), 45 (emphasis mine).

4 See *The Protestant Religion Truely Stated and Justified* (London: 1692), 87–91.

5 See *Inst.* 2: 2: 7–8.

6 *Richard Baxter: Puritan and Mystic* ,133.

7 See *Atonement and Justification*, 115ff.

that Baxter 'formed his opinions early and rarely changed them substantially'.[1] However, Dr Nuttall's 'atheological' though otherwise-useful biographical treatment of Baxter is disappointingly defective, especially in view of the importance Baxter attached to his rigorous and perpetually-published theology of the Gospel. One looks in vain for any reference to Davenant, Twisse or Amyraut (but there is a passing reference to Calvin and other 'contemporaries—like Ussher—whom he had admired'[2]). While Keeble states his preference for Nuttall's *Richard Baxter* over Powicke's pair of volumes 'as biography', he acknowledges that the latter contain 'valuable discussions of Baxter's thought and writings'.[3] A case in point is Powicke's assessment that Baxter's 'divergence from [orthodoxy] was all in the direction of a freer evangelism, and did not prevent him from retaining what he held to be the substantial truth of Calvinism together with due regard to elements of truth in Arminianism'.[4]

However, when Dr Nuttall does drift into theological matters, one detects a liberal ecumenical agenda at work. His discussion of Baxter's alleged-affinities with Socinianism and Unitarianism provides fuel for those orthodox Trinitarians who, justifiably suspicious, would dismiss Baxter's legacy on such grounds. Not wishing to misrepresent anyone—including Dr Nuttall—he does admit (after quoting a sympathetic statement by the Unitarian scholar Alexander Gordon) that 'it may seem strange that Baxter should be claimed as a founding-father by the section of Dissent which in time came to hold the Arminian, Arian and Socinian tenets which he explicitly repudiated'.[5]

That said, on the previous page, historian Nuttall outlines Baxter's contribution to the 'Fundamentals of Religion' conference held in London in 1654. Predictably unwelcome to those arguing for a more detailed confessional basis, Baxter's minimalist proposals sounded dangerous, as Dr Nuttall makes clear:

> For [Baxter] pleaded that the Apostles' 'Creed, Lord's Prayer, and Decalogue alone' should be offered 'as our essentials or Fundamentals';

---

1   *Richard Baxter* (London: Thomas Nelson, 1965), 130.

2   Ibid. 128.

3   *The Autobiography of Richard Baxter*, ed. N. H. Keeble (London: Dent, 1974), p. xxix.

4   F. J. Powicke, *Richard Baxter Under the Cross* (London: Jonathan Cape Ltd, 1927, Quinta edition), 245.

5   Ibid. 123.

and when other commissioners complained, 'A Socinian or a Papist will subscribe all this, I answered them, So much the better.' It is no wonder that he was misunderstood; or that his desire for Christian unity was ineffective, then and always.[1]

As with Keeble's partial quoting, Nuttall creates a false impression by omitting a highly-significant caveat in Baxter's full statement; he argued that should 'Papists and Socinians' subscribe to such a confessional basis, the way to proceed would be to 'call them to account whenever in preaching or writing they contradict or abuse the truth to which they have subscribed'.[2] In other words, neither Rome nor Rationalists would find support for their distinctives in Baxter's '*Confession of Faith*'! Such a qualification explains why Dr Nuttall was correct to conclude that Baxter 'explicitly repudiated' heretical notions; but omitting a key part of his statement—as did Roger Thomas (1968)[3], Hywel R. Jones (1969)[4] and D. M. Lloyd-Jones (1969)[5]—leaves the reader imagining that Baxter was happy to tolerate anti-Trinitarian ideas. In short, the Unitarians or so-called 'Rational Dissenters' have no friend in Richard Baxter, even though he would wish to win them to the 'Truth'. His emphasis on 'Scripture-sufficiency' meant that revelation and faith must always take precedence over 'natural' reason. He made this clear in his *Arrogancy of Reason*, a part of *The Unreasonableness of Infidelity* (1655).[6] For all the importance Baxter attached to 'sanctified' reason (in due subordination to 'faith'), the Unitarian community abused his insights to justify an anti-Christian agenda. And what impertinence it is to imply that those who affirm the Deity of Christ and the Holy Trinity are '*irrational* Dissenters!

It is now time to examine the evidence for Baxter's affinities with Calvin. Of course, many would say that Baxter should be tested by the Bible rather

---

1   Ibid. 122.

2   Baxter, *RB*, I, ii, 52, p. 198.

3   See Roger Thomas, 'The Rise of the Reconcilers' in *The English Presbyterians: From Elizabethan Puritanism to Modern Unitarianism* (London: George Allen & Unwin, 1968), 59.

4   See Hywel R. Jones, 'The Death of Presbyterianism' in *By Schisms Rent Asunder* (London: Puritan and Reformed Studies Conference, 1969), 37.

5   See D. M. Lloyd-Jones, 'Can We Learn from History' in *By Schisms Rent Asunder* (London: Puritan and Reformed Studies Conference, 1969), 82; also D. M. Lloyd-Jones, *The Puritans: Their Origins and Successors* (Edinburgh: The Banner of Truth Trust, 1987), 231.

6   See Richard Baxter, *The Autobiography of Richard Baxter*, ed. J. M. Lloyd Thomas (London: J. M. Dent, 1931), 285.

than Calvin's teaching. As far as I am concerned, this is axiomatic and goes without saying. Indeed, in Baxter's day, the vast majority of his theological contemporaries claimed to be Bible-based. However, if it hasn't yet dawned on my readers, I now declare my belief that John Calvin is the greatest theologian since the Apostle Paul. That said, while I would be careful not to invest the Genevan reformer with infallibility, I believe that when it comes to the distinctive doctrines of Christianity, no one can match him for biblical integrity, accuracy and consistency. Therefore, it is the 'authentic' Calvin I have in mind, not the caricature usually invoked when the word 'Calvinism' is used. I therefore seek to demonstrate that, by and large, 'authentic Calvinism' is the proper benchmark by which to test Baxter, not the exaggerated version which he repeatedly collided with.

Another reason for appealing to Calvin is that Packer *et al* invalidly appeal to the reformer against Baxter in favour of Owen.[1] I have demonstrated this in my *Atonement and Justification*. While the overlap falls short in two important (though reconcilable) details, it is evidently the case that there are several important precedents for Baxter's views in Calvin's teaching. So, having already quoted Baxter's unambiguous admiration for Calvin, I explore their respective teachings on the subjects of justification and the atonement. For those who might find this a tedious exercise, please feel free to return to my 'celebration' of Baxter. However, if you do, you are likely to end up with important theological reservations about him that you could have avoided. Be assured, I will endeavour to be as brief and clear as possible (including—unless impossible—an avoidance of any scholastic terms which always tended to clutter the discussion).

Starting with the charge discussed above that Baxter maintains the believer's faith is his righteousness before God, note the similarity between Baxter and Calvin:

> *Baxter:* 'the formal reason of [faith's] office as to our justification is its being the performed condition of the Covenant' ... and 'our faith now is instead of our innocency ... Paul saith, that faith is imputed to us for righteousness. To deny this sense, is to use violence with the text'.[2]

---

1   See J. I. Packer, 'The Doctrine of Justification in Development and Decline among the Puritans', *By Schisms Rent Asunder* (Puritan and Reformed Studies Report, 1969), 21.

2   *Catholick Theologie*, I. ii. 82, 86.

Calvin: '… what can the formal or instrumental cause be but faith?'[1] 'For it is not said that faith was imputed to him as a part of his righteousness but simply as righteousness. Hence his faith was truly in place of righteousness for him.'[2]

In his corresponding comment on Romans 4: 4–5, Calvin is careful to eliminate all trace of merit in man:

Calvin: 'Faith is reckoned as righteousness not because it brings any merit from us, but because it lays hold of the goodness of God'.[3]

Baxter also flatly denies that merit has any place:

Baxter: 'Faith is counted for righteousness [in the believer], by the Covenant of Grace; that is, God accepteth it as the qualification or condition, which must be found in him (without such meritorious works) to make him partaker of that pardon, adoption and salvation given by Grace, upon consideration of the meritorious Righteousness of Christ'.[4]

So, where is the problem? "The word 'condition'", some would say. "Isn't that Arminian talk?" Viewing the human response to the Gospel in terms of the sinner's *duty* to repent and believe (albeit performed only by grace), Baxter had no time for his antinomian critics' nervousness regarding 'conditions'. Anticipating Baxter, Calvin exhibits no such qualms:

Calvin: 'Repentance and faith must needs go together … God receiveth us to mercy, and daily pardoneth our faults through his free goodness: and that we be justified because Jesus Christ hath reconciled him unto us, inasmuch as he accepteth us for righteous though we be wretched sinners: in preaching this, it behoveth us to add, how *it is upon condition that we return unto God:* as was spoken of heretofore by the prophets'.[5]

Baxter's critics have often penalised him for questioning justification by faith alone, on the basis that he taught justification as a 'process' or 'continuum', starting at conversion and ending at the Day of Judgement. Such a view is

---

1   *Institutes*, III. xiv. 17
2   *Comm.* Galatians 3: 6.
3   *Comm.* Romans 4: 4.
4   *Paraphrase*, Romans 4: 5.
5   *Sermons on Timothy and Titus*, 1181–2 (emphasis mine).

frequently found, not only in his 'polemical' works,[1] but also in the very 'practical' works so highly commended by Packer.[2] Indeed, as cited by Samuel Clifford (using an edition different from the one quoted elsewhere in this book), his position was early made clear in his *Aphorismes*: 'That faith justifies as the great principal master duty of the Gospel, or chief part of its condition: but that gospel-works do justify as the secondary less principal parts of the condition of the Covenant'.[3] He continued:

> *Baxter.* 'I acknowledge that the very first point of justification is by faith alone, without either the concomitancy, or cooperation of works; for they cannot be performed in an instant: but the continuance and accomplishment of justification, is not without the joint-procurement of obedience'.[4]

> *Baxter.* 'Justification begun, is continued by the same God, Christ, merit, covenant; but not by the same condition only. I have oft proved out of many Scriptures, that forgiving others, repentance of after-sins, praying for pardon, sincere obedience, etc. are by God made conditions of continuance ...'[5]

Suggesting perhaps a more lenient view of Baxter than I allowed in *Atonement and Justification*, it is simply a slur to suggest that he taught some idea of justification by meritorious works. :

> *Baxter.* 'So far as we are sinners, a pardon is our righteousness: but so far as we are holy, it is not so ... [sincere obedience] is the justification by works (as many are willing to call it, to make it odious) which I assert and defend, and which I judge so necessary to be believed ...'[6]

In brief, what then is Baxter saying? Coupling one's understanding of Ephesians 2: 8–10 with that of James 2: 24, it is plain that, for Paul and James, true saving faith is a 'good works-producing faith'. Therefore, faith

---

1   'Justification is not a momentaneous act, begun and ended immediately upon our believing: but a continued act; which though it be in its kind complete from the first, yet is it still in doing, till the final justification at the judgement day' (*Aphorismes of Justification*, 149).

2   Notably in the early sections of *The Saints' Everlasting Rest* (1650).

3   Clifford, *Defence*, 17; *Aphorismes of Justification* (1649), 289.

4   Clifford, *Defence*, 17; Baxter, *Aphorismes*, 302.

5   Clifford, *Defence*, 17; Baxter, *The Substance of Mr Cartwright's Exceptions Considered* (1675), 252.

6   *Rich: Baxter's Confession of his Faith* 1655), Preface, pp. (ix, x)(n.p.) See also *CT*, I. ii. 69ff.

unaccompanied by obedience cannot save. This is not for one moment to deny that defective obedience will always require forgiveness, until one's dying day. That said, Baxter clearly found precedents in Calvin for such teachings:

> Calvin: 'We dream not of a faith which is devoid of good works, nor of a justification which can exist without them'.[1]

He also suggests that justification is no less dependent on the believer's obedience than it is on Christ's righteousness:

> Calvin: '... we cannot be justified freely by faith alone, if we do not at the same time live in holiness'.[2]

Calvin further describes the conditional passage, 'But if we walk in the light, ... the blood of Christ cleanses us from all sin' (1 John 1: 7) as 'remarkable':

> Calvin: 'From it we learn ... that the expiation of Christ, effected by his death, belongs properly to us when we cultivate righteousness ... For Christ is Redeemer only to those who are turned from iniquity and begin a new life'.[3]

Calvin clearly anticipates Baxter's emphasis that 'gospel-works do justify as the secondary less principal parts of the condition of the Covenant'. Stressing like Baxter that the obedience of Christ is the meritorious foundation of salvation, Calvin yet says:

> Calvin: '... there is nothing to prevent the Lord from embracing works as inferior causes. But how so? In this way: Those whom in mercy he has destined for the inheritance of eternal life, he, in his ordinary administration, introduces to the possession of it by means of good works ... For this reason, he sometimes makes eternal life a consequent of works'.[4]

Within weeks of his death in 1564, Calvin reflected on the idea of 'sola fide'. His remarkable statement clearly anticipated the kind of things Baxter felt compelled to affirm in the face of the antinomian threat:

---

1   *Institutes*, III. xvi. 1.
2   *Comm.* 1 Cor. 1: 30.
3   *Comm.* 1 Jn. 1: 7.
4   *Institutes*, III. xiv. 21.

Calvin: 'Thus it still remains true, that faith without works justifies, although this needs prudence and a sound interpretation; for this proposition, that faith without works justifies is true and yet false, according to the different senses which it bears. The proposition, that faith without works justifies by itself, is false, because faith without works is void ... faith cannot justify when it is without works, because it is dead, and a mere fiction.'[1]

Making sense of Calvin's hesitancy, an additional comment on the unbiblical 'sola fide' idea is in order. After all, since it is rejected in James 2: 24, Luther was wrong to add 'allein' ('alone') at Romans 3: 28 in his German New Testament (1522). I have explained elsewhere that 'faith alone' should not be seen as a statement about a believer's *psychological* response to Christ but as *synecdochal* 'shorthand' for 'faith in Christ alone'.[2] This is evidently how Paul intended 'faith' to be understood, as in Romans 3: 26; 'faith' always assumes and connotes an object, viz. in this instance, Christ. In short, *Christ is the only one trusted in*, a vital truth which excludes every idea of human merit, a truth jealously guarded by Calvin, and also Richard Baxter. Despite his Calvin-like insistence that love and obedience are necessary concomitants with trust in the Saviour's saving work, Baxter always taught properly-defined 'sola fide'.

The first detailed but resolvable difference between Calvin and Baxter concerns the meaning of the term 'justification'. I have demonstrated in my *Atonement and Justification* that, unlike, Beza, Owen and other 'over-orthodox' Calvinists who insisted that justification is *more* than just forgiveness, Calvin regularly insists that 'justification' and 'pardon' are really the same thing.[3] In the process of showing, as Baxter was to do, that justification is a 'continuum', Calvin argues that at every stage of his life, the believer's justification is always that of 'forgiveness'. 'Therefore we must have this blessedness not once only', he concludes.[4] He bases his argument on Psalm 32, where David describes his experience 'after a lengthy period of training in the service of God'. Thus, says Calvin, there is such a thing as the 'commencement of justification', and also 'the unending continuance of free righteousness throughout our whole life'.[5]

---

1   *Comm.* Ezek. 18: 14–17.
2   See *Atonement and Justification*, 176–7.
3   Ibid. 171.
4   *Institutes*, III. xiv. 11.
5   *Comm.* Rom. 3: 21; 4: 6.

In short, 'justification' (= 'pardon') is a daily requirement, not a once-for-all event. In this respect, the doctrine of continuous justification is found in the Lord's Prayer: 'Give us this day our daily bread, and forgive us our debts ...' (Matt. 6: 11–12). Calvin could not be clearer: '[Christ] bids all His disciples daily to have recourse to the remission of sins'.[1] As we have seen in Baxter, Calvin also recognised the conditional nature of our pardon: '... as we forgive our debtors'. While the meritorious sacrifice of Christ is the *cause* of our pardon, 'The condition is made to prevent anyone daring to approach God to seek forgiveness without being quite free and clear of hatred'.[2]

Whatever was true of a later orthodoxy, Calvin did not subscribe to the 'lightning-flash', once-for-all idea of justification, an idea with as much potential for antinomianism as the doctrine of eternal justification. This was no part of his polemic against Rome. His uncluttered continuum view is exegetically valid and thoroughly coherent. From an exegetical point of view, Paul's use of the aorist *dikaiothentes* in Romans 5: 1, 'Being justified by faith ...' merely proves that whenever any sins are confessed, either at conversion or subsequently, the believer is—there and then—pardoned or justified. From a translation perspective, this makes the AV 'being justified' more accurate than Packer's ESV 'since we have been justified'. Unlike the latter, the former is not time-specific. Indeed, it is an over-simplification to regard the aorist as a simple past. Greek tenses have to do with the *state* of the action (complete, incomplete or indefinite) rather than the *time* of the action (past, present or future). It is simple action without indicating it as either completed or incompleted.

In view of the equivalence between 'justification' and 'pardon', it is arguably incorrect to suggest that justification, unlike the 'new birth', is a once for all 'lightning-flash' event in the Christian's life. It is true that, at conversion, all sins hitherto committed are forgiven immediately. However, to say that such an instantaneous justification is a valid ticket for every sin thereafter is to 'over do' the legal metaphors of the Epistle to the Romans. There Paul clearly imagines a court trial. Justification of the accused relates only to crimes hitherto committed (Romans 3: 25?). Any future violations or the law would demand a further trial for justification to occur. It is true, the meritorious basis of all justification is the once for all sacrifice of Christ. But

---

1　*Comm.* Matt. 6: 12.
2　Ibid.

to say that the sinner's justification is complete—and that all our sins, past, present and future were all pardoned at the cross because the gracious basis of acquittal is complete—is to confuse a single cause with a multiplicity of effects. Baxter sums up the absurdity at the heart of this error: 'They say all sin past, present, and to come, are pardoned, even that not committed (that is no sin)'.[1] In short, sin is not forgiven until it is committed and repented of. Justification is never in advance. A believer's life is a continuum of instants. At any instant, 'I have been justified' and 'I am being justified' are perfectly compatible statements. The just man is living by faith.

It is striking that, as well as rejecting the 'lightning-flash' concept, Baxter almost did adopt Calvin's definition of 'justification = pardon':

> Baxter: 'I think it had been well for the church, if we had used less in our disputes the term justification … If we had treated more fully about remission of sin alone, and under that term … I think the church would reap much benefit by it. Doubtless we might much easier convince a papist … when so many of ours do take remission and justification for the same thing'.[2]

Had Baxter persisted with this observation, his overall teaching about justification (with its multiplicity of senses) would have met with fewer objections. That said, his stress on obedience as a kind of secondary basis of justification really endorses Calvin's clear teaching that justification can never be divorced from, or unaccompanied by, obedience. *The difference between the two theologians is merely verbal.*

The second equally-resolvable difference concerns the doctrine of imputation. Before proceeding, this much must be clarified, that—as Samuel Clifford pointed out above—Baxter argues for the 'true' idea of imputation over against the 'false'. He denies that a strict 'sameness' exists between the meritorious work of Christ (his 'being', 'doing' and 'suffering') and what is imputed to the believer. His 'actions', though for our benefit, were not 'ours'. As for our Saviour's death, Baxter argued that Christ paid not the *identical* punishment but a *substituted equivalent*. Since our sins are threatened with eternal punishment, Christ would be in hell if He paid the same satisfaction. In short, a proper biblical doctrine of penal substitution means

1 *A Defence of Christ and Free Grace* (1690), 12.

2 *Rich: Baxter's Confession of his Faith* (1655), p. (vii).

that *both* Christ *and* His sufferings were 'in the place' of all we deserve. Including the so-called 'double-payment' objection to universal atonement, I have made the intricacies of this issue clear elsewhere.[1] Hence Packer is incorrect to state Baxter's view of the atonement as 'penal and vicarious but not substitutionary'.[2] In short, it was an *equivalent* substitution, not an *exact* substitution. I have also elsewhere[3] questioned Packer's famous (though flawed) 1958 promotion of Owen's doctrine of 'limited atonement'.[4]

What Baxter rejects is the incoherence of the Beza-Owen theory of imputation. If this is correct, then, says Baxter regarding Christ's 'doing', 'we could need no pardon, for he that is reputed to be innocent, by fulfilling all the law, is reputed never to have sinned ... Therefore, such an imputation of Christ's righteousness to us would make his satisfaction null or vain'.[5] In short, the logic of Owen's defective and contradictory view makes the cross unnecessary and redundant!

At this point, Baxter's thought is in line with Johannes Piscator who made explicit what is implicit in Calvin, that Christ's sufferings rather than his 'active righteousness' are imputed to believers. For this reason, justification consists only in the remission of sins, a view which Baxter agreed would have been 'beneficial' to the church in debates on the subject. *It was his fear of antinomian abuse that made him uneasy with this simple solution, as if Calvin's view did not include the very safeguards Baxter was anxious to maintain. Put simply, Baxter was afraid of easy-believeism. So was Calvin.*

Further evidence of Baxter's growing sympathy with the Calvin-Piscator position is a highly-significant statement made a year before his death:

Baxter: And although my own judgement be for the imputation of Christ's passive, active, and habitual righteousness, dignified by the Divine as the full and the sole meritorious cause of all grace and glory, as making up the condition of his Mediatorial Covenant imposed on

1   See *Atonement and Justification*, 127–31.

2   Introduction , *The Reformed Pastor* (Edinburgh: The Banner of Truth Trust, 1974), 10.

3   See 'Geneva Revisited or Calvinism Revised', in *Churchman* 100. 4 (London: Church Society, 1986), 323–34; also: 'Calvin & Calvinism: Amyraut ET AL', in Alan C. Clifford (ed), *John Calvin 500: A Reformation Affirmation* (Norwich: Charenton Reformed Publishing, 2011), 37–79.

4   See 'Introductory Essay' to *The Death of Death in the Death of Christ* (London: The Banner of Truth Trust, 1959).

5   *Richard Baxter's Catholick Theologie*, I. ii. 59.

him by God; yet I intreat the learned reader to peruse the writings of those great divines that are for the imputation of the passive only ...[1]

At this point, Baxter recommends the theologians of Heidelberg (Ursinus, Olevianus, Pareus) and Saumur (Cameron, De la Place):

'... and all that party of famous French divines [including Amyraut and Daillé] who all effectually confute the false sense of imputation of the Active Righteousness ... as if we had done it by Christ, and were the subjects of it ...[2]

It is equally clear that Calvin would have had fewer reservations over Baxter's view of imputation than over Owen's. Although the Genevan reformer unambiguously defines salvation in terms of the death of Christ, he does not deny that 'the *ground* of pardon' extends to 'the whole life of Christ'.[3] Yet, for exegetical reasons (judging by his remarks on Romans 5: 8 and 18), Calvin would have no time for Owen's insistence that justification is *more* than pardon, or that Paul thought the obedience of Christ in question was *more* than his death. As he carefully points out, the obedience in question is *dikaioma*, the 'righteous act' of the cross.

It is interesting to compare Baxter's own *Paraphrase*[4] comments on Romans 5 with Calvin's. In many ways, this work is probably the most accessible source of Baxter's views in their entirety. Indeed, instead of responding exhaustively to works by other authors *ad hoc* (as was his wont!), Baxter's direct engagement with the sacred text demanded a more disciplined response to the issues, if only for reasons of brevity. Romans 5: 9 is especially important since, if the Beza-Owen view of twofold-imputation is correct, then Paul was only half right, and therefore half wrong, if being 'justified by his blood' states the full basis of justification. We thus find Baxter in complete harmony with Calvin. They evidently concur in holding that the merit of Christ's sacrifice is imputed to the believer:

Baxter: 'And if [God] loved us so far, as to give his Son to die for us when we were mere guilty sinners, we may be sure that now he hath

---

1   *The Scripture Gospel Defended* (1690), 74. See also, Alan C. Clifford, 'Justification: the Calvin-Saumur Perspective', *The Evangelical Quarterly*, 79. 4 (2007).

2   Ibid.

3   *Inst.* II. xvi. 5.

4   *A Paraphrase on the New Testament* (1685).

made and accepted us as righteous, pardoning all our sin for the sacrifice of the blood of Christ, he will certainly save us from damnation'.[1]

This much is clear: the gap between Calvin and Baxter on one hand, and Owen on the other is far from insignificant. Contrary to the stances of Packer and Clark, Owen is simply out of step with both the Bible and Calvin, and Packer especially was simply out of order when attempting to dismiss Baxter's view with Calvin's support.

Lastly, it is striking to see the close correspondence between Calvin and Baxter regarding the formula of Christ's triple office of Prophet, Priest and King, together with its implications for the nature of saving faith. Indeed, Baxter works out the full implications of the formula in a way Calvin certainly hints at.[2] Faith therefore has a comprehensive, tripartite character, each of its three constituents—belief, trust and obedience—relating to the corresponding office of Christ: the assent of the mind, the trust of the heart and the obedience of the will constitute justifying faith's response to Christ. 'Whenever justification and life is promised to faith, all these three are the essential parts of it'.[3] Therefore, 'The object of justifying, saving faith, is one only undivided Christ'.[4] and 'There is no justification by a partial faith'.[5] Thus, to deny any one element of faith would negate a corresponding office in Christ.

As I have demonstrated, on this issue John Owen's view—with its antinomian implications—is seriously defective.[6] Contrary to Clark's dubious commendation, Owen is no safe guide on the subject. Furthermore, in criticising Baxter's view of faith,[7] Packer ('supported' by Hywel Jones[8]) fails to see the full implications of the very theory he praises Calvin for expounding.[9] As for the antinomian hostility towards Baxter's so-called

---

1   Ibid. *Comment* on Rom. 5: 9.

2   Calvin writes that 'the name of Christ refers to those three offices' (*Institutes*, II. xv. 2), and 'faith embraces Christ as he is offered by the Father' (III. ii. 8). Therefore, 'He unites the offices of King and Pastor towards believers, who voluntarily submit to him' (II. xv. 5).

3   *Catholick Theologie*, I. ii. 45.

4   *Directions and Persuasions to Sound Conversion* (1658), (1981 ed.) at p.592.

5   *Catholick Theologie*, I. ii. 86.

6   See *Atonement and Justification*, 206.

7   See 'The Doctrine of Justification in Development and Decline among the Puritans', 27.

8   See 'The Death of Presbyterianism', 37.

9   J. I. Packer, 'Calvin the Theologian', in *John Calvin*, ed. G. Duffield (Abingdon: Sutton

'neonomianism', I refer the reader to my defence of his position.[1] Simply put, Baxter rightly argues that Christians are not 'lawless' since faith involves submission to Christ as King, who governs his people by his 'Law of Grace' (see Romans 8: 2; 1 Corinthians 9: 21; Galatians 6: 2).

Therefore, on the subject of justification, nothing more need be said to vindicate Richard Baxter. As I argued in *Atonement and Justification*,[2] one or two residual problems regarding James 2: 24 were dealt with by John Tillotson. Notwithstanding a slight but significant exegetical difference, Tillotson resolved the issue in line with the thrust and spirit of Calvin's and Baxter's identical emphases.[3] It must be said, that there is nothing 'disastrous' or 'poisonous' in what amounts to Baxter's personal testimony penned a year before his death:

I abhor the opinion of any works necessary to justification or salvation, or to any common blessings in the sense of Paul; such as make the reward to be of debt, and not of grace. I think few men living, are less tempted to magnify or trust to any worth of their own, than I am. I look not for a bit of bread, or an hour's ease, or life, or the pardon, or acceptance of one duty, or of my holiest affections (so faulty are they by their great imperfection) but merely from the free grace of God, and the merits and intercession of Christ. ... The faith by which we are justified, is that true Christianity which includeth our believing consent to God the Father, Son, and Holy Ghost; our belief of Christ, and our thankful acceptance of him to be our Teacher, Intercessor or Priest, and King, with his offered Grace; and that this acceptance is with desire, love, and hope, expressed in a holy contract or covenant. This is the soul's marriage with Christ, and allegiance to him, and it includeth the renouncing our trust in all creatures, or in any righteousness of our own, so far as they would usurp the least part of Christ's office, works, or honour. None of all this is justification by works.[4]

Courtenay Press, 1966), 168.

1   See *Atonement and Justification*, 192–4.

2   Ibid. 194ff.

3   See also, Alan C. Clifford, 'The Gospel and Justification' (Norwich: 2016 at at http://www. nrchurch.co.uk/

4   *A Defence of Christ and Free Grace* (1690), To the Reader [p. 7], 24.

2. The Extent of the Atonement

Having touched briefly on the subject of the atonement in Samuel Clifford's *Defence* and examined its nature, we have also noted Baxter's high regard for Calvin in general. When Baxter set forth his views on the atonement, he was careful to cite[5] (among others) Calvin's views on several biblical texts: Romans 5: 18; 1 Corinthians 8: 11; 2 Peter 2: 1 and 1 John 2: 2. They are as follows:

> *Comment on Romans 5: 18:* 'Paul makes grace common to all men, not because it in fact extends to all, but because it is offered to all. Although Christ suffered for the sins of the world, and is offered by the goodness of God without distinction to all men, yet not all receive him'.

> *Comment on 1 Corinthians 8: 11:* 'For one can imagine nothing more despicable than this, that while Christ did not hesitate to die so that the weak might not perish, we, on the other hand, do not care a straw for the salvation of the men and women who have been redeemed at such a price. This is a memorable saying, from which we learn how precious the salvation of our brothers ought to be to us, and not only that of all, but of each individual, in view of the fact that the blood of Christ was poured out for each one … If the soul of every weak person costs the price of the blood of Christ, anyone, who, for the sake of a little bit of meat, is responsible for the rapid return to death of a brother redeemed by Christ, shows just how little the blood of Christ means to him. Contempt like that is therefore an open insult to Christ'.

> *Comment on 2 Peter 2: 1:* 'Christ redeemed us to have us as a people separated from all the iniquities of the world, devoted to holiness and purity. Those who throw over the traces and plunge themselves into every kind of licence are not unjustly said to deny Christ, by whom they were redeemed'.

Although Baxter does not claim a total concurrence of view in the final example, he highlights Calvin's partial endorsement:

> *Comment on 1 John 2: 2:* 'He put this in for amplification, that believers might be convinced that the expiation made by Christ extends to all

---

who by faith embrace the Gospel. But here the question may be asked as to how the sins of the whole world have been expiated. I pass over the dreams of the fanatics, who make this a reason to extend salvation to all the reprobate and even to Satan himself. Such a monstrous idea is not worth refuting. Those who want to avoid this absurdity have said that *Christ suffered sufficiently for the whole world but effectively only for the elect. This solution has commonly prevailed in the schools.* Although *I allow the truth of this*, I deny that it fits the passage. For John's purpose was only to make this blessing common to the whole church'.

Although Calvin had his reasons for exegeting the text a little differently in his commentary, he approved of its unqualified use in Articles III and IV of the Sixth Session of the Council of Trent: "Him God set forth to be a propitiation through faith in his blood for our sins, and not for ours only, but also for the sins of the whole world ... But though he died for all, all do not receive the benefit of his death, but those only to whom the merit of his passion is communicated ..." Calvin stated unambiguously: "The third and fourth heads I do not touch ..."[1]

I have provided a large quantity of similar Calvin extracts elsewhere.[2] However, Baxter's brief selection is enough to suggest that Calvin did not subscribe to the doctrine of limited atonement associated with his successor Theodore Beza, John Owen and others. Besides expressing his debt to Calvin, Baxter also spoke highly of the Synod of Dort (1618–19):

In the article of the extent of redemption, wherein I am most suspected and accused, I do subscribe to the Synod of Dort, without any exception, limitation, or exposition, of any word, as doubtful and obscure.[3]

This is remarkable since the famous Synod is forever associated with the famous mnemonic 'TULIP', the 'L' standing for 'Limited Atonement'. How then is Baxter's commendation to be understood? Simply because the 'Owenite' understanding of the mnemonic does not square with the actual

---

1 John Calvin, *Tracts and Treatises* (Edinburgh: Calvin Translation Society, 1851), iii. 93, 109.

2 See Alan C. Clifford, *CALVINUS: Authentic Calvinism, A Clarification* (Norwich: Charenton Reformed Publishing, 1996; 2nd ed. 2009.

3 *Rich: Baxter's Confession of his Faith* (1655), 25; cited in William Orme (ed), *The Practical Works of the Revd. Richard Baxter* (London: James Duncan, 1830), i. 456.

wording of the Canons themselves. The reason why Baxter could vouch for them is that they state the following:

'The death of the Son of God is the only and most perfect sacrifice and satisfaction for sins, of infinite value and worth, abundantly sufficient to expiate the sins of the whole world ... That, however, many who have been called by the gospel neither repent nor believe in Christ but perish in unbelief does not happen because of any defect or insufficiency in the sacrifice of Christ offered on the cross, but through their own fault ... For this was the most free counsel of God the Father, that the life-giving and saving efficacy of the most precious death of His Son should extend to all the elect'.[1]

This being Baxter's view, it is generally the case that many who shout 'TULIP' have never actually read what the Canons say. One may add that the word 'limited' is nowhere used. Furthermore, a case could be made for redefining 'L' as Limitless Atonement'! The point is, of course that the Canons affirm two correlated aspects to the atonement, as Baxter himself always did.

To vindicate Baxter's stance on this subject, we need a little theological context. We must first understand that, according to the 'Limited Atonement' teaching of Theodore Beza, John Owen and others, Christ died for the elect ALONE. According to the 'Universal Atonement' teaching of Jakob Arminius, John Wesley and others, Christ died for ALL (yet salvation is uncertain for anyone). Richard Baxter—agreeing with Augustine, Martin Luther, Thomas Cranmer and John Calvin *et al*, and urging an avoidance of extremist exegesis—maintained that the Bible demands a balanced view of 'universality' and 'particularity'.

Largely using a careful representative selection of Baxter's *Paraphrase* and other 'practical' statements (instead of his rather technical and tricky posthumous treatise on *Universal Redemption*), also highlighting the evangelistic and pastoral implications of his teaching, the case may be set out as follows:

---

1   See The Canons of Dort, Arts. 3, 6, 7, *The Creeds of the Evangelical Protestant Churches*, ed. H. B. Smith and P. Schaff (London: Hodder & Stoughton, 1877), 586f.

I

Richard Baxter's basic view of the Gospel to be preached universally (see Mark 16: 15)

For God, who is Love itself, so far loved lapsed and lost mankind, as that he gave his only begotten Son to be incarnate, and to be their Redeemer, by his meritorious Life, and Death, and Resurrection, and to make them this promise, covenant and offer, that whoever truly believeth in him, should have his sin forgiven; and should not perish, but have everlasting blessed life.[1]

II

His refusal to 'explain away' the 'universal' texts of the Bible

When God saith so expressly that Christ died for all [2 Cor. 5: 14–15], and tasted death for every man [Heb. 2: 9], and is the ransom for all [1 Tim. 2: 6], and the propitiation for the sins of the whole world [1 Jn. 2: 2], it beseems every Christian rather to explain in what sense Christ died for all, than flatly to deny it.[2]

III

His explanation of the four texts cited above

(1) 2 Corinthians 5: 14–15: For we have cause to judge, that they are great things, which our Redemption intimateth, even that Christ, who died for all, found all men dead in Sin and Misery; and that he therefore redeemed them by his Death, that they who are recovered by him should not hereafter live to themselves, but to him that died for them and rose again.[3]

(2) Hebrews 2: 9: [Christ's] death was suffered in the common nature of Man, and the sins of all men had a causal hand in it, and it was by God's Grace the purchasing cause of the conditional Covenant of Grace, and of all the good that men receive, so he died to bring Man to Glory with himself.[4]

---

1 *A Paraphrase on the New Testament* (London, 1685), Comment on John 3: 16. Hereinafter, *Paraphrase*.
2 *The Universal Redemption of Mankind* (London, 1694), 286.
3 *Paraphrase*, Comment on 2 Corinthians 5: 14–15.
4 *Paraphrase*, Comment on Hebrews 2: 9.

(3) 1 Timothy 2: 6: For it must move us to pray for all, in compliance with this Will of God, that would have all Men saved; because there is One God who is good to all, and One Mediator between God and Mankind, who took on him the Common Nature of all men, and gave himself a Ransom for all ...[1]

(4) 1 John 2: 2: For he is the Propitiation for our sins by virtue of his Sacrifice, now interceding for us in heaven: And he is a propitiation sufficient for the sins of the whole World (so far as that none of them shall be damned for want of a sufficient Sacrifice, but only for want of accepting his Grace) and actually effecting the Pardon of all in the world, who believingly trust and accept him and his Grace.[2]

IV
His view of the Atonement-based provision of the universal Gospel offer

[We see] the wonderful love and mercy that God hath manifested in giving his Son to be the Redeemer of the world, and which the Son hath manifested in redeeming them by his blood; for all his full preparation by being *a sufficient sacrifice for the sins of all*; for all his personal excellencies, and that full and glorious salvation that he hath procured; and for all his free offers of these, and frequent and earnest invitation of sinners ... [He] declareth his person and nature, and the great things that he hath done and suffered for man; his redeeming him from the wrath of God by his blood, and procuring a grant of salvation with himself. Furthermore, the same gospel maketh an offer of Christ to sinners, that if they will accept him on his easy and reasonable terms, he will be their Saviour, the Physician of their souls, their Husband, and their Head.[3]

V
His distinction between the 'general' and 'special' aspects
of the atonement in relation to predestination

[God's people] are a small part of lost mankind, whom God hath from eternity predestined to [everlasting] rest, for the glory of his mercy, and given to his Son, to be by him in a *special manner* redeemed, and fully

---

1   *Paraphrase*, Comment on 1 Timothy 2: 5–6.
2   *Paraphrase*, Comment on 1 John 2: 1–2.
3   *Making Light of Christ and Salvation* (London, 1656), 4–5, emphasis mine.

recovered from their lost estate, and advanced to this higher glory; all which Christ doth, in due time, accomplish accordingly by himself for them, and by his Spirit upon them.[1]

... Christ is, in *some sense, a ransom for all*, yet not in that *special manner* as for his people. He hath brought others under the Conditional Gospel-Covenant; but them under the absolute. He hath, according to the tenor of his covenant, *procured salvation for all*, if they will believe; but he hath *procured for his chosen even this condition of believing*.[2]

Christ's blood hath purchased the Church in a *fuller sense* than he is said to *die for all*.[3]

Husbands, imitate Christ, in loving your wives, as Christ did his Church, for which (in a *special sense*) he gave himself by death, ...[4]

VI
His view of God's provision and man's responsibility

Whoever is damned, it is not because no ransom was made for him, or because it was not sufficient for him ... God hath made an Universal Act of Grace or Oblivion, giving pardon of all sin, and right to life in Christ, to all men, without exception, on condition of believing acceptance, and hath commissioned his Ministers to offer this gift to all men, to the utmost of their power, and entreat them to accept it; ... Few Christians have the face to affirm, that this universal Conditional Pardon and Gift (or Law of Grace) is no fruit of the Death of Christ.[5]

VII
Affirming the biblical teaching on predestination and election, Baxter makes plain that evangelistic preaching is to be motivated not by God's secret eternal decrees and absolute purposes but His revealed conditional purposes, desires and promises (see Deuteronomy 29: 29)

It is further proved by the sufferings of his Son, that God takes no

---

1   *The Saints Everlasting Rest* (London, 1658), 125, emphasis mine. Hereinafter *Saints' Rest*.

2   *Saints Rest,* 126, emphasis mine.

3   *Paraphrase*, Comment on Acts 20: 28, emphasis mine.

4   *Paraphrase*, Comment on Ephesians 5: 25, emphasis mine.

5   *Paraphrase*, Note on 1 Tim. 2: 5–6.

pleasure in the death of the wicked. Would he have ransomed them from death at so dear a rate? Would he have astonished angels and men by his condescension; would God have dwelt in flesh, and have come in the form of a servant, and have assumed humanity into one person with the Godhead? Would Christ have lived a life of suffering, and died a cursed death for sinners, if he had rather taken pleasure in their death?

Suppose you saw him but so busy in preaching and healing of them, as you find him in Mark 3: 21, or so long in fasting, as in Matt. 4, or all night in prayer, as in Luke 6: 12, or praying with the drops of blood trickling from him instead of sweat, as Luke 22: 44, or suffering a cursed death upon the cross, and pouring out his soul as a sacrifice for our sins,—would you have thought these the signs of one that delights in the death of the wicked?

Think not to extenuate it by saying, that it was only for his elect. For it was thy sin, and the sin of all the world, that lay upon our redeemer; and his sacrifice and satisfaction is sufficient for all, and the fruits of it are offered to one as well as to another; but it is true, that it was never the intent of his mind, to pardon and save any that would not by faith and repentance be converted.

If you had seen him weeping and bemoaning the state of disobedient impenitent people, Luke 19: 41, 42, or complaining of their stubbornness, as Matt. 23: 37, 'O Jerusalem, Jerusalem, how oft would I have gathered thy children together, even as a hen gathereth her chickens under her wings, and ye would not!' Or if you had seen and heard him on the cross, praying for his persecutors, 'Father, forgive them, for they know not what they do' [Luke 23: 34]; would you have suspected that he had delighted in the death of the wicked, even of those that perish by their wilful unbelief?

When God hath so loved (not only loved, but so loved) the world as to give his only-begotten Son, that whosoever believeth in him (by an effectual faith) should not perish, but have everlasting life', [John 3: 16], I think he hath hereby proved, against the malice of men and angels, that he takes no pleasure in the death of the wicked, but had rather that they would turn and live .[1]

---

1   *A Call to the Unconverted* (London, 1658), 98–100 (paragraphing and emphasis mine).

This quotation, along with the earlier one from *Making Light of Christ,* provides an easy refutation of Murray A. Capill's inadequate and defective criticism, that Baxter's 'preaching of the cross' was 'so slight'.[1] He backs up this false charge by another, that Baxter's Amyraldianism was the source of his theological 'deficiencies'. Adding insult to injury, he shows an uncritical acquiescence in J. I. Packer's 'Owenite' agenda. It is simply absurd for Capill to accuse Baxter of emphasising the believer's 'commitment to Christ–evangelical obedience–rather than his finished work for us'.[2] Had he personally examined the Baxter sources instead of depending on second-hand opinions, he would have drawn a very different conclusion. Recalling also the glorious passages on the sufferings of the Saviour in *The Saints' Everlasting Rest* (1649), as well as reading Baxter's *Call to the Unconverted* for himself, Capill should have examined Baxter's follow-up book *Directions and Persuasions to a Sound Conversion* (1658). I make no apology for the length of the following quotation. Besides refuting his critic, does any passage more eloquently and ecstatically set forth the all-sufficiency of Christ's redemption?

The most sweet and conspicuous end of our redemption, was the demonstration of God's love and mercy to mankind, and that he might make known the riches of his glory on the vessels of mercy prepared unto glory. Of all God's attributes, there is none shines more illustriously in the work of our redemption than love and mercy. 'Hereby perceive we the love of God, because he laid down his life for us.' By the creation and sustaining of us we perceive the love of God, but more abundantly by our redemption. 'In this was manifested the love of God towards us, because that God sent his only begotten Son into the world, that we might live through him.'

O wonderful love, which condescends to such rebels, and embraces such unworthy and polluted sinners, and pities them even in their blood! Even after we had sold ourselves to Satan, cast away the mercies of our creation, had all come short of the glory of God, and were sentenced to death and ready for the execution, then did this wonderful love step in, and rescue and recover us. Not staying till we repented and cried for

---

1   Murray A. Capill, *Preaching With Spiritual Vigour, Including Lessons from the Life and Practice of Richard Baxter* (Fearn, Ross-shire: Mentor, Christian focus Publications, 2003), 117.

2   Ibid. 117–18.

mercy, and cast ourselves at his feet; but seeking us in the wilderness, and finding us before we felt that we were lost, and being found of us before we sought him, and beginning to us in the depth of our misery. 'Herein is love, not that we loved God, but that he loved us, and sent his Son to be the propitiation for our sins.'

Though God love us not in our sin and misery before our conversion, so far as in that state to justify us, adopt us, and take pleasure in us, or have communion with us in the Spirit, yet doth he so far love us in that state, as to redeem us by the blood of Christ and tender us his salvation, and to bring his chosen effectually to entertain his offer. 'And thus the love of God is shed abroad in our hearts by the Holy Ghost which is given to us; for when we were yet without strength, in due time Christ died for the ungodly, and commended his love towards us, in that while we were yet sinners, Christ died for us. — Greater love hath no man than this, that a man lay down his life for his friend.'

What was the Son of God, but love incarnate? Love born of a virgin; love coming down from heaven to earth, and walking in flesh among the miserable, seeking and saving that which was lost: was it not love that spoke those words of life, those comfortable promises, those necessary precepts, those gracious encouragements which the gospel doth abound with? Was it not love itself that went preaching salvation to the sons of death, and deliverance to the captives, and offered to bind up broken hearts? Was it not love that invited 'the weary and heavy laden,' and that sent even to 'the highways, and the hedges to compel men to come in, that his house may be filled?' Was it not love itself that went up and down healing diseases and doing good; that suffered them for whom he suffered, to scorn him and spit upon him, buffet him, and condemn him; that being reviled, reviled not again; that gave his life an offering for sin, died, and prayed for them that murdered him? No wonder if the gospel be it that teaches us to call God by the name of love itself, for it is the gospel that hath most fully revealed him to be so ...

But if we should come down to the particular benefits of Christ's death, and see what love is manifested in them, even in our calling, our justification, our adoption or sanctification, our preservation, and our everlasting glorification, we should find ourselves in an ocean that hath neither banks nor bottom; and when we have fathomed as far as we can, we must be contented to stand and admire it, and to say with the beloved apostle, 'Behold what manner of love the Father hath bestowed on us, that we should be called the sons of God!'[1]

Concluding this theological vindication of Richard Baxter's soteriology, Joel Beeke's warnings to unwary readers regarding his alleged 'Arminian tendencies' and faulty views of justification[2] may be disregarded as abusive misrepresentation. The same may be said of Beeke's utterly unscholarly criticism of me.[3] For those who charge Baxter with leanings towards Roman Catholicism, probably the most accurate evaluation of Baxter is found in Hans Boersma's excellent and comprehensive study: 'Despite [some] eclectic agreement with some Roman Catholics, Baxter remains firmly entrenched within the Reformed tradition'.[4] I am at least grateful to Dr Packer for rejecting the stigmatization that Baxter's view of justification was Roman Catholic.[5] Those who insist on this slur should not forget Baxter's numerous treatises against 'popery', all of which confirm his unambiguous claim to be 'Protestant'.[6] I would only add that after Calvin, Baxter—opposed to both legalistic and antinomian distortions of the Gospel—remains arguably the best spokesman for the authentic Bible-based Christianity of the Protestant Reformation.

That said, I wish to conclude with a pastoral and evangelistic emphasis, in keeping with Baxter's life-long passionate preoccupation. We begin with a quote:

BAXTER'S PASTORAL HEART

The persons for whom 'eternal rest' is designed—the 'people of God'— are 'the chosen of God from eternity' (John 17: 2). That they are but a

---

1 *Directions and Persuasions to a Sound Conversion* (London: 1658), 'Direction V'.

2 'Reading the Puritans' at https://www.uniontheology.org/resources/historical/reading-the-puritans

3 See *A Puritan Theology: Doctrine for Life*, Joel R. Beeke & Mark Jones (Grand Rapids, MI: Reformation Heritage Books, 2012), 491ff.

4 Hans Boersma, *A Hot Pepper Corn: Richard Baxter's Doctrine of Justification in Its Seventeenth-Century Context of Controversy* (Zoetermeer, the Netherlands: Uitgeverij Boekencentrum, 1993), 330.

5 See J. I. Packer, 'The redemption and restoration of man in the thought of Richard Baxter', D. Phil. thesis (Oxford, 1954), 302–3; Boersma, 323–4.

6 J. M. Lloyd Thomas (ed), *The Autobiography of Richard Baxter* (London: J. M. Dent, 1931), 293.

small part of mankind is too apparent in scripture and experience. They are the 'little flock', to whom 'it is their Father's good pleasure to give the kingdom' (Luke 12: 32). Fewer they are than the world imagines; yet not so few as some drooping spirits think, who are suspicious that God is unwilling to be their God, when they know themselves willing to be His people.[1]

The evidence we have considered is surely conclusive. Baxter showed the way to preach the Gospel. Happily, many 'limited atonement' preachers have been better than their creed. At the 2006 Amyraldian Association Conference, Stephen M. Quinton highlighted Baxter's claim that Theodore Beza's 'pupil' William Perkins of Cambridge could not avoid universal atonement language in his evangelistic preaching.[2] Having exposed the defects in Owen's theology, Quinton concluded his thoroughly persuasive case thus:

> It was Richard Baxter amongst the Puritans who maintained Calvin's emphasis in this area, rather than John Owen. ... The subject raised ... is a vital one. It is important for those that preach the gospel. It is important for hearers of the gospel also. What is the message we are to preach to sinners? Is it a certain or uncertain message of salvation? Do we tell sinners what Christ has done for them or what he may have done for them? Is our message relevant for some or for all? What is the object of faith that sinners are to put their trust in? The subject raises further questions. How are we to persuade men? What language do we use? Do we reason with men as Baxter did that they should accept the provision that is truly provided for them in the death of Christ. Do we plead with men to accept it? Do we declare with Calvin, Baxter and as we have seen Perkins that it is a great sin to reject Christ's love, and to despise and trample on the blood of Christ. Do we weep over lost sinners? Are sinners who refuse Christ guilty of rejecting something or nothing?[3]

At the same conference, Dr J. E . Hazlett Lynch challenged all present with truly 'Baxterian' passion:

---

1   *Saints Rest* (ed. London: The Religious Tract Society, 1833), 68.

2   Stephen M. Quinton, 'The Object of Faith in the Theology of John Owen and Richard Baxter' in *Christ for the World*, 2006 Amyraldian Association Conference Report, ed. Alan C. Clifford (Norwich: Charenton Reformed Publishing, 2007), 124–5.

3   Ibid. 127.

Further, we give the impression to our hearers that it doesn't really matter whether they are saved or lost. Our preaching is so dispassionate! Why? Because our theological system has become a virtual strait-jacket for us, so that we cannot, or perhaps, will not, plead with lost sinners to be saved. I mean, what 'reformed' preacher wants to be in the position where the non-elect are being saved under their preaching?

Lack of passion in our evangelistic preaching conveys the very clear message to our hearers, that (1) we don't care; (2) God doesn't care; and (3) the church does not care! Now this says a lot about us and the church, but nothing about God! It says that we have lost a heart of compassion for perishing sinners. It says that we are unlike our Saviour and his apostles! Remember the passion and emotion that arose in Jesus when he viewed unrepentant Jerusalem?[1] He *wept* over the city. The Son of God *wept*! The Saviour of the world was broken-hearted at what he saw. He wept over those who would eventually be lost because they rejected him and his Gospel, and the eternal salvation offered therein.[2]

Relating to personal assurance, with a personal testimony, David F. Bond[3] concluded in a manner Baxter would heartily approve of:

Raymond Blacketer, in *The Glory of the Atonement*, insists that, 'The theory of universal atonement simply postpones the question of assurance'.[4] To the contrary, I discovered by experience that the hypothesis of a strictly limited atonement postponed assurance for me for several years.

So I thank God for the unambiguous truth of John 3: 16, that God, in His love, reached out in Christ Crucified to the whole world, which included me. I thank God for the truth of Hebrews 2: 9 that:

We see Jesus, who was made a little lower than the angels, for the

---

1   Luke 19: 41.

2   J. E. Hazlett Lynch, 'Evangelistic Preaching—Amyraldian Style!' in *Christ for the World*, 2006 Amyraldian Association Conference Report, ed. Alan C. Clifford (Norwich: Charenton Reformed Publishing, 2007), 150–65.

3   David. F. Bond, 'Amyraldianism and Assurance' in *Christ for the World*, 2006 Amyraldian Association Conference Report, ed. Alan C. Clifford (Norwich: Charenton Reformed Publishing, 2007), 92–108.

4   *The Glory of the Atonement*, ed. Charles Hill & Frank James (Downers Grove, Illinois: Inter Varsity Press, 2004), 321.

suffering of death crowned with glory and honour, that He, by the grace of God, *might taste death for everyone.*

I thank God for the practical discovery with Calvin that:

Whenever our sins press hard on us, whenever Satan would drive us to despair, we must hold up this shield, that God does not want us to be overwhelmed in everlasting destruction, for He has ordained His Son to be the Saviour of the world. [1]

I thank God for enabling me to rise above the problems of excessive introspection as I learnt with Calvin that:

The true looking of faith ... is placing Christ before one's eyes and beholding in Him the heart of God poured out in love. Our firm and substantial support is to rest on the death of Christ as its only pledge.[2]

I conclude by affirming with Amyraut in his *Brief Treatise on Predestination and its Dependent Principles:*

Now one does not know how to express the consolation with which this doctrine fills those who have felt the efficacy of the grace God and of the preaching of the Gospel of Christ. [3]

We give Richard Baxter the last word, being a quote from his first and much-maligned book:

The Love of God to the World was the first womb where the work of Redemption was conceived, John 3: 16.[4]

---

1   *Comm.* John 3: 16.

2   Ibid.

3   Moïse Amyraut, *Brief Treatise on Predestination*, trans. Richard Lum (Norwich: Charenton Reformed Pubishing, 2000), 91.

4   *Aphorismes of Justification (*1649; Hague *alias* Cambridge, 1655), 13.

1. Richard Baxter

2. Baxter's house

THE
Saints Everlasting Reſt:
OR, A
TREATISE
Of the Bleſſed State of the S A I N T S
in their enjoyment of G O D in Glory.

Wherein is ſhewed its Excellency and Certainty;
the Miſery of thoſe that loſe it; the way to Attain it,
and aſſurance of it; and hcw to live in the continual
delightful Foretaſts of it, by the help of Meditation.

Written by the Author for his own uſe, in the
time of his languiſhing, when God took him off
from all Publike Imployment; and afterwards
Preached in his weekly Lecture:

By *Richard Baxter*, Teacher of the Church of
Kederminſter in *Worceſterſhire*.

The Seventh Edition, Reviſed by the Author.

---

*My fleſh and my heart faileth; but God is the ſtrength of my heart, and my
portion for ever*, Pſal. 73. 26.

*If in this life only we have hope in Chriſt, we are of all men the moſt miſe-
rable*, 1 Cor. 15. 19.

*Set your affections on things above, and not on things on the Earth. For ye
are dead, and your life is hid with Chriſt in God. When Chriſt, who is
our life, ſhall appear, ven ſhall ye alſo appear with him in glory*,
Col. 3. 2, 3, 4.

Becauſe I live, ye ſhall live alſo, John 14. 9.

London, Printed for *Thomas Underhill* and *Francis Tyton*, and are to be ſold
at the Sign of the blew Anchor and Bible in *Pauls* Church-yard,
and at the three Daggers in Fleet-ſtreet. 1658.

3. Baxter's *Saints' Rest* (title page)

Making light of

CHRIST

AND

SALVATION

Too oft the Issue of Go-
spel-Invitations.

Manifested in a S E R M O N preached at *Laurence Jury* in *London*.

By R I C H. B A X T E R, Teacher
of the Church of Christ at *Kederminster* in *Worcestershire.*

Heb. 2. 34. *How shall we escape , if we
neglect so great salvation?*

LONDON,
Printed by *R. White,* for *Nevil Simmons*
Bookseller in *Kederminster;* 1 6 8 6.

4. Baxter's Making Light of Christ (title page)

A
CALL

TO THE

Unconverted

TO

Turn and *Live*,

AND

Accept of Mercy while Mercy may be had, as ever they would find Mercy in the day of their extremity :

From the Living God.

By his unworthy Servant
R I C H A R D B A X T E R.

To be Read in Families where any are Unconverted.

London, Printed by R. *W.* for *Nevil Sim-mons* Book-feller in *Kederminfter*, and are to be fold by him there ; and by *Nathaniel Ekins*, at the Gun in *Pauls* Church-Yard. 1658.

5. Baxter's *Call to the Unconverted* (title page)

THE
REASONS

OF THE

Chriſtian Religion.

The FIRST PART,
OF
GODLINESS:

Proving by *NATURAL EVIDENCE* the Being of *GOD*, the Neceſſity of *HOLINESS*, and a *future Life* of *Retribution*; the Sinfulneſs of the World; the Deſert of Hell; and what hope of Recovery Mercies intimate.

The SECOND PART,
OF
CHRISTIANITY:

Proving by *Evidence Supernatural* and *Natural*, the certain Truth of the *CHRISTIAN* Belief: and anſwering the *Objections* of *Unbelievers*.

Firſt meditated for the well-ſetling of his own Belief; and now publiſhed for the benefit of others, By RICHARD BAXTER.

It openeth alſo the true Reſolution of the Chriſtian Faith.

Alſo an APPENDIX, defending the *Soul's Immortality* againſt the *Somatiſts* or *Epicureans*, and other *Pſeudo-philoſophers*.

LONDON,
Printed by R. *White*, for *Fran. Titon*, at the *three Daggers* in *Fleet-ſtreet*. 1667.

6. Baxter's *Reasons for the Christian Religion* (title page)

WHICH IS THE

True Church?

The whole Chriftian World, as Headed only
B Y

CHRIST,

(Of which the Reformed are the foundeft part)
O R, T H E

POPE of ROME
And his SUBJECTS as fuch ?

IN THREE PARTS.

I. The *Papifts* Confufion in explaining the terms of the
    Queftions; not able to bear the light.
II. A Defence of a Difputation concerning the continued
    Vifibility of the Church of which the Proteftants
    are members.
III. A Defence of the feveral Additional proofs of the
    faid Vifibility.

By *RICHARD BAXTER.*

*Written efpecially to inftruct the younger unexperienced Scholars how to
deal with thefe Deceivers, in thefe dangerous times.*

LONDON; Printed, and are to be fold by *Richard Janeway*, in
Butcher-hall-Lane. 1 6 7 9.

7. Baxter's *Which is the True Church?* (title page)

A
PARAPHRASE
ON THE
New Teſtament,
With NOTES,
DOCTRINAL and PRACTICAL.

By PLAINNESS and BREVITY fitted to the Uſe of Religious FAMILIES, in their daily Reading of the Scriptures; and of the younger and poorer ſort of Scholars and Miniſters, who want fuller helps.

With an Advertiſement of Difficulties in the
REVELATIONS

By RICHARD BAXTER.

1. Tim. 3. 16. *Great is the myſtery of Godlineſs. God was manifeſted in the fleſh, Juſtified in the Spirit; Seen of Angels: Preached to the Gentiles: Believed on in the World. Recieved up into Glory.*
1. Joh. 4. 16. *God is Love, and he that dwelleth in Love, dwelleth in God: And God in him.*
Joh. 1. 4. *In him was Life, and the Life was the Light of Men.*
Joh. 20. 17. *Go to my Brethren, and ſay to them, I aſcend unto my Father and your Father, and unto my God and your God.*
2. Pet. 3. 11. *Seeing that all theſe things ſhall be diſſolved, what manner of perſons ought ye to be in all holy converſation and godlineſs: Looking for, and haſting unto the coming of the day of God.* 13. *We, according to his promiſe, look for new heavens and a new earth, wherein dwelleth righteouſneſs.*
Luk. 23. 43. *To day ſhalt thou be with me in Paradiſe.*
Joſh. 24. 15. *Chooſe you this day whom you will ſerve, But as for me and my houſe, we will ſerve the Lord.*

LONDON,
Printed for B. *Simmons,* at the *Three Cocks,* and *Tho. Simmons,* at the *Princes Arms,* in *Ludgate-ſtreet.* MDCLXXXV.

8. Baxter's *Paraphrase on the New Testament* (title page)

9. Baxter before Judge Jeffreys

A
Defence of Christ,
AND
Free Grace:
Againſt the
SUBVERTERS,
Commonly Called,
Antinomians or *Libertines*;
WHO
Ignorantly Blaſpheme CHRIST on Pretence
of extolling Him.

IN A
DIALOGUE
Between
An Orthodox Zealot,
AND
A Reconciling Monitor.

WRITTEN
On the occaſion of the reviving of thoſe Errours, and the Re-
printing and Reception of Dr. *Criſpes* Writings, and the danger of ſubverting many Thouſand honeſt Souls by the Notions of *Free Grace*, and Juſtification, miſ-underſtood and
abuſed by injudicious, unſtudyed, prejudiced Preachers.

By RICHARD BAXTER.

London, Printed for *Tho. Parkhurſt* at the *Bible* and *Three Crowns*,
at the lower End of *Cheapſide*, near *Mercers-Chapel*, 1690.

10. Baxter's *Defence of Christ & Free Grace* (title page)

THE
Grand Question
RESOLVED,

What we muſt do to be *SAVED.*

INSTRUCTIONS
FOR A
Holy Life.

BY
The late Reverend Divine
Mr RICHARD BAXTER

*Recommended to the Bookseller a few days before his death, to be
immediately printed for the good of souls.*

Acts 16. 30.
Sirs, What muſt I do to be Saved?

LONDON,

Printed for THO. PARKHURST, at the Bible
And Three Crowns, Cheapside. 1692.

11. Baxter's *Grand Question Resolved* (reconstructed title page)

Universal Redemption

OF

Mankind,

BY THE

Lord Jesus Chrift:

Stated and Cleared by the late Learned
Mr. Richard Baxter.

Whereunto is added a fhort Account of
Special Redemption, by the fame
Author.

---

2 Cor. 5. 14, 15. *For the love of Chrift conftraineth us be-
caufe we thus judge, that if one dyed for all, then were all
dead, and that he dyed for all, that they which live fhould
not henceforth live unto themfelves, but unto him which dyed
for them, and rofe again.*

Mors Chrifti in Sacra Scripturâ proponitur ut Univer-
fale remedium omnibus & fingulis hominibus exordina-
tione Dei & naturâ rei ad faluem applicabile. *Davenant
de morte Chrifti.*

LONDON. Printed for John Salusbury at the
Rifing-Sun in Cornhill, 1694.

12. Baxter's *Universal Redemption* (title page)

ELISHA'S CRY

AFTER

ELIJAH's GOD

Confider'd and Apply'd,

With Reference to the DECEASE of the late Reverend

Mr. Richard Baxter.

Who left this Life *Decemb.* 8*th*, 1691.

And Preach'd in Part on *Decemb.* 18*th*, *An. Eod.*
Being the LORD's-DAY,

At *Rutland-Houfe* in *Charter-houfe-Yard*, LONDON.

By *Matthew Sylvefter*, His unworthy Fellow-Labourer in the *Gofpel* there, for near Four of the laft Years of His Life and Labours.

And there was much Murmuring among the People concerning him: for fome faid, He is a Good Man. Others faid, nay; but he deceiveth the People. Joh. vii. 12.
But thou haft fully known my Doctrine, Manner of Life, Purpofe, Faith, Long-fuffering, Charity, Patience, Perfecutions, Afflictions, 2 Tim. iii. 10, 11.
The Law of Truth was in his Mouth, and Iniquity was not found in his Lips: He walked with me in Peace and Equity, and did turn many away from Iniquity. Mal. ii. 6.
My Father! my Father! the Chariot of Ifrael, and the Horfemen thereof! And he faw him no more: 2 King. ii. 14.
Quis cohortari ad virtutem ardentius; quis a vitiis acrius revocare; Quis vituperare Improbos afperius, Quis Laudare bonos ornatius, Quis cupiditatem vehementius frangere accufando poteft? Quis mœrorem levare mitius confolando? Cicer. De Orat. lib. 2.

LONDON,
Printed for *T. Parkhurft*, *J. Robinfon*, *J. Lawrence*, and *J. Dunton.* 1696.

13. Sylvester's funeral sermon (title page)

14. Dr William Bates

A
Funeral-Sermon

FOR THE

Reverend, Holy and Ex-
cellent DIVINE,

Mr. *Richard Baxter*,

Who deceafed *Decemb.* 8. 1691.

WITH

An Account of His LIFE.

By *WILLIAM BATES*, D.D.

LONDON,

Printed for *Brab. Aylmer*, at the *Three
Pigeons* againſt the *Royal Exchange*
in *Cornhill.* 1692.

15. Bates' funeral sermon (title page)

16. Dr Edmund Calamy

AN

ABRIDGEMENT

OF

Mr. Baxter's

HISTORY

OF HIS

LIFE and *TIMES.*

WITH

An Account of the Minifters, *&c.*
who were Eje&ed after the Reftauration,
of King *Charles* II.

Their Apology for themfelves, and their Adherents,
containing the Grounds of their Nonconformity:
Their Treatment in the Reign of King *Charles,*
and King *James*; and after the Revolution: And
the continuation of their Hiftory, to the paffing
of the Bill againft Occafional Conformity, in 1711.

The Second Edition: In Two VOLUMES. Vol. I.

By Edmund Calamy, *D. D.*

LONDON:

Printed for *John Lawrence,* at the *Angel* in the *Poultry*;
J. Nicholfon, and *J.* and *B. Sprint* in *Little-Britain*;
R. Robinfon in St. *Paul's* Church-yard, and *N. Cliffe,*
and *D. Jackfon* in *Cheapfide.* 1713.

17. Calamy's *Abridgement of Baxter's History* (title page)

THE PRACTICAL

WORKS

Of the Late Reverend and Pious

M#### RICHARD BAXTER,

In Four VOLUMES.

With a Preface ; Giving fome Account of the Author, and of this Edition of his Practical Works.

VOLUME I.

CONTAINING,

The Chriftian Directory ; *with the forementioned* Preface.

VOLUME II.

CONTAINING,

Reafons of the Chriftian Religion.	A Saint or a Brute.
Unreafonablenefs of Infidelity.	Mifchiefs of Self-ignorance, &c.
More Reafons for the Chriftian Religion.	Right Method for fettled Peace of Confcience.
Treatife of Converfion.	God's Goodnefs Vindicated.
Call to the Unconverted.	Directions for weak diftemper'd Chriftians.
Now or Never.	The Character of a Sound Confirm'd Chriftian.
Directions and Perfuafions to a found Converfion	

VOLUME III.

CONTAINING,

The Saints Everlafting Reft.	Divine Life.
Treatife of Self-denial.	Divine Appointment of the Lord's Day.
Crucifying the World by the Crofs of Chrift.	Obedient Patience.
Life of Faith.	Dying Thoughts.

VOLUME IV.

CONTAINING,

Compaffionate Counfel to Young Men.	Catholick Unity.
Mother's Catechifm.	True and only way of Concord.
Catechizing of Families.	The True Catholick.
Poor Man's Family-Book.	One Thing Neceffary.
Confirmation and Reftauration, &c.	True Chriftianity.
Gildas Salvianus, or the Reformed Paftor.	Making light of Chrift.
Vain Religion.	Two Treatifes of Death and Judgment.
Cain and *Abel.*	Eleven Sermons on fpecial Occafions.
Knowledge and Love.	Directions for Juftices of Peace.

Together with Alphabetical Tables to each VOLUME.

LONDON:

Printed for *Thomas Parkhurft* at the *Bible* and *Three Crowns* in *Cheapfide* ; *Jonathan Robinfon* at the *Golden Lyon* in St. *Paul's Church-Yard*, and *John Lawrence* at the *Angel* in the *Poultrey.* 1707.

18. Baxter's *Practical Works* (Calamy edition title page)

PART II
BAXTER'S GOSPEL

5. Making Light of Christ and Salvation

TO THE READER

READER,

Being called on in London to preach, when I had no time to study, I was fain to preach some sermons that I had preached in the country a little before. This was one, which I preached at St Laurence, in the church where my reverend and faithful brother in Christ, Mr Richard Vines, is pastor: when I came home I was followed by such importunities by letters to print the sermon, that I have yielded thereunto, though I know not fully the ground of their desires. Seeing it must [go] abroad, will the Lord but bless it to the cure of thy contempt of Christ and grace, how comfortable may the occasion prove to thee and me! It is the slighting of Christ and salvation, that undoes the world. O happy man if thou escape but this sin! Thousands do split their souls on this rock which they should build them on. Look into the world, among rich and poor, high and low, young and old, and see whether it appear not by the whole scope of their conversations that they set more by something else than Christ? And for all the proclamations of his grace in the gospel, and our common professing ourselves to be his disciples, and to believe the glorious things that he hath promised us in another world, whether it yet appear not by the deceitfulness of our service, by our heartless endeavours to obtain his kingdom, and by our busy and delightful following of the world, that the most who are called Christians do yet in their hearts make light of Christ; and if so, what wonder if they perish by their contempt? Wilt thou but soberly peruse this short discourse, and consider well as thou readest of its truth and weight, till thy heart be sensible what a sin it is to make light of Christ and thy own salvation, and till the Lord that bought thee be advanced in the estimation and affections of thy soul, thou shalt hereby rejoice, and fulfil the desires of

Thy servant in the faith,
RICHARD BAXTER

MAKING LIGHT OF CHRIST AND SALVATION,

TOO OFT
THE ISSUE OF GOSPEL INVITATIONS

"But they made light of it."—Matt. xxii. 5.

THE blessed Son of God, that thought it not enough to die for the world, but would himself also be the preacher of grace and salvation, doth comprise in this parable the sum of his gospel. By the king that is here said to make the marriage is meant God the Father, that sent his Son into the world to cleanse them from their sins, and espouse them to himself. By his Son, for whom the marriage is made, is meant the Lord Jesus Christ, the eternal Son of God, who took to his Godhead the nature of man, that he might be capable of being their Redeemer when they had lost themselves in sin. By the marriage is meant the conjunction of Christ to the soul of sinners, when he giveth up himself to them to be their Saviour, and they give up themselves to him as his redeemed ones, to be saved and ruled by him; the perfection of which marriage will be at the day of judgment, when the conjunction between the whole church and Christ shall be solemnized. The word here translated *marriage,* rather signifieth the marriage-feast; and the meaning is, that the world is invited by the gospel to come in and partake of Christ and salvation, which comprehendeth both pardon, justification, and right to salvation, and all other privileges of the members of Christ. The invitation is God's offer of Christ and salvation in the gospel; the servants that invite them are the preachers of the gospel, who are sent forth by God to that end; the preparation for the feast there mentioned, is the sacrifice of Jesus Christ, and the enacting of a law of grace, and opening a way for revolting sinners to return to God. There is a mention of sending second messengers, because God useth not to take the first denial, but to exercise his patience till sinners are obstinate. The first persons invited are the Jews; upon their obstinate refusal they are sentenced to punishment: and the Gentiles are invited, and not only invited, but by powerful preaching, and miracles, and effectual grace, compelled; that is, infallibly prevailed with to come in. The number of them is so great that the house is filled with guests: many come sincerely, not only looking at the pleasure of the feast, that is, at the pardon of sin, and deliverance from the wrath of God, but also at the honour of the marriage, that is, of the Redeemer, and their profession by giving up themselves to a holy conversation: but some come in only for the feast, that is, justification by Christ, having not the wedding-garment of sound resolution for obedience in their life, and looking only at themselves in believing, and not to the glory of their Redeemer; and these are sentenced to everlasting misery, and speed as ill as those that came not in at all; seeing a faith that will not work is but like that of the devil; and they that look to be pardoned and saved by it are mistaken, as James sheweth, chap. ii. 24.

The words of my text contain a narration of the ill entertainment that the gospel findeth with many to whom it is sent, even after a first and second invitation. They made light of it, and are taken up with other things. Though it be the Jews that were first guilty, they have too many followers among us Gentiles to this day.

THE DOCTRINE OF THE PASSAGE.—For all the wonderful love and mercy that God hath manifested in giving his Son to be the Redeemer of the world, and which the Son hath manifested in redeeming them by his blood; for all his full preparation by being a sufficient sacrifice for the sins of all; for all his personal excellencies, and that full and glorious salvation that he hath procured; and for all his free offers of these, and frequent and earnest invitation of sinners; yet many do make light of all this, and prefer their worldly enjoyments before it. The ordinary treatment of all these offers, invitations, and benefits, is by contempt.

Not that all, do so, or that all continue to do so, who were once guilty of it; for God hath his chosen whom he will compel to come in. But till the Spirit of grace overpower the dead and obstinate hearts of men, they hear the gospel as a common story, and the great matters contained in it go not to the heart.

The method in which I shall handle this doctrine is this.

I. I shall shew you what it is that men make light of.

II. What this sin of making light of it is.

III. The cause of the sin.

IV. The use of the doctrine.

The thing that carnal hearers make light of is,

1. The doctrine of the gospel itself, which they hear regardlessly. 2. The benefits offered them therein: which are, 1. Christ himself. 2. The benefits which he giveth.

Concerning Christ himself, the gospel, 1. Declareth his person and nature, and the great things that he hath done and suffered for man; his redeeming him from the wrath of God by his blood, and procuring a grant of salvation with himself. Furthermore, the same gospel maketh an offer of Christ to sinners, that if they will accept him on his easy and reasonable terms, he will he their Saviour, the Physician of their souls, their Husband, and their Head.

2. The benefits that he offereth them are these. 1. That with these blessed relations to him, himself and interest in him, they shall have the pardon of all their sins past, and be saved from God's wrath, and be set in a sure way of obtaining a pardon for all the sins that they shall commit hereafter, so they do but obey sincerely, and turn not again to the rebellion of their unregeneracy. 2. They shall have the Spirit to become their Guide and Sanctifier, and to dwell in their souls, and help them against their enemies, and conform them more and more to his image, and heal their diseases, and bring them back to God. 3. They shall have right to everlasting glory when this life is ended, and shall be raised up thereto at the last; besides many excellent privileges in the way, in means, preservation, and provision, and the foretaste of what they shall enjoy hereafter: all these benefits the gospel offereth to them that will have Christ on his reasonable terms. The sum of all is in 1 John v. 11, 12, "This is the record, that God hath given us eternal life, and this life is in his Son: he that hath the Son hath life, and he that hath not the Son hath not life."

II

What this sin of the making light of the gospel is.

1. To make light of the gospel is to take no great heed to what is spoken, as if it were not a certain truth, or else were a matter that little concerned them; or as if God had not written these things for them. 2. When the gospel doth not affect men, or go to their hearts; but though they seem to attend to what is said, yet men are not awakened by it from their security, nor doth it work in any measure such holy passion in their souls, as matters of such everlasting consequence should do: this is making light of the gospel

of salvation. When we tell men what Christ hath done and suffered for their souls, and it scarce moveth them: we tell them of keen and cutting truths, but nothing will pierce them: we can make them hear, but we cannot make them feel; our words take up in the porch of their ears and fancies, but will not enter into the inward parts; as if we spake to men that had no hearts or feeling: this is a making light of Christ and salvation. Acts xxviii. 26, 27, "Hearing ye shall hear, and shall not understand; seeing ye shall see, and shall not perceive. For the heart of this people is waxed gross, and their ears are dull of hearing, and their eyes have they closed," &c.

3. When men have no high estimation of Christ and salvation, but whatsoever they may say with their tongues, or dreamingly and speculatively believe, yet in their serious and practical thoughts they have a higher estimation of the matters of this world, than they have of Christ, and the salvation that he hath purchased; this is a making light of him. When men account the doctrine of Christ to be but a matter of words and names, as Gallio (Acts xviii. 4), or as Festus (Acts xxv. 19), a superstitious matter about one Jesus who was dead, and Paul saith is alive; or ask the preachers of the gospel, as the Athenians, "What will this babbler say?" Acts xvii. 18: this is contempt of Christ.

4. When men are informed of the truths of the gospel, and on what terms Christ and his benefits may be had, and how it is the will of God that they should believe and accept the offer; and that be commandeth to do it upon pain of damnation; and yet men will not consent, unless they could have Christ on terms of their own: they will not part with their worldly contents, nor lay down their pleasures, and profits, and honour at his feet, as being content to take so much of them only as he will give them back, and as is consistent with his will and interest, but think it is a hard saying, that they must forsake all in resolution for Christ: this is a making light of him and their salvation. When men might have part in him and all his benefits if they would, and they will not, unless they may keep the world too: and are resolved to please their flesh, whatever comes of it; this is a high contempt of Christ and everlasting life. In Matt. xiii. 21; Luke xviii. 23, you may find examples of such as I here describe.

5. When men will promise fair, and profess their willingness to have Christ on his terms, and to forsake all for him, but yet do stick to the world and their sinful courses; and when it comes to practice, will not be removed by

all that Christ hath done and said; this is making light of Christ and salvation, Jer. xlii. 5, compared with xliii. 2.

III

The causes of this sin are the next thing to be inquired after. It may seem a wonder that ever men, that have the use of their reason, should be so sottish as to make light of matters of such consequence. But the cause is,

1. Some men understand not the very sense of the words of the gospel when they hear them; and how can they be taken with that which they understand not? Though we speak to them in plain English, and study to speak it as plain as we can, yet people have so estranged themselves from God, and the matters of their own happiness, that they know not what we say; as if we spoke in another language, and as if they were under that judgment, Isa. xxviii. 11, "With stammering lips, and with another tongue, will he speak to this people."

2. Some that do understand the words that we speak, yet because they are carnal, understand not the matter. "For the natural man receiveth not the things of the Spirit of God, neither can he know them, because they are spiritually discerned," 1 Cor. ii. 14. They are earthly, and these things are heavenly, John iii. 12. These things of the Spirit are not well known by bare hearsay, but by spiritual taste, which none have but those that are taught by the Holy Ghost (1 Cor. ii. 12), that we may know the things that are given us of God.

3. A carnal man apprehendeth not a suitableness in these spiritual and heavenly things to his mind, and therefore he sets light by them, and hath no mind of them. When you tell him of everlasting glory, he heareth you as if you were persuading him to go play with the sun: they are matters of another world, and out of his element; and therefore he hath no more delight in them than a fish would have to be in the fairest meadow, or than a swine hath in a jewel, or a dog in a piece of gold: they may be good to others, but he cannot apprehend them as suitable to him, because he hath a nature that is otherwise inclined: he savoureth not the things of the Spirit, Rom. viii. 5.

4. The main cause of the slighting of Christ and salvation is, a secret root of unbelief in men's hearts. Whatsoever they may pretend, they do not soundly and thoroughly believe the Word of God: they are taught in general to say the gospel is true; but they never saw the evidence of its truth so far,

as thoroughly to persuade them of it; nor have they got their souls settled on the infallibility of God's testimony, nor considered of the truth of the particular doctrines revealed in the Scripture, so far as soundly to believe them. Oh did you all but soundly believe the words of this gospel, of the evil of sin, of the need of Christ, and what he hath done for you, and what you must be and do if ever you will be saved by him; and what will become of you for ever if you do it not; I dare say it would cure the contempt of Christ, and you would not make so light of the matters of your salvation. But men do not believe while they say they do, and would face us down that they do, and verily think that they do themselves. There is a root of bitterness, and an evil heart of unbelief, that make them depart from the living God, Heb. ii. 12; iv. 1, 2, 6. Tell any man in this congregation that he shall have a gift of ten thousand pounds, if he will but go to London for it; if he believe you, he will go; but if he believe not, he will not; and if he will not go, you may be sure he believeth not, supposing that he is able. I know a slight belief may stand with a wicked life; such as men have of the truth of a prognostication, it may be true, and it may be false; but a true and sound belief is not consistent with so great neglect of the things that are believed.

5. Christ and salvation are made light of by the world, because of their desperate hardness of heart. The heart is hard naturally, and by custom in sinning made more hard, especially by long abuse of mercy, and neglect of the means of grace, and resisting the Spirit of God. Hence it is that men are turned into such stones: and till God cure them of the stone of the heart, no wonder if they feel not what they know, or regard not what we say, but make light of all: it is hard preaching a stone into tears, or making a rock to tremble. You may stand over a dead body long enough, and say to it, O thou carcass, when thou hast lain rotting and mouldered to dust till the resurrection, God will then call thee to account for thy sin, and cast thee into everlasting fire, before you can make it feel what we say, or fear the misery that is never so truly threatened: when men's hearts are like the highway that is trodden to hardness by long custom in sinning, or like the clay that is hardened to a stone by the heat of those mercies that should have melted them into repentance; when they have consciences seared with a hot iron as the apostle speaks (1 Tim. iv. 2), no wonder then if they be past feeling, and working all uncleaness with greediness do make light of Christ and everlasting glory. Oh that this were not the case of too many of our hearers! Had we but *living souls* to speak to, they would hear, and feel, and not make

light of what we say. I know they are naturally alive, but they are spiritually dead, as Scripture witnesseth, Eph. ii. 3. Oh if there were one spark of the life of grace in them, the doctrine salvation by Jesus Christ would appear to them to be the weightiest business in the world! Oh how confident should I be, methinks, to prevail with men, and to take them off this world, and bring them to mind the matters of another world, if I spake but to men that had life, and sense, and reason! But when we speak to blocks and dead men, how should we be regarded? Oh how sad a case are these in, that are fallen under this fearful judgment of spiritual madness and deadness! To have a blind mind, and a hard heart, to be sottish and senseless (Mark iv. 12; John xii. 40), lest they should be converted, and their sin should he forgiven them.

6. Christ and salvation are made light of by the world. because they are wholly enslaved to their sense, and taken up with lower things: the matters of another world are out of sight, and so far from their senses, that they cannot regard them; but present things are nearer them, in their eyes, and in their hands. There must be a living faith to prevail over sense, before men can be so taken with things that are not seen, though they have the Word of God for their security, as to neglect and let go things that are still before their eyes. Sense works with great advantage, and therefore doth much in resisting faith where it is; no wonder then if it carry all before it, where there is no true and lively faith to resist, and to lead the soul to higher things. This cause of making light of Christ and salvation is expressed here in my text: one went to his farm, and another to his merchandise: men have houses and lands to look after; they have wife and children to mind; they have their body and outward estate to regard; therefore they forget that they have a God, a Redeemer, a soul to mind: these matters of the world are still with them. They see these, but they see not God, nor Christ, nor their souls, nor everlasting glory. These things are near at hand, and therefore work naturally, and so work forcibly; but the others are thought on as a great way off, and therefore too distant to work on their affections, or be at the present so much regarded by them. Their body hath life and sense, therefore if they want meat, or drink, or clothes, will feel their want, and tell them of it, and give them no rest till their wants be supplied, and therefore they cannot make light of their bodily necessities; but their souls in spiritual respects are dead, and therefore feel not their wants, but will let them alone in their greatest necessities; and be as quiet when they are starved and languishing to destruction, as if all were well, and nothing ailed them. And hereupon poor people are wholly taken

up in providing for the body, as if they had nothing else to mind. They have their trades and callings to follow, and so much to do from morning to night, that they can find no time for matters of salvation: Christ would teach them, but they have no leisure to hear him: the Bible is before them, but they cannot have time to read it; a minister is in the town with them, but they cannot have time to go to enquire of him what they should do to be saved: and when they do hear, their hearts are so full of the world, and carried away with these lower matters, that they cannot mind the things which they hear. They are so full of the thoughts, and desires, and cares of this world, that there is no room to pour into them the water of life. The cares of the world do choke the word, and make it become unfruitful, Matt. xiii. 32. Men cannot serve two masters, God and mammon; but they will lean to the one, and despise the other, Matt. vi. 24. He that loveth the world, the love of the Father is not in him, 1 John ii. 15, 16. Men cannot choose but set light by Christ and salvation, while they set so much by any thing on earth. It is that which is highly esteemed among men that is abominable in the sight of God, Luke xvi. 15. Oh, this is the ruin of many thousand souls! It would grieve the heart of any honest Christian to see how eagerly this vain world is followed every where and how little men set by Christ and the world to come; to compare the care that men have for the world, with the care of their souls: and the time that they lay out on the world, with that time they lay out for their salvation: to see how the world fills their mouths, their hands, their houses, their hearts, and Christ hath little more than a bare title: to come into their company, and hear no discourse but of the world; to come into their houses, and hear and see nothing but for the world, as if this world would last for ever, or would purchase them another. When I ask sometimes the ministers of the gospel how their labours succeed, they tell me, People continue still the same, and give up themselves wholly to the world; so that they mind not what ministers say to them, nor give any full entertainment to the word, and all because of the deluding world: and O that too many ministers themselves did not make light of that Christ whom they preach, being drawn away with the love of this world! In a word, men of a worldly disposition do judge of things according to worldly advantages, therefore Christ is slighted; "He is despised and rejected of men, they hide their faces from him, and esteem him not, as seeing no beauty or comeliness in him, that they should desire him," Isa. liii. 3.

7. Christ and salvation are made light of, because men do not soberly

consider of the truth and weight of these necessary things. They suffer not their minds so long to dwell upon them, till they procure a due esteem, and deeply affect their heart; did they believe them and not consider of them, how should they work! Oh when men have reason given them to think and consider of the things that most concern them, and yet they will not use it, this causeth their contempt.

8. Christ and salvation are made light of, because men were never sensible of their sin and misery, and extreme necessity of Christ and his salvation; their eyes were never opened to see themselves as they are; nor their hearts soundly humbled in the sense of their condition: if this were done, they would soon be brought to value a Saviour: a truly broken heart can no more make light of Christ and salvation, than a hungry man of his food, or a sick man of the means that would give him ease; but till then our words cannot have access to their hearts: while sin and misery are made light of, Christ and salvation will be made light of; but when these are perceived an intolerable burden, then nothing will serve the turn but Christ. Till men be truly humbled, they can venture Christ and salvation for a lust, for a little worldly gain, even for less than nothing: but when God hath illuminated them, and broken their hearts, then they would give a world for a Christ; then they must have Christ or they die; all things then are loss and dung to them in regard of the excellent knowledge of Christ, Phil. iii. 8. When they are once pricked in their hearts for sin and misery, then they cry out, "Men and brethren, what shall we do?" Acts ii. 37. When they are awakened by God's judgments, as the poor jailer, then they cry out, "Sirs, what shall I do to be saved?" Acts xvi. 30. This is the reason why God will bring men so low by humiliation, before he brings them to salvation.

9. Men take occasion to make light of Christ by the commonness of the gospel; because they do hear of it every day, the frequency is an occasion to dull their affections; I say, an occasion, for it is no just cause. Were it a rarity it might take more with them; but now, if they hear a minister preach nothing but these saving truths, they say, We have these every day: they make not light of their bread or drink, their health or life, because they possess them every day; they make not light of the sun because it shineth every day; at least they should not, for the mercy is the greater; but Christ and salvation are made light of because they hear of them often; this is, say they, a good, plain, dry sermon. Pearls are trod into the dirt where they are common:

they loathe this dry manna: "The full soul loathes the honey-comb; but to the hungry every bitter thing is sweet." Prov. xxvii. 7.

10. Christ and salvation are made light of, because of this disjunctive presumption; either that he is sure enough theirs already, and God that is so merciful, and Christ that hath suffered so much for them, is surely resolved to save them; or else it may easily be obtained at any time, if it be not yet so. A conceited facility to have a part in Christ and salvation at any time doth occasion men to make light of them. It is true, that grace is free, and the offer is universal, according to the extent of the preaching of the gospel; and it is true, that men may have Christ when they will; that is, when they are willing to have him on his terms; but he that hath promised thee Christ if thou be willing, hath not promised to make thee willing: and if thou art not willing now, how canst thou think thou shalt be willing hereafter? If thou canst make thine own heart willing, why is it not done now? Can you do it better when sin hath more hardened it, and God may have given thee over to thyself? O sinners! you might do much, though you are not able of yourselves to come in, if you would now subject yourselves to the working of the Spirit, and set in while the gales of grace continue. But did you know what a hard and impossible thing it is to be so much as willing to have Christ and grace, when the heart is given over to itself, and the Spirit hath withdrawn its former invitations, you would not be so confident of your own strength to believe and repent; nor would you make light of Christ upon such foolish confidence. If indeed it be so easy a matter as you imagine, for a sinner to believe and repent at any time, how comes it to pass that it is done by so few; but most of the world do perish in their impenitency when they have all the helps and means that we can afford them? It is true, the thing is very reasonable and easy in itself to a pure nature; but while man is blind and dead, these things are in a sort impossible to him, which are never so easy to others. It is the easiest and sweetest life in the world to a gracious soul to live in the love of God, and the delightful thoughts of the life to come, where all their hope and happiness lieth: but to a worldly, carnal heart, it is as easy to remove a mountain as to bring them to this. However, these men are their own condemners; for if they think it so easy a matter to repent and believe, and so to have Christ, and right to salvation, then have they no excuse for neglecting this which they thought so easy. O wretched, impenitent soul! what mean you to say when God shall ask you, Why did you not repent

and love your Redeemer above the world, when you thought it so easy that you could do it at any time?

IV

Use 1. We come now to the application: and hence you may be informed of the blindness and folly of all carnal men. How contemptible are their judgments that think Christ and salvation contemptible! And how little reason there is why any should be moved by them, or discouraged by any of their scorns or contradictions!

How shall we sooner know a man to be a fool, than if he know no difference between dung and gold? Is there such a thing as madness in the world, if that man be not mad that sets light by Christ, and his own salvation, while he daily toils for the dung of the earth? And yet what pity is it to see that a company of poor, ignorant souls will be ashamed of godliness, if such men as these do but deride them! or will think hardly of a holy life, if such as these do speak against it! Hearers, if you see any set light by Christ and salvation, do you set light by that man's wit, and by his words, and hear the reproaches of a holy life as you would hear the words of a madman, not with regard, but with a compassion of his misery.

Use 2. What wonder if we and our preaching be despised, and the best ministers complain of ill success, when the ministry of the apostles themselves did succeed no better? What wonder if, for all that we can say or do, our hearers still set light by Christ and their own salvation, when the apostles' hearers did the same? They that did second their doctrine by miracles, if any men could have shaken and torn in pieces the hearts of sinners, they could have done it; if any could have laid them at their feet, and made them all cry out as some, 'What shall we do?' it would have been they. You may see then that it is not merely for want of good preachers that men make light of Christ and salvation. The first news of such a thing as the pardon of sin, and the hopes of glory, and the danger of everlasting misery, would turn the hearts of men within them, if they were as tractable in spiritual matters as in temporal: but, alas, it is far otherwise. It must not seem any strange thing, nor must it too much discourage the preachers of the gospel, if when they have said all that they can devise to say, to win the hearts of men to Christ, the most do still slight him; and while they bow the knee to him, and honour him with their lips, do yet set so light by him in their hearts, as to prefer every fleshly pleasure or commodity before him. It will be thus with many: let us be glad that it is not thus with all.

Use 3. But for closer application, seeing this is the great condemning sin, before we inquire after it into the hearts of our hearers, it beseems us to begin at home, and see that we, who are preachers of the gospel, be not guilty of it ourselves. The Lord forbid that they that have undertaken the sacred office of revealing the excellencies of Christ to the world, should make light of him themselves, and slight that salvation which they do daily preach. The Lord knows we are all of us so low in our estimation of Christ, and do this great work so negligently, that we have cause to be ashamed of our best sermons; but should this sin prevail in us, we were the most miserable of all men. Brethren, I love not censoriousness; yet dare not befriend so vile a sin in myself or others, under pretence of avoiding it: especially when there is so great necessity that it should be healed first in them that make it their work to heal it in others. Oh that there were no cause to complain that Christ and salvation are made light of by the preachers of it! But, 1. Do not the negligent studies of some speak it out? 2. Doth not their dead and drowsy preaching declare it? Do not they make light of the doctrine they preach, that do it as if they were half asleep, and feel not what they speak themselves?

3. Doth not the carelessness of some men's private endeavours discover it? What do they for souls? how slightly do they reprove sin! How little do they when they are out of the pulpit for the saving of men's souls!

4. Doth not the continued neglect of those things wherein the interest of Christ consisteth discover it? 1. The church's purity and reformation. 2. Its unity.

5. Do not the covetous and worldly lives of too many discover it, losing advantages for men's souls for a little gain to themselves? And most of this is because men are preachers before they are Christians, and tell men of that which they never felt themselves. Of all men on earth there are few that are in so sad a condition as such ministers: and if, indeed, they do believe that Scripture which they preach, methinks it should be terrible to them in their studying and preaching it.

Use 4. Beloved hearers, the office that God hath called us to, is by declaring the glory of his grace, to help under Christ to the saving of men's souls. I hope you think not that I come hither today on any other errand. The Lord knows I had not set a foot out of doors but in hope to succeed in this work for your souls. I have considered, and often considered, what is the matter that so many thousands should perish when God hath done so much for their salvation; and I find this that is mentioned in my text is the cause. It is one of the wonders of the world, that when God hath so loved the world as to send his Son, and Christ hath made a satisfaction by his death sufficient for them all, and offereth the benefits of it so freely to them, even without money or price, that yet the most of the world should perish; yea, the most of those that are thus called by his word! Why, here is the reason, when Christ hath done all this, men make light of it. God hath shewed that he is not unwilling; and Christ hath shewed that he is not unwilling that men should be restored to God's favour and be saved; but men are actually unwilling themselves. God takes not pleasure in the death of sinners, but rather that they return and live, Ezek. xxxiii. 11. But men take such pleasure in sin, that they will die before they will return. The Lord Jesus was content to be their Physician, and hath provided them a sufficient plaster of his own blood: but if men make light of it, and will not apply it, what wonder if they perish alter all? This Scripture giveth us the reason of their perdition. This, sad experience tells us, the most of the world is guilty of. It is a most lamentable thing to see how most men do spend their care, their time, their pains, for known vanities, while God and glory are cast aside; that he who is all should seem to them as nothing, and that which is nothing should seem to them as good as all; that God should set mankind in such a race where heaven or hell is their certain end, and that they should sit down, and loiter, or run after the childish toys of the world, and so much forget the prize that they should run for. Were it but possible for one of us to see the whole of this business as the all-seeing God doth; to see at one view both heaven and hell, which men are so near; and see what most men in the world are minding, and what they are doing every day, it would be the saddest sight that could be imagined. Oh how should we marvel at their madness, and lament their self-delusion! Oh poor distracted world! what is it you run after? and what is it that you neglect? If God had never told them what they were sent into the world to do, or whither they were going, or what was before them in another world, then they had been excusable; but he hath told them over and over, till they were weary of it. Had he left it doubtful, there had been some excuse; but it is his sealed word, and they profess to believe it, and would take it ill of us if we should question whether they do believe it or not.

Beloved, I come not to accuse any of you particularly of this crime; but seeing it is the commonest cause of men's destruction, I suppose you will

judge it the fittest matter for our inquiry, and deserving our greatest care for
the cure. To which end I shall, 1. Endeavour the conviction of the guilty. 2.
Shall give them such considerations as may tend to humble and reform them.
3. I shall conclude with such direction as may help them that are willing to
escape the destroying power of this sin. And. for the first, consider,

1

It is the case of most sinners to think themselves freest from those sins that
they are most enslaved to; and one reason why we cannot reform them, is
because we cannot convince them of their guilt. It is the nature of sin so
far to blind and befool the sinner, that he knoweth not what he doth, but
thinketh he is free from it when it reigneth in him, or when he is committing
it: it bringeth men to be so much unacquainted with themselves, that they
know not what they think, or what they mean and intend, nor what they
love or hate, much less what they are habituated and disposed to. They are
alive to sin, and dead to all the reason, consideration, and resolution that
should recover them, as if it were only by their sinning that we must know
they are alive. May I hope that you that hear me to-day are but willing to
know the truth of your case, and then I shall be encouraged to proceed to
an inquiry. God will judge impartially; why should not we do so? Let me,
therefore, by these following questions, try whether none of you are slighters
of Christ and your own salvation. And follow me, I beseech you, by putting
them close to your own hearts, and faithfully answering them.

1. Things that men highly value will be remembered, they will be matter
of their freest and sweetest thoughts. This is a known case.

Do not those then make light of Christ and salvation that think of them
so seldom and coldly in comparison of other things? Follow thy own heart,
man, and observe what it daily runneth after; and then judge whether it
make not light of Christ.

We cannot persuade men to one hour's sober consideration what they
should do for an interest in Christ, or in thankfulness for his love, and yet
they will not believe that they make light of him.

2. Things that we highly value will be matter of our discourse; the judgment
and heart will command the tongue. Freely and delightfully will our speech
run after them. This also is a known case.

Do not those then make light of Christ and salvation, that shun the
mention of his name, unless it be in a vain or sinful use? Those that love

not the company where Christ and salvation is much talked of, but think it troublesome, precise discourse: that had rather hear some merry jests, or idle tales, or talk of their riches or business in the world. When you may follow them from morning to night, and scarce have a savoury word of Christ; but perhaps some slight and weary mention of him sometimes; judge whether these make not light of Christ and salvation. How seriously do they talk of the world (Psal. cxliv. 8, 11) and speak vanity! but how heartlessly do they make mention of Christ and salvation!

3. The things that we highly value we would secure the possession of, and therefore would take any convenient course to have all doubts and fears about them well resolved. Do not those men then make light of Christ and salvation that have lived twenty or thirty years in uncertainty whether they have any part in these or not, and yet never seek out for the right resolution of their doubts? Are all that hear me this day certain they shall be saved? Oh that they were! Oh, had you not made light of salvation, you could not so easily bear such doubtings of it; you could not rest till you had made it sure, or done your best to make it sure. Have you nobody, to inquire of, that might help you in such a work? Why, you have ministers that are purposely appointed to that office. Have you gone to them, and told them the doubtfulness of your case, and asked their help in the judging of your condition? Alas, ministers may sit in their studies from one year to another, before ten persons among a thousand will come to them on such an errand! Do not these make light of Christ and salvation? When the gospel pierceth the heart indeed, they cry out, "Men and brethren, what shall we do to be saved?" Acts xvi. 30. Trembling and astonished, Paul cries out, "Lord, what wilt thou have me to do?" Acts ix. 6. And so did the convinced Jews to Peter, Acts ii. 37. But when hear we such questions?

4. The things that we value do deeply affect us, and some motions will be in the heart according to our estimation of them. O sirs, if men made not light of these things, what working would there be in the hearts of all our hearers! What strange affections would it raise in them to hear of the matters of the world to come! How would their hearts melt before the power of the gospel! What sorrow would be wrought in the discovery of their sins! What astonishment at the consideration of their misery! What unspeakable joy at the glad tidings of salvation by the blood of Christ! What resolution would be raised in them upon the discovery of their duty! Oh what hearers should we have, if it were not for this sin! Whereas now we are liker to weary them,

or preach them asleep with matters of this unspeakable moment. We talk to them of Christ and salvation till we make their heads ache: little would one think by their careless carriage that they heard and regarded what we said, or thought we spoke at all to them.

5. Our estimation of things will be seen in the diligence of our endeavours. That which we highliest value, we shall think no pains too great to obtain. Do not those men then make light of Christ and salvation, that think all too much that they do for them; that murmur at his service, and think it too grievous for them to endure? that ask of his service as Judas of the ointment, What need this waste? Cannot men be saved without so much ado? This is more ado than needs. For the world they will labour all the day, and all their lives; but for Christ and salvation they are afraid of doing too much. Let us preach to them as long as we will, we cannot bring them to relish or resolve upon a life of holiness. Follow them to their houses, and you shall not hear them read a chapter, nor call upon God with their families once a day: nor will they allow him that one day in seven which he hath separated to his service. But pleasure, or worldly business, or idleness, must have a part. And many of them are so far hardened as to reproach them that will not be as mad as themselves. And is not Christ worth the seeking? Is not everlasting salvation worth more than all this? Doth not that soul make light of all these, that thinks his ease more worth than they? Let but common sense judge.

6. That which we most highly value, we think we cannot buy too dear: Christ and salvation are freely given, and yet the most of men go without them, because they cannot enjoy the world and them together. They are called but to part with that which would hinder them from Christ, and they will not do it. They are called but to give God his own, and to resign all to his will, and let go the profits and pleasures of this world, when they must let go either Christ or them, and they will not. They think this too dear a bargain, and say they cannot spare these things: they must hold their credit with men; they must look to their estates: how shall they live else? They must have their pleasure, whatsoever becomes of Christ and salvation: as if they could live without Christ better than without these: as if they were afraid of being losers by Christ, or could make a saving match by losing their souls to gain the world. Christ hath told us over and over, that if we will not forsake all for him we cannot be his disciples, Matt. x. Far are these men from forsaking all, and yet will needs think that they are his disciples indeed.

7. That which men highly esteem, they would help their friends to as well

as themselves. Do not those men make light of Christ and salvation, that can take so much care to leave their children portions in the world, and do so little to help them to heaven? that provide outward necessaries so carefully for their families, but do so little to the saving of their souls? Their neglected children and friends will witness, that either Christ, or their children's souls, or both, were made light of.

8. That which men highly esteem, they will so diligently seek after, that you may see it in the success, if it be a matter within their reach. You may see how many make light of Christ, by the little knowledge they have of him, and the little communion with him, and communication from him; and the little, yea, none of his special grace in them. Alas! how many ministers can speak it to the sorrow of their hearts, that many of their people know almost nothing of Christ, though they hear of him daily! Nor know they what they must do to be saved: if we ask them an account of these things, they answer as if they understood not what we say to them, and tell us they are no scholars, and therefore think they are excusable for their ignorance. Oh if these men had not made light of Christ and their salvation, but had bestowed but half as much pains to know and enjoy him as they have done to understand the matters of their trades and callings in the world, they would not have been so ignorant as they are: they make light of these things, and therefore will not be at the pains to study or learn them. When men that can learn the hardest trade in a few years, have not learned a catechism, nor how to understand their creed, under twenty or thirty years' preaching, nor can abide to be questioned about such things; doth not this shew that they have slighted them in their hearts? How will these despisers of Christ and salvation be able one day to look him in the face, and to give an account of these neglects?

2

Thus much I have spoken in order to your conviction. Do not some of your consciences by this time smite you, and say, I am the man that have made light of my salvation? If they do not, it is because you make light of it still, for all that is said to you. But because, if it be the will of the Lord, I would fain have this damning distemper cured, and am loth to leave you in such a desperate condition, if I knew how to remedy it, I will give you some considerations, which may move you, if you be men of reason and understanding, to look better about you; and I beseech you to weigh them, and make use of them as we go, and lay open our hearts to the work of grace, and sadly bethink you what a case you are in, if you prove such as make light of Christ.

Consider, 1. Thou makest light of him that made not light of thee who didst deserve it. Thou wast worthy of nothing but contempt. As a man, what art thou but a worm to God? As a sinner, thou art far viler than a toad: yet Christ was so far from making light of thee and thy happiness, that he came down into the flesh, and lived a life of suffering, and offered himself a sacrifice to the justice which thou hadst provoked, that thy miserable soul might have a remedy. It is no less than miracles of love and mercy, that he hath shewed to us: and yet shall we slight them after all?

Angels admire them, whom they less concern (1 Pet. i. 12), and shall redeemed sinners make light of them? What barbarous, yea, devilish, yea, worse than devilish ingratitude is this! The devils never had a saviour offered them, but thou hast, and dost thou yet make light of Him?

2. Consider, the work of man's salvation by Jesus Christ is the masterpiece of all the works of God, wherein he would have his love and mercy to be magnified. As the creation declareth his goodness and power, so doth redemption his goodness and mercy; he hath contrived the very frame of his worship so, that it shall much consist in the magnifying of this work; and after all this, will you make light of it? "His name is Wonderful," Isa. ix. 6. "He did the work that none could do," John xv. 24. "Greater love could none shew than his," John xv. 13. How great was the evil and misery that he delivered us from! the good procured for us! All are wonders, from his birth to his ascension; from our new birth to our glorification, all are wonders of matchless mercy—and yet do you make light of them?

3. You make light of matters of greatest excellency and moment in the world: you know not what it is that you slight: had you well known, you could not have done it. As Christ said to the woman of Samaria (John iv. 10), Hadst thou known who it is that speakest to thee, thou wouldst have asked of him the waters of life: had they known they would not have crucified the Lord of glory, 1 Cor. ii. 8. So had you known what Christ is, you would not have made light of him; had you been one day in heaven, and but seen what they possess, and seen also what miserable souls must endure that are shut out, you would never sure have made so light of Christ again.

O sirs, it is no trifles or jesting matters that the gospel speaks of. I must needs profess to you, that when I have the most serious thoughts of these things myself, I am ready to marvel that such amazing matters do not overwhelm the souls of men; that the greatness of the subject doth not so overmatch our understandings and affections, as even to drive men beside themselves, but that God hath always somewhat allayed it by the distance: much more that men should be so blockish as to make light of them. O Lord, that men did but know what everlasting glory and everlasting torments are; would they then bear us as they do? would they read and think of these things as they do? I profess I have been ready to wonder, when I have heard such weighty things delivered, how people can forbear crying out in the congregation; much more how they can rest till they have gone to their ministers, and learned what they should do to be saved, that this great business might be put out of doubt. Oh that heaven and hell should work no more on men! Oh that everlastingness should work no more! Oh how can you forbear when you are alone to think with yourselves what it is to be everlastingly in joy or in torment! I wonder that such thoughts do not break your sleep; and that they come not in your mind when you are about your labour! I wonder how you can almost do any thing else! how you can have any quietness in your minds! how you can eat, or drink, or rest, till you have got some ground of everlasting consolations! Is that a man or a corpse that is not affected with matters of this moment? that can be readier to sleep than to tremble when he heareth how he must stand at the bar of God? Is that a man or a clod of clay that can rise and lie down without being deeply affected with his everlasting estate? that can follow his worldly business, and make nothing of the great business of salvation or damnation; and that when they know it is hard at hand! Truly, sirs, when I think of the weight of the matter, I wonder at the very best of God's saints upon earth that they are no better, and do no more in so weighty a case. I wonder at those whom the world accounteth more holy than needs, and scorns for making too much ado, that they can put off Christ and their souls with so little; that they pour not out their souls in every supplication; that they are not more taken up with God; that their thoughts be not more serious in preparation for their account. I wonder that they be not a hundred times more strict in their lives, and more laborious and unwearied in striving for the crown, than they are. And for myself, as I am ashamed of my dull and careless heart, and of my slow and unprofitable, course of life; so the Lord knows I am ashamed of every sermon that I preach: when I think what I have been speaking of, and who sent me, and what men's salvation or damnation is so much concerned in it, I am ready to tremble, lest God should judge me as a slighter of his truth, and the souls of men, and lest in the best sermon I should be guilty of their blood. Methinks we should not speak a word to men in matters of such consequence without tears, or the greatest earnestness that possibly we can: were not we too much guilty of the sin which we reprove, it would be so. Whether we are alone, or in company, methinks our end, and such an end, should still be in our mind, and as before our eyes; and we should sooner forget any thing, and set light by any thing, or by all things, than by this.

Consider, 4. Who is it that sends this weighty message to you? Is it not God himself? Shall the God of heaven speak, and men make light of it? You would not slight the voice of an angel, or a prince.

5. Whose salvation is it that you make light of? Is it not your own? Are you no more near or dear to yourselves than to make light of your own happiness or misery? Why, sirs, do you not care whether you be saved or damned? is self-love lost? are you turned your own enemies? As he that slighteth his meat doth slight his life; so if you slight Christ, whatsoever you may think, you will find it was your own salvation that you slighted. Hear what he saith, "All they that hate me love death," Prov. viii. 36.

6. Your sin is greater, in that you profess to believe the gospel which you make so light of. For a professed infidel to do it that believes not that ever Christ died, or rose again; or doth not believe that there is a heaven or hell; this were no such marvel: but for you that make it your creed, and your very religion, and call yourselves Christians, and have been baptized into this faith, and seemed to stand to it, this is the wonder, and hath no excuse. What! believe that you shall live in endless joy or torment, and yet make no more of it to escape torment, and obtain that joy! What! believe that God will shortly judge you, and yet make no more preparation for it! Either say plainly, I am no Christian, I do not believe these wonderful things, I will believe nothing but what I see; or else let your hearts be affected with your belief, and live as you say you do believe. What do you think when you repeat the creed, and mention Christ's judgment and everlasting life?

7. What are these things you set so much by, as to prefer them before Christ and the saving of your souls? Have you found a better friend, a greater and surer happiness than this? Good Lord! what dung is it that men make so much of, while they set so light by everlasting glory! What toys are they that they are daily taken up with, while matters of life and death are neglected! Why, sirs, if you had every one a kingdom in your hopes, what were it in comparison of the everlasting kingdom? I cannot but look upon all the glory

and dignity of this world, lands and lord-ships, crowns and kingdoms, even as on some brain-sick, beggarly fellow, that borroweth fine clothes, and plays the part of a king or a lord for an hour on a stage, and then comes down, and the sport is ended, and they are beggars again. Were it not for God's interest in the authority of magistrates, or for the service they might do him, I should judge no better of them. For as to their own glory, it is but a smoke: what matter is it whether you live poor or rich, unless it were a greater matter to die rich than it is? You know well enough that death levels all. What matter is it at judgment, whether you be to answer for the life of a rich man or a poor man? Is Dives then any better than Lazarus? O that men knew what a poor deceiving shadow they grasp at, while they let go the everlasting substance! The strongest. and richest, and most voluptuous sinners, do but lay in fuel for their sorrows, while they think they are gathering together a treasure. Alas! they are asleep, and dream that they are happy; but when they awake, what a change will they find! Their crown is made of thorns: their pleasure hath such a sting as will stick in the heart through all eternity, except unfeigned repentance do prevent it. O how sadly will these wretches be convinced, ere long, what a foolish bargain they made in selling Christ and their salvation for these trifles! Let your farms and merchandise then save you if they can; and do that for you that Christ would have done. Cry then to thy Baal to save thee! Oh what thoughts have drunkards and adulterers, &c. Of Christ, that will not part with the basest lust for him! "For a piece of bread," saith Solomon, "such men do transgress," Prov. xxviii. 11.

8. To set so light by Christ and salvation, is a certain mark that thou hast no part in them, and if thou so continue, that Christ will set as light by thee: "Those that honour him he will honour, and those that despise him shall be lightly esteemed," 1 Sam. ii. 30. Thou wilt feel one day that thou canst not live without him; thou wilt confess then thy need of him; and then thou mayest go look for a saviour where thou wilt; for he will be no saviour for thee hereafter, that wouldst not value him, and submit to him here. Then who will prove the loser by thy contempt? O what a thing will it be for a poor miserable soul to cry to Christ for help in the day of extremity, and to hear so sad an answer as this! Thou didst set light by me and my law in the day of thy prosperity, and I will now set as light by thee in thy adversity. Read Prov. i. 24, to the end. Thou that, as Esau, didst sell thy birthright for a mess of pottage, shalt then find no place for repentance, though thou seek it with tears, Heb. xii. 17. Do you think that Christ shed his blood to save

them that continue to make light of it? and to save them that value a cup of drink or a lust before his salvation? I tell you, sirs, though you set so light by Christ and salvation, God doth not so: he will not give them on such terms as these: he valueth the blood of his Son, and the everlasting glory; and he will make you value them if ever you have them. Nay, this will be thy condemnation, and leaveth no remedy. All the world cannot save him that sets light by Christ, Heb. ii. 3; Luke xiv. 24. None of them shall taste of his supper, Matt. x. 37. Nor can you blame him to deny you what you made light of yourselves. Can you find fault if you miss of the salvation which you slighted?

9. The time is near when Christ and salvation will not be made light of as now they are. When God hath shaken those careless souls out of their bodies, and you must answer for all your sins in your own name; oh then what would you give for a saviour! When a thousand bills shall be brought in against you, and none to relieve you then you will consider, Oh! Christ would now have stood between me and the wrath of God: had I not despised him, he would have answered all. When you see the world hath left you, and your companions in sin have deceived themselves and you, and all your merry days are gone; then what would you give for that Christ and salvation that now you account not worth your labour! Do you think when you see the judgment set, and you are doomed to everlasting perdition for your wickedness, that you should then make as light of Christ as now? Why will you not judge now as you know you shall judge then? Will he then be worth ten thousand worlds? and is he not now worth your highest estimation and dearest affection?

10. God will not only deny thee that salvation thou madest light of, but he will take from thee all that which thou didst value before it: he that most highly esteems Christ shall have him, and the creatures so far as they are good here, and him without the creature hereafter, because the creature is not useful; and he that sets more by the creature than by Christ, shall have some of the creature without Christ here, and neither Christ nor it hereafter.

So much of these considerations, which may shew the true face of this heinous sin.

What think you now, friends, of this business? Do you not see by this time what a case that soul is in that maketh light of Christ and salvation? What need then is there that you should take heed lest this should prove your own case! The Lord knows it is too common a case. Whoever is found guilty at the last of this sin, it were better for that man he had never been born. It were better for him he had been a Turk [Muslim] or Indian [Hindu], that never had heard the name of a Saviour, and that never had salvation offered to him: for such men "have no cloak for their sin," John xv. 22. Besides all the rest of their sins, they have this killing sin to answer for, which will undo them. And this will aggravate their misery, that Christ whom they set light by must be their Judge, and for this sin will he judge them. Oh that such would now consider how they will answer that question that Christ put to their predecessors, "How will ye escape the damnation of hell ?" Matt. xxiii. 33: or, "how shall we escape if we neglect so great salvation?" Heb. ii. 3. Can you escape without a Christ? or will a despised Christ save you then? If he be accursed that sets light by father or mother (Deut. xxvii. 16), what then is he that sets light by Christ? It was the heinous sin of the Jews, that among them were found such as set light by father and mother, Ezek. xxii. 7. But among us, men slight the Father of spirits! In the name of God, brethren, I beseech you to consider how you will then bear his anger which you now make light of! You that cannot make light of a little sickness or want, or of natural death, no, not of a tooth-ache, but groan as if you were undone; how will you then make light of the fury of the Lord, which will burn against the contemners of his grace! Doth it not behove you beforehand to think of these things?

3

Hitherto I have been convincing you of the evil of the sin, and the danger that followeth: I come now to know your resolution for the time to come. What say you? Do you mean to set as light by Christ and salvation as hitherto you have done; and to be the same men after all this? I hope not. Oh let not your ministers that would fain save you, be brought in as witnesses against you to condemn you; at least, I beseech you, put not this upon me. Why, sirs, if the Lord shall say to us at judgment, Did you never tell these men what Christ did for their souls, and what need they had of him, and how nearly it did concern them to look to their salvation, that they made light of it? We must needs say the truth; Yea, Lord, we told them of it as plainly as we could; we would have gone on our knees to them if we had thought it would have prevailed; we did entreat them as earnestly as we could to consider these things: they heard of these things every day; but, alas, we could never get them to their hearts: they gave us the hearing, but they made light of all that we could say to them. Oh! sad will it prove on your side, if you force us to such an answer as this.

But if the Lord do move the hearts of any of you, and you resolve to make light of Christ no more; or if any of you say, We do not make light of him; let me tell you here in the conclusion what you must do, or else you shall be judged as slighters of Christ and salvation.

And first I will tell you what will not serve the turn.

1. You may have a notional knowledge of Christ, and the necessity of his blood, and of the excellency of salvation, and yet perish as neglecters of him. This is too common among professed Christians. You may say all that other men do of him: what gospel passages had Balaam! Jesus I know, and Paul I know, the very devils could say, who believe and tremble, James ii. 19.

2. You may weep at the history of Christ's passion, when you read how he was used by the Jews, and yet make light of him, and perish for so doing.

3. You may come desirously to his word and ordinances. Herod heard gladly; so do many that yet must perish as neglecters of salvation.

4. You may in a fit of fear have strong desires after a Christ, to ease you, and to save you from God's wrath, as Saul had of David to play before him; and yet you may perish for making light of Christ.

5. You may obey him in many things so far as will not ruin you in the world, and escape much of the pollutions of the world by his knowledge, and yet neglect him.

6. You may suffer and lose much for him, so far as leaveth you an earthly felicity; as Ananias; and the young man, Matt. xix. 16–22. Some parcels of their pleasures and profits many will part with in hope of salvation, that shall perish everlastingly for valuing it no more.

7. You may be esteemed by others a man zealous for Christ, and loved and admired upon that account, and yet be one that shall perish for making light of him.

8. You may verily think yourselves, that you set more by Christ and salvation than any thing, and yet be mistaken, and be judged as contemners of him: Christ justifieth not all that justify themselves.

9. You may be zealous preachers of Christ and salvation, and reprove others for this neglect, and lament the sin of the world in the like expression as I have done this day; and yet if you or I have no better evidence to prove our hearty esteem of Christ and salvation, we are undone for all this.

4

You hear, brethren, what will not serve the turn; will you now hear what persons you must be if you would not be condemned as slighters of Christ? O search whether it be thus with your souls or no!

1. Your esteem of Christ and salvation must he greater than your esteem of all the honours, profits, or pleasures of this world, or else you slight him: no less will be accounted sincere, nor accepted to your salvation. Think not this hard, when there is no comparison in the matters esteemed. To esteem the greatest glory on earth before Christ and everlasting glory, is a greater folly and wrong to Christ, than to esteem a dog before your prince, would be folly in you, and a wrong to him. Scripture is plain in this; "He that loveth father or mother, wife, children, house, land, or his own life, more than me, is not worthy of me, and cannot be my disciple," Matt. x. 37; Luke xiv. 26.

2. You must manifest this esteem of Christ and salvation in your daily endeavours and seeking after him, and in parting with any thing that he shall require of you. God is a Spirit, and will not take a hypocritical profession instead of the heart and spiritual service which he commandeth. He will have the heart or nothing; and the chief room in the heart too: these must be had.

If you say that you do not make light of Christ, or will not hereafter; let me try you in these few particulars, whether indeed you mean as you say, and do not dissemble.

1. Will you for the time to come make Christ and salvation the chiefest matter of your care and study? Thrust them not out of your thoughts as a needless or unprofitable subject; nor allow it only some running, slight thoughts, which will not affect you. But will you make it your business once a day to bethink you soberly, when you are alone, what Christ hath done for you, and what he will do, if you do not make light of it; and what it is to be everlastingly happy or miserable? And what all things in this world are in comparison of your salvation; and how they will shortly leave you; and what mind you will be then of, and how will esteem them? Will you promise me now and then to make it your business to withdraw yourselves from the world, and set yourselves to such considerations as these? If you will not, are not you slighters of Christ and salvation, that will not be persuaded soberly to think on them? This is my first question to put you to the trial, whether you will value Christ or not.

2. Will you for the time to come set more by the Word of God, which contains the discovery of these excellent things, and is your charter for

salvation, and your guide thereunto? You cannot set by Christ, but you must set by his word: therefore the despisers of it are threatened with destruction, Prov. xiii. 13. Will you therefore attend to the public preaching of this Word; will you read it daily; will you resolve to obey it whatever it may cost you? if you will not do this, but make light of the Word of God, you shall be judged as such as make light of Christ and salvation, whatever you may fondly promise to yourselves.

3. Will you for the time to come esteem more of the officers of Christ, whom he hath purposely appointed to guide you to salvation; and will you make use of them for that end? Alas, it is not to give the minister a good word, and speak well of him, and pay him his tithes duly, that will serve the turn: it is for the necessity of your souls that God hath set them in his church; that they may be as physicians under Christ, or his apothecaries to apply his remedies to your spiritual diseases, not only in public, but also in private: that you may have some to go to for the resolving of your doubts, and for your instruction where you are ignorant, and for the help of their exhortations and prayers. Will you use hereafter to go to your ministers privately, and solicit them for advice? And if you have not such of your own as are fit, get advice from others; and ask them, What you shall do to be saved? how to prepare for death and judgement? And will you obey the Word of God in their mouths? If you will not do this much, nor so much as inquire of those that should teach you, nor use the means which Christ hath established in his church for your help, your own consciences shall one day witness that you were such as made light of Christ and salvation. If any of you doubt whether it be your duty thus to ask counsel of your teachers, as sick men do of their physicians, let your own necessities resolve you, let God's express Word resolve you; see what is said of the priests of the Lord, even before Christ's coming, when much of their work did lie in ceremonials: "My covenant was with him of life and peace: and I gave them to him (to Levi) for the fear wherewith he feared me, and was afraid before my name. The law of truth was in his mouth, and iniquity was not found in his lips; he walked with me in peace and equity, and did turn many away from iniquity. For the priest's lips should keep knowledge, and they should seek the law at his mouth: for he is the messenger of the Lord of hosts," Mal. ii. 5–7.

Nay, you must not only inquire, and submit to their advice, but also to their just reprehensions, and church censures; and without proud repining submit to the discipline of Christ in their hands, if it shall be used in the congregations whereof you are members.

4. Will you for the time to come make conscience of daily and earnest prayer to God, that you may have a part in Christ and salvation? Do not go out of doors till you have breathed out these desires to God; do not lie down to rest till you have breathed out these desires: say not, God knoweth my necessity without so often praying; for though he do, yet he will have you to know them, and feel them, and exercise your desires and all the graces of his Spirit in these duties: it is he that hath commanded to pray continually, though he know your needs without it, 1 Thess. v. 17. Christ himself spent whole nights in prayer, and encourageth us to this course, Luke xviii. 1. If you will not be persuaded to this much, how can you say that you make not light of Christ and salvation?

5. Will you for the time to come resolvedly cast away your known sins at the command of Christ? If you have been proud, or contentious, or malicious, and revengeful, be so no more. If you have been adulterers, or swearers, or cursers, be so no more. You cannot hold these, and yet set by Christ and salvation.

What say you? Are you resolved to let them go? If not, when you know it is the will of Christ, and he hath told you such shall not enter into his kingdom, do not you make light of him?

6. Will you for the time to come serve God in the dearest as well as in the cheapest part of his service? not only with your tongues, but with your purses and your deeds? Shall the poor find that you set more by Christ than this world? Shall it appear in any good uses that God calls you to be liberal in, according to your abilities? "Pure religion and undefiled before God is this, to visit the fatherless and the widows in their affliction." James i. 27. Will you resolve to stick to Christ, and make sure this work of salvation, though it cost you all that you have in the world? If you think these terms too dear, you make light of Christ, and will be judged accordingly.

7. Will you for the time to come make much of all things that tend to your salvation; and take every help that God offereth you, and gladly make use of all his ordinances? Attend upon his strengthening sacraments; spend the Lord's own day in these holy employments; instruct your children and servants in these things, Deut. vi. 6, 7; get into good company that set their faces heavenward, and will teach you the way, and help you thither; and take heed of the company of wicked scorners, or foolish, voluptuous, fleshly

men, or any that would hinder you in this work. Will you do these things? Or will you shew that you are slighters of Christ by neglecting them?

8. Will you do all this with delight; not as your toil, but as your pleasure? And take it for your highest honour that you may be Christ's disciples, and may be admitted to serve and worship him; and rejoice with holy confidence in the sufficiency of that sacrifice by which you may have pardon of all your failings, and right to the inheritance of the saints in light? If you will do these things sincerely, you will shew that you set by Christ and salvation; else not.

Dearly beloved in the Lord, I have now done that work which I came upon; what effect it hath, or will have, upon your hearts, I know not, nor is it any further in my power to accomplish that which my soul desireth for you. Were it the Lord's will that I might have my wish herein, the words that you have this day heard should so stick by you, that the secure should be awakened by them, and none of you should perish by the slighting of your salvation. I cannot now follow you to your several habitations to apply this word to your particular necessities; but O that I could make every man's conscience a preacher to himself that it might do it, which is ever with you!—That the next time you go prayerless to bed, or about your business, conscience might cry out, Dost thou set no more by Christ and thy salvation? That the next time you are tempted to think hardly of a holy and diligent life (I will not say to deride it as more ado than needs), conscience might cry out to thee, Dost thou set so light by Christ and thy salvation? That the next time you are ready to rush upon known sin, and to please your fleshly desires against the command of God, conscience might cry out, Is Christ and salvation no more worth, than to cast them away, or venture them for thy lusts? That when you are following the world with most eager desires, forgetting the world to come, and the change that is a little before you, conscience might cry out to you, Is Christ and salvation no more worth than so? That when you are next spending the Lord's day in idleness or vain sports, conscience might tell you what you are doing. In a word, that in all your neglects of duty, your sticking at the supposed labour or cost of a godly life, yea, in all your cold and lazy prayers and performances, conscience might tell you how unsuitable such endeavours are to the reward; and that Christ and salvation should not be so slighted.

I will say no more but this at this time. It is a thousand pities that when God hath provided a Saviour for the world, and when Christ hath suffered so much for their sins, and made so full a satisfaction to justice, and purchased so glorious a kingdom for his saints, and all this is offered so freely to sinners, to lost, unworthy sinners, even for nothing, that yet so many millions should everlastingly perish because they make light of their Saviour and salvation, and prefer the vain world and their lusts before them. I have delivered my message, the Lord open your hearts to receive it. I have persuaded you with the word of truth and soberness; the Lord persuade you more effectually, or else all this is lost. Amen.

6. THE GRAND QUESTION RESOLVED

WHAT WE MUST DO TO BE SAVED:

INSTRUCTIONS
FOR A
Holy Life.

BY
The late reverend Divine

MR RICHARD BAXTER.

Recommended to the Bookseller a few days before his death,
to be immediately printed for the good of souls.

ACTS xvi. 30. Sirs! What shall I do to be saved?

LONDON:
Printed for THO. PARKHURST, at the Bible
and Three Crowns, Cheapside. 1692.

THE GREAT CASE RESOLVED, HOW TO BE CERTAINLY SAVED.

Instructions for a Holy Life
I. THE NECESSITY, REASON, AND MEANS OF HOLINESS.
II. THE PARTS AND PRACTICE OF A HOLY LIFE.
For personal direction and for family instruction. With two short Catechisms and Prayers.

READER,

IGNORANT persons cannot remember long and many words, nor understand a brief style and few words. This maketh it impossible to write a Catechism that shall not be unsuitable either to the understanding or the memory of such. I must therefore desire the Teacher to make up the unavoidable defect, by opening the meaning,—especially of the Catechisms,— to the children and servants, when they have learned and say the words. Read the Instructions often to them and press all as you go, on their affections. For, the bare words without a present guide may else be all lost.

I. *The necessity, reason, and means of Holiness.*

1. To keep up the resolutions of the converted. And
2. To instruct those in families that need them.

Though the saving of souls be a matter of inexpressible importance,[1] yet—the Lord have mercy upon them!—what abundance are there that think it not worthy of their serious enquiry, nor the reading of a good book, one hour in a week! For the sake of these careless slothful sinners, I have here spoken much in a little room, that they may not refuse to read and consider so short a lesson, unless they think their souls worth nothing. Sinner! As thou wilt shortly answer it before God, deny not to God, to thyself and me, the sober pondering and faithful practising these few directions:—

I. Begin at home, and know thyself. Consider what it is to be a man.[2] Thou art made a nobler creature than the brutes. They serve thee, and are governed by thee; and death ends all their pains and pleasures. But thou hast reason to rule thyself and them; to know thy God, and foresee thy end, and know thy way, and do thy duty. Thy reason, and free-will, and executive

---

1   Mark 8: 36; Matthew 6: 33; Job 21: 14; 22: 17; Psalm 1: 2–3; 14: 12.
2   Psalm 8: 4–6; Genesis 1: 26–7; 9: 6; Colossians 3: 10.

power, are part of the image of God upon thy nature: so is thy dominion over the brutes, as, under him, thou art their owner, their ruler, and their end. But thy holy wisdom, and goodness, and ability, is the chief part of his image on which thy happiness depends. Thou hast a soul that cannot be satisfied in knowing, till thy knowledge reach to God himself:[1] nor can it be disposed by any other; nor can it or the societies of the world, be well governed according to its nature, without regard to his sovereign authority and without the hopes and fears of joy and misery hereafter;[2] nor can it be happy[3] in anything but seeing and loving and delighting in this God as he is revealed in the other world. And is this nature given thee in vain? If the nature of all things be fitted to its use and end,[4] then it must be so with thine.

II. By knowing thyself then, thou must needs know *that there is a God*:[5] and that he is thy maker and infinite in all perfections; and that he is thy Owner, thy Ruler and thy Felicity or End. He is mad that seeth not that such creatures have a cause or maker: and that all the power and wisdom and goodness of the world, is caused by a power and wisdom and goodness which is greater than that of all the world. And who can be our Owner but he that made us? And who can be our highest Governor but our Owner, whose infinite power wisdom and goodness maketh him only fit thereto? And if he be our Governor, he must needs have laws, with rewards for the good and punishments for the bad; and must judge and execute accordingly. And if he be our chiefest Benefactor, and all that we have is from him, and all our hope and happiness is in him, nothing can be more clear than that the very nature of man doth prove that in hope of future happiness, he should absolutely assign himself to the will and disposal of this God, and that he should absolutely obey him,[6] and that he should love and serve him with all his power: it being impossible to love, obey and please that God too much who is thus our cause, our end, our all.

III. By knowing thus thyself and God, it is easy to know what primitive

---

1   John 17: 3; 1 John 4: 6–7; Jeremiah 9: 24.

2   Luke 12: 4–5.

3   Psalm 16: 5–11.

4   Isaiah 45: 18.

5   Psalm 14: 1; Genesis 1: 1; Revelation 1: 8; Romans 1: 19–20; Psalm 46: 10; 9: 10; 100 and 23; 19: 1–3; 47: 7; Ezekiel 18: 4; Genesis 18: 25; Malachi 1: 6.

6   Matthew 22: 37; Jeremiah 5: 22; 2 Corinthians 5: 8–9; Titus 2: 14; 2 Corinthians 8: 5; 6: 16–18; 1 Peter 2: 9; Psalm 10; 37: 4; 40: 8; Colossians 3: 1–2; Matthew 6: 20–21; 2 Corinthians 4: 17–18.

holiness and godliness is. Even this hearty, entire and absolute resignation of the soul to God, as the infinite power, wisdom, and goodness: as our Creator, our Owner, Governor, and Felicity or End: fully submitting to his disposal, obeying his laws, in hope of his promised rewards and fear of his threatened punishments: and loving and delighting in himself and all his appearances in the world: and desiring and seeking the endless right and enjoyment of him in heavenly glory, and expressing these affections in daily prayer, thanksgiving and praise. This is the use of all thy faculties, the end and business of thy life, the health and happiness of thy soul. This is that holiness or godliness which God doth so much call for.

IV. And by this it is easy to know what *a state of sin and ungodliness is.*[1] Even the want of all this holiness, and the setting of carnal self instead of God. When men are proudly great and wise and good in their own eyes, and would dispose of themselves and all their concernments, and would rule themselves and please themselves, according to the fleshly appetite and fancy: and therefore love most the pleasures and profits and honours of the world as the provision to satisfy the desires of the flesh: and God shall be no further loved, obeyed, or pleased than the love of fleshly pleasures will give leave, nor shall have anything but what the flesh can spare: this is a wicked, a carnal, an ungodly state; though it break forth in various ways of sinning.

V. By this, *experience may tell you that all men*[2]—yea all till grace renew them—are in this ungodly miserable state: though only the Scripture tells us how this came to pass. Though all are not fornicators nor drunkards nor extortioners nor persecutors nor live not in the same way of sinning; yet selfishness and pride and sensuality and the love of worldly things, ignorance and ungodliness are plainly become the common corruption of the nature of man; so that their hearts are turned to the world from God, and filled with impiety, filthiness and injustice; and their reason is but a servant to their senses; and their mind and love and lip is carnal;[3] and this carnal mind is enmity to the holiness of God, and cannot be subject to his law. This corruption is hereditary, and is become, as it were, a nature to us, being the mortal malady of all our natures. And it is easy to know that such an unholy, wicked nature, must needs be loathsome to God and unfit for the

---

1   Psalm 14: 1; Hebrews 12: 14; Romans 8: 12–13; John 3: 34; 5: 6; 1 John 2: 15–16; Romans 13: 14–15; 6: 16; Luke 18: 23; 14: 26, 33.

2   Romans 3; Psalm 14; Ephesians 2: 2–3; Romans 5: 12, 17, 39; John 3: 6.

3   Romans 8: 5–7.

happy enjoyment of his love, either here or in the life to come:[1] for what communion hath light with darkness?

VI. Hence then it is easy to see what grace is needful to a man's salvation. So odious a creature, such an unthankful rebel that is turned away from God and set against him, and defiled with all this filth of sin, must needs be both renewed and reconciled,[2] sanctified and pardoned, if ever he will be saved. To love God and be beloved by him and to be delighted herein, in the might of his glory, is the heaven and happiness of souls: and all this is contrary to an unholy state. Till men have new and holy hearts, they can neither see God nor love him nor delight in him nor take him for their chief content: for the flesh and world have their delight and love. And till sin be pardoned,[3] and God is reconciled to the soul, what joy or peace can it expect from him whose nature and justice engageth him to loathe and punish it?

VII. And experience will tell you *how insufficient you are for either of these two works yourselves:*[4] *to renew your souls or to reconcile them unto God.* Will a nature that is carnal resist and overcome the flesh and abhor the sin which it most dearly loveth? Will a worldly mind overcome the world? When custom hath rooted your natural corruptions, are these easily rooted up? O how great and hard a work is it to cause a blind unbelieving sinner to set his heart on another world and lay up all his hopes in heaven, and to cast off all the things he seeth for that God and glory which he never saw. And for a hardened, worldly, fleshly heart to become wise and tender and holy and heavenly, and abhor the sin which it most fondly loveth! And what can we do to satisfy justice and reconcile such a rebel soul to God?

VIII. Nature and experience having thus acquainted you with your sin and misery, and what you want, will further tell you that *God*[5] *doth not yet deal with you according to your deserts.* He giveth you life, and time, and mercies, when your sins had forfeited all these. He obligeth you to repent and turn unto him. And therefore experience telling you that there is some hope, and that God hath found out some way of shewing mercy to the children of wrath, reason will command you to enquire of all that are fit to teach you what way of remedy God hath made known. And as you very

---

1   Psalm 4: 3; 2 Corinthians 6: 14, 17.
2   Psalm 32: 1–2; 1 Corinthians 6: 11; Titus 2: 14; 3: 5–7; Hebrews 14: 14 (? sic); Matthew 5: 8.
3   Romans 5:1–3.
4   Psalm 97: 7–8, 15; 1 Corinthians 2: 11, 21; Hebrews 14: 12 (? sic); 2 Peter 1: 3.
5   Acts 14: 27; 17: 24–28; Romans 1: 19, 20; 2: 4; Job 33: 14–25; Matthew 12: 42, 43.

soon discover that the religion of heathens and Mahometans is so far from shewing the true remedy that they are part of the disease itself: so you may learn that a wonderful Person[1] the Lord Jesus Christ, hath undertaken the office of being the Redeemer and Saviour of the world: and that he who is the eternal Word and Wisdom of the Father, hath wonderfully appeared in the nature of man, which he took from the virgin Mary, being conceived by the Holy Ghost: and that we might have a Teacher sent from Heaven[2] infallibly and easily to acquaint the world with the will of God and the unseen things of life eternal: how God bare witness of the Truth by abundant, open and uncontrolled miracles:[3] how he conquered Satan and the world,[4] and gave us an example of perfect righteousness[5] and underwent the scorn and cruelty of sinners, and suffered the death of the cross as a sacrifice for our sins to reconcile us unto God: how he rose again the third day and conquered death, and lived forty days longer on earth, instructing his apostles and giving them commission to preach the Gospel to all the world, and then ascended bodily into heaven, while they gazed after him: how he is now in heaven, both God and man in one Person, the Teacher and King and High-priest of his Church. Of him must we learn the way of life: by him must we be ruled as the physician of souls. All power is given him in heaven and in earth. By his sacrifice and merits and intercession must we be pardoned and accepted with the Father: and only by him must we come to God. He hath procured and established a covenant of grace, which baptism is the seal of: Even that God will in him be our God and reconciled Father, and Christ will be our Saviour, and the Holy Ghost will be our Sanctifier, if we will unfeignedly consent; that is if penitently and believingly we give up ourselves to God the Father, Son and Holy Ghost, in these resolutions. This covenant in the tenor of it is a deed of gift, of Christ and pardon and salvation to all the world: if by true faith and repentance they will turn to God. And this shall be the law according to which he will judge all that hear it at the last: for he is made the judge of all, and will raise all the dead, and justify his saints and judge them unto endless joy and glory, and condemn the unbelievers,

---

1   Isaiah 9: 6, 7; 53; John 3: 16, 19; 1: 3–4; 3: 2.

2   John 1: 18.

3   Acts 2: 22; Hebrews 2: 3–4.

4   Matthew 4.

5   1 Peter 2: 22–25; Matthew 26: 27–28; Acts 1; Hebrews 4; Ephesians 1: 22, 23; Romans 5: 1, 3, 9; Hebrews 8: 9, 13; 8: 6–7; 7: 25; 1 John 5: 10, 12; John 5: 22; 3: 18–19; Matthew 25.

impenitent and ungodly,[1] unto endless misery. The soul alone is judged at death, and body and soul at the resurrection. This Gospel the apostles preached to the world; and that it might be effectual to man's salvation, the Holy Ghost was first given to inspire the preachers of it,[2] and enable them to speak in various languages, and infallibly to agree in One, and to work many great and open miracles to prove their word to those they preached to. And by this means they planted the Church;[3] which ordinary ministers must increase and teach and oversee, to the end of the world, till all the elect be gathered in. And the same Holy Spirit hath undertaken it as His work[4] to accompany this Gospel and by it to convert men's souls, illuminating and sanctifying them; and by a secret regeneration[5] to renew their natures and bring them to that knowledge and obedience and love of God which is the primitive holiness for which we were created and from which we fell. And thus by a Saviour and a Sanctifier must all be reconciled, and renewed that will be glorified with God in heaven. All this you may learn from the Sacred Scriptures which were written by the inspiration of the Holy Spirit[6] and sealed by multitudes of open miracles,[7] and contain the very image and superscription of God, and have been received and preserved by the Church as the certain word of God, and blessed by him through all generations, to the sanctifying of many souls.

IX. When you understand all this it is time for you to look home[8] and understand now *what state your souls are in*. That you were made capable of holiness and happiness, you know: that you and all men are fallen from God and holiness and happiness unto self and sin and misery, you know: that you are so far redeemed by Christ, you know, as to have a pardoning and saving covenant tendered you, and Christ and mercy offered to your choice. But whether you are truly penitent believers and renewed by the Holy Ghost and so united unto Christ, this is the question yet unresolved, this is the work that is yet to do, without which there is no salvation, and if thou die

---

1   Luke 16.
2   Acts 2; John 17: 23.
3   Matthew 28: 19–20; Acts 14: 23; Acts 20; 26: 17- 18.
4   Romans 8: 9.
5   Titus 3: 5, 6; John 13: 5–6.
6   2 Timothy 3: 16.
7   Hebrews 2: 3–4.
8   2 Corinthians 13: 5; Psalm 4: 4; 2 Peter 1: 10.

before it is done, woe to thee that ever thou wast a man! Except a man be regenerated by the Spirit[1] and converted and made a new creature, and of carnal be made spiritual, and of earthly be made heavenly, and of selfish and sinful be made holy and obedient to God, he can never be saved, no more than the devil himself can be saved. And if this be so—as nothing is more sure—I require thee now, who readest these words, as thou regardest thy salvation, as thou wouldst escape hell-fire and stand with comfort before Christ and his angels at the last, that thou soberly consider whether reason command thee not to try thy state: whether thou art thus renewed by the Spirit of Christ or not,[2] and to call for help to those that can advise thee[3] and follow on the search till thou know thy case. And if thy soul be a stranger to this sanctifying work, whether reason command thee not, without any delay, to make out to Christ, and beg his Spirit, and cast away thy sins, and give up thyself entirely to thy God, thy Saviour and Sanctifier, and enter into his covenant, with a full resolution never to forsake him; to deny thyself and the desires of the flesh and this deceitful, transitory world, and lay out all thy hopes on heaven, and speedily, whatever it cost thee, to make sure of the felicity which hath no end? And darest thou refuse this when God and conscience do command it? And further I advise you,

X. Understand how it is that *Satan hindereth souls from being sanctified*, that you may know how much to resist his wiles. Some he deceiveth by malicious suggestions that holiness is nothing but fancy or hypocrisy:[4] and God and death and heaven and hell were fancies, this might be believed. Some he debaucheth by the power of fleshly appetite and lust, so that their sins will not let their reason speak: some he keepeth in utter ignorance by the evil education of ignorant parents and the negligence of ungodly soul-murdering teachers:[5] some he deceiveth by worldly hopes, and keepeth their minds so taken up with worldly things, that the matters of eternity can have but some loose and uneffectual thoughts, or as bad as none: some are entangled in ill company,[6] so make a scorn of a holy life, and feed them with continual diversions and vain delights: and some are so hardened in

---

1   John 3: 5; 2 Corinthians 5: 17; Romans 8: 7–9; Philippians 3: 18–20.
2   Acts 16: 14.
3   Acts 2: 37; 16: 30; 11: 33; 2 Corinthians 6: 1–2; Revelation 2: 7.
4   Acts 24: 14; 28: 22; 24: 5–6.
5   Malachi 2: 7–9; Hosea 4: 9.
6   Proverbs 13: 20.

their sin[1] that they are even past feeling, and neither fear God's wrath nor
care for their salvation, but hear these things as men asleep, and nothing
will awake them. Some are discouraged with a conceit that godliness is a
life so grievous,[2] sad and melancholy, that rather than endure it they will
venture their souls, come on it what will-as if it were a grievous life to
love God and hope for endless *joys*; and a pleasant life to love the world
and sin, and live within a step of hell!—Some that are convinced do put
off their conversion with delays, and think it's time enough hereafter: and
are purposing and purposing till it be too late, and life and time and hope
be ended.[3] And some that see there is a necessity of holiness are cheated
by some dead opinion or names or shews and images of holiness:[4] either
because they hold a strict opinion or because they are baptized with water
and observe the outward parts of worship: and perhaps because they offer
God a great deal of lip-service and lifeless ceremony, which never savoured
of a holy soul. Thus deadness, sensuality, worldliness and hypocrisy do
hinder millions from sanctification and salvation.

XI. If ever thou wouldest be saved, *oppress not reason by sensuality or diversions*:
but sometimes retire for sober consideration.[5] Distracted and sleepy reason
is unuseful. God and conscience have a great deal to say to thee: which in a
crowd of company and business thou art not fit to hear. It is a doleful case[6]
that a man who hath a God, a Christ, a soul, a heaven, a hell to think of,
will allow them none but running thoughts, and not once in a week bestow
one hour in man-like serious consideration of them.[7] Sure thou hast no
greater things to mind. Resolve then sometimes to spend half an hour in
the deepest thoughts of thy everlasting state.

XII. *Look upon this world and all its pleasures as a man of reason, who foreseeth
the end*: and not as a beast that liveth by sense or present objects.[8] Do I need
to tell thee, man, that thou must die? Cannot carcases and dust instruct

---

1   Ephesians 4: 18–19.

2   Malachi 1: 13.

3   Matthew 25: 3, 8, 12; 24: 43, 44.

4   John 8: 39, 42, 44; Romans 3: 1–2; Galatians 4: 29; Matthew 13: 19–22; 15: 2–3, 6; Galatians 1: 1.

5   Psalm 4: 4; Haggai 1: 5; Deuteronomy 32: 7–29.

6   Isaiah 1: 3.

7   Job 34: 27; Jeremiah 23: 20; Psalm 119: 59.

8   2 Corinthians 4: 8; Deuteronomy 32: 29; 1 John 2: 17; 1 Corinthians 7: 31; Luke 12: 19–20;
John 14: 1–2; 1 Thessalonians 5: 13.

thee to see the end of earthly glory and all the pleasures of the flesh? Is it a controversy whether thy flesh must shortly perish? And wilt thou yet provide for it before thy soul? What a sad farewell must thou shortly take of all that worldlings sell their souls for! And O how quickly will this be! Alas! man, the day is even at hand: a few days more and thou art gone! and darest thou live unready, and part with heaven for such a world as this?

XIII. And then think soberly on the life to come:[1] what it is for a soul to appear before the living God and be judged to endless joy or misery! If the devil tempt thee to doubt of such a life, remember that nature and Scripture and the world's consent, and his own temptations are witnesses against him. O man canst thou pass one day in company or alone in business or in idleness, without some sober thoughts of everlastingness? Nothing more sheweth that the hearts of men are asleep or dead than that the thoughts of endless joy or pain, so near at hand, constrain them not to be holy and overcome not all the temptations of the flesh as toys and inconsiderable things.

XIV. *Mind well, what mind most men are of when they come to die!*[2] Unless it be some desperate forsaken wretch do they not all speak well of a holy life? And wish that their lives had been spent in the most fervent love of God and strictest obedience to his laws? Do they then speak well of lust and pleasures and magnify the wealth and honours of the world? Had they not rather die as the most mortified saints, than as careless, fleshly worldly sinners? And dost thou see and know this, and yet wilt thou not be instructed to be wise in time?

XV. *Think well what manner of men these were whose names are now honoured for their holiness.*[3] What manner of life did St Peter and St Paul, St Cyprian, St Augustine, and all other saints and martyrs live? Was it a life of fleshly sports and pleasures? Did they deride or persecute a holy life? Were they not more strictly holy than any that thou knowest? And is he not self-condemned that honoureth the names of saints and will not imitate them?

XVI. Think what the difference is *between a Christian and an heathen.*[4] You are loath to be heathens or infidels. But do you think a Christian excelleth them but in opinion? He that is not holier than they, is worse, and shall suffer more than they.

---

1   Luke 12: 4; Ecclesiastes 12: 7; 2 Peter 3: 11; 2 Corinthians 4: 18; Philippians 3: 18, 20.
2   Numbers 23: 10; Matthew 25: 8; 8: 21–22; Proverbs 1: 28–29.
3   Matthew 23: 29–33; Hebrews 11: 38; John 8: 39.
4   Matthew 10: 15; Romans 2; Acts 10: 34–5.

XVII. Think what the difference is *between a godly Christian and an ungodly.*[1] Do not all the opposers of holiness among us yet speak for the same God and Christ and Scripture: and profess the same creed and religion, with those whom they oppose? And is not this Christ the author of our holiness, and this Scripture the commander of it? Search and see, whether the difference be not this, that the godly are serious in their profession, and the ungodly are hypocrites, who hate and oppose the practise of the very things which themselves profess: whose religion serveth but to condemn them while their lives are contrary to their tongues.

XVIII. Understand what the devil's policy is by *raising so many sects and factions and controversies about religion in the world:*[2] even to make some think that they are religious because they can prate for their opinions, or because they think their party is the best, because their faction is the greatest or the best; the uppermost or the suffering side. And to turn holy, edifying conference into vain jangling; and to make men atheists–suspecting all religion and true to none–because of men's diversity of minds. But remember that [the] Christian religion is but one, and a thing easily known by its ancient rule; and the universal church containing all churches, is but one. And if carnal interest or opinions so distract men that one party saith `We are all the Church,' and another saith 'It is we'—as if the kitchen were all the house or one town or village all the kingdom—wilt thou be mad with seeing this distraction? Hearken sinner, all those sects in the Day of Judgment shall concur as witnesses against thee if thou be unholy: because however else they differed,[3] all of them that are Christians professed the necessity of holiness and subscribed to that Scripture which requireth it. Though thou canst not easily resolve every controversy thou may'st easily know the true religion, it is that which Christ and his apostles taught, which all Christians have professed, which Scripture requireth: which is first pure and then peaceable:[4] most spiritual, heavenly, charitable, and just.

XIX. *Away from that company*[5] *which is sensual,* and an enemy to reason, sobriety and holiness, and consequently to God, themselves and thee. Can

---

1 Romans 2: 28–29; Matthew 25: 28; Luke 19: 22: Acts 24: 15; Galatians 4: 29.

2 Ephesians 4: 14; Acts 20: 30; 1 Corinthians 11: 19; 2 Timothy 4: 3; 2: 14, 16; 1 Timothy 1: 5–6; Titus 3: 9; Ephesians 4: 3 etc.; 1 Corinthians 12; Matthew 12: 25; Romans 2: 12, 27–29.

3 Galatians 1: 7–8; Matthew 28: 20.

4 James 3: 17.

5 Ephesians 5: 11; Proverbs 23: 20; 2 Corinthians 6: 17–18; Psalm 15: 4; Deuteronomy 13: 3.

they be wise for thee that are foolish for themselves? Or friends to thee that are undoing themselves? Or have any pity on thy soul when they make a jest of their own damnation? Will they help thee to heaven who are running so furiously to hell? Chuse better familiars if thou woulds't be better.

XX. *Judge not of a holy life by hearsay*, for it cannot so be known.[1] Try it awhile and then judge as thou findest it. Speak not against the things thou knowest not. Hadst thou but lived in the love of God, and the lively belief of endless glory, and the delights of holiness, and the fears of hell but for one month or day: and with such a heart hadst cast away thy sin[2] and called upon God and ordered thy family in a holy manner, especially on the Lord's day, I dare boldly say experience would constrain thee to justify a holy life.[3] But yet I must tell thee it is not true holiness if thou but try it with exceptions and reserves.[4] If therefore God hath convinced thee that this is his will and way, I adjure thee as in his dreadful presence, that thou delay no longer[5] but resolve, and absolutely give up thyself to God as thy heavenly Father, thy Saviour and thy Sanctifier, and 'make an everlasting covenant with him,' and then he and all his mercies will be thine: his grace will help thee and his mercy pardon thee: his ministers will instruct thee and his people pray for thee and assist thee: his angels will guard thee and his Spirit comfort thee: and when flesh must fail and thou must leave this world, thy Saviour will then receive thy soul and bring it into the participation of his glory: and he will raise thy body and justify thee before the world and make thee equal to the angels: and thou shalt live in the sight and love of God and in the everlasting pleasures of his glory. This is the end of faith and holiness. But if thou harden thy heart and refusest mercy[6] everlasting woe will be thy portion, and then there will be no remedy.

And now, Reader, I beg of thee and I beg of God on my bended knees that these few words may sink into thy heart and that thou wouldest read them over and over again and bethink thee as a man that must shortly die. Whether any deserve thy love and obedience more than God? And thy

---

1   John 5: 40; Luke 14: 29–30; John 6: 35, 37, 45.

2   Isaiah 55: 6–7.

3   Matthew 11: 19.

4   Luke 14: 33.

5   Revelation 22: 17; John 1: 12; Revelation 2 and 3; 1 John 5: 12, 13; Psalm 34: 7; Psalm 73: 26; Matthew 25; Luke 20: 39; Hebrews 2: 3; 1 Thessalonians 2: 12.

6   Luke 19: 27; Proverbs 29: 1 and 1: 10, etc.

thankful rememberance more than Christ? And thy care and diligence more than thy salvation? Is there any felicity more desirable than heaven? Or any misery more terrible than hell? Or anything so regardable as that which is everlasting? Will a few days' fleshly pleasures pay for the loss of heaven and thy immortal soul? Or will thy sin and thy prosperity be meet at death and in the day of judgment? If thou art a man, and as ever thou believest that there is a God and a world to come, and as thou carest for thy soul, whether it be saved or damned, I beseech thee, I charge thee, think of these things! think of them once a day at least! think of them with thy most sober, serious thoughts! Heaven is not a May-game and hell is not a flea-biting! Make not a jest of salvation or damnation! I know thou livest in a distracted world where thou mayest hear some laughing at such things as these, and scorning at a holy life, and fastening odious reproaches on the godly, and merrily drinking and playing and feasting away their time, and then saying that they will trust God with their souls and hope to be saved without so much ado! But if all these men do not change their minds and be not shortly down-in-the-mouth, and would not be glad to eat their words, and wished that they had lived a holy life, though it had cost them scorn and suffering in the world, let me bear the shame of a deceiver for ever. But if God and thy conscience bear witness against thy sin and tell thee that a holy life is best, regard not the gain-sayings of a bedlam-world, which is drunk with the delusions of the flesh. But give up thy soul and life to God by Jesus Christ in a faithful covenant! Delay no longer, man, but resolve, resolve immediately, resolve unchangeably: and God will be thine and thou shalt be his for ever. Amen. Lord have mercy on this sinner and so let it be resolved by thee in him.

II. The Parts and Practice of a holy life for personal and family instructions. All is not done when men have begun a religious life.[1] All trees that blossom prove not fruitful, and all fruit comes not to perfection. Many fall off who seemed to have good beginnings; and many dishonour the name of Christ, by their scandals and infirmities. Many do grieve their teachers' hearts and lamentably disturb the Church of Christ, by their ignorance, errors, self-conceitedness, unruliness, headiness, contentiousness, sidings and divisions: insomuch that the scandals and the feuds of Christians are[2] the

---

1   1 Corinthians 1: 25; Hebrews 4: 1; 2 Peter 22: 22; 1 Corinthians 3; Galatians 3 and 4; Matthew 13: 41; 18: 7.

2   Philippians 3: 18–19; Acts 20: 30.

great impediments of the conversion of the infidel and heathen world, by the exposing Christianity to their contempt and scorn, as if it were but the error of men as unholy and worldly and proud as others, that can never agree among themselves. And many by their passions and selfishness are a trouble to their families and neighbours where they live. And more by their weaknesses and great distempers, are snares, vexations and burdens to themselves. Whereas Christianity in its true constitution is a life of such holy light and love,[1] such purity and peace, such fruitfulness and heavenliness, as, if it were accordingly shewed forth in the lives of Christians, would command admiration and reverence from the world and do more to their conversion than swords or words alone can do: and it makes Christians useful and amiable to each other and their lives a feast and pleasure to themselves. I hope it may prove some help to those excellent ends and to the securing men's salvation, if in a few, sound experienced directions I open to you the duties of a Christian life.

I. *Keep still the true form of Christian doctrine, desire and duty, orderly printed on your minds.*[2] that is, understand it clearly and distinctly and remember it, I mean the great points of religion contained in Catechisms. You may still grow in the clearer understanding of your Catechisms, if you live an hundred years. Let not the words only but the matter, be as familiar in your minds as the rooms of your house are. Such solid knowledge[3] will establish you against seduction and unbelief and will be still within you a ready help for every grace and every duty, as the skill of an artificer is for his work. And for want of this when you come among infidels or heretics, their reasonings may seem unanswerable to you, and shake if not overthrow your faith. And you will easily err in lesser points and trouble the Church with your dreams and wranglings. This is the calamity of many professors, that while they will be most censorious judges in every controversy about Church-matters they know not well the doctrine of the Catechism.

II. *Live daily by faith on Jesus Christ*[4] *as the Mediator between God and you.* Being well-grounded in the belief of the Gospel and understanding Christ's office, make use of him still in all your wants. Think on the fatherly love of God, as coming to you through him alone: and of the Spirit as given by

---

1   Matthew 5: 16; 1 Peter 2: 18; 2 Corinthians 1: 21.

2   2 Timothy 1: 13; 3: 7; Hebrews 5: 12; Philippians 1: 9; Romans 15: 14.

3   Ephesians 4: 13–14; Colossians 1: 9; 2: 2; 3: 10; 1 Timothy 6: 4.

4   John 17: 3; Ephesians 3: 17–18; Matthew 28: 19; Ephesians 1: 22, 23; 4: 6, 16; Romans 5; 2 Corinthians 12: 9; John 16: 33; 1 John 5: 4; Hebrews 4: 14, 16, etc.

him your head: and of the covenant of grace as enacted and sealed by him: and of the ministry as sent by him: and of all times and helps and hopes as procured and given by him. When you think of sin and infirmity and temptations, think also of his sufficient, pardoning, justifying and victorious grace. When thou thinkest of the world, the flesh and the devil, think how he overcometh them. Let his doctrine and the pattern of his most perfect life, be always before you as your rule. In all your doubts and fears and wants go to him in the Spirit and to the Father by him and him alone. Take him as the root of your life and mercies, and live as upon him and by his life; and when you die resign your soul to him that they may be with him 'where he is and see his glory.' To live as Christ and use him in every want and address to God, is more than a general confused believing in him.

III. *To believe in the holy Ghost as to live and work by him, as the body doth by the soul.*[1] You are not baptized into his name in vain;[2] but too few understand the sense and reason of it. The Spirit is sent by Christ for two great works. 1. To the apostles and prophets to inspire them infallibly to preach the Gospel[3] and confirm it by miracles and leave it on record for following ages in the Holy Scriptures. 2. To all his members[4] to illuminate and sanctify them to believe and obey this sacred doctrine—beside his common gift to many to understand and preach it. The Spirit having first indited the Gospel doth by it first regenerate and after govern, all true believers. He is not now given us for the revealing of new doctrines but to understand and obey the doctrine revealed and sealed by him long ago.[5] As the sun doth by its sweet and discreet influence both give and cherish the natural life of things, sensitive and vegetative: so doth Christ by his Spirit our spiritual life.[6] As you do no work but by your natural life you should do none but by your spiritual life. You must not only believe and love and pray by it, and manage all your calling by it: for 'holiness to the Lord' must be written upon all. All things are sanctified to you because you being sanctified to God devote all to him and use all for him; and therefore must do all in the strength and conduct of the Spirit.

---

1   Galatians 5: 16, 25.
2   Matthew 28: 19.
3   John 16: 13; Hebrews 2: 34.
4   1 Corinthians 12: 12–13; Romans 8: 9, 13; John 3: 5–6.
5   2 Timothy 3: 15–16; Jude 19–20.
6   Ezekiel 36: 27; Isaiah 44: 3; Romans 8: 1, 5; 1 Corinthians 6: 11; Zechariah 14: 20.

IV. *Live wholly upon God as all in all.*[1] as the first efficient, principal dirigent[2] and final cause of all things. Let faith, hope and love be daily feeding on him. Let 'our Father which art in heaven' be first inscribed on your hearts that he may seem most amiable to you and you may boldly trust him, and filial love may be the spring of duty. Make use of the Son and the Spirit to lead you to the Father: and of faith in Christ to kindle and keep alive the love of God. God's love is our primitive holiness and especially called, with its fruits our sanctification' which 'faith in Christ' is but a means to. Let it be your principal end in studying Christ, to see the goodness, love and amiableness of God in him. A condemning God is not so easily loved as a gracious, reconciled God. You have so much of the Spirit as you have love to God. This is the proper gift of the Spirit to all the adopted sons of God, to cause them with filial affection and dependence to cry 'Abba Father.' Know not, desire not, love not any creature but purely as subordinate to God. Without him, let it be nothing to you, but as the glass without the face or scattered letters without the sense or as the corps without the soul. Call nothing prosperity or pleasure but his love:[3] and nothing adversity or misery but his displeasure and the cause and the fruits of it. When anything would seem lovely and desirable which is against him, call it 'dung.'[4] And hear that man as Satan and the serpent[5] that would entice you from him; and count him but vanity, a worm and dust, that would affright you from your duty to him. Fear him much but love him more. Let love be the soul and end of every duty.[6] It is the end and reason of all the rest: but it hath no end or reason but its object. Think of no other heaven and end and happiness of man but love the final act and God the final object. Place not your religion in anything but the love of God, with its means and fruits. Own no grief, desire or joy but a mourning, a seeking and a rejoicing love.

V. *Live in the belief and hopes of heaven, and seek it as your part and end*; and daily delight your souls in the forethoughts of the endless sight and love

---

1   1 Corinthians 10: 31; Romans 11: 36; 2 Corinthians 5: 7–8; 1 John 3: 1; Romans 5: 1–3; Matthew 22: 37; Ephesians 1: 6; 2 Corinthians 5: 19; Galatians 4: 4–6.

2   Sic: = 'director.' C.

3   Psalm 30: 5; 63: 3.

4   Philippians 3: 7–8.

5   Matthew 16: 13.

6   2 Thessalonians 3: 5; 2 Corinthians 13: 14.

of God.[1] As God is seen on earth but as in a glass so is he proportionably enjoyed. But when mourning, seeking love hath done, and sin and enemies are overcome, and we behold the glory of God in heaven, the delights of love will then be perfect. You may desire more on earth than you may hope for. Look not for a kingdom of this world, nor for Mount Zion in the wilderness. Christ reigneth on earth—as Moses in the camp—to guide us to the Land of the promise. Our perfect blessedness will be when the kingdom is delivered up to the Father and God is all in all. A doubt, or a strange, heartless thought of heaven, is water cast on the sacred fire, to quench your holiness and your joy. Can you travel one whole day to such an end, and never think of the place that you are going to? Which must be intended[2] in every righteous act—either notedly or by the ready unobserved act of a potent habit. When earth is at the best it will not be heaven. You live no further by faith, like Christians, than you either live for heaven in seeking it or else upon heaven in hope and joy.

VI. *Labour to make religion your pleasure and delight.* Look oft to God, to heaven, to Christ, to the Spirit, to the promises, to all your mercies. Call over your experiences, and think what matter of high delight is still before you, and how unseemly it is, and how injurious to your profession for one that saith he hopeth for heaven, to live as sadly as those that have no higher hopes than earth. How should that man be filled with joy, who must live in the joys of heaven for ever! Especially rejoice when the messengers of death do tell you that your endless joy is near. If God and heaven with all our mercies in the way, be not reason enough for a joyful life, there can be none at all. Abhor all suggestions which would make religion seem a tedious, irksome life. And take care that you represent it not so to others; for you will never make them in love with that which you make them not perceive to be delectable and lovely. Not as the hypocrite, by forcing and framing his religion to his carnal mind and pleasure: but bringing up the heart to a holy suitableness to the pleasures of religion.

VII. *Watch as for your souls against this flattering, tempting world:*[3] especially when it is represented as more sweet and delectable than God and holiness

---

1 Colossians 3: 1–4; Matthew 6: 19–21; 2 Corinthians 4: 17–18; 7; Luke 12: 20; Hebrews 6: 20; 1 Corinthians 15: 28; Ephesians 4: 6; 1: 23; Philippians 3: 18, 20; Psalm 73: 25–26; John 18: 36.

2 Psalm 1: 2–3; : 84: 2, 10; 63: 3, 5; 37: 4; 91: 19; 119: 47, 70; Isaiah 58: 14; Psalm 112: 1; Romans 14: 17; 5: 1, 3, 5; 1 Peter 1: 8; Matthew 5: 11, 12; Psalm 32: 11.

3 Galatians 6: 14; 1 John 2: 15–16; James 1: 27; 4: 4–5; 1 John 5: 4–5; Romans 12: 2; Galatians

and heaven. This world with its pleasures, wealth and honours, is it that is put in the balance by Satan, against God and holiness and heaven: and no man shall have better than he chooseth and prefereth. The bait taketh advantage of the brutish part when reason is asleep: and if by the help of sense it get the throne, the beast will ride and rule the man: and reason becomes a slave to sensuality. When you hear the serpent, see his sting and see death attending the forbidden fruit. When you are rising look down and see how far you have to fall! His reason as well as faith, is weak, who for such fools-gawds as the pomp and vanities of this world, can forget God and his soul and death and judgment, heaven and hell, yea and deliberately command them to stand by. What knowledge or experience can do good on that man who will venture so much for such a world, which all that have tried it, call vanity at the last? How deplorable then is a wordling's case! Oh fear the world when it smileth or seems sweet and amiable. Love it not if you love your God and your salvation.

VIII. *Fly from temptations and crucify the flesh and keep a constant government over your appetite and senses.*[1] Many who had no designed, stated vice or worldly interest, have shamefully fallen by the sudden surprise of appetite and lust. When custom hath taught those to be greedy and violent, like a hungry dog or a lusting boar, it is not a sluggish wish or purpose that will mortify or rule them. How dangerous a case is that man in who hath so greedy a beast continually to restrain! that if he do but neglect his watch an hour, is ready to run him headlong into hell! Who can be safe that standeth long on so terrible a precipice? The tears and sorrows of many years may perhaps not repair the loss which one hour or act may bring. The case of David and many others, are dreadful warnings. Know what it is you are most in danger of: whether lust and idleness or excess in meats or drinks or play: and there set your strongest watch for your preservation. Make it your daily business to mortify that lust, and scorn that your brutish sense or appetite should conquer reason. Yet trust not purposes alone: but away from the temptation. Touch not, yea look not on the tempting bait: keep far enough off if you desire to be safe. What miseries come from small beginnings! Temptation leads to sin, and small sins to greater, and those to hell. And sin and hell are

---

1: 4; Titus 2: 12; Matthew 19: 24; Luke 12: 16–21; 16: 25; James 1: 11; 5: 1–4; Luke 8: 14; Hebrews 11: 26.

1   Romans 8: 1, 13; Galatians 5: 24; Romans 13: 14; Galatians 5: 17; Jude 8, 23; 2 Peter 2: 10; Ephesians 2: 3; 1 Peter 2: 11; Matthew 6: 13; 26: 41; Luke 8: 13.

not to be played with. Open your sin or temptation to some friend, that shame may save you from danger.

IX. *Keep up a constant, skilful government over your passions and your tongues.*[1] To this end keep a tender conscience, which will smart when in any of these you sin. Let holy passions be well-ordered; and selfish, carnal passions, be restrained. Let your tongues know their duties to God and man[2] and labour to be skilful and resolute in performing them. Know all the sins of the tongue, that you may avoid them: for your innocency and peace do much depend on the prudent government of your tongues.

X. *Govern your thoughts with constant skilful diligence.*[3] In this, rigid habits and affections will do much by inclining them unto good. It's easy to think on that which we love. Be not unfurnished of matter for your thoughts to work upon: and often retire yourselves for serious meditation. Be not so solitary and deep in musings as to over-stretch your thoughts and confound your minds or take you off from necessary converse with others. But be sure that you be considerate and dwell much at home, and converse most with your consciences and your God, with whom you have the greatest business. Leave not your thoughts unemployed or ungoverned, scatter them not abroad upon impertinent vanities! O that you knew what daily business you have for them. Most men are wicked, deceived and undone, because they are inconsiderate and dare not or will not, retiredly and soberly use their reason : or use it but as a slave in chains in the service of their passion, lust and interest. He was never wise or good or happy, who was not soberly and impartially considerate. How to be good, to do good and finally enjoy good, must be the sum of all your thoughts. Keep them first holy, then charitable, clean and chaste. And quickly check them when they look towards sin.

XI. *Let time be exceeding precious in your eyes, and carefully and diligently redeem it.*[4] What haste doth it make! and how quickly will it be gone! and then how highly will it be valued when a minute of it can never be recalled! O what important business have we for every moment of our time, if we should live a thousand years! Take not that man to be well in his wits or to know

---

1   James 1: 19; 3: 17; 1 Peter 3: 4; Matthew 5: 5; Ephesians 4: 2, 3; Colossians 3: 12.

2   James 1: 26; 3: 5–6; Psalm 34: 13; Proverbs 18: 21.

3   Deuteronomy 15: 9; 2 Corinthians 10: 5; Genesis 6: 5; Psalm 10: 4; 94: 19; 119: 113; Proverbs 12: 5; 15: 26; Psalm 119: 59; Proverbs 30: 32; Jeremiah 4: 14; Deuteronomy 32: 29.

4   Ephesians 5: 16; John 14: 1–2; Acts 17: 21; 1 Corinthians 7: 29; 2 Corinthians 6: 2; John 9: 4; Luke 19: 42, 44; Psalm   39: 4; Matthew 25: 10, 12.

his God, his end, his work or his danger, who hath time to spare. Redeem it not only from needless sports and plays and idleness and curiosity and compliment and excess of sleep and chat and worldliness: but also from the entanglements of lesser good which would hinder you from greater. Spend time as men that are ready to pass into another world, where every minute must be accounted for; and it must go with us for ever as we lived here. Let not health deceive you into the expectation of living long, and so into a senseless negligence. See your glass running and keep a reckoning of the expense of time: and spend it just as you would review it when it is gone.

XII. *Let the love of all in their several capacities, become as it were your very nature:*[1] and doing them all the good you can be very much of the business of your lives. God must be loved in all his creatures, his natural image on all men and his spiritual image on his saints. Our neighbour must be loved as our natural selves, that is, our natural neighbour as our natural self, with a love of benevolence: and our spiritual neighbour as our spiritual self, with a love of complacence. In opposition to complacence we may hate our sinful neighbour, as we must ourselves, much more. But in opposition to benevolence we must neither hate ourselves, our neighbour or our enemy. O that men knew how much of Christianity doth consist in love and doing good. With what eyes do they read the Gospel who see not this in every page? Abhor all that selfishness, pride and passion which are the enemies of love: and those opinions and factions and censurings and back-bitings, which would destroy it. Take him that speaketh evil of another to you without a just cause and call, to be Satan's messenger, entreating you to hate your brother or to abate your love. For to persuade you that a man is bad is directly to persuade you so far to hate him. Not that the good and bad must be confounded: but love will call none bad without constraining evidence. Rebuke back-biters. Hurt no man and speak evil of no man; unless it be not only just but necessarily to some greater good. Love is lovely: they that love shall be beloved; hating and hurting makes men hateful. "Love thy neighbour as thyself," and "do as thou wouldst be done by," are the golden rules of our duty to men: which must be deeply written on your hearts. For want of this there is nothing so false, so bad, so carnal which you may not be drawn to think or say or

---

1   1 Timothy 1: 5–6; Matthew 19: 19; Romans 13: 10; 1 John 1: 16; Ephesians 4: 2, 15–16; Colossians 2: 2; 1: 4; 1 Timothy 6: 11; James 3: 17; Philippians 2: 1–2; 1 Thessalonians 4: 9; John 13: 35; Matthew 5: 44–45; 1 Corinthians 13; James 4: 11; Galatians 6: 10; Titus 2: 14; Philippians 2: 20–21; Romans 15: 1, 3.

brethren. Selfishness and want of love do as naturally tend to ambition and covetousness, and thence to cruelty against all that stand in the way of their desires, as the nature of a wolf to kill the lambs. All factions and contentions and persecutions in the world, proceed from selfishness and want of charity. Devouring malice is the devilish nature. Be as zealous in doing good to all as Satan's servants are in hurting. Take it as the use of all your talents, and use them as you would hear of it at last. Let it be your business and not a matter on the by: especially for public good and men's salvation. And what you cannot do yourselves, persuade others to. Give them good books: and draw them to the means which are most like to profit them.

XIII. *Understand the right terms of Church-communion*: especially the unity of the universal church and the universal communion which you must hold with all the parts and the difference between the Church as visible and invisible. For want of these how woeful are our divisions! Read oft 1 Corinthians 12, and Ephesians iv: 1–17; John 17: 21–23; Acts 4: 32; 2: 42; 1 Corinthians 1: 10–13; 3: 3, 12–13; Romans 16: 17; Philippians 2: 1–4; 1 Thessalonians 5: 12–13; Acts 20: 30; 1 Corinthians 11: 19; Titus 3: 10; James 3; Colossians 1: 4; Hebrews 10: 25; Acts 8: 12–13, 37; 1 Corinthians 1: 2, 13; 3: 3–4; 11: 18, 21. Study these well. You must have union and communion in faith and love with all the Christians in the world. And refuse not local communion when you have a just call so far as they put you not on sinning. Let your usual meeting be with the purest church, if you lawfully may—and still respect the public good-but sometimes occasionally communicate with defective, faulty churches, so be it they are true Christians and put you not on sin: that so you may show that you own them as Christians, though you disown their corruptions. Think not your presence maketh all the faults of ministry, worship or people to be yours—for then I would join with no Church in the world. Know that as the mystical church consisteth of heart-covenanters, so doth the Church as visible consist of verbal-covenanters, which make a credible profession of consent: and that nature and scripture teacheth us to take every man's word as credible, till perfidiousness forfeit his credit: which forfeiture must be proved, before any sober profession can be taken for an insufficient title. Grudge not then at the communion of any professed Christian in the Church visible[1]–though we must do our part to cast out the obstinately impertinent by discipline: which, if we cannot do, the fault is not

---

1   Matthew 13: 29, 41.

ours. The presence of hypocrites is no hurt but oft a mercy to the sincere. How small else would the Church seem in the world! Outward privileges belong to outward covenanters and inward mercies to the sincere. Division is wounding and tends to death.[1] Abhor it if you love the Church's welfare or your own. 'The wisdom from above is first pure then peaceable.' Never separate what God conjoineth. It is the earthly, sensual, devilish wisdom which causeth bitter envying and strife and confusion and every evil word. 'Blessed are the peace-makers.'

XIV. *Take heed of pride and self-conceitedness in religion.*[2] If once you over-value your own understandings, your crude conceptions and gross mistakes will delight you as some supernatural light; and instead of having compassion on the weak, you will be unruly and despisers of your guides and censorious contemners of all that differ from you, and persecutors of them if you have power, and will think all intolerable that take you not as oracles and your word as law. Forget not that the Church hath always suffered by censorious, worldly professors on the one hand—and O what divisions and scandals have they caused!—as well by the profane and persecutors on the other. Take heed of both: and when contentions are afoot be quiet and silent and not too froward, and keep up a zeal for love and peace.

XV. *Be faithful and conscionable in all your relations.* Honour and obey your parents and other superiors. Despise not and resist not government. If you suffer unjustly by them, be humbled for those sins, which cause God to turn your protectors into afflictors. And instead of murmuring and rebelling against them, reform yourselves and then commit yourselves to God. Princes and pastors I will not speak to: subjects and servants and children, must obey their superiors as the officers of God.

XVI. *Keep up the government of God in your families.*[3] Holy families must be the chief preservers of the interest of religion in the world. Let not the world turn God's service into a customary, lifeless form. Read the scripture and edifying books to them; talk with them seriously about the state of their souls and everlasting life; pray with them fervently; watch over them diligently; be angry against sin and meek in your own cause; be examples

---

1   John 16: 2; 1 Corinthians 1: 10; Romans 16: 17; James 3: 14–18.
2   1 Timothy 3: 6; Colossians 2: 18; 1 Corinthians 8: 1; 4: 6; 1 Timothy 6: 4; 1 Peter 5: 5; James 3: 1, 17; Ephesians 5–6; Colossians 3–4; Romans 13: 1, 7; 1 Peter 2: 13, 15.
3   *Command* 4; Joshua 24: 15; Deuteronomy 6: 6–8; Daniel 6.

of wisdom, holiness and patience; and see that the Lord's day be spent in holy preparation for eternity.

XVII. *Let your callings be managed in holiness and laboriousness.*[1] Live not in idleness; be not slothful in your work be you bound or free; in the sweat of your brows you must eat your bread, and labour the six days that you may have to give to him that needeth: slothfulness is sensuality as well as filthier sins. The body that is able must have fit employments as well as the soul, or else body and soul will fare the worse; but let all be but as the labour of a traveller, and aim at God and heaven in all.

XVIII. *Deprive not yourself of the benefit of an able, faithful pastor,*[2] to whom you may open your case in secret, or at least of a holy faithful friend:[3] and be not displeased at their free reproofs.[4] Woe to him that is alone! How blind and partial we are in our own cause! and how hard it is to know ourselves without an able, faithful helper! You forfeit this great mercy when you love a flatterer, and angrily defend your sin.

XIX. *Prepare for sickness, sufferings and death.*[5] Over-value not prosperity nor the favours of man. If selfish man prove false and cruel to you, even those of whom you have deserved best, marvel not at it, but pray for your enemies, persecutors and slanderers, that God would turn their hearts and pardon them. What a mercy is it to be driven from the world to God, when the love of the world is the greatest danger of the soul! Be ready to die and you are ready for anything. Ask your hearts seriously, what is it that I shall need at a dying hour? And let it speedily be got ready and not be to seek in the time of your extremity.

XX. *Understand the true method of peace of conscience:* and judge not the state of your souls upon deceitful grounds. As presumptuous hopes do keep men from conversion and embolden them to sin: so causeless fears do hinder our love and praise of God, by obscuring his loveliness: and they destroy our thankfulness and our delight in God, and make us a burden to ourselves and a grievous stumbling-block to others. The general grounds of all your

---

1   Hebrews 13: 5; *Command* 4; 2 Thessalonians 3: 10, 12; 1 Thessalonians 4: 7; 1 Timothy 5: 13; Proverbs 31; 1 Corinthians 7: 29.

2   Malachi 2: 7.

3   Ecclesiastes 4: 10, 11.

4   Proverbs 12: 1; 15: 30–31; Hebrews 3: 13.

5   Luke 12: 40; 2 Peter 1: 10; Philippians 1: 21, 23; Jeremiah 9: 4–5; Matthew 7: 4–5; 2 Corinthians 5: 1–2, 4, 8.

comfort are (1) the gracious nature of God[1] (2) the sufficiency of Christ[2] and (3) the truth and universality of the promise[3] which giveth Christ and life to all, if they will accept him. But this acceptance is the proof of your particular title, without which these do but aggravate your sin. Consent to God's covenant is the true condition and proof of your title to God as your Father, Saviour and Sanctifier, and so to the saving blessings of the covenant: which consent, if you survive, must produce the duties which you consent to. He that heartily consenteth that God be his God, his Saviour and Sanctifier, is in a state of life. But this includeth[4] the rejection of the world. Much knowledge, and memory, and utterance, and lively affection, are all very desirable. But you must judge your state by none of these, for they are all uncertain. But 1. If God and holiness and heaven have the highest estimation by your practical judgment, as being esteemed best for you: 2. And be preferred in the choice and resolution of your wills and that habitually before all the pleasures of the world: 3. And be first and chiefly sought in your endeavours: this is the infallible proof of your sanctification. Christian, upon long and serious study and experience I dare boldly commend these Directions to thee, as the way to God, which will end in blessedness. The Lord resolve and strengthen thee to obey them. This is the true constitution of Christianity: this is true godliness: and this is to be religious indeed: all this is no more than to be seriously such as all among us in general would prefer to be. This is the religion which must difference you from hypocrites, which must settle you in peace and make you an honour to your profession and a blessing to those that dwell about you. Happy is the land, the church, the family, which doth consist of such as these! These are not they that either persecute or divide the church or that make their religion a servant to their policy, to their ambitious designs or fleshly lusts; nor that make it the bellows of sedition or rebellion or of an envious hurtful zeal or a pistol to shoot at the upright in heart. These are not they that have been the shame of their profession, to hardening of ungodly men and infidels, and that have caused the enemies of the Lord to blaspheme. If any man will make a religion of or for his lusts: of Papal tyranny, or Pharisaical formality, or of his

---

1   Exodus 34: 6.

2   Hebrews 7: 25.

3   John 4: 42; John 3: 16; 1 Timothy 4: 10; 2: 4; Matthew 28: 19–20; Revelation 22: 17; Isaiah 55: 1–3. 6–7.

4   Luke 14: 26, 33; 1 John 2: 15; Matthew 6: 19, 20–1, 33; Colossians 3: 1, 2; Romans 8: 1, 13.

private opinions, or of proud censoriousness and contempt of others: and of faction and unwarrantable separations and divisions and of standing at a more observable distance from common professors of Christianity than God would have them, or yet of pulling up the hedge of discipline and laying Christ's vineyard common to the wilderness—the storm is coming when this religion founded on the sand will fall "and great will be the fall thereof." When the religion which consisteth in faith and love to God and man, in mortifying the flesh and crucifying the world, in self-denial, humility and patience in sincere obedience and faithfulness in all relations, in watchful self-government, in doing good and in a divine and heavenly life, though it will be hated by the ungodly world—shall never be a dishonour to your Lord nor deceive or disappoint your soul.

A Short Catechism

Quest. I. What is the Christian Religion?

Ans. The Christian Religion is the baptismal-covenant made and kept: wherein God the Father, Son and Holy Ghost, doth give Himself to be our reconciled God and Father, our Saviour and Sanctifier: and we believingly give up ourselves accordingly to Him, renouncing the "flesh, the world and the devil." Which covenant is to be oft renewed, specially in the sacrament of the Lord's Supper.

Quest. 2. Where is our covenant-part and duty fullier opened?

Ans. I. In the Creed, as the sum of our belief.

2. In the Lord's Prayer, as the sum of our desires.

3. And in the Ten Commandments (as given us by Christ, with the Gospel-explanations) as the sum of our practice. Which are as followeth—

The Creed.

I believe in God the Father Almighty, Maker of heaven and earth; and in Jesus Christ his only Son our Lord, who was conceived by the Holy Ghost, born of the virgin Mary, suffered under Pontius Pilate, was crucified, dead, and buried: he descended into hell; the third day he rose again from the dead; he ascended into heaven, and sitteth on the right hand of God the Father Almighty; from thence he shall come to judge the quick and the dead. I believe in the Holy Ghost; the holy catholic church; the communion of saints; the forgiveness of sins; the resurrection of the body; and the life everlasting. Amen.

The Lord's Prayer.

Our Father, which art in heaven, Hallowed be thy name. Thy kingdom come. Thy will be done on earth, as it is in heaven. Give us this day our daily bread, and forgive us our debts, as we forgive our debtors. And lead us not into temptation; but deliver us from evil: For thine is the kingdom, and the power, and the glory, for ever. Amen.

The Ten Commandments.

I. I am the Lord thy God, which have brought thee out of the land of Egypt, out of the house of bondage. Thou shalt have no other gods before me.

II. Thou shalt not make unto thee any graven image, or any likeness of any thing that is in heaven above, or that is in the earth beneath, or that is in the water under the earth: Thou shalt not bow down thyself to them, nor serve them: for I the Lord thy God am a jealous God, visiting the iniquity of the fathers upon the children unto the third and fourth generation of them that hate me; and shewing mercy unto thousands of them that love me, and keep my commandments.

III. Thou shalt not take the name of the Lord thy God in vain: for the Lord will not hold him guiltless that taketh his name in vain.

IV. Remember the Sabbath-day, to keep it holy. Six days shalt thou labour, and do all thy work: but the seventh day is the sabbath of the Lord thy God: in it thou shalt not do any work, thou, nor thy son, nor thy daughter, thy man-servant, nor thy maid-servant, nor thy cattle, nor thy stranger that is within thy gates: for in six days the Lord made heaven and earth, the sea, and all that in them is, and rested the seventh day: wherefore the Lord blessed the sabbath-day, and hallowed it.

V. Honour thy father and thy mother: that thy days may be long upon the Land which the Lord thy God giveth thee.

VI. Thou shalt not kill.

VII. Thou shalt not commit adultery.

VIII. Thou shalt not steal.

IX. Thou shalt not bear false witness against thy neighbour.

X. Thou shalt not covet thy neighbour's house, thou shalt not covet thy neighbour's wife, nor his man-servant, nor his maid-servant, nor his ox, nor his ass, nor any thing that is thy neighbour's.

Quest. 3. Where is the Christian Religion most fully opened and entirely contained?

Ans. In the Holy Scriptures, especially of the New Testament: where, by Christ and his Apostles and Evangelists, inspired by His Spirit, the history of Christ and His Apostles is sufficiently delivered, the promises and doctrines of faith are perfected, the covenant of grace more clearly opened and church-offices, worship and discipline established: on the understanding whereof the strongest Christians may increase while they live on earth.

The explained Profession of the Christian Religion.

I. I believe that there is One God, an infinite Spirit of life, understanding and will: perfectly powerful, wise and good: the Father, the Word and the Spirit, the Creator, Governor and End of all things: our absolute Owner, our most just Ruler and our most gracious Benefactor and most amiable Lord.

II. I believe that man being made in the image of God, an embodied spirit of life, understanding and will, with holy suavity, wisdom and love, to know and love and serve his Creator here and for ever, did by wilful sinning fall from his God, his holiness and innocency, under the wrath of God, the condemnation of his Law, and the slavery of the flesh, the world and the devil. And that God so loved the world that He gave His only Son to be their Redeemer, who being God and one with the Father, took our nature and became man: being conceived of the Holy Ghost, born of the virgin Mary, called Jesus Christ, who was perfectly holy [and] sinless, fulfilling all righteousness, overcame the devil and the world and gave Himself a sacrifice for our sins, by suffering a cursed death on the cross, to ransom us and reconcile us unto God: and was buried and went among the dead: the third day He rose again, having conquered death. And He fully established the covenant of grace, that all that truly repent and believe shall have the love of the Father, the grace of the Son and the communion of the Holy Spirit; and if they love God and obey him sincerely to the death, they shall be glorified with him in heaven for ever; and the unbelievers, impenitent and ungodly shall go to everlasting punishment. And having commanded his Apostles to preach the Gospel to all the world and promised His Spirit, He ascended into heaven: where He is the glorified Head over all things to the Church and our prevailing Intercessor with the Father: who will there receive the departed souls of the justified: and at the end of this world will come again and rouse all the dead and will judge all according to their works and justly execute his Judgment.

III. I believe that God the Holy Spirit was given by the Father and the Son, to the prophets, apostles and evangelists, to be their infallible guide in preaching and recording the doctrine of salvation: and the witness of its certain truth, by his manifold Divine operations: and to question, illuminate and sanctify all the believers, that they may renounce the flesh, the world and the devil. And all that are thus sanctified are one holy and catholic Church of Christ and must live in holy communion and have the pardon of their sins and shall have everlasting life.

The *Covenant or Covenants.*—Believing in God the Father, Son and Holy Spirit, I do perfectly, absolutely and resolutely give up myself to Him, my Creator and reconciled God and Father, my Saviour and Sanctifier: and repenting of my sins I renounce the devil, the world and the sinful desires of the flesh: and denying myself and taking up my cross, I consent to follow Christ the captain of my salvation, in hope of His promised grace and glory.

A short Catechism for those that have learned the first.

Quest. 1. What do you believe concerning God?

Ans. There is one only God, an infinite Spirit of life, understanding and will, most perfectly powerful, wise and good: the Father, the Word and the Spirit: the Creator, Governor and End of all things: our absolute Owner, our most just Ruler, and our most gracious and most amiable Father.

Quest. 2. What believe you of the Creation, and the nature of man and the law which was given to him?

Ans. God created all the world: and made man in his own image, an embodied spirit of life, understanding and will, with holy liveliness, wisdom and love: to know and love serve his Maker here and for ever: and gave him the inferior creatures for his use; but forbad him to eat of the tree of knowledge upon pain of death.

Quest. 3. What believe you of man's fall into sin and misery?

Ans. Man being tempted by Satan, did by wilful sinning fall from his holiness, his innocency, and his happiness, under the justice of God, the condemnation of his Law, and the slavery of the flesh, the world and the devil; whence sinful, guilty and miserable natures are propagated to all mankind: and no mere creature is able to deliver us.

Quest. 4. What believe you of man's Redemption by Jesus Christ?

Ans. God so loved the world that He gave His only Son to be their

Saviour: Who being God and One with the Father, took our nature and became man: being conceived by the Holy Ghost, born of the virgin Mary and called Jesus Christ: Who was perfectly holy, without sin, fulfilling all righteousness: and overcame the devil and the world; and gave himself a sacrifice for our sins, by suffering a cursed death on the Cross to ransom us and reconcile us unto God: and was buried and went among the dead: the third day He rose again, having conquered death; and having sealed the New Covenant with His blood, He commanded His apostles and other ministers, to preach the Gospel to all the world: and promised the Holy Ghost: and then ascended into heaven, where He is God and man, the glorified Head over all things to His Church, and our prevailing intercessor with God the Father.

Quest. 5. What is the New Testament or Covenant or law of grace?

Ans. God through Jesus Christ doth freely give to all mankind Himself, to be their reconciled God and Father, the Son to be their Saviour, and the Holy Spirit to be their Sanctifier, if they will believe and accept the gift and will give up themselves to Him accordingly: repenting of their sins and consenting to forsake the devil, the world and the flesh, and sincerely, though not perfectly, to obey Christ and the Spirit to the end, according to the law of nature and the gospel institutions, that they may be glorified in heaven for ever.

Quest. 6. What believe ye of the Holy Ghost?

Ans. God the Holy Ghost was given by the Father and the Son to the prophets, apostles and evangelists, to be their infallible guide in preaching and recording the doctrine of salvation: and the witness of its certain truth by his manifold Divine operations. And He is given to quicken, illuminate and sanctify all true believers, and to save them from the devil, the world and the flesh.

Quest. 7. What believe you of the holy Catholic Church, the communion of saints and the forgiveness of sins?

Ans. All that truly consent to the baptismal covenant, are one sanctified Church or Body of Christ, and have communion in the same spirit of faith and love, and have the forgiveness of all their sins: and all that by baptism sensibly covenant and that continue to profess Christianity and holiness, are the universal visible Church or state: and must keep holy communion with love and peace in the particular Churches: in the doctrine, worship and order instituted by Christ.

Quest. 8. What believe you of the Resurrection and everlasting life?

Ans. At death the souls of the justified go to happiness with Christ, and the souls of the wicked to misery: and at the end of the world Christ will come in glory and will raise the bodies of all men from death and will judge all according to their works: and the righteous shall go into everlasting life where being made perfect themselves, they shall see God and perfectly love and praise Him, with Christ and all the glorified Church: and the rest into everlasting punishment.

Quest. 9. You have told me what you believe: Tell me now what is the full resolution and desire of your will concerning all this which you believe.

Ans. Believing in God the Father, Son and Holy Spirit, I do presently, absolutely and resolutely give up myself to Him, my Creator and reconciled God and Father, my Saviour and my Sanctifier! And repenting of my sins I renounce the devil, the world and the sinful desires of the flesh. And denying myself and taking up my cross, I consent to follow Christ, the captain of my Salvation: in hope of the grace and glory promised. Which I daily desire and beg as He hath taught me saying Our Father which art in heaven, etc.

Quest. 10. What is the practice which by this covenant you are obliged to?

Ans. According to the law of nature and Christ's institutions I must—desiring perfection—sincerely obey Him in a life of faith and hope and love: loving God as God for Himself above all, and loving myself as His servant, especially my soul, and seeking its holiness and salvation: and loving my neighbour as myself. I must avoid all idolatry of mind and body, and must worship God according to His Word, by learning and meditating on His Word: by prayer, thanksgiving, and praise and use of his Sacrament.[1]

I must not profane but holily use His holy name: I must keep holy the Lord's Day, especially in communion with the Church-assemblies: I must honour and obey my parents, magistrates, pastors and other rulers: I must not wrong my neighbour in thought, word or deed, in his soul, his body, his chastity, estate, right or propriety [=property]: but do him all the good I can: and do as I would be done by: which is summed up in the Ten Commandments 'God spake these words, saying,' etc.

A Prayer for Families in the method of the Lord's Prayer, being but an Exposition of it. Most glorious God, who art power and Wisdom and Goodness itself,

---

1   The Lord's Supper and other Church-ordinances are referred to in the VIIIth day's Conference, and more fully in my *Universal Concord.*

the Creator of all things: the Owner, the Ruler and the Benefactor of the world: though by sin, original and natural we were Thy enemies, the slaves of Satan and our flesh, and under Thy displeasure and the condemnation of Thy Law: yet Thy children redeemed by Jesus Christ Thy Son, and regenerated by Thy Holy Spirit, have leave to call Thee their reconciled Father. For by Thy covenant of grace Thou hast given them Thy Son to be their Head, their Teacher and their Saviour: and in Him Thou hast pardoned, adopted and sanctified them: sealing and preparing them for Thy celestial kingdom and beginning in them that holy life and light and love which shall be perfected with Thee in everlasting Glory. O with what wondrous love hast Thou loved us, that of rebels we should be made the sons of God! Thou hast advanced us to this dignity that we might be elevated wholly to Thee as Thine own, and might delightfully obey Thee and actively love Thee with all our heart: and so might glorify Thee here and forever.

O cause both us and all Thy churches, and all the world, to hallow Thy great and holy name! and to live to Thee as our ultimate end: that Thy shining image and holy soul may glorify Thy divine perfection.

And cause both us and all the earth to cast off the tyranny of Satan and the flesh and to acknowledge Thy supreme authority and to become the kingdoms of Thee and Thy Son Jesus, by a willing and absolute subjection. O perfect Thy kingdom of grace in ourselves and in the world and hasten the kingdom of glory.

And cause us and thy churches and all people of the earth no more to be ruled by the lusts of the flesh and their erroneous conceits, and by self-will, which is the idol of the wicked: but by Thy perfect wisdom and holy will revealed in Thy laws. Make known Thy Word to all the world and send them the messengers of grace and peace: and cause men to understand, believe and obey the Gospel of salvation, and that with such holiness, unity and love, that the Earth which is now too like hell may be made liker unto heaven: and not only Thy scattered, imperfect flock but those also who in their carnal and ungodly minds do now refuse a holy life and think Thy word and ways too strict, may desire to imitate even the heavenly Church: where Thou art obeyed and loved and praised, with high delight, in harmony and perfection:

And because our being is the subject of our well-being, maintain us in the life which Thou hast here given us, until the work of life be finished: and give us such health of mind and body and such protection and supply of all our wants as shall fit us for our duty and make us contented with our daily bread and patient if we want it. And save us from the love of the riches and honours and pleasures of this world; and the pride, and idleness and sensuality which they cherish. And cause us to serve Thy Providence by our diligent labours, and to serve Thee faithfully with all that Thou givest us. And let us not make provision for the flesh to satisfy its desires and lusts.

And we beseech Thee of Thy mercy, through the sacrifice and propitiation of Thy beloved Son, forgive us all our sins, original and actual, from our birth to this hour: our omissions of duty and committing what Thou didst forbid: our sins of heart and word and deed; our sinful thoughts and affections, our sinful passions and discontents, our secret and our open sins, our sins of negligence and ignorance and rashness: but especially our sins against knowledge and conscience, which have made the deepest guilt and wounds. Spare us O Lord and let not our sins so find us out as to be our ruin: but let us so find them out as truly to repent and turn to Thee! Especially punish us not with the loss of Thy grace! Take not Thy Holy Spirit from us and deny us not Thy assistance and holy operations. Seal to us by that Spirit the pardon of our sins, and lift up the light of Thy countenance upon us and give us the joy of Thy favour and salvation. And let thy love and mercy so fill us not only with thankfulness to Thee: but with love and mercy to our brethren and our enemies, that we may heartily forgive them that do us wrong, as through Thy grace we hope we do. And for the time to come, suffer us not to cast ourselves wilfully into temptations: but carefully to avoid them and resolutely to resist and conquer what we cannot avoid. And O sanctify those inward sins and lusts which are our constant and most dangerous temptations: and let us not be tempted by Satan or the world, or tried by Thy judgments above the strength which Thy grace shall give us. Save us from a fearless confidence in our own strength. And let us not dally with the snare nor taste the bait nor play with the fire of Thy wrath: but cause us to fear and depart from evil: lest before we are aware we be entangled and overcome and wounded with our guilt and with Thy wrath, and our end should be worse than our beginning. Especially save us from those radical sins of error and unbelief, pride, hypocrisy, hardheartedness, sensuality, slothfulness and the love of the present world and the loss of our love to Thee, to Thy kingdom and Thy ways.

And save us from the malice of Satan and of wicked men and from the evils which our sins would bring upon us.

And as we crave all this from Thee, we humbly render our praises with our future service to Thee! Thou art the king of all the world and more than the life of all the living! Thy kingdom is everlasting! Wise and just and merciful is Thy government. Blessed are they that are Thy faithful subjects. But who hath hardened himself against Thee and hath prospered? The whole creation proclaimeth Thy perfection: But it is to heaven where the blessed see Thy glory and the glory of our Redeemer, where the angels and saints behold Thee, admire Thee, adore Thee, love Thee, and praise Thee with triumphant, joyful songs, the holy, holy, holy God, the Father, Son and Holy Ghost, who was and is and is to come. Of Thee and through Thee and to Thee are all things. To Thee be glory for ever. Amen.

A Short Prayer for Families.

Most glorious, ever-living God, Father, Son and Holy Ghost, infinite in Thy power, wisdom and goodness! Thou art the Author of all the world, the Redeemer of lost mankind, and the Sanctifier of Thine elect! Thou hast made us living, reasonable souls, placed awhile on earth in flesh, to seek and know and love and serve Thee, which we should have done with all our soul and might. For we and all things are Thine own and Thou art more to us than all the world. This should have been the greatest business care and pleasure of our lives. We were bound to it by Thy Law and invited by Thy love and mercy and the promise of a reward in heaven. And in our baptism we were devoted to this Christian life of faith and holiness, by a solemn covenant and vow. But with grief and shame we do confess that we have been too unfaithful to that covenant and too much neglected the Lord our Father, our Saviour and our Sanctifier, to whom we were devoted. And have too much served the flesh and the world and the devil which we renounced. We have added to our original sin, the guilt of unthankfulness for a Saviour and resisting the Spirit and grace that should have renewed, governed and saved us. We have spent much of our lives in fleshly and worldly vanity and wilfully neglected the greatest work of making a sure preparation for death and judgment and our endless state. In a custom of sinning we have hardened our hearts against Thy Word and warnings and the reproofs of thy ministers and of our consciences that have oft told us of our sin and danger and called us to repent. And now O Lord! our convinced souls confess that we deserve to be forsaken by Thee and left to our own lust and folly and to the deceits of Satan and unto endless misery. But seeing Thou hast given a Saviour to lost man and a pardoning covenant through the merits of Christ, promising forgiveness and salvation to every true, penitent, believer, we thankfully accept Thy offered mercy and penitently bewail our sin and cast our miserable souls upon Thy grace and the sacrifice, merits and intercession of our Redeemer.

Forgive all the sins of our hearts and lives; and as a reconciled Faher take us as Thy adopted children in Christ. O give us Thy renewing Spirit to be in us a powerful and constant author of holy light and love and life, to fit us for all our duty and for communion with Thee and for everlasting life. And to dwell in us as Thy witness and seal of our adoption. Let Him be better to our souls than our souls are to our bodies, teaching us Thy word and will, and bringing all our love and will to a joyful compliance with Thy will and quickening our dull and drowsy hearts to a holy and heavenly conversation. Let Him turn all our sinful pleasures and desires unto the delightful love of Thee and of Thy ways and servants. Save us from the great sins of selfishness pride and worldliness, and give us self-denial, humility and a heavenly mind, that while we are on earth, our hearts may be in heaven, where we hope to live in Thy joyful love and praise, with Christ and all His holy ones for ever. Let us never forget that this life is short and that the life to come is endless: that our souls are precious and our bodies vile and must shortly turn to rottenness and dust: that sin is odious and temptation dangerous and judgment dreadful to unprepared, guilty souls: and that to them a Saviour and His grace and Spirit there is no salvation. Cause us to live as we would die, and let no temptation, company or business, draw us to forget our God and our everlasting state. –

Lord bless the world, and specially these kingdoms, with wise, godly, just and peaceable princes and inferior judges and magistrates; and guide, protect and perfect them for the common good and the promoting of godliness and suppressing of sin. And bless all Churches with able, godly, faithful Pastors, that are zealous lovers of God and goodness and the people's souls. And save the nations and churches from oppressing tyrants and deceivers, and from malignant enemies to serious piety. And cause subjects to live in just obedience and in love and peace. Bless Families with wise, religious governors, who will carefully instruct their children and servants and restrain them from sin and keep them from temptation. Teach children and servants to fear God and honour and obey their governors.

O our Father which art in heaven, let Thy name be hallowed: Let Thy kingdom come: Let Thy will be done on earth as it is in heaven: Give us this day our daily bread: Forgive us our trespasses as we forgive them that trespass against us: Lead us not into temptation but deliver us from evil: for Thine is the kingdom, the power and the glory for ever. Amen.

Before Meal.

Most gracious God, who hast given us Christ and with Him all that is necessary to life and godliness: we thankfully take this our food as the gift of Thy bounty, procured by His merits. Bless it to the nourishment and strength of our frail bodies to fit us for Thy cheerful service. And save us from the abuse of Thy mercies by gluttony, drunkenness, idleness and sinful fleshly lusts, for the sake of Jesus Christ our only Saviour and Lord. Amen.

After Meat.

Most merciful Father, accept of our thanks for these and all Thy mercies: and give us yet more thankful hearts. O give us more of the great mercies proper to Thy children, even Thy sanctifying and comforting Spirit, assurance of Thy love through Christ and a treasure and a heart and conversation in heaven. And bring and keep us in a constant readiness for a safe and comfortable death: for the sake of Jesus Christ our Lord and only Saviour. Amen.

FINIS

PART III
BAXTER'S LEGACY

7. THE GOSPEL ACCORDING
TO JOHN CALVIN

NOTE: Under the title *Geneva Revisited or Calvinism Revised: The case for theological reassessment,* this article was published in *Churchman: a Journal of Anglican theology* in Autumn 1986.[1] A separate sheet listed planned items for 1987. The tenth article was to be: Jim Packer, 'A Reply to Alan Clifford'. However, the editor informed me that nothing was ever received from Dr Packer. One wonders why ...

In recent years, the precise character of Calvin's 'Calvinism' has been extensively discussed.[2] Numerous scholarly contributions have been occasioned by Dr R. T. Kendall's provocative monograph *Calvin and English Calvinism to 1649* (1979). The discussion seems to suggest on balance, that a significant theological gap does exist between Calvin and later Calvinists,[3] although many remain unconvinced. Various factors might explain a widespread reluctance to revise what is regarded as the traditional view of Calvin, with all that this might entail for Reformed orthodoxy. (Could our venerated Calvin be wrong. or are we out of step after all?). Tradition is a powerful obstacle to theological revision. The situation may he compounded by personal psychological factors: there is a sense of security in a clear-cut. unquestioned theological stance vis-à-vis the fluctuating uncertainties of

---

1   *Churchman, a Journal of Anglican theology*, Vol. 100.4 (1986), 323–34.

2   For a comprehensive survey of the literature, see Roger Nicole, 'John Calvin's view of the Extent of the Atonement' in *The Westminster Theological Journal*, Vol. 47 (1985), 197–225. Also, R. Buick Knox, 'John Calvin—An Elusive Churchman' in *The Scottish Journal of Theology*, Vol. 34, (1981), 147–156.

3   After an exhaustive study of the evidence, Dr Curt Daniel is persuaded that John Calvin did not teach, nor believe in, the doctrine of limited atonement See his unpublished Ph.D. thesis, 'John Gill and Hypercalvinism' (Edinburgh, 1983), Appendix A: Did John Calvin teach Limited Atonement?

much alternative theology. A generation of Reformed scholars and preachers have established their reputations on the strength of their commitment to the 'Five Points', and acceptance within the Reformed fraternity will not be lightly jeopardised.

Whereas an idiosyncratic individualism, and a 'unity-at-any-price' ecumenism are alike to be shunned, the true scholar will ever be ready to reach new conclusions if the evidence is deemed sufficiently compelling. In addition to the 'truth-value' of any viewpoint, it will appear all the more attractive if it possesses a distinct tendency to reconcile opposing positions. Although truth, rather than deliberate compromise, must ever lead the way, the pursuit of an orthodox *via media* will ever be a legitimate concern for the evangelical scholar.

Whilst evangelicalism continues to he divided on many issues, no division has had such lasting and far reaching effects as the Calvinist-Arminian controversy. In the words of Alan Sell, the dispute has never been 'solved, but only shelved'.[1] This author pleads for a renewed concern for 'doctrinal clarity, provided it could be fostered without acrimony'.[2] It is the belief of the present writer that the recent debates about Calvin and Calvinism provide a unique opportunity to reassess a controversy of such obvious and fundamental importance.

It would be historically inaccurate and theologically unjust to apportion blame unequally to the parties in dispute. However, it seems probable to conclude that predestinarian theology in the hands of Theodore Beza was the immediate stimulus for the Arminian reaction, rather than Calvin's own balanced and essentially Christological theology.[3] As one reaction prompted another, so the seventeenth century Calvinists repudiated Arminianism with Bezan scholasticism, rather than Calvin's balanced biblicism. The dispute therefore became a contest between two equally-anomalous positions. *Sub-orthodox* evangelicalism, i.e. Arminianism, was opposed by *ultra-orthodox* evangelicalism, i.e. High Calvinism. This was how the divines of Saumur in France (John Cameron, Moïse Amyraut and others),[4] Richard Baxter 'the

---

1   A. P. F. Sell, *The Great Debate* (Worthing: Walter, 1982), 95.

2   Ibid.

3   This is not to question Calvin's own rigid teaching on predestination but merely to acknowledge a difference in perspective compared with Beza's approach. See Dr Buick Knox's comment in 'John Calvin—An Elusive Churchman', 148.

4   See Brian G. Armstrong, *Calvinism and the Amyraut Heresy* (Madison: University of Wisconsin

apostle of Kidderminster'[1] and others in England evaluated the issues. In nineteenth century Scotland, it was the conviction of Ralph Wardlaw that High Calvinism provided too easy an excuse for the Arminians to reject true Calvinism.[2] Once this consideration is grasped, it is unjust to regard Amyraldianism *alias* Baxterianism as merely another variation on the theme of theological heterodoxy.

A failure accurately to define Calvinism in terms of John Calvin's actual soteriology has confused the entire discussion for too long. High Calvinist dogmas have prejudiced biblical exegesis in those areas central to the debate itself, viz, the nature, design, extent and application of the atonement. To assist us in substantiating these arguments, it will be useful to consider a number of evangelical theologians, ranging from that doyen of Puritan high Calvinism, Dr John Owen, to John Wesley, the very personification of English Arminianism.

Any attempt at theological reconstruction almost inevitably involves the demolition of 'myths'. This is regrettably necessary where the incisive and brilliant contribution of Dr J. I. Packer is concerned, whose advocacy of the orthodoxy of John Owen is well known. Dr Packer remains an unflinching supporter of Owen, believing that the Puritan wrote the very last word on the subject of the atonement.[3] He is evidently confirmed in the myth, more recently perpetuated by Paul Helm,[4] that no significant differences exist between the theologies of John Calvin and John Owen. Dr Packer's own statement, that the Synod of Dort taught what Calvin would have said 'had he faced the developed Arminian thesis'[5] is entirely questionable, especially if he thinks that Dort speaks for Owen. Since Calvin had no quarrel with the Council of Trent over the atonement,[6] it is arguable to suggest that, election apart, Calvin would have been happy with the Arminian thesis. He would

---

Press, 1969).

1   See Baxter's *Catholick Theologie* (London: 1675), II. 50, and his Preface to *Certain Disputations of Right to Sacraments* (London: 1658).

2   *Discourses on the Nature and Extent of the Atonement of Christ* (Glasgow: Blackie, 1854), p. lxxvii.

3   See Introductory Essay to *The Death of Death in the Death of Christ* (London: The Banner of Truth Trust, 1959), 23.

4   See *Calvin and the Calvinists* (Edinburgh: The Banner of Truth Trust, 1982).

5   'Calvin the Theologian' in *John Calvin*, ed. G. Duffield (Abingdon: Sutton Courtenay Press, 1966), 151.

6   See Calvin, *Tracts and Treatises* (Edinburgh: Calvin Translation Society, 1851), iii. 93, 109. Even William Cunningham admits the Tridentine view was universalist, without seeing the implication

have objected to their denial of election and predestination (based on faith foreseen) but not to the idea of universal atonement *per se*. In short, later Calvinism represented a policy of 'over kill' in its handling of the controversy. This is especially true of the Westminster divines, and even more so in the case of John Owen.

It must be said that even the theology of Dort only represents a half way stage in the transition from the theology of Calvin and the other reformers to the theology of Owen. In other words, contrary to the verdict of some,[1] even Dort Calvinism is not so 'high' as subsequent developments. Indeed, it is a popular fallacy to associate Owen with Dort, when one discovers Richard Baxter asserting 'In the article of the extent of redemption, wherein I am most suspected and accused, I do subscribe to the Synod of Dort, without any exception, limitation, or exposition, of any word, as doubtful and obscure'.[2] Only from Baxter's perspective is it true to say that Dort's theology expresses the mind of Calvin.

Fundamental to the Dort Canons' conception of the atonement is the formula 'sufficient for all, efficient for the elect'. This conception was properly the view of the Calvinistic universalists, rather than the particularists. One may suggest however, that Article 3 of the second Dort Canon is marginally ambiguous, in that its concept of the sufficiency of the atonement does not distinguish between Beza's idea of mere (or undesigned) sufficiency and what Bishop John Davenant called an ordained (or designed) sufficiency.[3] It is clear that Owen follows the Bezan tradition, whereas Davenant and Baxter follow Calvin.[4] Unlike Beza and Owen, Davenant and Baxter would concur with Calvin's comment on the thief on the cross, '… our Lord made effective for him his death and passion which He suffered and endured for all mankind'.[5]

---

of Calvin's endorsement of the view. See *The Reformers and the Theology of the Reformation* (1862; Edinburgh: The Banner of Truth Trust, 1967 rep.), 401.

1   See J. R. de Witt, 'The Arminian Conflict and the Synod of Dort' in *The Manifold Grace of God* (Puritan Conference Report, 1968). Daniel is also incorrect to link Owen with Dort without qualification. see 'John Gill and Hypercalvinism', 533. n. 114.

2   See William Orme's Memoir of' Baxter in *The Practical Works of the Rev. Richard Baxter* (London: James Duncan, 1830), i. 456.

3   *A Dissertation on the Death of Christ* (London: Hamilton, Adams & Co., 1832), 401.

4   Contrary to Kendall's claim, it is clear that Calvin accepts the formula in his Comment on 1 John 2: 2. although he denies that it has relevance to the text itself.

5   *Sermons on the Saving Work of Christ*, tr. Nixon (Grand Rapids: Baker Book House, 1950, 1980 rep.), 151.

In the words of John Cameron, Calvin's use of the 'sufficient for all/efficient for the elect' formula involves a more 'ample' concept of sufficiency'.[1] Owen's use of this is very different. It implies that the atonement would have been sufficient for all had God intended it. In short, according to Owen's thesis, the atonement was only sufficient for whom it was efficient.[2]

Dr Packer's sympathy for Owen's theology of the atonement involves him in a further anomaly, especially where his adherence to Reformed Anglican orthodoxy is concerned. A close examination of the Parker Society volumes reveals that the Anglican reformers embraced a theology of the atonement closely akin to John Calvin's. John Hooper[3] and Hugh Latimer[4] are particularly clear in this respect. It is perfectly clear from Cranmer's Prayer Book[5] and the Thirty-nine Articles[6] that the Reformed Anglican Church never committed its clergy to the doctrine of limited atonement. John Wesley argued this point with Rowland Hill in view of Article XXXI, the Communion service and the Catechism.[7] Whereas George Whitefield was entirely correct to challenge Wesley on the latter's implicit rejection of Article XVII, 'Of Predestination and Election',[8] Wesley had a case against Whitefield, Hill and Toplady where the extent of the atonement was concerned. John Goodwin, Owen's Arminian contemporary, argued this point with even greater force than Wesley was able to muster. Indeed, Goodwin shows how familiar he was with Calvin and the other Reformation divines, whose views on the atonement he enlisted

1   Armstrong, *Calvinism and the Amyraut Heresy*, 59.

2   See Owen, *The Death of Death* (Banner of Truth ed.), 184. This idea dictates Owen's view of his famous 'triple choice' question. viz. Christ died for 'either all the sins of all men, or all the sins of some men, or some of the sins of all men' (ibid., 61). Unlike Owen, Calvin and Baxter embrace the first choice with respect to the atonement's sufficiency. and the second choice with respect to its efficiency. This is also the teaching of the famous *Heidelberg Catechism* (1563) in its answer to Q. 37. Christ suffered the wrath of God 'against the sins of the whole human race'.

3   See *Later Writings of Bishop Hooper* (Cambridge: Parker Society, 1852), 31.

4   See *Sermons* (Cambridge: Parker Society, 1844), 521.

5   Statements in both the Communion service and the Catechism show a clear understanding of a universal dimension in the atonement.

6   See Article XXXI and also Articles II and XV.

7   See *Remarks on Mr. Hill's 'Review of all the Doctrines Taught by Mr. John Wesley'* (1772) in *Works*, ed. T. Jackson (London: John Mason, 1841), x. 368 and 'A Dialogue Between a Predestinarian and His Friend', in ibid., 25.

8   See 'A Letter to the Revd. John Wesley' in Whitefield's *Journal,* ed. Murray (London: The Banner of Truth, 1960), 563f.

against his High Calvinist critics.[1] Wesley's case is further substantiated by the views of John Jewel[2] and Richard Hooker[3] in the late sixteenth century, and more recent statements by John Newton,[4] and J. C. Ryle.[5] In short, Dr Packer is in as anomalous a position for going 'beyond' Anglican Calvinism, as Arminian Anglicans are for failing to embrace it. It was for the *via media* that Baxter was pleading, a position arguably identical to Calvin's original biblical insights.

Hitherto, John Owen's exposition of the theology of the atonement has been considered unanswerable and irrefutable. However, there is good reason to suggest that the chief strength of his argument lies not so much in his exegesis of the biblical data, but in the distinctly Aristotelian methodology he employs in the process. Although some attention has been drawn to Owen's Aristotelianism,[6] its most damaging feature has not been detected. Owen is not so much to be penalised for the use of the syllogistic method as such, but for ignoring, or distorting, textual data in his deductive operations. Owen's logical starting points are sometimes suspect, and he often argues 'beyond' the data, rather than within it, to the utter detriment of Scriptural paradox. For instance, Owen would never acquiesce in Calvin's acceptance of the paradox between the generality of the provision of grace and its particular, efficacious application. Of course, Calvin sees a direct correlation between the universal offer of gospel grace and a universal atonement.[7]

Another example of Owen's Aristotelianism is his 'means–end' thinking. He argues for a single, exclusivist teleology in the atonement, viz. the one end in the death of Christ was the salvation of the elect, and the procurement

---

1   See Goodwin's *Redemption Redeemed* (London: 1651), 549f.

2   See Jewel's *Apologia Ecclesiae Anglicanae* in *Works* (Cambridge: Parker Society, 1848), iii. 66.

3   See Hooker's *Laws of Ecclesiastical Polity* in *Works*, ed. Keble (Oxford: Clarendon Press), iii. 17.

4   See Newton's sermon 'The Lamb of God, the Great Atonement' in *Works* (1820; fac. Edinburgh: Banner of Truth Trust, 1985), iv. 190–195.

5   See Ryle's *Expository Thoughts on the Gospels: St. John*, Vol. 1 (London: W. Hunt & Co., 1865; The Banner of Truth Trust, 1987) for his notes on John 3: 16.

6   See J. B. Torrance, 'The Incarnation and Limited Atonement' in *The Evangelical Quarterly*, Vol. LV (April 1983), 86.

7   See Calvin's *Comments* on Matthew 23: 37 and Romans 5: 18. In an otherwise valuable survey of the literature, Roger Nicole fails to grasp this. He is thus involved in an incoherent exposition of Calvin's position (see 'John Calvin's view of the Extent of the Atonement', 213, 217). Judging by Nicole's remarks on Calvin's logic (at p. 210), he is clearly unwilling to share the reformer's version of the ultimate paradox.

of grace for them alone. The entire drift of Owen's argument in the Death of Death would lead one to imagine that Owen would find no place for the popular idea of common grace in his soteriology. However, this is not the case.[1] In short, Owen, cannot really validate the distinction he still employs, along with Baxter, the Westminster divines and Calvin, between common and special grace. It is hardly surprising to find Hypercalvinists like Hussey, Brine and Gill in the next century discarding the notion of common grace whilst they pursued the rigorous logic of Owen's *Death of Death*. Baxter's point is that the Bible does not support the kind of exclusive particularity of the atonement implied by Owen. The doctrine of common grace suggests other, even 'lower' ends, than the admittedly chief end of the redemption of the elect. It is important also to remember, that Owen did not confine his idea of common grace to providence alone, since it did have a place in the *ordo salutis*.[2] In other words, one is committed to a dualistic hermeneutic of the kind obvious in Calvin and latent in the Scriptures themselves, e.g. Deut. 29: 29; Matthew 22: 14; 1 Tim. 4: 10. Indeed, a precise correlation obtains between common grace and special grace, and the 'sufficient for all/ efficient for the elect' formula. The universal provision of grace by means of an all sufficient atonement is as much part of the design of the atonement as its effectual application to the elect. Owen is thus forced to choose either Baxter's position if he wishes to retain common grace, or Gill's position if the atonement is strictly limited.

The position therefore emerges more clearly that the atonement, as with the entire scheme of redemption, possesses general as well as particular features. Unless this synthesis, rooted in plain text after plain text, is adhered to, then no gospel statement is safe from distortion. The Gospel is therefore universal in provision (see John 3: 16), though particular in application (see John 6: 37). When High Calvinism stressed the latter at the expense of the former,[3] it was natural for the Arminians to commit the reverse mistake. Each viewpoint

---

1   See Owen's *Display of Arminianism* in *The Works of John Owen, DD*, ed. W. H. Goold (Edinburgh: Johnstone & Hunter, 1850), x. 134.

2   See also Berkhof's concessionary comment about common grace, together with the cautionary remark that the common/special grace distinction is not intended to suggest two kinds of grace, in *Systematic Theology* (London: The Banner of Truth Trust, 1963 rep.), 436 and 435 respectively.

3   John Owen is guilty of this, in a way Calvin is not. Compare Owen's exposition of John 3: 16 in *The Death of Death in the Death of Christ* (London: The Banner of Truth Trust, 1959), 207f with Calvin's *Comment* on the verse.

distorted the aspect it suppressed, viz. the Arminian rejected sovereign election, as the High Calvinist rejected universal atonement. One may conclude that if Arminianism is the rationalism of the 'left', then High Calvinism is the rationalism of the 'right'. Both positions, albeit from opposing perspectives, suppressed textual data in the interests of theory. True Calvinism accepts the biblical paradox of the fact of election and the fact of a universal atonement. It is surely significant that when Amyraut was charged with heterodoxy at this point, he appealed to Calvin's own teaching in his *Defense de la doctrine de Calvin* (1644) and other writings. Pierre du Moulin—'the French John Owen'—was as much out of order in his treatment of Amyraut as was Owen in his treatment of Baxter.

John Owen is at his most reprehensible when he employs Aristotle's metaphysical substance/accidents theory. As is clear from the *Death of Death*,[1] Owen employs the commercial theory of the atonement to argue its particularity in both design and application. This is why he adopts the modified idea of sufficiency referred to above. The atonement—viewed *quantitatively*—is only sufficient for whom it is efficient, because it only relates to the debts of the elect.[2] In arguing with these commercial metaphors, Owen [employing a medieval scholastic distinction] insists that the Lord Christ 'paid' the same price owed by the elect to God on account of their transgressions—the *solutio eiusdem*.[3] Richard Baxter (following the Dutch jurist-theologian Grotius at the only point he could do so with any real justification) argued that, in virtue of the obvious differences between our Lord's limited sufferings, and the eternal sufferings of the lost, Christ only 'paid' a *qualitative* equivalent—the *solutio tantidem*.[4] It is at this point that, in reply to Baxter, Owen resorts to Aristotle's dubious substance/accidents theory to argue a 'sameness' between our Lord's sufferings and the pains of the damned.[5] In short, our Lord's agonies were 'substantially' the same, but 'accidentally' equivalent.[6] In other words, Owen is forced to concede that there is only a *similarity*, not a *sameness* at all. Had Baxter been as nimble as

---

1   See *Death of Death*, 153f.

2   Ibid., 155 and 184.

3   Ibid., 155.

4   See *Aphorismes of Justification* (Hague *alias* Cambridge, 1655), 301f.

5   See *Death of Death*, 157f and *Of the Death of Christ, the Price He Paid* in *The Works of John Owen, DD*, ed. W. H. Goold (Edinburgh: Johnstone & Hunter, 1850), x. 437f.

6   *Of the Death of Christ*, 448.

David Hume at this point,[1] he would have exploded Owen's case. However, Aristotle had a few more years to reign in seventeenth century scholastic circles. We are now able to see how Owen's questionable commercialism falls to the ground, and with it, the classical case for the doctrine of limited atonement.

It is surely important to note that numerous Reformed theologians have rejected what is surely the raison d'être of limited atonement, in most cases retaining the theory against their better judgment. Charles Hodge,[2] R. L. Dabney,[3] and Andrew Fuller[4] are but three. Thomas Chalmers seems to have seen the full implications of this, whilst virtually embracing an Amyraldian position.[5] Andrew Fuller made the valuable point that if the commercial theory is correct, then believers appear at the throne of grace as claimants rather than suppliants.[6] As Joseph Bellamy of New England observed,[7] the commercial theory implies that those who 'claim' the benefits of the atonement have some prior knowledge of their election. Of course, the very pastoral problem suggested by this kind of thinking explains the tragedy of the Hypercalvinism of Hussey, Brine, Gill and the Gospel Standard Strict Baptists, with all its associated personal misery. It seems therefore perfectly just to suggest that Owen, through the *embryonic* Hypercalvinism of the *Death of Death*,[8] made his contribution to this 'downgrade', equally pernicious as the opposite one from Baxterianism to Unitarianism.[9] On the other, and more

---

1   The metaphysical point here, as highlighted by philosopher David Hume with irrefutable cogency (see *A Treatise of Human Nature* (London: J. M. Dent, 1962), I. vi), is that a 'thing' is what its 'accidents' are. Once the accidents or properties are logically separated from the substance, what can be meaningfully said about the 'substance'? Equivalence in 'accidents' can only mean equivalence of the 'thing'. Even William Cunningham shows little sympathy for Owen's position, thus failing to grasp the significance of the issue. See *Historical Theology* (1862; rep. London: The Banner of Truth Trust, 1960), ii. 307.

2   See *Systematic Theology* (London: J. Clarke, 1960 rep.), ii. 555.

3   See *Discussions: Evangelical and Theological* (London: The Banner of Truth Trust, 1967 rep.), ii. 305f.

4   See *The Gospel Worthy of All Acceptation* in *Works* (London: Holdsworth & Ball, 1824), i. 134.

5   See *Institutes of Theology* (Edinburgh: Sutherland & Knox, 1849), ii. 403f.

6   *The Gospel Worthy of All Acceptation*, 134.

7   *True Religion Delineated* (Edinburgh, 1788), 311.

8   Owen was 'better than his creed', still teaching 'free offers of grace', whereas developed Hypercalvinism denied the 'free offer'.

9   See J. I. Packer's Introduction to Baxter's *The Reformed Pastor* (Edinburgh: The Banner of Truth Trust, 1974), 10.

healthy hand, Calvin taught that Christ is the mirror of election. Election is only known indirectly by faith in Christ, and the gospel call takes place within the context of a universal atonement. Those who reject the gospel do not 'pay' over again what Christ 'paid' for them. He suffered the *tantundem*;[1] they will 'pay' the *idem*.[2] Assuming the commercialist analogy, there is no duplication of payment, in which case, Toplady's oft-quoted lines do not apply as a proof of limited atonement.[3]

The *idem-tantundem* distinction sheds light on the question of substitution. Just as the provision of atonement in Israel was coextensive with the nation, yet not all actually partook of the benefit (many being disobedient and impenitent), so the provision of Calvary extends to all the world, though many do not actually believe. In this respect, there is really something 'on offer', antecedent to its actual reception, making full sense of the idea of the atonement's universal sufficiency. Furthermore, as in the Old Testament the lamb and its sufferings were substituted for the deserved sufferings of guilty Israel, so likewise Christ and His sufferings were substituted for the deserved pains of mankind. Dr Packer criticised Baxter for arguing that God relaxed the law rather than satisfying it,[4] but it is noteworthy that even Owen grants a relaxation of the law with respect to the persons suffering. Baxter was surely correct to pursue the point that God relaxed the law both with regard to the persons *and* their sufferings. Baxter's point is surely irrefutable when he argues that the law did not permit the notion of the punishment of a substitute in the place of the offender. Thus Christ's sacrifice satisfied the law-giver as above His law.[5] Coupled with the infinite dignity of the suffering Saviour, His sufferings were regarded as a satisfactory equivalent for all that is deserved by mankind. The 'exact payment' idea would involve the unthinkable thought that the Saviour would suffer eternally in hell while the sinner was in heaven. This consideration apart, only a rehabilitation of Aristotle can give validity to Owen's argument, a thought unlikely to appeal to evangelical scholars.

---

1   An 'equivalent compensation'.

2   The same, exact payment.

3   'Payment God cannot twice demand. First at my bleeding Surety's hand. And then again at mine.' See *Diary and Hymns of Augustus Toplady* (London: Gospel Standard Baptist Trust, 1969), 193.

4   See 'The Doctrine of Justification ... Among the Puritans' in *By Schisms Rent Asunder* (Puritan Conference Report, 1969), 27.

5   See *Catholick Theologie* (London: 1675), I. ii, 40.

Dr Packer is correct to point out the dangers of Baxter's dependence on the Governmental theory of Grotius. Even then, the Puritan's worst crime is to 'overdo' political analogies to the point of using every aspect of secular government to illustrate sacred themes. As R. L. Dabney suggests, the objection chiefly relates to the form of government in question, not the fact of government itself'.[1] This said, in fairness to Baxter, there are monarchical analogies in the Bible, and he does not depend so heavily on notions of governmental expediency or utilitarianism as does the Dutchman. In short, Baxter does consider that the atonement relates chiefly to the satisfaction of divine justice, rather than the mere deterrence of sin, especially in his later works. What Baxter did see, viz. that Owen was guilty of *over* using commercial metaphors, applies equally to his own *over-use* of political metaphors. In this respect, both men were in error. After all, analogy is not identity. There is a difference between God's rule and secular kingship, and there is a difference between sins and debts. In other words, the atonement is incorrectly viewed in either political or commercial terms, as understood in the seventeenth century. It must surely he viewed, as by the Amyraldian A. H. Strong, in ethical terms.[2] The atonement was a *qualitative* mystery, rather than a *quantitative* transaction. It is because of this particular insight that Baxter has the 'edge' over Owen in the exposition of the 'universalist' texts like John 3: 16 and 1 John 2: 2. etc. Even while allowing for election as the ultimate explanation of the applied particularity of redemption, Baxter is able to resist the temptation to 'particularise' the universal expressions as Owen repeatedly does, i.e. 'world' = 'world of the elect'; 'all' = 'all the elect', etc. It would, of course, be better to treat the whole matter as did Calvin and the other reformers, without regard to the metaphysical complexities of the 'commercialism *versus* politicism' era of the seventeenth century. Nonetheless, it seems correct to conclude that Baxter rather than Owen is the true heir of Calvin's Scriptural theology.

Having dealt with the major thesis of John Owen's *Death of Death,* a few residual problems should be tackled. It is commonly argued that if the atonement relates to any who perish, then the blood of Christ was shed in vain. Closely related to this objection is the one which says that none will

---

1 See *Discussions: Evangelical and Theological*, i. 469. In the same volume appears Dabney's penetrating discussion 'God's Indiscriminate Proposals of Mercy' (282f) in which he entertains a much broader conception of the love of God than ever Owen would allow.

2 See *Systematic Theology* (New York: A. C. Armstrong, 1891), 409f.

be found in hell for whom Christ died. How can they be justly punished if Christ died for them? Quite apart from the fact that the Apostles Paul and Peter saw no theoretical difficulties here,[1] it may be said that if the atonement is the ground upon which the gospel is universally preached, then that particular 'end' is accomplished. Furthermore, the atonement is also the basis upon which those who reject the gospel are justly punished. Indeed, the question may be returned, if it is the duty of mankind to believe the gospel, and unbelief is guilty disobedience (see 2 Thess. 1: 8; Romans 1: 5), what are unbelievers guilty of rejecting if Christ was not given for them? However awesome the thought, are there not those who are condemned, precisely because they have spurned God's conditional offers of mercy?

It must of course be appreciated, that all three positions—High Calvinist, Amyraldian and Arminian—are confronted by the insoluble difficulty of reconciling the ultimate paradox of divine sovereignty on one hand, and human responsibility on the other. Closely correlating with this is the additional paradox between divine election and universal invitations of grace. At the centre of the latter paradox is the question, 'For whom did Christ die?' The important thing is to answer this question without suppressing or distorting any aspect of the paradox. It has been already shown that the High Calvinist answers the question from the perspective of election, thus denying that Christ died for any other than the elect. Similarly, the Arminian replies to the question from the perspective of the universal offer, thus denying election (in the Calvinist sense, of course). What the Amyraldian does is to live with the paradox *without adjusting it as the other parties do.* An analogy will illustrate the position as follows. God's revealed truth may be likened to a house. 'Upstairs' is the realm of God's secret will, the decree of electing grace, the efficacious application of the atonement to the elect, and their perseverance in grace. 'Downstairs' is the realm of God's conditional will and indiscriminate offers of mercy, a universally sufficient atonement and exhortations to persevere in grace. The Arminian tends to think he lives in a 'bungalow', whereas the High Calvinist tends to live 'upstairs' all the time. However, the Amyraldian recognises that both floors have scriptural data for their support, seeking always the wisdom to know when, and how, to use the 'stairs'. It may be said that Baxter was wonderfully agile in this

---

1   See Romans 14: 15; 1 Corinthians 8: 11 and 2 Peter 2: 1. It has to be said that, at this point, Owen's exegesis of these verses is totally unconvincing.

respect! He realised that the 'world' was not to be greeted with the good news by shouting from an 'upstairs room', but by proclaiming it from the 'front door'. However, he knew his Bible well enough to know that the final success of evangelistic endeavour was guaranteed by 'higher' considerations than mere human nature.

In common with the teaching of Calvin and the sixteenth century reformers, Richard Baxter believed that the question 'For whom did Christ die?' must be answered in terms of the kind of dualistic hermeneutic we have illustrated. In short, Christ died for all sufficiently (pardon being conditional), though for the elect absolutely and efficiently. He believed that the evidence of the Bible allowed no other interpretation which did not, at one and the same time, offer violence to the data. He summed up his position as follows:

> When God saith so expressly that Christ died for all, and tasted death for every man, and is the ransom for all, and the propitiation for the sins of the whole world, it beseems every Christian rather to explain in what sense Christ died for all men, than flatly to deny it.[1]

It is refreshing to find Baxter making a straightforward, albeit indirect reference to certain texts in the New Testament. His one object, after all the metaphysical and logical jousting was over, was to leave his fellow disputants with the Verbum Dei. He believed that the task of the theologian was to make a balanced response to all the evidence, and he believed also that his version of the issues alone met that requirement. As we have seen, Baxterianism was the seventeenth century expression of Calvinism, rather than a heterodox theology. Of course, judged by the criteria of High Calvinism, it was bound to look like a compromise with Arminianism, as surely as the Arminians thought Baxterianism to be too Calvinistic! Baxter considered that, at their best, both High Calvinism and Arminianism were but emphasising opposite sides of the same coin. They were both, in differing though complementary senses, semi-Calvinist. He saw that as the Arminian was not all wrong, so the High Calvinist was not all right, and vice versa.

If Baxter and his theological companions are right, then Arminianism appears no more 'heretical' than High Calvinism arguably seems. The men

---

1 *Universal Redemption of Mankind* (London: 1694), 286. Baxter simply appeals, albeit indirectly, to a sequence of texts, viz. 2 Corinthians 5: 14–15; Hebrews 2: 9; 1 Timothy 2: 6 and 1 John 2: 2.

of the *via media* would therefore have no difficulty in singing with Charles Wesley:

> O for a trumpet voice,
> On all the world to call!
> To bid their hearts rejoice
> In Him who died for all;
> For all my Lord was crucified,
> For all, for all my Saviour died.[1]

and:

> See all your sins on Jesus laid:
> The Lamb of God was slain,
> His soul was once an offering made
> For every soul of man.[2]

Considerations of election apart, these verses are as much the authentic voice of true Calvinism as they are of Arminianism. It is only on the level of the atonement's application that the Calvinist parts company with the Arminian. The true Calvinist *alias* Amyraldian *alias* Baxterian is therefore in a unique position to attempt a reconciliation between the opposing wings of Evangelicalism. True Calvinism has a strong sympathy with what is demonstrably Scriptural in both viewpoints, although it could not agree with both in everything. Although Richard Baxter had little success in healing the divisions of his day,[3] it remains true that the theological ground he occupied is the most likely meeting place for a united evangelicalism. True, an entrenched traditionalism might render such thoughts powerless, but a reconsideration of the issues as outlined above must surely create new possibilities. In which case, our return visit to Geneva via Canterbury, Kidderminster and Saumur will have proved a worthwhile beginning to the task of theological reassessment and reconciliation.

---

1   *Methodist Hymn Book* (London: Methodist Conference, 1933), Hymn 114 verse 7.

2   Ibid., Hymn 1 verse 6.

3   See N. H. Keeble's excellent study, *Richard Baxter: Puritan Man of Letters* (Oxford: Clarendon Press, 1982), 22f.

POSTSCRIPT

Immersed in my *Atonement and Justification* research in the early 1980s, I was interested to see an advertisement for Paul Helm's reply to R. T. Kendall's *Calvin and English Calvinism to 1649* (Oxford, 1979). Contacting the Banner of Truth by 'phone, I was informed that the first consignment of *Calvin and the Calvinists* was not expected from the printer for another couple of weeks. Surprise, surprise, it must have been delivered the next day: a copy arrived on our Great Ellingham doormat after two days!

Rapidly reading and digesting the book, I then 'phoned Bob Horn, editor of the *Evangelical Times*, offering a book review. "Oh, we haven't even received our review copy yet, so yes, thanks." Duly typed, the review appeared in the October 1982 edition. This eventually led to extensive correspondence between myself and the author. These fascinating and revealing exchanges have yet to see the light of day. My doctorate was awarded in 1984, Oxford published *A&J* in 1990, and *Calvinus* appeared in 1996. The rest is history.

WILL THE REAL JOHN CALVIN PLEASE STAND UP?

Evangelical Times (October 1982)
CALVIN AND THE CALVINISTS
By Paul Helm
Banner of Truth. 84 pages. £2.25
Would the real John Calvin please stand up?

When R. T. Kendall's *Calvin and English Calvinism to 1649* appeared in 1979, it sent shock-waves throughout the reformed evangelical world. It claimed to prove that what many had assumed to be 'Calvinism' was in fact a misunderstanding and distortion of the teaching of John Calvin himself. Paul Helm's book is a reply to Dr Kendall's monograph. It is an attempt to prove that Puritan theology is wholly consistent with Calvin's own position.

This much is sure, the controversy aroused by Dr Kendall will only be aggravated by this book, in view of the serious charges it makes. Dr Kendall is accused of 'cavalier and unscholarly use of evidence' (53) and of 'scouring the literature for evidence to support his view!' (80). In the nature of the case, facts alone can settle the dispute, when prejudice can only raise the temperature.

Mr Helm deals with the two areas of principal concern in a clear and methodical manner. The nature and extent of the atonement are covered in pp.1–50, and the application of the benefits of redemption to the believer occupy pp.51–81. Helm compares 'Kendall's Calvin' with 'the original' throughout, and he attempts to demonstrate that doctrinal agreement exists between Calvin and the Puritans.

With regard to the second area of concern. Mr Helm has little difficulty in showing that Calvin did allow a distinction between faith and assurance, and that the Westminster Confession does not teach an Arminian-style legalism. There is not therefore the disparity between Calvin and the Westminster Puritans over the nature of Christian experience argued by Dr Kendall. With regard to the nature and extent of the atonement, it is doubtful whether Mr Helm has proved his point. Indeed, it is arguable that he is guilty of the very thing he accuses Dr Kendall of doing. In short. Mr Helm's use of evidence is often selective and merely deductive. I do not believe that he presents the true John Calvin either!

Mr Helm is correct to argue that Calvin did accept the formula 'Christ died for all sufficiently, but for the elect efficaciously (or effectively)' (39). He is also right in describing Dr Kendall's view as 'novel', that Calvin taught an unlimited atonement, but a limited intercession (35). However, this does not prove Mr Helm's point that Calvin taught a puritan-style doctrine of limited atonement.

There is clearly some uneasiness on p.18. and not a little contradiction when we are told that Calvin 'does *not commit himself* to definite atonement', yet 'There are passages in Calvin which show that he held to the doctrine of limited atonement, …' What Mr Helm fails to do is to see the full implications of Calvin's adherence to the 'sufficient for all/efficient for the elect' distinction. Calvin taught a dualism, which applies to the gospel as a whole—to the atonement, to Christ's intercession, to the will of God and the workings of divine grace through the Holy Spirit. Calvin made it plain that Christ prayed for all indiscriminately as well as the elect; see *Sermons on Isaiah's Prophecy* (1956), 143, and Calvin's comment on John 17: 9, tr. T. H. L. Parker (1961), 140). Dr Kendall seems to have missed this vital evidence.

Calvin's view of the intercession of Christ runs parallel with his view of the atonement. Directly contrary to Mr Helm's claim on p.46, Calvin says: 'It is incontestable that Christ came for the expiation of the sins of the whole world', adding that 'God reconciles the world to Himself, reaches to all, but that it is not sealed on the hearts of all to whom it comes so as to be effectual' (*The Eternal Predestination of God*, tr. J. K. S. Reid (1961), 148–9).

In like manner, Calvin says on Colossians 1: 14 that 'by the sacrifice of His death all the sins of the world have been expiated'. For further evidence, see Calvin's comments on Matthew 26: 1, 12–14, 26; Mark 14: 24; John 1: 29, 3: 16; Romans 5: 18; 1 Corinthians 8: 11–12; 2 Peter 2: 1 and 3: 9. In other words. Calvin taught a universal atonement, but a restricted application of it. In this respect, the Puritans—and John Owen in particular, went 'beyond' Calvin (and Scripture too?). It is a serious omission in Mr Helm's book that he does not discuss Owen's contribution *vis-à-vis* Calvin. Had he done so, his main argument would have been destroyed.

Dr Kendall's somewhat exaggerated and inaccurate claims aside, it is still true that 'Calvin's Calvinism' and 'Puritan Calvinism' are different. Mr Helm rightly says that the Amyraldians (a 'middle' group between later Calvinists and the Arminians) viewed Christ's work as a whole in universal terms (36). The truth is, they viewed it in the same dualistic way that Calvin had done. Furthermore, they argued—as did Richard Baxter in this country—that condemnation of their position involved a condemnation of Calvin also, a point demonstrated by Brian G. Armstrong's excellent study *Calvinism and the Amyraut Heresy* (1969).

The implications of all this are obvious. The questions raised are numerous. It seems that Mr Helm has difficulty in placing Calvin within the tradition which glories in his name. Calvin's actual views are something of an embarrassment to that tradition, if not an outright rebuke to it. If this controversy leads us to re-examine Calvin. and also to an uninhibited view of the Word of God, then it will have served a useful purpose.

Alan C. Clifford

8. The Gospel According to John Davenant

Introduction to the Quinta Press edition of John Davenant's Dissertation on the Death of Christ

Quinta Press is to be congratulated for making this new edition of Bishop Davenant's excellent treatise available to a new generation of readers. It is welcome for two reasons. *First,* in the context of past and ongoing debates between Calvinists and Arminians over the extent of the Atonement, the author's long-neglected treatise remains an invaluable and significant contribution to a proper understanding of this fundamental subject. Indeed, for reasons to be explained, what one may call the 'Davenant dimension' has been sadly lacking for too long. Michael G. Thomas is right to say that 'Not only does Davenant deserve to be better known, but he also should be better understood'.[1]

The *second* reason for welcoming this new edition of Davenant's *Dissertation on the Death of Christ* is that it compensates for the deletion of it from the recently-issued [2005] single volume Banner of Truth Trust facsimile of the author's original two-volume *Commentary on Colossians*[2]—where it appeared at the end of Volume 2. It is surely regrettable if not disingenuous that the publisher of the facsimile nowhere indicates that the dissertation has been deleted. Since the translator's 'Life of the Author' is retained, readers are informed that a 'translation' of the dissertation is 'annexed to this work'.[3] Disconcerted readers will thus look in vain for it in the facsimile!

---

1 G. Michael Thomas, *The Extent of the Atonement: A Dilemma for Reformed Theology from Calvin to the Consensus* (Carlisle: Paternoster Press, 1997), 150.

2 *An Exposition of the Epistle of St Paul to the Colossians* by The Right Revd John Davenant, D. D., translated from the original Latin; with a life of the Author by Josiah Allport (two volumes, London: Hamilton, Adams & Co., 1831).

3 At p. xlviii.

As to why the Banner of Truth Trust excised Davenant's dissertation, we are left in no doubt. In an e-mail to Dr Hazlett Lynch, editor Jonathan Watson said that The Banner wanted to make his *Commentary on Colossians* available and to include it in the Geneva Series of Commentaries. The only edition they had to work with was an old two volume edition which had appended to it Davenant's *Dissertation on the Death of Christ*—hence the references to the latter work in the translator's Introduction, which they could not excise due to the nature of the photolitho process. They decided not to publish it, partly because of the sheer size of the book (the Commentary alone runs to 952 pp), and partly because, in their view, the work was less valuable than other works they have published on the Death of Christ, namely Owen's *The Death of Death* and Smeaton's two volumes on the *Atonement*, to name but two.

So there we have it. A theological agenda rather than commercial considerations really explains the deletion. Davenant's *Dissertation* is 'less valuable' than Owen's *Death of Death*. However, one may ask, "less valuable for whom?" In his 'Introductory Essay' to the 1959 Banner of Truth edition of John Owen's treatise, Dr J. I. Packer stated that 'Owen was not impressed'[1] with Davenant's 'Amyraldian' *Dissertatio de Morte Christi*. Indeed, Owen himself was utterly uncompromising in his verdict. Davenant's treatise was 'repugnant unto truth itself.'[2]

If Owen and his disciples are correct, then our friends at the Quinta Press should be having sleepless nights. Being Christian publishers, is it right or safe to be printing and selling such a 'false' theological work on such a central subject as the death of our Lord Jesus Christ? Surely not, if Owen is correct. However, in the opinion of the present writer, despite unpersuasive and misleading attempts to vindicate John Owen's 'limited atonement' ultra-orthodoxy,[3] there are substantial grounds not only to congratulate the Quinta Press but to reassure them that they are rendering a necessary and valuable service to the Church of Christ in republishing Davenant's noble work. In short, despite the criticisms of Owen, Packer and others, his treatise is 'very helpful' to say the least. The purpose of this introduction is to explain why.

---

1 Introductory Essay to John Owen's *Death Of Death In The Death Of Christ* (London: The Banner of Truth Trust, 1959), 23, n. 5.

2 Owen, *Works*, ed. W. H. Goold (Edinburgh: Johnstone & Hunter, 1850), x. 432.

3 See Carl R. Trueman, *The Claims of Truth: John Owen's Trinitarian Theology* (Carlisle: Paternoster Press, 1998).

Despite the concern of the Banner of Truth Trust to shield its readers from Davenant's 'unhelpful' theology of redemption, the commentary itself teaches the author's 'Amyraldian' views unambiguously. Commenting on the text 'In whom we have redemption through his blood, even the forgiveness of sins' (*Colossians 1: 14*), Davenant declares:

It demonstrates also the infinite love of God towards the human race, who willingly sent his own Son to redeem miserable mortals. ... It must also be observed, that the Apostle does not say we have redemption by the Son of God, but *in* him. For *by* Christ the whole world is said to be redeemed, inasmuch as he offered and gave a sufficient *ransom* for all; but *in* him the elect and faithful alone have effectual redemption, because they alone are *in* him.[1]

To avoid further embarrassment, the Banner of Truth would have done better to delete translator Allport's 'Life of the Author' as well as the dissertation, since it includes a thoroughly sympathetic account of Davenant's 'proto-Amyraldian' contribution at the Synod of Dort (1618–19). An outline of his career[2] enables us to see the significance of the new edition of the dissertation in its proper context.

The information supplied by Allport reminds us that Davenant was probably the most eminent of the five English deputies[3] commissioned by King James I to attend the famous Synod. A graduate of Cambridge University, John Davenant (1576–1641) received his DD at the age of thirty-three and was elected Lady Margaret's Professor of Divinity in 1609. Later, in 1621, the King appointed him Bishop of Salisbury, a position he was to occupy until his death in 1641. Among several publications, Davenant's Latin commentary on Colossians[4] was published at Cambridge in 1627, a third edition appearing

---

1   *Exposition of Colossians*, i. 163–4.

2   See also Morris Fuller, *The Life, Letters & Writings of John Davenant, DD* (London: Methuen, 1897).

3   The others were Dr George Carleton, Bishop of Llandaff, Dr Joseph Hall, Dean of Worcester (and later Bishop of Norwich), Dr Samuel Ward, Master of Sydney Sussex College, Cambridge, and Walter Balcanqual, a presbyter of the Church of Scotland (see Nicholas Tyacke, 'The British Delegation to the Synod of Dort' in *Anti-Calvinists: The Rise of English Arminianism c. 1590–1640* (Oxford: Clarendon Press, 1987). While these men had little sympathy for the supralapsarian Calvinism of some in the Synod, 'None of the British delegates ... can meaningfully be described as Arminian' (Tyacke, 99).

4   *Expositio Epistolae D. Pauli ad Colossenses* (Cambridge: 1627).

in 1639. Before his death in 1641, he published a reply to a thoroughly
'Arminian' tract by Samuel Hoard, Rector of Morton in Essex.[1] Hoard's
work is one of the earliest assaults upon what may be regarded as classical
'Anglican Calvinism'. Davenant's reply[2] was not merely a re-statement of the
orthodoxy of the *Thirty-nine Articles*. It was also an expression of the views
he maintained at the Synod of Dort more than twenty years earlier. It is
highly relevant to note that, in France, Hoard's tract also occasioned a reply
from Moïse Amyraut, Professor of Theology at the Reformed Academy of
Saumur—his *Defence of the Doctrine of Calvin*.[3] It is remarkable to note the
concurrence of sentiment in these two replies. Davenant's final and fullest
statement on the subject of the Atonement, and one of two Latin treatises,
was his *Dissertation on the Death of Christ*. Written in 1627, it was initially a
victim of the new 'anti-Calvinist' licensing laws of King Charles I;[4] the work
was published posthumously in 1650[5] (but only translated and published by
Allport in English in 1832).

In view of Owen's summary dismissal of Davenant's dissertation, what are
we to make of its 'orthodoxy'? While John Calvin is not the only authority
cited by Davenant in his dissertation, he was conscious of doing what he
himself did in his *Animadversions*[6] and Amyraut does in several treatises[7]—
defending 'the doctrine of Calvin'. Accordingly he states:

> The death of Christ is the universal cause of the salvation of mankind,
> and Christ himself is acknowledged to have died for all men sufficiently
> ... by reason of the Evangelical covenant confirmed with the whole
> human race through the merit of his death ... [This] evangelical covenant
> [is the basis on which] 'Christ .... sent his Apostles into all the world

---

1   *God's Love to Mankind, manifested by disproving his absolute Decree for their Damnation* (London: 1633).

2   *Animadversions written by the Right Rev. Father in God, John, Lord Bishop of Salisbury, upon a treatise intituled, God's Love to Mankind* (Cambridge: 1641).

3   *Defensio doctrinae J. Calvini de absoluto reprobationis decreto* (Saumur: Isaac Desbordes, 1641). This work appeared in French in 1644. See Brian G. Armstrong, *Calvinism and the Amyraut Heresy* (Madison: University of Wisconsin Press, 1969), 99.

4   See Tyacke, *Anti-Calvinists*, 181ff.

5   *Dissertationes Duae; prima, de Morte Christi; altera, De Praedestinatione et Electione, &c* (Cambridge: 1650).

6   *Animadversions*, 142.

7   See Armstrong, 142.

(*Mark 16: 15,16*). ... On which words of promise, the learned Calvin has rightly remarked, that 'this promise was added that it might allure the whole human race to the faith.'[1]

Earlier, Davenant had quoted[2] (among others) a statement by Calvin which Amyraut also cited against his critics:

Paul makes grace common to all, not because it in fact extends to all, but because it is offered to all. Although Christ suffered for the sins of the world, and is offered by the goodness of God without distinction to all men, yet not all receive him. [3]

Such citations as these ought surely to arouse suspicions regarding Owen's perspective on Davenant's dissertation. In which case, in view of Davenant's and Amyraut's use of Calvin, it might be useful to provide a summary of Calvin's actual teaching. Here, I repeat material published elsewhere.

As his writings make abundantly clear, the great reformer John Calvin taught a doctrine of the atonement significantly different from that of later Calvinists. Indeed, he would hardly recognise the theory of limited atonement as his offspring. The key to understanding Calvin's very different view of the extent and efficacy of Christ's death is his view of the divine will. While Calvin believed God's will to be one, he insists that it is set before us in Scripture as double—secret and revealed.[4] Conscious of its rational incomprehensibility (yet no more problematic than the doctrine of the Trinity), Calvin argued for this divine dichotomy from Deut. 29: 29 and elsewhere. As it relates to redemption, God's revealed will is universal and conditional but the secret will or counsel is restricted

---

1 Allport, 401, 419; Quinta, 71, 85.

2 Allport, 37; Quinta, 19.

3 *Comment on Romans 5: 18*. Roger Nicole admits that 'the passage ... comes perhaps closest to providing support for Amyraut's thesis'. Without actually quoting the passage at this point, Dr Nicole flies in the face of the obvious when he adds: 'it may well refer simply to the relevance of the sacrifice of Christ to a universal offer, without actually asserting a substitutionary suffering for all mankind' (*Moyse Amyraut (1596–1664) and the Controversy on Universal Grace*, Harvard University thesis, 1966), 83, n. 38. Even Richard Muller admits that 'Calvin's teaching was ... capable of being cited with significant effect by Moïse Amyraut against his Reformed opponents' (*The Unaccommodated Calvin*, (Oxford: OUP, 2000), 62).

4 *Comments* on Ezekiel 18: 23; Matthew 23: 37; 2 Peter 3: 9.

and absolute.[1] While predestination and election relate to the latter, Calvin usually relates the Gospel to the former.[2] Hence the death of Christ is presented by Calvin as universal according to God's revealed intention or decree, but limited in efficacy according to God's secret decree.[3] In his biblical comments, without speculating on any temporal or logical priority in the decrees, Calvin seems to stress one or the other according to strictly contextual considerations.

Accepting the delicate balance of this acute antinomy, it is truly remarkable that one who has been condemned for severe logicality should embrace a concept branded by its detractors as illogical. Yet Calvin insisted that humility of mind is demanded in the face of transcendent truth. After his death, his finely tuned biblical balance was effectively destroyed by the ultra-orthodoxy of Theodore Beza (1519–1605) and the reactionary sub-orthodoxy of Jakob Arminius (1560–1609). Their theological antagonism notwithstanding, they agreed on the priority of strict rational consistency. Thus the two strands in Calvin's composite thought were separated with unhappy soteriological results. While Beza insisted on an atonement limited by decree, design and efficacy, Arminius—denying divine foreordination—taught an unlimited, hypothetical atonement.

---

1   *Concerning the Eternal Predestination of God*, tr. J. K. S. Reid (London: James Clarke, 1961), 105–6; *Sermons on Timothy and Titus*, tr. L. T. [sic] (1579; fac. Edinburgh: The Banner of Truth Trust, 1983), 1181–2.

2   *Comments* on John 12: 47; 2 Peter 1: 16.

3   Comments on Matthew 26: 24; Romans 5: 18; 1 Peter 1: 20; *Sermons on Christ's Passion*, tr. L. Nixon (Grand Rapids: Baker Book House, 1950), 151; *Concerning the Eternal Predestination of God*, 102–3. Professor Paul Helm rejects what he dismisses as a 'proof-text' use of Calvin's teaching in relation to debates 'that only arose after his death' (Review of my *Amyraut Affirmed* in *Evangelicals Now* (November, 2004). While it is true that the reformer never *formally* addressed the issue of the extent of the atonement, yet he constantly and consistently presented his views *exegetically*. To say his views are not relevant and appropriate source material for later discussion is simply absurd. After all, would Professor Helm exclude Calvin's views on predestination from a discussion of seventeenth-century Calvinistic orthodoxy? The simple answer to Helm's charge of anachronism is that some things are eternal. Accordingly Nigel Westhead concludes that 'Calvin's language and thought forms *do* fit the contours of the later disputes very well and he speaks in a remarkably similar way to later disputants. His thought easily transplants to the 17th century debates. In any case all we can do is accept what Calvin did say in his own time on the controverted texts' (see Clifford, *Spotlight on Scholastics* (Norwich: Charenton Reformed Publishing, 2005), 11).

Thus the two sides of a supra-logical, paradoxical coin were rent asunder. The opposing positions were alike rationalistic; theologians adjusted and modified textual evidence which conflicted with their particular perspective. Whereas the Arminians made election conditional and God's redemptive purpose contingent, the high Calvinists squeezed the universal language of Scripture into a rigidly particularist mould. Calvin would have rejected this double-distortion of his theology.[1]

Having outlined the 'authentic Calvinism' of John Calvin (the very soteriology defended and propagated by both Amyraut and Davenant), it is also essential to possess a correct grasp of the teaching of the Canons of Dort, not least because of Davenant's decisive influence and contribution. It is a fact that the Canons were a compromise statement reflecting 'broader' and 'narrower' views of the Lombardian formula 'sufficient for all, efficient for the elect'.[2] The likes of Bishop Davenant and the other English delegates at Dort, together with the divines from Bremen and Hesse, represented this 'broader view'. For them, notwithstanding doctrines of predestination and the atonement's particular application to the elect, the following articles relate to an *intended provision* ('for the sins of the whole world') in Christ's sacrifice and not merely to its intrinsically infinite value derived from His person (a view shared by all parties):

The death of the Son of God is the only and most perfect sacrifice and satisfaction for sin; and is of infinite worth and value, abundantly sufficient to expiate the sins of the whole world. ... That, however, many who have been called by the gospel neither repent nor believe in Christ but perish in unbelief does not happen because of any defect or insufficiency in the sacrifice of Christ offered on the cross, but through their own fault. ... [This] was the most free counsel of God the Father, that the life-giving and saving efficacy of the most precious death of His Son should extend to all the elect.[3]

---

1 See *Calvinus: Authentic Calvinism, A Clarification* (Norwich: Charenton Reformed Publishing, 1996), 11–12; *Amyraut Affirmed, or Owenism, a caricature of Calvinism* (Norwich: Norwich: Charenton Reformed Publishing 2004), 7–8.

2 See Armstrong, 59–60.

3 H. B. Smith and P. Schaff, *The Creeds of the Evangelical Protestant Churches* (London: Hodder & Stoughton, 1877), 586.

It should be remembered that King James I and Archbishop Abbot (besides insisting that no discussion of Anglican episcopacy should be allowed at Dort) had charged the English delegates to be 'peremptory on the point of introducing into the decisions of the Synod, the Universality of Christ's Redemption'.[1] Davenant's role in securing this was crucial. Francis Gomarus, the supralapsarian Dutch 'Beza-ist' stood for a rigidly exclusive definition of limited atonement, a position resisted by Davenant and his friends. Heated discussions created a rift even within the English delegation when Bishop Carleton nearly yielded to pressure from Gomarus. Allport narrates the dramatic developments:

The doctrine of redemption as a blessing to be universally proposed and offered to all men, was so little relished by the Synod, that it is clear, nothing but a threatened loss of the English deputies induced its insertion. In fact, it led to so much unpleasant discussion, that it appears the Bishop [Carleton] would have given way: but Davenant declared he would sooner cut off his hand than rescind any word of it; in which he was supported by Ward; and it was ultimately agreed to.[2]

As if to confirm that the 'Three Forms of Unity' [*Belgic Confession, Heidelberg Catechism*[3] and *Canons of Dort*] and the Anglican *Thirty-nine Articles* were

---

1   'Life of Bishop Davenant' in *An Exposition of the Epistle of St Paul to the Colossians* by The Right Revd John Davenant, D. D., translated from the original Latin; with a life of the Author by Josiah Allport (London: Hamilton, Adams & Co.,), i. p. xv.

2   Ibid. p. xvi.

3   Reflecting the *Heidelberg Catechism's* answer to Q. 37 (which states that 'Christ bore in body and soul the wrath of God against the sin of the whole human race'), David Pareus (1548–1622) expressed the 'Heidelberg' position at Dort. Too old to attend the Synod personally, his views on the atonement were heard *in absentia*. Significantly, the words of the *Heidelberg Catechism* are woven into his statement as cited by Davenant: 'The cause and matter of the passion of Christ was the sense and sustaining of the anger of God excited against the sin, not of some men, but of the whole human race; whence it arises, that the whole of sin and of the wrath of God against it was endured by Christ, but the whole of reconciliation was not obtained or restored to all' (see Allport, ii. 356; Quinta, 34–5). Not surprisingly, many catechism commentators have been quick to distance the *Heidelberg Catechism* from a 'broader' understanding. However, in so doing, they have reflected not the views of the catechism's authors, Ursinus and Olevianus (surely the best guides as to its meaning) but a later and 'higher' orthodoxy of the Westminster type. Notwithstanding the Heidelberg divines' commitment to election and predestination, they nonetheless—like Calvin and Davenant—maintained a universal dimension to the atonement. Ursinus affirmed that as Christ 'died for all, in respect to the sufficiency of his ransom; and for the faithful alone in respect

entirely consistent (whatever advocates of the later *Westminster Confession of Faith* were to say), Dr Samuel Ward wrote thus to Archbishop Ussher:

> We were careful that nothing should be defined which might gainsay the Confession of the Church of England, which was effected, for that they were desirous to have all things in the canons defined *unanimi consensu*. We foreign divines, after the subscription to the canons, and a general approbation of the Belgic Confession, and Catechism, which is the Palatine's, as containing no dogmata repugnant to the Word of God, ... were dismissed. In our approbation of the Belgic Confession, our consent was only asked for doctrinals, not for matters touching discipline [episcopacy or presbytery]. We had a solemn parting in the Synod, and all was concluded with a solemn feast.[1]

In view of the seeming soundness of Davenant and his colleagues, enough has surely been said to raise questions about John Owen's theological stance. Is it correct to regard him as 'the Calvin of England' and, as the Banner of Truth affirmed, 'the greatest British theologian of all time'?[2] While the second question involves a value judgement, the first is more than doubtful from a purely factual perspective. In view of the significant differences between Calvin and Beza—and even Richard Muller, for all his pleas that doctrinal and scholastic continuity existed, acknowledges that the latter was 'more rationalistic' than the former[3]—it may be argued that Owen was 'the

---

of the efficacy of the same, so also he willed to die for all in general, as touching the sufficiency of his merit ... But he willed to die for the elect alone as touching the efficacy of his death' (*The Commentary on the Heidelberg Catechism*, ed. G. W. Williard (Phillipsburg: Presbyterian and Reformed publishing Company, 1985), 223). Consistent with his colleague, Olevianus declared that Christ 'was being tried before God, laden with your sin and my sin and that of the whole world' (*A Firm Foundation: An Aid to Interpreting the Heidelberg Catechism* (tr. & ed. L. D. Bierma (Grand Rapids/ Carlisle: Baker Books/Paternoster Press 1995), 65).

1 Ibid. p. xvii.

2 See Alan C. Clifford, *Atonement and Justification: English Evangelical Theology 1640–1790—An Evaluation* (Oxford: Clarendon Press, 1990, rep. 2002), 3–4.

3 R. A. Muller, *Christ and the Decree* (Grand Rapids: Baker Book House, 1988), 12. For Calvin and Beza, see G. M. Thomas, *Extent of the Atonement*, 47–8 and Jonathan D. Moore, 'Theodore Beza (1519–1605)' in *Evangelical Times* (November, 2005), 19–20. Whether or not Calvin gave unqualified approval to Beza's 'rationalising' *Tabula praedestinationis* (1555), Thomas is more cautious than Moore in this respect in view of a lack of epistolary or other documentary proof. Even if Calvin did not object—and he probably didn't—to Beza's systematic portrayal of the *ordo salutis* from a purely *abstract* perspective, he evidently did not share his successor's aversion to 'a two-

Beza of England'. Following Beza rather than Calvin, Owen's soteriology is flawed in a number of respects (as I have argued elsewhere). *First*, it is *exegetically* defective. Quite apart from other textual distortions, the 'limited love' exegesis of John 3: 16[1] in the *Death of Death* has no prototype in Calvin's theology. *Second*, it is *theologically* defective. Since his approach is driven more by ultra-orthodox dogma than scriptural data, universalist texts are 'explained away' in the interests of deductive theological consistency.[2] *Third*, it is *philosophically* defective. In his discussion of the purpose and nature of the Atonement, Owen's entire approach was conditioned by the scholastic categories of medieval Aristotelianism.[3] This is not to deny that Owen's opponent Richard Baxter—who championed Davenant's teaching—also employed a scholastic methodology.[4] However, unlike Baxter's significantly different scholastic mode, Owen's had a more detrimental influence on his understanding of biblical teaching. Sadly, his embryonic hypercalvinism produced the semi-justifiable Wesleyan over-reaction of the next century.

It is undeniable that for Owen, his 'method' influenced the 'content' of his theology. So much so, that we may say Owen's Gospel is not Calvin's Gospel. For this reason, his rejection of Davenant's treatise as 'repugnant unto truth' has no credibility. Where the doctrine of the Atonement is concerned, it may be safely argued that 'over-orthodox' Owen (as Richard Baxter called

---

fold counsel of God' and its consequent 'errors' (*Tabula*, VII, par. 3). What is undeniable is that Calvin—with clear implications for his doctrine of universal redemption—continued to adopt the two-fold will of God distinction in *A Harmony of the Gospels* (1555), *Sermons on Ephesians* (1558) and the final edition of the *Institutes* (1559). While Beza tampered with the text of Calvin's *Eternal Predestination* (1552; see J. K. S. Reid edition, 105, n. 2), presumably in the interests of 'tightening up' the latter's teaching and eliminating his 'errors', Calvin continued to use the distinction between the absolute and conditional wills of God in his uncompleted 1564 lectures on *Ezekiel* (see *Comment* on 18: 23). Perpetuating Calvin's theological programme, the Amyraldians rightly resisted Bezan rationalism and the 'limited atonement' mentality it produced. For all his attempts to close the gap between Calvin and Beza, Muller fails to do so with regard to the extent of the atonement (see the 'Appendix' to my *The Good Doctor: Philip Doddridge of Northampton—A Tercentenary Tribute* (Norwich, 2002), 255–6). For an accurate brief assessment of Beza's scholastic rationalism, see Michael Jinkins, 'Theodore Beza: Continuity and Regression in the Reformed Tradition', *The Evangelical Quarterly* (64. 2) 1992.

1   A. C. Clifford, *Atonement and Justification,* 152–3.

2   Ibid. 96, 161

3   Ibid. 95ff; 129.

4   Contrary to Carl Trueman's criticism of me, I never denied Baxter's scholastic activity. See my *Spotlight on Scholastics* (Norwich: 2005), 4 and *Atonement and Justification*, 23, 106–7, 143.

him[1]) was no friend of the Canons of Dort, Calvin, or the early Reformed confessions, including the formularies of the Anglican Church in which he was ordained.[2] From a 'Davenantian perspective', Baxter's commendations of Calvin and Dort make perfect sense. While Owen's editor, W. H. Goold, found it difficult to reconcile Baxter's rejection of Owen's view of the atonement with his admiration for the divines of Dort[3] Baxter could happily declare: 'In the article of the extent of redemption, wherein I am most suspected and accused, I do subscribe to the Synod of Dort, without any exception, limitation, or exposition, of any word, as doubtful and obscure'.[4]

The solution to Goold's perplexity is not difficult to find for, unlike the Westminster Confession, and contrary to their popular image, the Canons of Dort contain a clear statement about the universal sufficiency of the atonement. It is from the very same perspective that Amyraut himself was able to rebut the charge of heterodoxy at the National Synod of Alençon (1637).[5] In short, whilst neither Baxter nor Amyraut questioned the 'effectual application' of the atonement in the salvation of the elect, they were able to affirm—on the authority of the Synod of Dort—that there was a universal dimension to the atonement. As Amyraut himself eulogised Calvin, enlisting his support against his ultra-orthodox critics,[6] so Baxter expressed his admiration for the Genevan reformer in a way Owen never did: 'I know no man, since the Apostles' days, whom I value and honour more than Calvin, and whose judgement in all things, one with another, I more esteem and come nearer to'.[7]

---

1   *Reliquiae Baxterianae, or Mr Richard Baxter's Narrative of the Most Memorable Passages of his Life and Times*, ed. M. Sylvester (London: 1696), ii. 199.

2   Article XXXI explicitly affirms that 'The offering of Christ once made is that perfect redemption, propitiation, and satisfaction, for all the sins of the whole world, both original and actual; ...' Consistent with this, the prayer of consecration from the service of Holy Communion states that Christ made 'a full, perfect and sufficient sacrifice, oblation, and satisfaction, for the sins of the whole world'. The Catechism teaches the catechumen to believe that God the Son 'hath redeemed me, and all mankind' while it hastens to add, in Calvinist rather than Arminian fashion, that God the Holy Ghost 'sanctifieth me, and all the elect people of God'.

3   *The Works of John Owen*, ed. W. H. Goold (London: Johnstone & Hunter, 1850–5), x. 430.

4   Cited by W. Orme (ed), *The Practical Works of the Revd Richard Baxter* (London: James Duncan, 1830), i. 456.

5   See J. Quick, *Synodicon in Gallia Reformata* (London: 1692), ii. 354.

6   See Armstrong, 186f.

7   Cited in Philip Schaff, *The History of the Christian Church* (Edinburgh: T. & T. Clark, 1883), viii. 136. Neil Keeble's assessment is therefore wholly inaccurate: 'Though we may wonder that

Bringing Baxter into the picture is directly relevant to our appreciation of Davenant. Indeed, the former is perhaps the most famous proponent of 'the Davenant dimension'. For puritan Baxter, Davenant was one of 'The old Orthodox Protestant Bishops'[1] of the pre-Laudian type. No other English divine stamped his outlook more decisively on Baxter than did John Davenant. Writing to his 'dearly beloved friends' at Kidderminster in 1650, Baxter urged them 'to beware of extremes in the controverted points of religion. When you avoid one error, take heed you run not into another ... The middle way which Camero,[2] Ludov. Crocius,[3] Amyraldus,[4] (John) Davenant, &c. go, I think, is nearest the Truth'.[5]

Not surprisingly, Baxter owned a number of Davenant's works.[6] Even then, he insists that his theological understanding was formed prior to his acquaintance with them.[7] He confesses to admiring Amyraut, Davenant and others because they confirmed his own grasp of things. Thus, while he shunned the *Bezan* Calvinism of 'over-orthodox' Owen, Davenant's influence helped him to avoid the 'opposite error'. Writing in 1653 to Peter Ince, Baxter declared 'I am more firmly established against Arminianism than ever I was in my life; & much more since I ... went the way of the Synod of Dort, ...[8] In 1655, Augustine and Davenant were cited authorities in Baxter's response to enquiries about predestination and reprobation.[9] The publication of Baxter's 1649 manuscript on *Universal Redemption* was held back[10] because he considered works by Amyraut, Jean Daillé[11] and Davenant rendered it superfluous. He

---

Baxter could say 'I am no Arminian', it is no surprise to find him denying whole-hearted allegiance to Calvin' (*Richard Baxter: Puritan Man of Letters* (Oxford: Clarendon Press, 1982), 72).

1   N. H. Keeble and Geoffrey F. Nuttall (eds), *Calendar of the Correspondence of Richard Baxter* (Oxford: Clarendon Press, 1991), i. 358 (*Letter* 516). Hereafter Baxter, *Letter* 'n'.

2   John Cameron (c. 1580–1625) was Amyraut's mentor and predecessor at Saumur.

3   Lewis Crocius (1586–1655) was one of the 'moderate' Bremen delegates at the Synod of Dort.

4   Moïse Amyraut (1596–1664), Cameron's successor at Saumur.

5   Baxter, *Letter* 32.

6   Baxter, *Letter* 94, n.5.

7   See Hans Boersma, *A Hot Pepper Corn: Richard Baxter's Doctrine of Justification in its Seventeenth-Century Context* (Zoetermeer: Uitgeverij Boekencentrum, 1993), 26.

8   Baxter, *Letter* 148.

9   Baxter, *Letter* 225.

10   According to Baxter's late instructions, the work was eventually published posthumously by Joseph Read in 1694.

11   Daillé (1594–1670)—as a preacher, the 'French Baxter'—was a friend and former fellow student of Amyraut at Saumur, later pastor at Charenton, Paris.

asked, 'What need more than Davenant's *Dissertation* & Daillé's *Apology?*'[1]
While Baxter's Amyraldian friend John Howe (1630–1705)[2] shared Baxter's
enthusiasm for Davenant, he insisted that 'however about Redemption
Davenant and Amyraldus may have spoken many of your thoughts, yet their
books do not commonly fall into hands of young scholars (whose minds
while such are least prepossessed & almost *rasa tabula*) as yours are like to do'.[3]

Baxter and Howe were not the only seventeenth-century English admirers
of Davenant. While they were young men, Davenant's influence was felt
in the Westminster Assembly (1643–9). During the debates on redemption,
Edmund Calamy (1600–60) declared:

> I am far from universal redemption in the Arminian sense; but that that
> I hold is in the sense of our divines (e.g. Bishop Davenant) in the Synod
> of Dort, that Christ did pay a price for all ... that Jesus Christ did not
> only die sufficiently for all, but God did intend, in giving Christ, and
> Christ in giving himself, did intend to put all men in a state of salvation
> in case they do believe ...'[4]

Like Baxter and his grandfather, the Dissenting leader Dr Edmund Calamy
III (1671–1732) argued in the next century that 'the doctrine of particular
election' is consistent with 'a general love of God to the world'.[5] Allport
is careful to cite Calamy's exhortation to those who think more narrowly
to 'consult the learned and peaceable Bishop Davenant's *Animadversions
upon Hoard's Treatise*; a book not valued according to its worth'.[6] When
Gilbert Burnet, the Latitudinarian Bishop of Salisbury failed to make sense
of 'middle way' orthodoxy, Calamy was quick to point out 'that the learned
Davenant, one of his Lordship's predecessors in the See of Sarum, had not
only vigorously asserted and defended that middle way in the Synod of Dort,
in opposition to Remonstrants and Supralapsarians, but had also been at no

---

1   Baxter, *Letter* 314. Also 115, n. 1; 263n; 140, n. 4; 77, n. 3.

2   See David P. Field, *Rigide Calvinisme in a Softer Dresse: The Moderate Presbyterianism of John
Howe (1630–1705)* (Edinburgh: Rutherford House, 2004).

3   Baxter, *Letter* 436.

4   Quoted in A. F. Mitchell and J. Struthers (eds), *Minutes of the Sessions of the Westminster
Assembly of Divines* (Edinburgh: Blackwood, 1874), 152.

5   *Divine Mercy Exalted: or Free Grace in Its Glory* (London: 1703), p. iv.

6   Allport, l.

small pains to support it in several of his writings; of which his Lordship took not the least notice'.[1]

In the nineteenth century, J. C. Ryle, the first Bishop of Liverpool expressed the 'Davenant dimension' in no uncertain terms. Commenting on John 1: 29, he wrote that 'Christ's death is profitable to none but to the elect who believe on His name. ... But ... I dare not say that no atonement has been made, in any sense, except for the elect. ... When I read that the wicked who are lost, "deny the Lord that bought them," (2 Pet. 2: 1) and that "God was in Christ, reconciling the world unto himself," (2 Cor. 5: 19), I dare not confine the intention of redemption to the saints alone. Christ is for every man'. Commenting on John 3: 16 and appealing to Bishop John Davenant, Calvin and others, he concludes: 'Those who confine God's love exclusively to the elect appear to me to take a narrow and contracted view of God's character and attributes. ... I have long come to the conclusion that men may be more systematic in their statements than the Bible, and may be led into grave error by idolatrous veneration of a system'.[2]

Such a dismissal of Bezan orthodoxy is remarkable in a work published in facsimile by the Banner of Truth Trust. It directly challenges the Bezan orthodoxy of Owen's *Death of Death*. Ryle, who quotes copiously from Davenant's reply to Hoard and another pro-Amyraldian work on the *Gallican Controversy*[3] would doubtless have something to say about the deletion of Davenant's *Dissertation* from the new *Exposition of Colossians*.

Even more remarkable is a recent Banner of Truth publication about debates over the Atonement in nineteenth-century Wales.[4] An otherwise informative and valuable study, the book is published with a highly critical translator's introduction against the author's theological stance. Clearly out of sympathy with the tight 'limited atonement' orthodoxy of both translator and publisher, Owen Thomas cites at length a letter from the English delegates at the Synod of Dort to Archbishop Abbot, prefacing it with the remark

---

1   Ibid. l. See also C. G. Bolam, J. Goring, H. L. Short, R. Thomas, *The English Presbyterians: From Elizabethan Puritanism to Modern Unitarianism* (London: George Allen and Unwin, 1968), 134–5.

2   *Expository Thoughts on the Gospels: St John* (London: W. Hunt & Co., 1865), i. 61–2, 159.

3   Ibid. 159–60.

4   Owen Thomas, trans. John Aaron, *The Atonement Controversy in Welsh Theological Literature and Debate, 1701–1841* (Edinburgh: The Banner of Truth Trust, 2002).

that Drs Davenant and Ward in particular, were very decided in wishing for 'a wider interpretation' than the 'more limited view'.[1]

The author and many of his brethren were convinced that the scholastic 'Owenite' doctrine of limited atonement involved an 'unscriptural limitation'.[2] Thomas and his friends were persuaded that Article 18 of the Calvinistic Methodist *Confession of Faith* (1823) was 'wise above what is written'.[3] Indeed, this article *Of Redemption* is more 'particular' than the *Westminster Confession of Faith* equivalent. These arguments had significant effect. In 1874, the year Thomas's book was published, the General Assembly of the denomination (Carmarthen, 1874; Portmadoc, 1875) modified the interpretation of the article with an appendix stressing the universal sufficiency of the atonement.[4]

In short, the whole controversy concerned the true character of Calvinism. Despite the translator's criticisms, Owen Thomas had done his homework well. He was thoroughly aware that John Calvin and many other reformers both Continental and British did not teach the doctrine of limited atonement and that the Canons of Dort maintain a universal dimension in the atonement.[5] The first of these accurate and well-established observations is dismissed with a doubtful two-fold appeal to highly debateable studies by Robert A. Peterson and Paul Helm.[6] In all this highly biased discussion, the translator fails to perceive the integrity and accuracy of the author's case. The former's reference to 'classical Reformed teaching'[7] is question begging. By blaming 'moderate Calvinism' as 'Calvinism in decay',[8] John Aaron is effectively saying that 'Calvin's Calvinism' is dangerous!

---

1   Ibid. 124–5.

2   Ibid. 323.

3   Ibid. 323.

4   Ibid. 324.

5   Ibid. 123–4. See my *Window on Welsh Calvinism: Owen Thomas and D. Martyn Lloyd-Jones on the Atonement* (Norwich: Charenton Reformed Publishing, 2006) for selected 'Davenant dimension' citations from Augustine, John Wycliffe, Martin Luther, John Calvin, the Anglican Reformers, the Canons of Dort, John Davenant, Moïse Amyraut, William Twisse, Edmund Calamy, Richard Baxter, Philip Doddridge, Jonathan Edwards, Joseph Bellamy, Thomas Boston, Thomas Chalmers, Charles Hodge, Robert Dabney, J. C. Ryle, John Murray and D. Martyn Lloyd-Jones. These statements suggest that John Owen and his friends are 'out of step' with some of the wisest heads of the Church of Christ.

6   Ibid. 123, 6.

7   Ibid. p. xxxiii.

8   Ibid. p. xxxii.

The simple fact is that Owen Thomas and his friends saw the need to 'moderate' the 'ultra-Calvinism' of the day in order to return to a Bible-based 'Authentic Calvinism'. One may say that they sought to rescue the denomination from 'Owenistic Methodism' and to be true to correctly-defined 'Calvinistic Methodism'. In this respect, contrary to the standpoint of both translator and publisher, the author produced one of the most praise-worthy and illuminating studies in historical theology ever written. For us, it is important to note the 'Davenant dimension' in the theology of Owen Thomas. The author would doubtless welcome the Quinta Press edition of Davenant's *Dissertation*, an event which will simply reinforce and confirm his well-argued case. For us, we welcome the work with joy. Let us pray that, by the blessing of God, it will help restore 'compassionate Calvinism' to the Church of the twenty-first century and bring blessing to a desperately-needy world.

9. THE GOSPEL ACCORDING

TO MOÏSE AMYRAUT[1]

There are many who would dismiss our conference as an unwelcome and undesirable event in the Reformed Evangelical calendar. Generally dismissing Amyraldianism as a compromise between Arminianism and Calvinism, they fear a dilution and weakening of what they regard as 'orthodox' Calvinism. However, I believe that sufficient has been written within the last four decades at least to demonstrate that Amyraldian theology is both a reaffirmation of Calvin's original teaching[2] and, more importantly, a confirmation of the true message of the Word of God.[3] Yet, Amyraut continues to have a bad press. In systematic theologies and articles, his distinctive theological stance is usually misrepresented and marginalised.[4] As if the man had openly spurned the Reformation doctrine of Justification by Faith,[5] he is—in some circles at least—having difficulty in shaking off the unflattering epithet of 'the grave digger of the French Reformed Church',[6] a charge repeated as recently as 2003.[7]

---

1 'A Quick Look at Amyraut', a paper given at the 4th Amyraldian Association Conference held at Attleborough, Norfolk on 5 April 2006.

2 See especially Brian G. Armstrong, *Calvinism and the Amyraut Heresy: Protestant Scholasticism and Humanism in Seventeenth-Century France* (Madison: University of Wisconsin Press, 1969); see also further bibliographical data and argument in my *Calvinus* (Norwich: Charenton Reformed Publishing, 1996) and *Amyraut Affirmed* (Norwich: Charenton Reformed Publishing, 2004).

3 For a recent summary, see Paul T. Nimmo & David A. S. Ferguson, *Reformed Theology* (Cambridge: CUP, 2016), 52–3.

4 See L. Berkhof, *Systematic Theology* (London: The Banner of Truth Trust, 1958), 394 and R. L. Reymond, *New Systematic Theology of the Christian Faith* (Nashville: Thomas Nelson, 1998), 475–9. I have responded to these 'standard' dismissals in several publications (see note 2).

5 See Amyraut's concurrence with Calvin on this subject in Armstrong, 222ff.

6 See my refutation of this absurd accusation in *Calvinus*, 16 and *Amyraut Affirmed*, 52.

7 See Ian Hamilton, *Amyraldianism—is it modified Calvinism?* (Worcester: Evangelical Presbyterian Church in England and Wales, 2003), 26.

For the vast majority of students of church history and Christian biography, the Huguenot Amyraut (1596–1664) is an unknown figure compared with someone like his near-contemporary, the Puritan Richard Baxter (1615–91). Yet within a British historical context, Richard Baxter is generally regarded as the chief exponent of Amyraldianism. Even though, at one time, Baxter's doctrinal distinctives were identified as 'Baxterianism',[1] he tends to be styled as an 'Amyraldian'. Who then is the Frenchman whose teaching gave our English Baxter his theological identity? As we all should know, the Puritan is far from being a shadowy figure. His extraordinary ministry in seventeenth-century Kidderminster is celebrated by an appropriate local statue; his nationwide influence was diffused by such still-gripping page turners as *The Saints' Everlasting Rest* and *Call to the Unconverted;* and his lovely hymn 'Ye holy angels bright' is still enjoyed by modern worshippers. Neither must we ignore that his colourful and dramatic life is recorded in his autobiography with its exotic Latin title *Reliquiae Baxterianae.* Lastly, Baxter made a further mark on English church history by his courageous stand before the infamous Judge Jeffreys in 1685.

Turning to Moïse Amyraut, while he had an effective pastoral ministry, he never quite turned Saumur upside down, and this charming town in the Loire Valley exhibits no statue to commemorate him. Although he wrote a series of highly-significant theological works, he wrote no devotional or evangelistic classic, neither is a little-known hymn ever sung. Lastly, no *Reliquiae Amyraldianae* exists to perpetuate his memory. Our ignorance is chiefly due more to prejudice than the language and culture barrier, more formidable perhaps to overcome than the geological problems faced by the builders of the Channel Tunnel. On top of the 'foreign' nature of some features of French culture is French religion in general and that of Huguenot history in particular. This is where an almost unknown Englishman comes to our aid. I refer to a certain John Quick, the mere mention of whose name should explain the wording of my title. In short, my paper is not a ten-minute *hors d'oeuvre!*

My known passionate affinities with the Huguenots are due neither to Francophilia as such nor to French Protestant ancestry. For all that my roots are English, my interests are self-consciously spiritual and theological. If

---

1   See G. F. Nuttall, *Richard Baxter and Philip Doddridge: a Study in a Tradition* (London: Dr Williams's Library, 1954).

any precedents are needed for my enthusiasm, I would cite such English nineteenth-century writers as Samuel Smiles[1] and Richard Heath[2] if not the American historian Henry Baird (probably of Scottish descent). All these authors wrote significant accounts of the Huguenots, especially the latter whose comprehensive six-volume history was published between 1880 and 1895.[3] However, I feel a close affinity with the aforementioned English Presbyterian minister John Quick (1636–1706), the tercentenary of whose death falls later this month. This persecuted puritan was the first writer to chronicle and document the Huguenot epic for English readers in an extensive manner.[4] Being both a personally-acquainted commentator on their affairs and a participant in the struggles of English Nonconformity, Quick is a literary 'link man' and part of the broader story at the same time. So, before we take a look at Quick's look at Amyraut, it is necessary to take a 'quick look at Quick'![5]

The reason for John Quick's inclusion in our story will be apparent from a sketch of his little-known life. He was born at Plymouth in 1636. After graduating at Oxford in 1657 he was ordained at Ermington in Devon in 1659. Along with his illustrious puritan brethren—a more famous contemporary John Flavel (1628–91) ministered at nearby Dartmouth, Quick exercised a faithful and courageous ministry. He served at Kingsbridge with Churchstow and then at Brixton near Plymouth. Undeterred by the Act of Uniformity (1662), he continued to preach. He was arrested during the Lord's Day morning worship on 13 December 1663 and imprisoned at Exeter. At his trial, Quick was nearly acquitted on a technicality. However, since he refused to give up preaching, he was sent to prison. After suffering for a further eight weeks, he was liberated by Sir Matthew Hale. The Bishop of Exeter, Seth

---

1 See *The Huguenots—their settlements, churches, and industries in England and Ireland* (London: John Murray, 1880) and *The Huguenots in France after the Revocation of the Edict of Nantes* (London: Daldy, Isbister & Co., 1875).

2 *The Reformation in France* (London: The Religious Tract Society, 1886), 2 Vols.

3 See *History of the Rise of the Huguenots* (London: Hodder & Stoughton, 1880), 2 Vols; *The Huguenots and Henry of Narvarre* (London: Hodder & Stoughton, 1886), 2 Vols; *The Huguenots and the Revocation of the Edict of Nantes* (London: Hodder & Stoughton, 1895), 2 Vols.

4 In his otherwise excellent study, *Huguenot Heritage: The history and contribution of the Huguenots in Britain* (London: Routledge, 1985), Robin D. Gwyn makes no reference to John Quick.

5 The following material including a portrait may be found in my *Calvin Celebrated: The Genevan Reformer & His Huguenot Sons* (Norwich: Charenton Reformed Publishing, 2009), 52ff.

Ward then prosecuted Quick for preaching to the prisoners but the Lord's servant was acquitted, his unashamed 'guilt' notwithstanding!

King Charles II's indulgence of 1672 brought a brief respite for the persecuted puritan brotherhood. Quick was licensed to preach at Plymouth. When restrictions were imposed again the following year, he was imprisoned for three months with other nonconformists at the Marshalsea prison in Plymouth. On his release, Quick left the west of England for London. He then travelled to the Netherlands where he became a minister to the English church at Middleburg in 1679. Returning to London two years later, Quick gathered a Presbyterian congregation in a small meeting house in Middlesex Court, Bartholomew Close, Smithfield. On the eve of less troubled times, his London ministry—'successful to the conversion of many', said Dr Edmund Calamy—was relatively undisturbed. The 'Glorious Revolution' (1688) and the Toleration Act (1689) eventually brought persecution to an end. Known as a 'serious, good preacher' with a 'great facility and freedom in prayer', John Quick continued to serve his people faithfully until his death on 29 April 1706. He was buried in the Dissenters' burial ground at Bunhill Fields. His wife Elizabeth died in 1708. Their only daughter became the wife of Dr John Evans (1680?–1730) who completed the commentary on the Epistle to the Romans in Matthew Henry's immortal *Exposition.*

During his early ministry and subsequently, Quick became acquainted with the Huguenot refugees, some of whom landed at his native Plymouth from La Rochelle in 1681—the year the dreadful 'dragonnades' began. Accordingly, wrote Calamy, Quick 'was very compassionate to those in distress; at a great deal of pains and expense for the relief of the poor French Protestants, and his house and purse were almost ever open to them. He was a perfect master of their language, and had a peculiar respect for their churches, upon the account of their sound doctrine and useful discipline, and the noble testimony which they bore to religion by their sufferings'.

Consistent with his personal courage and pastoral gifts, John Quick combined scholarship with zeal for the truth. The blending of these qualities explains his authorship of a work of major Huguenot interest, the *Synodicon in Gallia Reformata.* This pair of fascinating folios was published in 1692. The work chiefly consists of the proceedings of all the National synods—twenty-nine in all—of the French Reformed Churches from the first held at Paris in 1559 to the last permitted by Louis XIV at Loudun in 1659. Besides an historical introduction, Quick included the Confession of Faith and Discipline of the Reformed Churches together with the Edict of Nantes (1598) and the Edict of Fontainebleau (1685) commonly known as the 'Revocation of the Edict of Nantes'. Pope Innocent XI's congratulatory letter to the French king is also included along with an account of the dreadful persecution of the immediate post-revocation period. The author's title-page claim—'A work never before extant in any language'—is noteworthy. A French 'edition' was later published at the Hague in 1710 by Jean Aymon. Unlike Aymon, Quick had direct access to original manuscript material borrowed from Huguenot refugees which he then collated and translated. Aymon then re-translated Quick's work back into French—which explains his repetition of some of Quick's inaccuracies! The *Synodicon* remains therefore a primary English source for Huguenot information during the early modern period.

Quick's interest in the Huguenots did not end with the *Synodicon*. Besides a few published sermons of his own, he also prepared for publication a selection of fifty brief—some quite lengthy—biographies of eminent pastors, theologians and martyrs of the French Reformed churches, the *Icones Sacrae Gallicanae*. He also produced a similar selection of twenty Puritans, the *Icones Sacrae Anglicanae*. These ambitious ventures failed with the death in 1700 of William Russell, Duke of Bedford (the dedicatee of the *Synodicon)* who had offered to finance the project. Advancing illness also prevented Quick from collecting subscriptions for the work. Following the author's death, the manuscript volumes were eventually deposited at what is now known as Dr Williams's Library. There they remain in their unpublished state although, since the originals decayed with time, a transcription was made of them in the nineteenth century by the Revd Hugh Hutton, MA, minister of Churchgate Presbyterian Church, Bury St Edmunds. The work took three years (1862–5), for which the then princely sum of £150 was paid!

This brings us to the thirty-fifth of Quick's fifty Huguenot biographies or *Icones*: 'The Life of Mons[r]. Amyraut, Pastor and professor in the Church and University of Saumur'. Interestingly, in the two major studies of Amyraut during the last fifty years by Dr Brian G. Armstrong[1] and Dr Frans Pieter van Stam,[2] this work was neglected. While Quick's *Synodicon* is frequently cited, his *Icones Sacrae Gallicanae* are ignored.[3] However, biographical information is

---

1   See Armstrong, *Calvinism.*

2   *The Controversy over the Theology of Saumur, 1635–1650: Disrupting Debates among the Huguenots in Complicated Circumstances* (Amsterdam & Maarsen: APA–Holland University Press, 1988).

3   Armstrong was aware of the work (see 292) but he neither quotes it nor cites it in his

cited from Pierre Bayle's *Dictionnaire historique et critique* (1696),[1] described by Armstrong as 'an under-valued and under-used source containing much that is still important and not readily accessible elsewhere'.[2] For information about Amyraut, Bayle states that his source was 'the memoirs communicated by M. Amyraut the son', a source also used by Quick. However, the latter's biography includes more personal features than Bayle revealed in his *Dictionnaire*. These generally unknown 'personal features' are a vital part of this presentation of Amyraut's life.

His ancestors coming originally from Alsace and later Orleans, Moïse Amyraut was born in September 1596 at Bourgueil in Anjou, a small town in the Loire Valley 40 km west of Tour. Provided an education in the humanities, his father sent him to study law at the university of Poitiers. Proving himself a diligent student working daily for 14 hours, Moïse graduated Licentiate after a year. Travelling home via Saumur, he visited M. Bouchereau, pastor of the Reformed Church, who recognised the young man's extraordinary abilities and piety. Being introduced to the Governor of Saumur, the famous Huguenot soldier-statesman and scholar The Lord Philippe du Plessis-Mornay, young Moïse was encouraged to abandon law and study theology. At first reluctant, his father agreed with the advice given. Studying other works by Tully, Demosthenes and Aristotle, Moïse felt drawn to theology and the Christian ministry through reading John Calvin's *Institutes of the Christian Religion*. He was admitted to the Reformed Academy at Saumur, founded by Lord du Plessis-Mornay in 1599. Moïse thus came under the influence of the Scottish theologian John Cameron (c. 1580–1625) who served as Professor of Theology from 1618–21. Cameron had a profound influence on Moïse who became his most famous pupil. Succeeding the Dutch Francis Gomarus at Saumur, Cameron challenged the ultra-orthodox theology of Calvin's successor Theodore Beza. Restless and outspoken, he became known as 'Bezae mastyx' or 'Beza's scourge'. Effectively signalling a return to the balanced biblicism of Calvin, Amyraut embraced and developed Cameron's 'authentic Calvinism', a *via media* between Arminianism and Bezaism. Such

---

bibliography (at 300). For Quick's *Icone* of Amyraut at Dr Williams's Library, see DWL 6, 38–39 (35).

1   See English translation: *The Dictionary Historical and Critical of Mr Peter Bayle* (London: 1734). References to the article on Amyraut in Volume 1 hereafter cited as 'Bayle'.

2   *Calvinism and the Amyraut Heresy*, 300. For Bayle, see Elizabeth Labrousse, *Bayle* (Oxford: OUP, 1983).

was Amyraut's admiration for Cameron that he imitated his gestures and even spoke French with a Scottish accent![1]

Little information is available about Amyraut for the years 1618–26. However, in 1626, he was called to succeed his life-long friend and former fellow student Jean Daillé as pastor at Saumur. Having commenced his ministry in the town in 1625, Daillé—the future preacher *par excellence*—was called to the great Reformed Temple at Charenton near Paris where he exercised a powerful and influential ministry until his death in 1670.[2] Having authored his first major publication *A Treatise Concerning Religions* (1631),[3] Amyraut was appointed as theology professor in the Academy in 1631. He joined the learned Hebraist Louis Capell and fellow theologian Josué de la Place[4] on the faculty. All three being disciples of Cameron, they exhibited a remarkable harmony 'as is rarely to be met with in academic land' says Bayle[5]. Writing more quaintly, Quick states that 'it was commonly said of them, that their three heads were covered with one bonnet, i.e. with one and the same nightcap'.[6]

Before we proceed, it is important to remember the religious and political context in which the Huguenots lived.[7] While they were a sizeable and significant minority, their liberties within Roman Catholic France were defined by the Edict of Nantes, granted during the reign of Henri IV in 1598.

---

1 Bayle, ii. 288–9.

2 For Daillé, see Bayle, ii. 580ff; Quick, *Icones*, 39; also my *Calvin Celebrated: The Genevan Reformer & His Huguenot Sons* (Norwich: Charenton Reformed Publishing, 2009), 8ff.

3 *Traitté des religions contre ceux qui les estiment toutes indifferentes* (Saumur: Girard & de Lerpiniere, 1631); English translation full title: *A Treatise Concerning Religions, in Refutation of the Opinion which accounts all indifferent, wherein is also evinced the necessity of a Particular Revelation, And the Verity and preeminence of the Christian Religion above the Pagan, Mahometan, and Jewish rationally Demonstrated* (London: 1660). See also David Llewellyn Jenkins, 'Amyraut on other Religions' in *Christ for the World*, Amyraldian Association Conference Report (Norwich: Charenton Reformed Publishing, 2007), 44–91.

4 See David Llewellyn Jenkins, *Saumur Redux: Josué de la Place & the Question of Adam's Sin* (Harleston, Norfolk: Leaping Cat Press, 2008).

5 Bayle, 261.

6 *Icones*, 962.

7 For a modern study, see Geoffrey Treasure, *The Huguenots* (New Haven and London: Yale University Press, 2013); also Mack P. Holt, ed., *Renaissance and Reformation in France* (Oxford: OUP, 2002); see also H. O. Wakeman, *The Ascendancy of France, 1598–1715* (London: Rivingtons, 1959); for an earlier useful overview, see A. J. Grant, *The Huguenots* (London: Thornton Butterworth/ Oxford: OUP, 1934).

After decades of religious conflict, the Edict guaranteed a degree of religious freedom and other public privileges. However, due to constant intrigue by the Jesuits and other Roman Catholic conservatives, the position of the Huguenots still made them vulnerable. As 'second class citizens', they enjoyed a fragile and frequently-violated peace. To practise the Reformed religion always demanded a combination of courage and wisdom. Throughout their public lives and ministries, the Huguenot pastors generally proved exemplary in this respect. It was during the National Synod of Charenton (1631) that Amyraut made his initial mark. Contrary to earlier custom, the Reformed delegates from the previous National Synod of Castres (1626) presented their complaints and grievances over violations of the Edict of Nantes before King Louis XIII *on their knees*. Determined to honour the King yet maintain their privileges as servants of Christ, Amyraut insisted that he would address His Majesty *standing*. Thus commissioned by the Synod, so he did. In fact, so impressive was Amyraut's demeanour in the whole matter, his courage, manners and integrity won him the esteem of Cardinal Richelieu.

Amyraut is chiefly remembered for setting the cat among the pigeons over the theology of predestination. When a Roman Catholic nobleman—otherwise sympathetic to the Reformed Faith—expressed doubts about what he perceived to be Calvin's teaching, Amyraut responded with his first work on the subject. However, his *Brief Treatise on Predestination* (1634)[1] aroused the wrath of the Reformed world when he expounded a position on election, the extent of the atonement and 'universal grace' at odds with accepted wisdom. Starting what Bayle described as a 'kind of civil war among the Protestant divines of France',[2] it soon became clear that Amyraut—heavily influenced by Calvin—was pursuing a very different theological agenda from 'orthodox' theologians like the 'French John Owen' Pierre du Moulin, but one that was not exposed to many of the *biblical* objections raised by many then and subsequently.

Rooted in a dualistic conception of the divine will (see *Deuteronomy 29: 29*), Calvin taught that Christ was offered as the Redeemer of the whole world according to God's 'revealed' conditional will albeit only received by elected believers according to God's 'hidden' absolute will. Notwithstanding the rationally-challenging paradox involved, Calvin maintained the doctrines of

---

1   *Brief Traitté de la predestination et de ses principales dependences* (Saumur: Isaac Desbordes, 1634).
2   Bayle, 261.

universal atonement and divine election side by side. Faced by clear biblical evidence for both, he refused to tamper with the scriptural texts. Logic was not allowed to dictate one emphasis at the expense of the other. Typical of his numerous statements on the extent of the atonement, Calvin commented thus on Romans 5: 18: 'Paul makes grace common to all, not because it in fact extends to all, but because it is offered to all. Although Christ suffered for the sins of the world, and is offered by the goodness of God without distinction to all men, yet not all receive him'.[1]

Unhappy with this kind of dualism, Calvin's rationalistic successor Theodore Beza deleted the 'universal' aspect of Calvin's scheme in favour of limited atonement, which in turn provoked the equally-rationalistic Jakob Arminius to delete the 'particular' aspect of Calvin's scheme in favour of conditional election. Unimpressed by either of the two deviants, Amyraut was persuaded that Calvin's original position alone possessed biblical integrity. For him, the only option was Calvin's 'authentic Calvinism'. Amyraut also insisted that Calvin's view, with its unique 'mind and heart-set', had enormous pastoral and evangelistic advantages. Roger Nicole admits that Calvin's comment on Romans 5: 18 'comes perhaps closest to providing support for Amyraut's thesis'.[2] Even Richard Muller admits that 'Calvin's teaching was ... capable of being cited with significant effect by Moïse Amyraut against his Reformed opponents'.[3] According to Dr van Stam, at a time when Bezan ultra-orthodoxy had replaced Calvin's balanced biblicism, 'Amyraut ... revealed the attraction which the theology of Calvin held for him. He demonstrated this preference in an array of books, in the process proving his familiarity with the writings of this reformer. ... Amyraut rediscovered Calvin, as it were, and was perhaps the Calvin-expert of the day. In any case, Amyraut fell under the spell of Calvin's theology'.[4] Thus historian Philip Benedict—who incorrectly imagines the Canons of the Synod of Dort (1618–19) to represent a *higher* orthodoxy than is the case—recognises

---

1   *Comment* on Romans 5: 18.

2   Dr Nicole flies in the face of the obvious when he adds: 'it may well refer simply to the relevance of the sacrifice of Christ to a universal offer, without actually asserting a substitutionary suffering for all mankind' (*Moyse Amyraut (1596–1664) and the Controversy on Universal Grace* (Harvard University thesis, 1966), 83, n. 38).

3   *The Unaccommodated Calvin* (Oxford: OUP, 2000), 62

4   *The Controversy over the Theology of Saumur* (Amsterdam & Maarssen: APA–Holland University Press 1988), 431.

Amyraut's position in France accurately when he says that 'the theologians of the Academy of Saumur ... consciously opposed Beza and appealed to Calvin instead. ... In effect they reversed the steps that had been taken in the passage from Calvin to Calvinism'.[1]

Amyraut's impeccable *authentic* Calvinist orthodoxy did not shield him from the charge of Arminianising heresy, even though he claimed an orthodoxy consistent with the Canons of Dort. He—with his fellow pastor Paul Testard of Blois who had also published a similarly 'heretical' piece—was tried and acquitted at the National Synod of Alençon (1637). The controversy was to rumble on for decades, not only in France but throughout Europe and beyond. Even today, ultra-orthodox blood pressure is often raised when anyone dares to defend and expound the tenets of Moïse Amyraut. Sadly, for most students of French church history, knowledge of Amyraut is confined to his theological notoriety. Since these theological issues are discussed in depth elsewhere, we will continue to explore the less-familiar features of Amyraut's life.

Returning home from the Synod of Alençon, all Saumur rejoiced at Amyraut's acquittal. The Academy flourished for many years with many students attending from all parts of France and beyond. Indeed, the Saumur Academy became the premier institution of its kind. Amyraut's personal reputation grew with the years, not least among the Roman Catholics. As we have noted, the King's chief minister Cardinal Richelieu greatly admired him.

What is striking is the way Amyraut maintained his Reformed convictions without compromise. Surrounded as the Reformed community in France was by a large and not always benign Roman Catholic majority, tensions were not always easy to handle, even during the 'golden years' (1629–61).[2] However, in the true spirit of the Gospel, Amyraut avoided the extremes of social hostility and a servile ecumenism. He demonstrated this when, to ingratiate himself at Rome, the Cardinal advanced a scheme to unite the Roman and Reformed communions in France. He commissioned the Jesuit Father Audebert to sound out the Reformed pastors. Intending to engage in talks with Amyraut, the Jesuit visited Saumur. Brought together by the King's Lieutenant, M. Villeneuve, Father Audebert soon discovered that Amyraut

---

1   *The Faith and Fortunes of France's Huguenots, 1600–85* (Aldershot: Ashgate, 2001), 227.

2   See Menna Prestwich, 'The Huguenots under Richelieu and Mazarin, 1629–61: A Golden Age?' in Irene Scouloudi, ed., *Huguenots in Britain and their French Background, 1550–1800* (London: Macmillan Press, 1987).

was quite inflexible. Regarding unity, the latter declared 'That this was a thing more to be wished than hoped for; that the opinions of both were so opposite that there was no probability nor possibility of concerting and adjusting them'.[1] When the Jesuit indicated that the Roman Catholics were ready to abandon the invocation of saints, the merit of good works, purgatory and papal supremacy, Amyraut was not to be taken in. These concessions were too few if they did not include the doctrine of the real presence in the Mass. At this point the Romanist refused to yield. Amyraut concluded the discussion insisting that without this, any unity was 'mere vanity'.[2]

Doctrinal debate over the doctrines of grace involved Amyraut in further controversy in the 1640s. When the English Arminian Samuel Hoard, Rector of Morton in Essex published an attack on predestination,[3] the impact of the work was also felt in France. Just as the English 'proto-Amyraldian' John Davenant replied to Hoard, so did Amyraut. It is fascinating to discover that both authors did not refute Hoard from a *Bezan* perspective.[4] They were conscious of doing so as 'authentic Calvinists'.[5] Amyraut could not have been more explicit in calling his reply *A Defence of the Doctrine of Calvin*.[6] Armstrong states that in this work, 'Amyraut clearly identifies his own teaching with that of Calvin. Of all his writings, this is the most important in demonstrating the distinctives of Amyraldianism as compared to the scholastic orientation of the orthodox'.[7] Persisting in the same stance that produced the heresy trial at Alençon in 1637, it was inevitable that Amyraut's critics would try to make more trouble for him at the next National Synod at Charenton in

---

1   *Icones*, 970.

2   Ibid. 970–1.

3   *God's Love to Mankind, manifested by disproving his absolute Decree for their Damnation* (London: 1633).

4   See my introduction to the Quinta Press edition of John Davenant's, *A Dissertation on the Death of Christ* (Weston Rhyn: Quinta Press, 2006).

5   See *Animadversions written by the Right Rev. Father in God, John, Lord Bishop of Salisbury, upon a treatise intituled, God's Love to Mankind* (Cambridge: 1641), 142.

6   Published first in Latin as *Defensio doctrinae J. Calvini de absoluto reprobationis decreto* (Saumur, 1641), the work appeared three years later in French as *Defense de la doctrine de Calvin* (Saumur: Isaac Desbordes, 1644).

7   *Calvinism and the Amyraut Heresy*, 99–100. For an Amyraut bibliography, see Armstrong, 290–8. Archbishop Marsh's Library in Dublin 'contains the largest single collection of the writings of Moyse Amyraut' (*Marsh's Library 1701–2001 Exhibition Catalogue* (Dublin: 2001), 154).

1644–5. As before, all attempts to discredit him proved fruitless.[1] Doubtless influenced by Amyraut's criticisms of Islam in his first major work,[2] this synod drew up a liturgy for receiving converted Muslims into membership of the Reformed Churches.[3]

This synod provides us with a glimpse of Amyraut's magnanimous nature when he defended his Saumur colleague Josué de la Place's views over the doctrine of imputed guilt. Properly speaking, Amyraut defended his friend's right to hold such a view (which again can claim some degree of precedent in Calvin!) even though he did not share it. He simply did not consider it sufficiently fundamental to dispute about publicly, and his eloquence won the day.

More important to his ongoing ministry among the churches, Amyraut was asked to write a 'paraphrase or commentary' on the Bible. He commenced this in 1644 with his commentary on Romans. Eventually he covered all the epistles, the Acts of the Apostles and the Gospel of John. He died before attempting a harmony of the Gospels. Like Calvin, he declined to do anything on the Book of Revelation.[4]

Personal tragedy hit the Amyrauts in 1645 when their only daughter died at the age of nineteen. To comfort his distressed wife, Amyraut wrote his *Treatise on the State of Believers after Death*.[5] Not initially intended for publication, it was only printed when others, impressed by the therapeutic quality of the work, urged him to do so. Published in 1646, it was translated into English and German. In this work, Amyraut the theologian was also Amyraut the pastor. Combining faithful exegesis with deep sympathy, he was able to minister effectively to the bereaved.

Amyraut was remarkable for the way he combined academic concerns and pastoral compassion. Many besides his students sought his wise solutions to their intellectual and personal perplexities. The Roman Catholics of Saumur knew that when students of their college had disputes with those of the Reformed Academy, they could rely on Amyraut to be reliable umpire. He was famous for his philanthropy to the poor, irrespective of religious

---

1   See Quick, *Synodicon*, ii. 455.

2   See Amyraut, *Traitté des religions*.

3   See Quick, *Synodicon*, ii. 449.

4   Quick, *Icones*, 976.

5   *Discours de l'estat des fideles apres la mort* (Saumur: Jean Lesnier, 1646); tr: *The Evidence of things not seen, or Diverse … Discourses Concerning the State of Good and Holy Men after Death* (London, n. d.).

affiliation. When the local monastery was burned down, the friars asked him to approach M. Hervart, the King's Controller of Revenue—who happened to be a Reformed man—to help with rebuilding costs. Quick tells us that 'the begging friars would be sure to knock at his doors, for they never missed of a good alms, their knapsacks being well filled. And he would tell them pleasantly, that he gave them candles that they might read more and study better'.[1]

Quick provides a challenging and beautiful picture of Amyraut the model pastor:

The poor of both religions loved and reverenced him as their common father, for he distributed his charity indifferently among them all. But yet he had a most particular concern for the sick, and how many and urgent so ever his businesses were, they should never dispense with him from visiting them on their beds of languishing, and administering spiritual physic, counsels and comforts suitable to their conditions and inward circumstances. He evaded not this office and service of love, neither for the sultry heats of the day, nor for the storms and bitter colds of the night. He hath quitted his own bed and repose to console dying persons'.[2]

As we discover the gracious character of Moïse Amyraut, it is important to repeat that he always maintained his Reformed convictions without compromise. For him, a compassionate heart and a sound head were not—as is often the case today—mutually exclusive. He proved this in June 1646 when, by order of the Privy Council, during the Roman Catholic Festival of Corpus Christi,[3] the Reformed families of Saumur were ordered to hang tapestries from their balconies as the idolatrous procession passed along the streets of the town. For Amyraut, this situation was a test case for Reformed fidelity. Responding to the instruction of the Seneschal—the chief judge of the city—that Amyraut should direct the Protestant people to obey the order, we see evidence of old-fashioned Calvinist courage. Quick's account reveals something of the drama and tension involved:

[Amyraut] had indeed always preached up subjection unto the higher

---

1 *Icones*, 977.
2 Ibid. 978.
3 Falling on the first Thursday after Trinity Sunday, the festival involved a colourful and pompous procession led by priests carrying what Quick calls 'their breaden God' consecrated in the Mass.

powers, but then it was in those matters in which conscience was not interested nor concerned, that he was so far from exhorting his flock to yield obedience in this case, that he would go immediately unto every house of the Reformed, and particularly charge them not in the least to obey this wicked order, nor in any wise to yield the least consent unto it, whatever they might suffer for it. And that he would be the first to give them an example and pattern of steadfastness and constancy, and patience in their religion. What he said he did. M. Amyraut was as good as his word. For he was not a reed shaken with the wind; but fixed and immovable in his holy purpose and resolutions as a rock. He therefore quits the High Priest's Hall, the Seneschal's house, and goes from house to house, admonishing and warning all his flock not to have to do in any wise with this idolatry. God's glory and the everlasting salvation of their precious souls were now at stake. They should quit themselves as men, as the ancient saints of God had done before them, rather suffer than sin, burn in the furnace than bow the knee to the King's golden image or impious decree.[1]

Such was the example of one decried as 'the grave digger of the French Reformed Church'!

The Corpus Christi episode illustrates the dilemma constantly facing the Huguenots. In their obedience to the Word of God, they always sought to 'Fear God' and 'Honour the King' (1 Peter 2: 17). In matters not involving religious conformity they endeavoured to be model subjects. Thus far they were happy to be 'politically correct'. However, should the King command anything contrary to their consciences as Reformed Christians, Peter's bold stand was theirs also: 'We ought to obey God rather than men' (Acts 5: 29). As Amyraut's behaviour made clear, the Huguenot was guided by 'Christian correctness', a stance which in no way could properly be construed as 'revolutionary'. Such was the influential teaching expounded in the final chapter of John Calvin's Institutes. While leaving room for the legitimacy of 'popular magistrates' in their public capacity to 'curb the tyranny of kings',[2] the duty of private Christians is to 'prove our obedience to them, whether

---

1   Icones, 978–80.
2   Institutes, IV. xx. 31.

in complying with edicts, or in paying tribute'[1] and cooperating in other civil matters.

Faced by royal tyranny, 'private men' must recognise that while 'the Lord takes vengeance on unbridled domination', our obligation is to 'obey and suffer'.[2] A faithful exegete of the Word of God, Calvin clearly had a high view of kingship. Citing 1 Peter 2: 17 and Proverbs 24: 21, he states that 'under the term honour, [the Apostle Peter] includes a sincere and candid esteem, and [Solomon], by joining the king with God, shows that he is invested with a kind of sacred veneration and dignity'.[3] Even when rulers are unjust, 'this feeling of reverence, and even of piety, we owe to the utmost of our rulers, be their characters what they may'.[4] This teaching explains why, after the execution of King Charles I in 1649, Huguenots like Amyraut distanced themselves from the English Puritan regicides. Agreeing with Calvin, Amyraut published his treatise *The Sovereignty of Kings* in 1650.[5] At a time when the political heritage of the United Kingdom is fast becoming an 'anything-goes' 'PC' democratic tyranny, no less hostile to Christians than the monarchical tyrannies of old, the teaching of Calvin and Amyraut is worthy of sober reflection today. Surely, the ultimate issue is not 'monarchy *versus* democracy' but the value consensus shared by both the governors and the governed within society, whatever theory of government operates at any one time.

Because of the religious affinities between the Huguenots and the Puritans (especially the Presbyterians), the English civil war created problems in France. Reformed believers were suspected of fomenting revolution against established order. Unlike England, France had already endured the sixteenth-century wars of religion, and, for Amyraut and his generation, the terrible siege of La Rochelle (1627–8) in which Cardinal Richelieu crushed Protestant political power in France forever, was very recent history. In another work, *An Apology for those of the Reformed Religion*,[6] Amyraut took the view that for all that was noble in Huguenot resistance to royal tyranny, just religious grievances were too often mixed up with dubious politics.

---

1 Ibid. IV. xx. 23.
2 Ibid. IV. xx. 31.
3 Ibid. IV. xx. 22.
4 Ibid. IV. xx. 29.
5 *Discours sur la souveraineté des rois* (Charenton: L. Vendosme, 1650).
6 *Apologie pour ceux de la Religion Reformeé* (Saumur: Isaac Desbordes, 1647).

These issues were brought into sharp focus during the civil disturbances in France known as the War of the Fronde (1648–53). Succeeding Cardinal Richelieu on his death in 1642 (and Louis XIII died the following year), Cardinal Mazarin's unpopular rule was challenged by the Paris Parlement which sought to limit royal power during the minority of Louis XIV. The revolt being suppressed by the Duke of Condé, he himself led a rebellion in 1650 which ended three years later. The entire conflict was civil rather than religious, being doubtless influenced by events in England. So when Condé used his protestant ancestry to gain Huguenot support in 1651, he was disappointed. Amyraut and his brethren preached obedience to the young King. Their allegiance was considered decisive. Count Harcourt summed up the situation when he declared to the deputies of Montauban, "The crown was tottering on the King's head, but you have steadied it."[1]

Returning from banishment, Cardinal Mazarin was no less grateful to the 'little flock'.[2] In 1652, Louis expressed appreciation for Huguenot support: "Our subjects aforesaid of the Pretended Reformed Religion have afforded us sure proofs of their affection and faithfulness, ... wherewith we are much pleased."[3] The King also promised to guarantee the Huguenot privileges provided in the Edict of Nantes. Thus the Huguenots rejoiced. Unlike the English Puritans, they had few misgivings about royalty. At that time, there was no reason to suspect that young Louis would one day become a monster persecutor. However, from 1656 onwards, Louis began to exhibit signs of a change of heart, an intolerant 'absolutist' disposition which eventually led to the terrible Dragonnades of 1681 and Revocation of the Edict of Nantes in 1685.

Amyraut became closely involved with the events of these tumultuous times. In January 1651, the Royal Court came to Saumur. According to custom, there was great pressure on the Reformed community to alter their weekly worship routine during the first three days of the royal visit. Amyraut was prepared to be accommodating on the understanding that their normal Lord's Day services would take place as usual. John Quick provides a fascinating account of what happened next:

---

1   Henry M. Baird, *The Huguenots and the Revocation of the Edict of Nantes* (London: Hodder & Stoughton, 1895), i. 395.

2   Ibid.

3   Ibid. 397.

The King came to Saumur the Monday night, and there was no sermon on Wednesday, but on the next Lord's Day the whole service was performed as usual. M. Amyraut preached in the afternoon. The King was just then got into his majority [actually his fourteenth year], and together with several young Lords walked out onto the tennis court, which was near adjoining unto the Temple of the Reformed. The Protestants were then singing the Psalm. The King being a perfect stranger to this action and melody demanded the meaning of it. Somebody answered it was part of the religious worship of the Huguenots. "Let's go in," said the King, "and see what they are doing." But some great ones then about him obstructed his resolution, and conducted him to his sports and divertisements.

One wonders what might have transpired in the soul of young Louis XIV had he come under the ministry of M. Amyraut. Quick continues:

Whilst the King was engaged in his play, some of the courtiers had the curiosity to get into the Temple, and the patience to tarry out the whole sermon. M. Amyraut preached upon those words of St Peter, 'Fear God. Honour the King' [1 Peter 2: 17]. When the action was ended, they declared their great satisfaction one unto the other, and commended the preacher highly, as a man of singular merit and eloquence. They went directly from the Temple to the racket court, and acquainted His Majesty with that excellent discourse of the Huguenot minister; yea and at night when Her Majesty [the Queen Mother] sat at table she was recreated with the punctual relation of it.[1]

Surprise at Amyraut's preaching is not difficult to explain. Roman Catholic propaganda created the impression that the Huguenots were a perpetual threat to church and state. Confronted by the reality of Huguenot piety, those in a position to judge for themselves were able to draw a different conclusion.

Arriving at Saumur the following week, even Cardinal Mazarin heard about the sermon and wanted to meet the preacher. Meeting at the Cardinal's lodgings, the two men sat by the fire and talked. When Amyraut assured Mazarin of Huguenot support for the King, the Cardinal was surprised and charmed at the manners and wisdom of the Reformed Pastor. A day or two later, while the King was on a hunting trip, the Cardinal visited the

---

1 Quick, *Icones*, 987.

nearby Abbey of St Bennet. On returning from his walk, which provided a panoramic view of Saumur, he asked his host the Count of Comminges where the Reformed Academy was. Pointing it out in the distance, the Cardinal wished to call on Amyraut. Welcomed at the college gate, he was invited to inspect the library. They discussed the Edict of Nantes and the perpetual obligation of the Kings of France to honour it. News of this encounter was the talk of the town. Many were asking what the Cardinal and the Professor discussed. They did not discuss theological differences on this occasion, as Amyraut later made clear. The Count of Guilaut said to the Queen Mother that had they discussed religion, the Cardinal would have more than met his match in M. Amyraut.[1]

Clearly, the Court and the Cardinal were impressed by the piety, learning and integrity of Amyraut. However, while they could not dismiss the Reformed Faith, time was to prove that their hearts remained hostile to the Gospel thus adorned by Amyraut and his brethren.

In the meantime, the Reformed Churches continued to flourish and the pastors enriched one another by periodic fellowship. In 1653, Jean Daillé called at Saumur on his way from Paris to La Rochelle to ordain his son Adrien at the Reformed Temple.[2] Quick reminds us that, since their student days, Amyraut and Daillé had remained 'dear friends'. Regarded as the greatest French preacher since Calvin, Daillé had fully supported his friend in his theological conflicts. Both men owed so much to their benefactor, The Lord du Plessis-Mornay. During this meeting, they enjoyed rich fellowship as guests of the godly noble Lord's grandson Lord de Villarnoul at his chateau at La Forêt-sur-Sèvre in lower Poitou. We may imagine the joys thus shared in the great hall of the chateau. Quick says that 'their discourses and conversation together did ravish and charm that religious family, and all the guests and strangers that had the happiness to be their auditors'.[3]

Quick also supplies a vivid and charming picture of student life at Saumur. He tells us that 'it was a constant custom with M. Amyraut in the summer evenings to walk in the fields about Saumur, especially after supper. He was always attended with some sixty or fourscore students in divinity, who propounded to him all those difficulties and knotty objections which occurred

---

1   Ibid. 978–92.

2   See my *Calvin Celebrated: The Genevan Reformer & His Huguenot Sons* (Norwich: Charenton Reformed Publishing, 2009), 82.

3   *Icones*, 995.

to them in their private studies'.[1] We can imagine the cut and thrust of provocative yet good-humoured discussion as professor and students fired questions at one another. Quick stresses the importance of these nocturnal excursions:

> These exercises did highly improve those young divines in knowledge, judgement, acumen and ability to defend the truth, and refute errors, and many of them afterwards proved most eminent ministers of the Gospel, and victorious champions of our holy Religion against all the subtle Popish aggressors. And it was these evening walks which occasioned the publication of sundry theological dissertations, which he emitted at diverse times from the press into the open world, and which otherwise might have been buried in the graves of perpetual silence.[2]

In the sharp winter of 1657, Amyraut had a bad fall after leaving the Temple. Carried home in great agony, he was thought to have broken his thigh. All were gravely concerned, including the Roman Catholics, and fear was expressed for his life. As soon as he recovered from shock, 'he began to speak and comfort those that attended him', says Quick, 'telling them that if the Lord should vouchsafe him that favour as to enjoy the benefit of his tongue and understanding to edify his brethren to the last of his life, he should account this the happiest providence which ever had befallen him'.[3] Amyraut had actually suffered a hip dislocation and torn ligaments. He was out of action for six months, during which time he attended to his voluminous correspondence, continuing also with his paraphrase on the Acts of the Apostles. Becoming more mobile with the aid of crutches, he was carried from place to place in a Sedan chair. At the end of August, accompanied by his daughter-in-law, he visited the small spa town of Bourbon in Burgundy, famous for its attractive vista of the Loire Valley. During his stay, many Reformed believers gathered in his apartment on the Lord's Day for worship, ministry and fellowship. They were 'edified', says Quick, 'by his excellent and fruitful sermons'.[4] One sermon in particular was highly

---

1   Ibid.
2   Ibid. The 'sundry theological dissertations' referred to by Quick are the *Theses Salmurienses* published in four volumes (Saumur, 1665; Geneva, 1665).
3   *Icones*, 996.
4   Ibid. 998.

valued. Finding relief from the *eaux de Bourbon*, he drew parallels between the healing effect of the waters and the grace of God in the Gospel.[1]

Making their way to Paris, Amyraut and his daughter-in-law were welcomed by M. Hervart (the King's Controller of Revenue and a Reformed man) at whose residence they stayed for three months. The Princess of Tarente, the godly daughter of the Huguenot Duke de la Force enjoyed their company and especially Amyraut's discussions on theological and devotional matters. Appearing frequently at the great Temple at Charenton, he preached sermons on the glory of Christ and the work of the Holy Spirit, which were published.[2]

Learning from M. Hervart that Amyraut was in town, Cardinal Mazarin welcomed a further opportunity to speak with the Reformed professor. When they first met, the Cardinal's position during the Fronde had been much less secure. Always impressed by Amyraut's personal integrity and learning, and recalling with pleasure his visit to the Saumur Academy and its library, the Cardinal now invited the Huguenot to see his house and library. While relations were respectful and even cordial, it should be remembered that synodical assemblies of the Reformed Churches could only be approved by the Government. During another visit, having been asked by the Reformed consistory of Paris to petition the Cardinal to authorise a new National Synod, Amyraut duly approached him on the subject. Suspicions about Reformed influence always lurking in the background, matters were never plain sailing. However, the Cardinal, urging Amyraut to be patient, invited him to put the request in writing, which he did.

Permission for the National Synod of Loudun was eventually granted. It was to prove the final synod ever allowed by Louis XIV as he increasingly pursued a Jesuit-inspired policy to exterminate the Reformed Churches of France. Indeed, the King and his advisers had good reason to respect Huguenot resolve. When the Synod commenced 'by His Majesty's Permission' on 10 November 1659, the King's Commissioner demanded that the Huguenots should be more submissive to His Majesty and less antagonistic to the Church of Rome. The Synod Moderator, the illustrious M. Jean Daillé rose to the occasion. While he affirmed the loyalty and submission of the Reformed Churches to the King 'as next under God'[3] in all things lawful, he refused to

---

1   *Discours chrestien sur les eaux de Bourbon* (Charenton: A. Cellier, 1658).
2   See *Cinq sermons prononcez a Charenton* (Charenton: A. Cellier, 1658).
3   *Synodicon*, ii. 511.

dilute their theological stance. He bravely affirmed that, 'As to those words *Antichrist*, found in our Liturgy, and *idolatry* and *deceit of Satan*, found in our Confession [of Faith], they be words declaring the grounds and reasons of our separation from the Romish Church, and doctrines which our fathers maintained in the worst of times, and which we are fully resolved as they, through the aids of Divine grace, never to abandon, but to keep faithfully and inviolably to the last gasp'.[1]

It is interesting to note that John Quick was writing his biography of Amyraut in 1696, eleven years after the Revocation of the Edict of Nantes (1685). Looking back wistfully, he wrote of the Synod of Loudun: 'I pray God, it may not be their last. It being six and thirty years since it was broken up [10 January 1660], and the churches in that kingdom are all ruined and desolate'.[2] The next synod was planned (DV) for Nîmes in 1662/3,[3] but it was never to be. However, according to the amazing providence of 'the wonderful Numberer',[4] and nine years after Quick's death, the next took place in the Cévennes in 1715, the very year Louis XIV died. But that is another and happier story![5]

It is appropriate here to mention that synods had a vital place in the life of the Reformed Churches of France. Respectful and courteous to both Anglican[6] and Roman Catholic churchmen, they remained committed to Reformed Faith and Order. Indeed, the Huguenots were as tenacious over their 'Order' as they were over their 'Faith'. Amyraut believed with Calvin and Beza that, according to clear New Testament teaching, 'elder' and 'bishop' were terms relating to one and the same individual,[7] as surely as 'elder' and 'deacon' denoted quite different roles.[8] He also taught that each church should be governed by a plural body or council of elders, that such a 'consistory'

---

1 Ibid. 513.

2 *Icones*, 999.

3 See Quick, *Synodicon*, ii. 582.

4 Ibid. i. p. clxiv.

5 See the account of Antoine Court in my *Calvin Celebrated: The Genevan Reformer & His Huguenot Sons* (Norwich: Charenton Reformed Publishing, 2009), 129ff.

6 Amyraut maintained friendly correspondence with Dr Cousins, future Bishop of Durham, whom he met in Paris. After the Restoration of Charles II, Amyraut congratulated his English friend. Quite unaware of the sufferings awaiting the Puritans at the Great Ejection of 1662, Amyraut dedicated his *Paraphrase on the Psalms* to the King (see Quick, *Icones*, 999, 1004).

7 See Titus 1: 5–7.

8 See 1 Timothy 3: 1–14.

was made up of 'Ministers of the Word' and 'ruling elders'.[1] Showing little sympathy for congregational independency, he also believed that synods had divine warrant.[2] They enabled churches to express connexional fellowship and solidarity. However, while French Reformed Church Order stated that provincial synods were to be 'subordinate' to national synods, it was only a 'self-subordination'. By referring to their 'churches' in plural terms, their approach was 'bottom-up' rather than 'top-down' as in the Presbyterian Church [singular] hierarchical system. Amyraut had already published a work on church order before the National Synod of Loudun.[3] At the Synod, he was commissioned to prepare a treatise showing the 'Conformity' of the discipline of the Reformed Churches of France with the 'ancient primitive Church'.[4] Dying before this work was finished, it was completed by his pupil Matthieu Larroque, Pastor of Quevilly near Rouen, whose treatise was later translated into English.[5]

As in England, where Anglicans regarded non-episcopally-ordained Puritans as not true ministers, so the French Roman Catholic clergy dismissed the orders of the Huguenot ministers. Ever concerned to combine courtesy with tenacity, Amyraut put his theory of church order to good use. When M. Pérréfix, Archbishop of Paris visited Saumur, he requested a meeting with Amyraut. Knowing the scriptural prohibition against bishops (= elders!) being 'lords' (*1 Peter 5: 3*), Amyraut refused to address Roman Catholic bishops as 'My Lord' unless they were peers of the realm (itself an arrangement the Huguenots were hardly in a position to correct). Once the Archbishop—not being a peer—realised he would only be addressed as 'Mr', he agreed to an unofficial private meeting with Amyraut. While he was quite a civil man, he was possibly tinged with jealousy where the Parisian preacher Jean Daillé was concerned. Quick's revealing report is not without a touch of humour:

They spent together in that conversation about three hours, discoursing of the affairs of the great world, and the most eminent persons for learning

---

1   See 1 Timothy 5: 17.

2   See Acts 15.

3   See *Du gouvernement de l'eglise contre ceux qui veulent abolir l'usage & l'autorité des synodes* (Saumur: Isaac Desbordes, 1653; 2nd ed. 1658, *Avec un appendice au livre du gouvernement de l'eglise où il est traité de la puissance des consistoires.*

4   *Icones*, 1001.

5   See *The Conformity of the Ecclesiastical Discipline of the Reformed Churches of France with that of the Primitive Christians* (London: 1691). For Larroque, see Quick, *Icone* 43.

and religion in the communion of both churches. This led them into a discourse of M. Daillé, a person of extraordinary parts and famous for his profound knowledge in the learned world. M. Amyraut observed that the Archbishop always spoke of him slightingly, and by the single name of Daillé; which made M. Amyraut never to mention him without a preface and title of honour.[1]

We have thus noticed that in those tense and potentially-explosive times, Amyraut was concerned to combine tenacity of conviction with courtesy and compassion. A beautiful example of the latter occurred in 1662, two years before he died. Following a bad harvest that year, there was a great shortage of corn in France.[2] Due to her wise management, Mme Amyraut had—Joseph-like—stocked up large reserves of corn at their country house in the Vale of Anjou. Says Quick, 'She had stacked it up in the barns and fields for sundry years of plenty together most abundantly'.[3] Urged to take financial advantage of the situation by selling the corn, the Amyrauts refused to follow what they construed as selfish and ungodly advice. Instead, while taking prudent care of his family and servants should bad harvests continue, they drew up a plan to distribute the corn freely to the poor, irrespective of religious persuasion. Observing Paul's directive to 'do good to all, especially to those who are of the household of faith' (*Galatians 6: 10*), first the Reformed poor, then the Roman Catholic poor benefited from their gracious generosity. Quick writes that 'the Roman Catholics whose hungry bellies and empty bowels were refreshed by him, loved and honoured him, calling him the common father of the poor, declaring that in his charities he made no distinction between them and those of his own religion'.[4]

At the commencement of the September vacation in 1663, the Amyrauts retired to their country house as usual. Within days Moïse became unwell, developing a high but intermittent fever. Instead of returning to Saumur for medical help, he stayed to enjoy a well-deserved rest. After several weeks, his condition deteriorating, Amyraut bowed to the inevitable and returned to

---

1 *Icones*, 1002–3. For further confirmation of Daillé's eminence, see Philip Benedict, *The Faith and Fortunes of France's Huguenots*, 254.

2 England's harvests were bad in the years 1658–61. See C. Hill, *The Century of Revolution, 1603–1714* (London: Nelson, 1961), 321.

3 *Icones*, 1005.

4 Ibid.

Saumur. Concern for his health grew and the sad news spread rapidly. Many anxious visitors called to see him, Roman Catholics as well as Reformed people. As his end drew near, he testified of his faith to a captive audience crowded around his bed. So moving were his last hours that Quick referred to Amyraut's death-bed utterances in a later funeral sermon. He did so to prove the dying man's fidelity to the Reformed Faith to the last:

> [He proved] the truth of the Christian religion, and of our Holy Reformed religion, by many unanswerable arguments. "This I have professed," said he; "I have preached this Holy Reformed religion well nigh forty years." And turning himself unto the Papists (for there were many then present in his chamber, spectators and witnesses of his last end) "Gentlemen," said he, "This is the only true religion, and out of it there is no salvation. That God to whom I am going knows that I do speak the very truth." This, and much more he uttered with a clear and audible voice; yea, and those very Papists heard him with much reverence and attention.[1]

He lingered several days, during which time many of his flock received their beloved pastor's final exhortations. Quick adds this further moving information:

> He had advised them to stand steadfast in the faith, and to hold fast to their profession without wavering, and to prepare against the evil times of sore trials which were approaching, for the God of judgement was at the door, and heavy judgements would begin at the house of God, and therefore how painful soever their cross and sufferings might be, they should not faint, nor prevaricate in, nor apostatise from their holy religion. For he protested to them in the presence of God to whose tribunal he was now a going, that it was the only true one in the whole world, and that out of it there was no salvation to be obtained. I say, after he had given them these and a great many other divine counsels, he blessed them in the name of the Lord'.[2]

The dying servant of God clearly foresaw the coming persecutions which afflicted the Reformed Churches of France two decades later. He had sufficient

---

1   *The Triumph of Faith* (London: 1698), 24.

2   *Icones*, 1007–8.

strength to repeat some of these exhortations to another pastor from Poitou who, passing through Saumur and hearing that Amyraut was dying, called to see him. Encouraging his rather diffident brother, Amyraut said: 'The doctrine I have taught my scholars in the university and my church in the city is the very truth of God, by which we must all be saved'.[1]

After giving his son directions about his will, Amyraut said farewell to his wife and family. Quick describes his last moments thus:

In the fifteen last moments of his life, he joined his hands together, and lifted them up with his eyes unto heaven, waiting as dying Jacob did for God's salvation. And in that posture breathed out his blessed soul into the arms of his Redeemer'.[2]

And so this honoured servant of Christ died on the 18 January 1664, aged sixty-eight years. His dearly beloved wife, who also became ill during her husband's sickness, survived him by only a few months. Their son—whose own son Moses eventually settled here—met John Quick in London after escaping to England at the time of the Revocation of the Edict of Nantes. Quick describes him as a man 'of serious piety, being an illustrious confessor of our Lord Jesus in these woeful times of tribulation'.[3] He later served as an Advocate in the High Court of Justice in the Hague. After presenting an engraving of his father to one of the greatest of Amyraut's pupils, Pierre du Bosc[4]—Minister of the Reformed Church at Caen in Normandy and described by Louis XIV as the greatest orator in France—added to the

---

1   Ibid. 1009. Of course, this includes his 'doctrinal distinctives', and many continued to dispute Amyraut's claim. However, through the good offices of the Prince of Tarente, some reconciliation was achieved in 1649 (see Quick, *Icones*, 967). In 1655, even Pierre du Moulin responded positively to a conciliatory letter from Amyraut. His 'Amyraldian distinctives' were eventually regarded—at least by some former enemies—as 'innocent' and 'inoffensive' instead of 'shocking doctrine' (Quick, *Icones*, 1004; Bayle, 262). Sadly, subscribers to supra-scriptural Westminster orthodoxy think otherwise.

2   Ibid. 1010.

3   Ibid. 1012.

4   For Du Bosc (1623–92), see Quick *Icone* 47; Bayle, ii. 91. For academic life at Saumur, see J.-P. Pittion, 'Intellectual life in the Académie of Saumur, 1633–1685 (Unpublished Ph.D. thesis, Trinity College, Dublin, 1970). This work is currently being prepared for publication. On a lighter note, Amyraut defended his young gentlemen against some dour critics of their high-spirited behaviour: "Our morose and supercilious critics had quite forgot that they had been also young lads" (*Icones*, 1016). Together with another student, Pierre du Bosc had been censured for his fashionable clothes!

portrait a personal Latin tribute to his professor. Thus translated, this worthy epitaph reads:

> From Moses down to Moses, none,
> Among the sons of men,
> With equal lustre ever shone,
> In manners, tongue and pen.[1]

Is it any wonder that Richard Baxter should be impressed by this man whose books he so much admired? Indeed, is it so dubious a privilege after all to be dubbed an Amyraldian?

---

1   Bayle says these words were an allusion to what the Jews said in praise of their famous Rabbi Moses Maimonides [1135–1204]: 'A Mose ad Mosem par Mosi non fuit ullus: More, ore & calamo, mirus uterque fuit' (*Dictionary*, 265).

10. The Gospel According
to Matthew Henry[1]

Son of the godly ejected Puritan Philip Henry (1631–96),[2] Matthew was born two months after the 'Great Ejection' on 18 October 1662 at Broad Oak, Flintshire. Blessed with the best of domestic piety, he professed personal faith in Christ from an early age. He came under the tuition of Thomas Doolittle at Islington, London in 1680. After a period back at Broad Oak, Matthew returned to London to study Law at Gray's Inn in 1685. In a letter dated 17 November, he relates a visit to Richard Baxter, then in prison following the latter's infamous trial at the hand of Judge Jeffreys. Returning home, Matthew was ordained, becoming a Presbyterian pastor at Chester in 1687. For over twenty years, he exercised a faithful and effective ministry, both in preaching and writing. Visiting London in 1704, he heard the aged Puritan John Howe (1630–1705). Invited to become pastor at Hackney in 1709, Matthew consulted Dr Edmund Calamy who encouraged him to accept. Deeply attached to his people at Chester, Matthew continued in a state of acute perplexity. The invitation being renewed, he finally accepted, commencing his ministry at Hackney in May 1712. The bonds remaining strong, Matthew Henry journeyed to see his former people at Chester in May 1714. Despite his intention to do so, he never returned south. *En route* from Chester to Hackney, Matthew Henry died at Nantwich on 22 June 1714 after a riding accident.

After three centuries, Matthew Henry's praise continues to be in Bible-believing churches. His *Exposition of the Old and New Testaments* remains an

---

1   A revision of a paper first given at the Matthew Henry Conference held at Chester University, 14–16 July 2014.

2   See A. G. Matthews, *Calamy Revised* (Oxford: Clarendon Press, 1934), 257; also Matthew Henry, *The Life of the Rev. Philip Henry, AM* in J. B. Williams, *Memoir of the Life, Character and Writings of the Revd Matthew Henry* ([1828] repr. Edinburgh: The Banner of Truth Trust, 1974).

honoured and useful tool for pastors and Bible students. Nineteenth-century
C. H. Spurgeon regarded Henry's *Exposition* as 'first among the mighty for
general usefulness'. The eighteenth-century Methodist evangelist George
Whitefield—who was born six months after Henry's death—testified that
'Henry's *Expositions* were of admirable use to lead me into all Gospel truths'.[1]

As his biographer, J. B. Williams makes clear, the famous Bible commentator
was an ardent admirer of the seventeenth-century 'Apostle of Kidderminster'
Richard Baxter, famous for his occupation of the theological middle ground
between sub-orthodox Arminianism and ultra-orthodox Owenism: 'The
practical works of Mr Baxter, especially, occupied a very exalted place in his
esteem; they are more frequently cited in his manuscripts than the productions
of any other author; and he caught, in a happy measure, the holy flame by
which they were animated'.[2]

Committed as he was to doctrinal and practical godliness, it is hardly
surprising to find Henry sharing Baxter's strong aversion for antinomianism.
That said, in the face of undeniable evidence supplied by himself, Williams
labours unconvincingly[3] to insist that Henry did not embrace Baxter's so-called
'neonomianism'—the idea that the Gospel is a [new] 'remedial law'. Indeed,
Henry states unambiguously that 'the gospel of Christ is a remedial law, and
you hope to have a remedy by it. It is a charter of privileges, and you hope
to be privileged by it; but how can you expect either remedy or privilege by
it, if you will not observe its precepts, nor come up to its conditions? The
gospel will never save you if it shall not rule you'.[4] He further states that,
in order to be saved, sinners 'must, therefore, take the benefit of a covenant
of grace, must submit to a remedial law; and *this* is it—repentance toward
God, and faith towards our Lord Jesus Christ'.[5]

Clearly then, Henry was undeterred by 'ultra-Calvinist' nervousness over
the language of conditionality. Like Baxter, while the notion of 'merit' is
ruled out, Henry refused to explain away the necessity of good works as

---

1   For Spurgeon and Whitefield details, see the 'blurb' for J. B. Williams, *Memoir of the Life,
Character and Writings of the Revd Matthew Henry* ([1828] repr. Edinburgh: The Banner of Truth
Trust, 1974).

2   John B. Williams, *Memoir,* 221.

3   Ibid. 240–2.

4   'A Word of Advice to the Wanton and Unclean' in *The Complete Works of Matthew Henry—
Treatises, Sermons, and Tracts* (Grand Rapids: Michigan: Baker Books, 1997), i. 106.

5   Henry on Mk 1: 15.

taught in Matthew 25. After all, as the 'fruit' from the 'root', 'good works' are the evidence of a 'living faith'. Henry could not be more 'Baxterian' when he insists that

An estate made by deed or will upon condition, when the condition is performed according to the true intent of the donor or testator, becomes absolute; and then, though the title be built purely upon the deed or will, yet the performing of the condition must be given in evidence: and so it comes in here; for Christ is the Author of eternal salvation to those only that obey him, and who patiently continue in well doing.[1]

Again, Henry's exposition of justifying faith is typically 'Baxterian':

Is justifying faith a working faith? Yes: for by works is faith made perfect, Jam. ii. 22. And will that faith justify us which does not produce good works? No: for by works a man is justified, and not by faith only, Jam. ii. 24. Is faith then dead without good works? Yes: for as the body without the spirit is dead, so faith without works is dead also, Jam ii. 26. And are good works dead without faith? Yes: for without faith it is impossible to please God, Heb. xi. 6. Must they both act together then? Yes: for that which avails is faith, which works by love, Gal. v. 6.[2]

Of arguably equal importance, Williams says nothing of Henry's views on the nature and extent of the atonement. On this issue too, Henry reflected the influence of Baxter's books, both the 'practical' and 'controversial' works. This claim is evident in his *A Scripture Catechism, in the Method of the Assembly's* (1702), a work mentioned but not discussed by Williams.[3] Recent biographies by Allan M. Harman and Philip H. Eveson also fail to acknowledge Henry's 'Baxterian/Amyraldian' view of the Gospel. The latter seems determined to present him as an 'Owenite', which is simply untrue.[4]

Judging by his *Scripture Catechism*, there can be no doubt that Presbyterian Matthew Henry was not comfortable with the strict 'Owenism' of the Westminster Standards. David P. Field writes that 'Despite the studied

---

1   Henry on Matthew 25: 35–6.

2   *A Scripture Catechism* in *The Complete Works of Matthew Henry—Treatises, Sermons, and Tracts* (Grand Rapids: Michigan: Baker Books, 1997), ii. 208.

3   Ibid. 225.

4   See Allan M. Harman, *Matthew Henry: His Life and Influence* (Fearn, Tain, Ross-shire: Christian Focus Publications, 2012), 71; Philip H. Eveson, *Matthew Henry* (Darlington: EP Books, 2012), 43, 89.

practicality of Matthew Henry's writings, [his] Neonomian and Amyraldian
tone is to be discerned—even in his catechism, based on the Westminster
Assembly's catechisms, and contrary to the claim of his biographer [J. B.
Williams], this does constitute sufficient evidence to number Matthew Henry
with the moderate Presbyterians in point of theology'.[1] In this respect,
he was one of a sizable cluster of 'Baxterians' including Dr William Bates
(1625–99), John Howe (1630–1705), Dr Daniel Williams (1643–1716), Dr
Edmund Calamy (1671–1732), Dr Philip Doddridge (1702–51) and others[2]
including lesser writers like Dr Abraham Clifford (1628–75)[3] and Samuel
Clifford (1630–99).[4] Rather than the ambiguous label 'Moderate Calvinists',
a good case may be made for calling them 'authentic Calvinists', judging by
the explicit views of John Calvin.[5]

Two examples may be cited. A great admirer of Baxter,[6] and untroubled
in believing that Christ died for his hearers indiscriminately, John Howe's
sublime evangelistic pleadings have a distinct Baxterian flavour:

God so loved the world, &c. (John 3: 16), and what could our Lord
himself have done more to testify his own love? … And what could be
so apt a means, sinner, to break thy heart, and conquer all thy former
enmity, as to behold thy Redeemer dying upon the cross for thee? They
shall look upon me whom they have pierced, and mourn, Zech. 12: 10.
And I, if I be lifted up, will draw all men to me; by which our Lord
said, signifying what death he should die, by being lift up on the cross,
John 12: 32, 33. Now what dost thou think of thyself, if such a sight
will not move thee?[7]

---

1   David P. Field, *Rigide Calvinisme in a Softer Dr.ess: The Moderate Presbyterianism of John Howe,
1630–1705* (Edinburgh: Rutherford House, 2004), 174.

2   Ibid. 167–79.

3   Ibid. 170. See Abraham Clifford, *Methodus Evangelica; or, the Gospel Method of God's Saving
Sinners by Jesus Christ* (London: 1676).

4   See Samuel Clifford, *An Account of the Judgement of the Late Reverend Mr Baxter* (London: 1701).

5   See Alan C. Clifford, *Calvinus: Authentic Calvinism, A Clarification* (Norwich: Charenton
Reformed Publishing, 1995).

6   Howe wrote warmly of Baxter's books. He insisted that 'however about Redemption Davenant
and Amyraldus may have spoken many of your thoughts, yet their books do not commonly fall
into hands of young scholars (whose minds while such are least prepossessed & almost *rasa tabula*)
as yours are like to do' (*Calendar of the Correspondence of Richard Baxter,* ed. Neil H. Keeble and
Geoffrey F. Nuttall (Oxford: Clarendon Press, 1991), i. 295, *Letter* 436).

7   John Howe, 'Man's Enmity to God and Reconciliation between God and Man' in *Works of*

In his justly-celebrated work, *The Redeemer's Tears Wept over Lost Souls*, Howe's tender portrayal of the love of Jesus towards even those who reject Him reveals his convictions over the availability of the atonement:

Thou dost not perish unlamented, even with the purest heavenly pity, ...[1]

Our second example comes from Dr. Edmund Calamy, a personal acquaintance of Matthew Henry. Concerned that we grasp a proper view of the Gospel, Baxter's champion presents the issues with perfect Baxterian balance:

Let us put things together, and take notice, that general grace and special are very reconcilable; ... The Scripture appears clear as to both; and where's the inconsistency? Why must we deny general grace to exalt that which is special [as John Gill did later]? Or deny and depress special grace, to advance that which is general [as John Wesley did later]? ... And is not this very consistent with our owning that 'God so loved the world' in general, as 'that He gave His only-begotten Son, that whosoever believeth in Him, might not perish, but might have everlasting life'? And on the other side, is not general grace sufficiently secured by our maintaining God's love to the world, and His willing the salvation of all men, on condition they turn to Him? ... and why then should we go about to dash these truths against each other which are fairly consistent, and agree well together? Let us beware of extremes: and stand upon our guard, lest for fear of one error, we fall into another.[2]

Calamy's explanation correlates with the Amyraldian view that a 'dualistic' or two-fold intention features in the Divine redemptive purpose.[3]

While Richard Baxter was the ever-brilliant master and passionate communicator, his 'dualistic' stance is also clear:

For all the wonderful love and mercy that God hath manifested in

---

the *English Puritan Divines: John Howe* (London: Thomas Nelson, 1846), 285.

1   Ibid. 65.

2   Edmund Calamy, *Divine Mercy Exalted: or Free Grace in its Glory* (London, 1703), 44–54. Parenthetic remarks mine.

3   See Alan C. Clifford, *Amyraut Affirmed* (Norwich: Charenton Reformed Publishing, 2004), 18, 49–50.

giving his Son to be the Redeemer of the world, and which the Son hath manifested in redeeming them by his blood; for all his full preparation by being a sufficient sacrifice for the sins of all; for all his personal excellencies, and that full and glorious salvation that he hath procured; and for all his free offers of these, and frequent and earnest invitation of sinners; yet many do make light of all this, and prefer their worldly enjoyments before it. The ordinary treatment of all these offers, invitations, and benefits, is by contempt. Not that all, do so, or that all continue to do so, who were once guilty of it; for God hath his chosen whom he will compel to come in. But till the Spirit of grace overpower the dead and obstinate hearts of men, they hear the gospel as a common story, and the great matters contained in it go not to the heart.[1]

Baxter's words regarding perspicuous Scripture sum up the convictions of these men:

When God saith so expressly that Christ died for all [2 Cor. 5: 14–15], and tasted death for every man [Heb. 2: 9], and is the ransom for all [1 Tim. 2: 6], and the propitiation for the sins of the whole world [1 Jn. 2: 2], it beseems every Christian rather to explain in what sense Christ died for all, than flatly to deny it. [2]

Returning to 'authentic Calvinist' Matthew Henry, his exposition of the atonement takes him beyond the confines of 'limited atonement'; but—to make an observation of immense significance—*not beyond the plain language of Holy Scripture*. Henry obviously shared Baxter's preference for directly-derived Bible-based language instead of the formulations of 'confessional correctness'.[3] In the 'Introduction' to the *Scripture Catechism*, he states this as his hermeneutical priority:

But another thing I aimed at, (and indeed the chief,) is to promote the knowledge of the Scriptures. Divine truths, methinks, sound best in divine language; and the things which God has revealed to us by his

---

1   Richard Baxter, *Making Light of Christ* (Norwich: Charenton Reformed Publishing, 2010), 18–19.
2   Richard Baxter, *The Universal Redemption of Mankind* (London, 1694), 286.
3   See Geoffrey F. Nuttall, *Richard Baxter* (London: Thomas Nelson, 1965), 121–2.

Spirit, cannot be conveyed in a more safe and proper vehicle, than by the words which the Holy Ghost teaches, (1 Cor. ii. 10, 13) ...[1]

What this boils down to is that if a 'Confession of Faith' was to be Dr.awn up using strictly biblical terminology, it is impossible to formulate an 'Owenite' article on 'limited atonement', viz, that 'Christ died for the elect *alone*'. Agreeing with Baxter rather than Owen, Henry states that

God chose [Christ] to be the Saviour of poor sinners, and would have him to save them in this way, by bearing their sins and the punishment of them; not the *idem*—the same that we should have suffered, but the *tantundem*—that which was more than equivalent for the maintaining of the honour of the holiness and justice of God in the government of the world.[2]

This extract from the well-known *Commentary* provides a rare example of non-biblical, scholastic terminology.[3] While its significance would be lost on most of his readers, it shows Henry's debt to Baxter's discussions about the nature of the atonement.

In his debates with John Owen, Baxter insisted that our Saviour Christ's satisfaction for sin did *not* involve the 'same' payment our sins deserve but a 'substituted' payment.[4] Since our sins are threatened with eternal punishment,

---

1   Matthew Henry, *A Scripture Catechism*, ii. 174.

2   Henry on Isa. 53: 6. See also Alan C. Clifford, *Atonement and Justification: English Evangelical Theology 1640–1790—An Evaluation* (Oxford: Clarendon Press, 1990), 128ff.

3   The *idem-tantundem* distinction is also maintained in *Matthew Henry's Unpublished Sermons on the Covenant of Grace*, ed. Allan Harman (Fearn, Tain, Ross-shire: Christian Focus Publications, 2002), 30.

4   Owen insisted that God's justice was only satisfied by Christ's payment of the same penalty or debt owed by the elect to God on account of their sins—the *solutio eiusdem*. Richard Baxter argued that, in virtue of the differences (in detail and duration) between Christ's sufferings and the actual sufferings of the lost, Christ only paid an equivalent debt—the *solutio tantidem*. Since the penalty of the law threatens eternal punishment to impenitent offenders, Christ clearly did not suffer the identical punishment, for his resurrection terminated his banishment. God therefore relaxed the law both with regard to the persons who should suffer (a fact Owen obviously agreed with) and the penalty suffered. Clearly, there was not the 'sameness' Owen pleads for. The *idem-tantundem* distinction automatically answers Owen's objection that if any suffer eternally for whom Christ died, then 'double-payment' is being demanded. But there is no duplication of payment. Those who reject the gospel do not suffer again what Christ has suffered for them. He 'paid' the *tantundem* or equivalent penalty; they will 'pay' the *idem* or exact price. Baxter was surely correct to state that

Christ would be in hell if He paid the same satisfaction. In short, a proper biblical doctrine of penal substitution means that *both* Christ *and* His sufferings were 'in the place' of all we deserve. Defending John Owen in a recently-published 'heavyweight tome' on 'definite atonement', Dr Garry Williams insists that the exact penal nature of the atonement necessarily points to a limited or 'definite' atonement.[1] Regarded as two 'clinching' contributions by the editors,[2] Dr Williams fails to grasp the cogency of Baxter's case that there is nothing in the nature of Christ's satisfaction to threaten the atonement's universality. Dr Williams also fails to detect Owen's flawed reliance on Aristotelian metaphysics in arguing for his '*idem*' view.[3] Even if

---

both Christ *and* his sufferings were inseparably substituted for the law's strict demands. Had the law not been relaxed with regard to the offender, none would be saved; had it not been relaxed with regard to the penalty, Christ himself would have suffered 'the everlasting torments of hell' (*Catholick Theologie* (London, 1675), I. ii. 40). Baxter's argument is irrefutable when he observes that the law did not permit the punishment of a substitute in the place of an offender: 'For the law made it due to the sinner himself. And another's suffering for him fulfilleth not the law (which never said, Either thou or another for thee shalt die) But [Christ's death] satisfied the Law-giver as he is above his own law, and could dispense with it, his justice being satisfied and saved' (ibid. 50). In other words, coupled with the infinite dignity of the suffering Saviour, his sufferings were accepted as a satisfactory equivalent for all that is deserved by mankind.

1   See Garry J. Williams, 'The Definite Intent of Penal Substitutionary Atonement' and 'Punishment God Cannot Twice Inflict' in *From Heaven He Came and Sought Her: Definite Atonement in Historical, Biblical, Theological and Pastoral Perspective,* ed. David & Jonathan Gibson (Wheaton, Illinois: Crossway, 2013), 461–515.

2   See the review feature 'Definite atonement' in *Evangelicals Now,* March 2014, 15.

3   The mammoth Crossway publication fails to vindicate the Owenite doctrine of 'limited atonement'. Owen clearly saw that his doctrine of limited atonement hung on the 'sameness' between Christ's sufferings and those deserved by the elect. However, he could only argue his case with the aid of Aristotle's metaphysics. His very language betrays him: 'When I say the same, I mean *essentially* the same in weight and pressure, though not in all the *accidents* of duration and the like; for it was impossible that he should be detained by death' (*Death of Death,* in *The Works of John Owen,* ed. W. H. Goold (London: Johnstone & Hunter, 1850–55), x. 269–70). Owen therefore resorts to Aristotle's dubious essence/accidents theory to prove his point. In Baxter's view, even this statement 'yieldeth the cause' (Appendix to *Aphorismes of Justification* (London, 1649), 138) but after learning of Baxter's criticism, Owen then granted that 'There is a sameness in Christ's sufferings with that in the obligation in respect of essence, and equivalency in respect of attendencies' (*Of the Death of Christ, the Price He Paid,* in *Works,* x. 448). But Owen's employment of this philosophical distinction simply obscures the fact that there is a real difference between Christ's temporary sufferings and the eternal sufferings deserved by the elect. He cannot establish his concept of 'sameness' without philosophical double-talk. If he is prepared to grant an equivalence in either respect, then he is forced to concede that there is only a similarity, and not a sameness

there is no necessary connection between Owen's strictly-commercialistic view of the atonement and his exact payment idea, Garry Williams also fails to see how Owen's commercial theory actually negates the idea of the atonement's universal sufficiency.[1] The 'over-orthodox doctor' (as Baxter called him)[2] really paid little more than lip-service to the time-honoured 'sufficient for all-efficient for the elect' distinction.[3] In other words, if the atonement is strictly limited, then the 'credit facilities' of the gospel are only sufficient for the elect. In short, it is only sufficient for whom it is efficient. Undoubtedly, on issues of such fundamental importance, Matthew Henry was persuaded by Baxter rather than Owen.

Just as Baxter's theology satisfied neither Arminians nor the over-orthodox 'High Calvinist Owenites', his 'disciple' Matthew Henry has not been to everyone's liking. J. B. Williams rightly concludes that, 'As a natural consequence, [Henry] has been sometimes claimed by Calvinists; at others by Arminians; and often rejected by both'.[4] The causes of their respective

---

at all. Clearly, Aristotle's metaphysical formula (see *Metaphysics*, tr. J. Warrington (London, 1956), 173, 46) only serves to permit unreal and meaningless distinctions. Despite Dr Carl Truman's unconvincing attempt to laugh off the point, philosopher Bertrand Russell was correct to describe this as a 'muddle-headed notion, incapable of precision' (*History of Western Philosophy* (London: George Allen & Unwin, 1961), 177). For Truman, see *The Claims of Truth: John Owen's Trinitarian Theology* (Carlisle: Paternoster Press, 1998), 216.

1   *From Heaven He Came,* 482. Dr Williams is surely correct to rescue Grotius *vis-à-vis* Socinus from the charge that his 'Governmental' theory of the atonement excludes the idea of God's retribution for sin (ibid. 490–2). Clearly, Baxter was aware of the Dutchman's exact teaching: 'Yet did [Christ] in the person of a mediator ... suffer the penalty, *nostro loco*, in our stead ... to satisfy God's wisdom, truth and justice, and to procure pardon and life for sinners ... The perfection of Christ's satisfaction consisteth not in its being instead of all the sufferings due to all for whom he died, but ... in its full sufficiency to those ends for which it was designed by the Father and Son ...' (*Catholick Theologie*, I. ii. 39).

2   Richard Baxter, *Reliquiae Baxterianae* (London: 1696), ii. 199.

3   Making the sufferings of Christ commensurate with the sins of the elect in a quantitative, commercialistic sense explains why Owen modified the sufficiency/efficiency distinction. His deliberate redefinition of it means that the atonement is only sufficient for whom it is efficient: '... it is denied that the blood of Christ was a sufficient price and ransom for all and everyone ...' (*Death of Death,* 296). Christ's sacrifice would have been a sufficient ransom 'if it had pleased the Lord to employ it to that purpose; ...' (ibid. 295). Baxter writes: '... they cannot without absurdity be interpreted to mean, that his death is sufficient for all if it had been a price for them; and not a sufficient price for them; For that were to contradict themselves ...' (*Universal Redemption,* 59).

4   Williams, *Memoir,* 242.

hesitations are evident in the *Scripture Catechism*.[1] In short, he believes the Bible teaches the kind of 'dual-aspect' view of the atonement found in Calvin, Amyraut, Baxter and numerous other divines in the Medieval and Reformed traditions, from Augustine to Ryle. While he clearly affirmed the 'special' efficacious salvation of the elect, Henry—like Baxter—acknowledged a 'general' universal dimension to the atonement, usually 'explained away' by those who take a strictly-exclusive particularist position.

Is Jesus Christ the Redeemer? Yes: there is one mediator between God and man, the man Christ Jesus, 1 Tim. ii. 5. Is he the only Redeemer? Yes: for there is no other name under heaven given among men, whereby we must be saved, Acts iv. 12. Is he a universal Redeemer? Yes: he gave himself a ransom for all, 1 Tim. ii. 6. Did he die to purchase a general offer? Yes: the Son of man was lifted up, that whosoever believes in him should not perish, John iii. 14, 15. Is all the world the better for Christ's mediation? Yes: for by him all things consist, Col. i. 17. Is it long of Christ then that so many perish? No: I would have gathered you, and you would not, Matt. xxiii. 37.[2]

Notwithstanding the wonderful fruitfulness of their ministries, it would have been an antidote to their exaggerated orthodoxy and a basis for theological harmony had Whitefield (in opposition to the Wesleys[3]) and Spurgeon (in opposition to Dr John Clifford[4]) followed Matthew Henry more closely. Whether or not they were ever acquainted with Henry's *Scripture Catechism*, they could have detected his soteriological stance in his expositions of Isaiah 53, John 3: 16 and other texts. Indeed, the biblical balance evident therein is a

---

1   See the Appendix.

2   *A Scripture Catechism*, 192. Elsewhere Henry affirms: 'The sacrifices of atonement were instituted only for Israel, but Christ being come he is the propitiation for the sins of the whole world (1 John 2: 2). The Gospel excludes none that do not by their own unbelief and impenitency exclude themselves' (*Unpublished Sermons*, 42).

3   John Wesley's commendation of Matthew Henry's *Exposition* is remarkably positive and extensive, despite misgivings over the latter's teachings on predestination and particular redemption. Sadly, the assumption is that Henry endorses the ultra-orthodoxy of John Owen, which is simply not the case. Henry's teaching on universal redemption *a la* Baxter is ubiquitous in his writings. See the Preface to John Wesley's *Explanatory Notes upon the Old Testament* in *Works of the Rev. John Wesley* (London: John Mason, 1842), xiv. 236–40.

4   See James Marchant, *Dr. John Clifford, CH—Life, Letters and Reminiscences* (London: Cassell and Company, 1924), 166.

rebuke to the schemes of both Arminius and John Owen, so justly criticised by J. C. Ryle in his own comments on John 3: 16: 'I have long come to the conclusion that men may be more systematic in their statements than the Bible, and may be led into grave error by idolatrous veneration of a system'.[1] Albert Barnes rightly affirmed that 'The fact that Christ died for all, and that all may be saved, should be a fixed and standing point in all systems of theology, and should be allowed to shape every other opinion, and to shed its influence over every other view of truth'.[2] Such was undoubtedly the opinion of Matthew Henry. He remains a sure guide for our understanding and experience of the glorious universal sufficiency of the Gospel of our Lord Jesus Christ:

> The laying of our sins upon Christ implies the taking of them off from us; we shall not fall under the curse of the law if we submit to the grace of the gospel ... It was the iniquity of us all that was laid on Christ; for in Christ there is a sufficiency of merit for the salvation of all, and a serious offer made of that salvation to all, which excludes none that do not exclude themselves.[3]

In short, for Henry as for Baxter, after all the theological jousting is over, the Bible rules. This is well illustrated by an exchange between Spurgeon and Clifford. Referring to his own Calvinistic beliefs, Spurgeon said to his London Baptist colleague, 'I cannot imagine, Clifford, why you do not come to my way of thinking.' Clifford replied, 'I only see you about once a month, but I read my Bible every day.'[4]

Among others who shared Matthew Henry's view of the Gospel, none perhaps had a greater impact in the 19th century than the seraphic Calvinistic Methodist preacher, John Jones, Talsarn. This 'Welsh Baxter' learned his theology from the writings of another much-neglected admirer of Matthew

---

1   See John C. Ryle, *Expository Thoughts on the Gospels: John, Volume 1* ([1865] repr. Edinburgh: The Banner of Truth Trust, 1999), 159. See also J. C. Ryle, *Ryle on Redemption: The Gospel According to John Charles Ryle*, ed. Dr Alan C. Clifford (Norwich: Charenton Reformed Publishing, 2014), 13.

2   Albert Barnes, *A Popular Family Commentary on the New Testament* (London: Blackie & Son, 1850), vi. 139.

3   Henry on Isaiah 53: 6.

4   Cited in Iain H. Murray, *The Forgotten Spurgeon* (Edinburgh: The Banner of Truth Trust (1966 repr. 1994), 187.

Henry, the Congregationalist Dr Edward Williams of Rotherham.[1] Rescuing
the Gospel from the cramping tendencies of John Elias's Owenism and the
widespread soul-destroying antinomian fatalism, John Jones, Talsarn preached
in a manner that would have delighted Matthew Henry. On a notable occasion
in 1835 during the Bala Methodist Association, he thus lifted up his voice
before a large open-air crowd:

> God in the Gospel calls upon you to repent, to believe, and to lead
> a pious and godly life. But He does not mean that you should do all
> this of your own individual resources. No; He intends that you should
> put yourselves as you are under the operation of the mighty forces of
> the Gospel; that you should faithfully employ the means which He
> has commanded. Turn the prow of your little vessel to the deep; let it
> sail upon the wide ocean of Christ's Atonement; spread the sails, and
> steer it on by the guidance of the Word of God. The winds will blow,
> the mighty forces of redemption will play upon your vessel; the tides
> will carry it, and you shall find your little bark one day in the haven of
> eternal rest. You have, my friends, something yourselves to do, and it
> is of no use at all to expect the operations of the Spirit of God, while
> we ourselves neglect our duty. 'But what can I do?' Can you not read?
> Open your Bible; look at it, read it; bring your mind into contact with
> the great saving forces, and wait for help from above. 'But I cannot pray.'
> Can you not try? Can you not bend your knee, and put it down on the
> ground? 'But I must pray from the heart, and this I cannot do.' Would
> you give Him your heart? Give Him your body, give Him your tongue;
> and if you cannot say a word, there is One up there who can open His
> lips to intercede for you. Try fairly; do your best for your own salvation.
> Do not, at least, rush headlong into perdition. I, indeed, have made up
> my mind long ago that I shall not go there so. If I must go to hell at all,
> I shall not go there straight along. No; I shall loiter a good deal about
> the Garden of Gethsemane; I shall go many a round about the hill of
> Calvary; I shall bend my knees daily at the throne of grace. I shall be
> good enough for hell, if I have to go there, after all these efforts. But,
> blessed be the name of God, we have every reason to believe that this is

---

1   See W. T. Owen, *Edward Williams, DD—His Life, Thought and Influence* (Cardiff: University
of Wales Press, 1963), 20.

the high road to heaven, and that no one ever went to hell in that way, and that no one ever will.[1]

APPENDIX

Q. 20 Did God leave all mankind to perish in the state of sin and misery?

… Go preach the gospel to every creature; he that believes shall be saved, and he that believes not shall be damned, Mark xvi. 15, 16. Is this good news to fallen man? Yes: Glory be to God in the highest, on earth peace, good-will towards men, Luke ii. 14. Does this covenant exclude any that do not exclude themselves? No: Whosoever will let him come, and take of the water of life freely, Rev. xxii. 17.

Q. 21. Who is the Redeemer of God's elect?

A. The only Redeemer of God's elect is the Lord Jesus Christ, who, being the eternal Son of God, became man; and so was, and continues to be, God and Man, in two distinct natures, and one person, for ever.

1. Did mankind need a Redeemer? Yes: for by our iniquities we had sold ourselves, Isa. i. 1. Did the elect themselves need a Redeemer? Yes: for we ourselves also were sometimes disobedient, Tit. iii. 3. Would there have been a Redeemer if Adam had not sinned? No: for they that be whole need not a physician, Matt. ix. 12. Could an angel have been our Redeemer? No: for his angels he charged with folly, Job iv. 18.

2. Is Jesus Christ the Redeemer? Yes: there is one mediator between God and man, the man Christ Jesus, 1 Tim. ii. 5. Is he the only Redeemer? Yes: for there is no other name under heaven given among men, whereby we must be saved, Acts iv. 12. Is he a universal Redeemer? Yes: he gave himself a ransom for all, 1 Tim. ii. 6. Did he die to purchase a general offer? Yes: the Son of man was lifted up, that whosoever believes in him should not perish,

---

1 Cited in Alan C. Clifford, *John Jones Talsarn—Pregethwr Y Bobl/The People's Preacher* (Norwich: Charenton Reformed Publishing, 2013), 71–2.

John iii. 14, 15. Is all the world the better for Christ's mediation? Yes: for by him all things consist, Col. i. 17. Is it long of Christ then that so many perish? No: I would have gathered you, and you would not, Matt. xxiii. 37.

3. Is Christ in a special manner the Redeemer of God's elect? Yes: I lay down my life for the sheep, John x. 15. Was their salvation particularly designed in Christ's undertaking? Yes: Thou hast given him power over all flesh, that he should give eternal life to as many as thou hast given him John xvii. 2 ...[1]

Q. 25 How does Christ execute the office of a Priest? ...

... Did Christ [offer his sacrifice] for the purchase of our pardon? Yes: for when he did it, he said, Father forgive them, Luke xxiii. 34. Was it designed to save us from ruin? Yes: he gave his life a ransom for many, Matt. xx. 28. And to reconcile us to God? Yes: for he made peace through the blood of his cross, Col. i. 20. Is this our plea for peace and pardon? Yes: Who is he that condemns? It is Christ that died, Rom. viii. 34. Is Christ then the great propitiation? Yes: he is the propitiation for our sins, and not for ours only, but for the sins of the whole world, 1 John ii. 2. And have we hereby access to God? Yes: he suffered the just for the unjust, that he might bring us to God, 1 Pet. iii. 18. And had the Old Testament saints the benefit of this sacrifice? Yes: for he was the Lamb slain from the foundation of the world, Rev. xiii. 8.[2]

Q. 29. How are we made partakers of the redemption purchased by Christ?

A. We are made partakers of the redemption purchased by Christ, by the effectual application of it to us by his Holy Spirit.

1. Is redemption purchased by Christ? Yes: he Obtained eternal redemption for us, Heb. ix. 12. Is he then the Author of it? Yes: he became the Author of salvation, Heb. v. 9. Is it redemption by price? Yes: Ye are bought with a price, 1 Cor. vi. 20. Is it a redemption by power? Yes: for he hath led captivity captive, Ps. lxviii. 18. Is this redemption offered to all? Yes: he

---

1   *Scripture Catechism*, 192.

2   Ibid. 196–7.

hath proclaimed liberty to the captives, Isa. lxi. 1. May all that will take the benefit of it? Yes: Ho, every one that thirsteth, come ye to the waters, Isa. lv. 1. Have all the world therefore some benefit by it? Yes: Go into all the world, and preach the gospel to every creature, Mark xvi. 15. But have all the world a like benefit by it? No: Thou wilt manifest thyself to us, and not unto the world, John xiv. 22.

2. Is it enough for us that there is a redemption purchased? No: for there are those who deny the Lord who bought them, 2 Pet ii. 1. Is it enough to hear of it? No: for to some it is a savour of death unto death, 2 Cor. ii. 16. Is it enough to have a name among the redeemed? No: Thou hast a name that thou livest, and art dead, Rev. iii. 1. Is it necessary therefore that we be partakers of the redemption? Yes: that we may say, Who loved me, and gave himself for me, Gal. ii. 20 ...[1]

---

[1] Ibid. 203.

II. The Gospel According
to Edmund Calamy[1]

Introduction

This paper has enabled me to complete unfinished business. I refer to a mid-1970s request from Mr Geoffrey Williams of the Evangelical Library to write an article on Dr Edmund Calamy for the Library's *Bulletin*. The story is this: over a period of about a month, Mr Williams wrote to me three times. The first letter hailed Dr Calamy as 'a great man'. Would I therefore produce an article on his life and ministry? As I began to gather material, a second letter arrived about ten days later. This expressed continuing interest but somewhat less enthusiastically. I continued with my reading. Then, after another week or two, a third letter was not only more cautious; the invitation to prepare an article was virtually cancelled. Utterly perplexed, I never did understand what had happened, until now.

My recent study of Calamy's contribution has enabled me to propose a solution to the 'perplexity'. Since Mr Williams was a Strict Baptist with Gospel Standard sympathies,[2] he possibly became aware of Dr Calamy's 'Baxterian' convictions. "So what?" one might say. Well, the Gospel Standard Articles of Faith roundly condemn Baxterianism.[3] In which case, Geoffrey Williams's early enthusiasm for an article probably cooled as he discovered Calamy's sympathies. In addition to this possible scenario, the 'Banner of Truth Reformed revival' largely reflected the WCF Presbyterian and Strict

---

1 'Calamy's Gospel Preaching', a paper presented at the Eighth Annual Conference of the Amyraldian Association on 20 April 2011.

2 Iain H. Murray, *D. Martyn Lloyd-Jones: The Fight of Faith 1939–1981* (Edinburgh: Banner of Truth Trust, 1990), 81.

3 See Article 28, 'Baxterianism Denied', *Articles of Faith and Rules* (Gospel Standard Trust Publications: Harpenden, 2008), 36.

Baptist outlooks. In this respect, Dr Edmund Calamy's face didn't quite fit with the prevailing varieties of 'confessional correctness'! (It is doubtful, so soon after my 1972 Westminster Conference paper on Philip Doddridge,[1] that Mr Williams had cause to suspect me. I was quite 'safe' at that time! Indeed, my convictions had yet to develop into what they are today.) That said, it is my personal conviction that Calamy's Christianity is—in several respects—a more faithful expression of Bible-based Gospel truth than the other alternatives.

Apart from modest attention from nonconformist scholars, Dr Calamy is a largely unsung hero of a depressing period in English church history. He is almost the least-known of the Gospel preachers we are considering in our conference. While he never had the impact of his hero Richard Baxter (and how many could claim that until George Whitefield appeared in 1735?), Calamy shared most of Baxter's convictions, a good deal of his piety and an equally-strong pastoral and evangelistic commitment. In addition, besides documenting the sacrifice of the ejected ministers of 1662, he perhaps more than any other preacher and theologian transmitted Baxter's wonderful legacy to the eighteenth century and beyond. At a time when frequently-persecuted Protestant Dissent struggled to justify its existence within late Stuart and early Hanoverian society, Dr David Wykes points out that Calamy emerged as the 'Champion of Nonconformity'.[2] His own fascinating autobiography illuminates the period in which he lived. For these reasons, we do well to explore the life and labours of Dr Edmund Calamy.

CALAMY'S LAND

The England of Calamy's day was fast becoming a political, social, moral and religious wilderness. Reaction to Puritan morality could be witnessed in every realm of life. Popular with the intellectuals was Deism, a system of thought which rejected both the supernatural and a supernatural, personal God. The Deists replaced the study of revealed theology by the study of natural theology, arguing that all that needed to be known about God could be derived from a scientific study of the created order. The Deists were not

---

1   Alan C. Clifford, *Not in Word only—the Forgotten Doddridge* (Westminster Conference, 1972).

2   David. L. Wykes, 'Calamy, Edmund (1671–1732)', *Oxford Dictionary of National Biography* (Oxford University Press, 2004).

atheists in the strict sense; they believed in a God who was the 'first cause' of the universe, but they rejected the personal God of the Bible. The Deists viewed God like a watchmaker who, having made and wound up the watch, leaves it to run down without any further involvement on His part. Deism stood for the authority of reason at the expense of revelation, and its advocates preached morality rather than religion. Calamy himself lamented, 'Are not too many among us so weary of revelation, as to be willing to return back to natural religion, or Deism?'[1]

Reactions to the new liberalism, incongruously styled 'The Enlightenment', were various. In the face of such a barrage upon the Christian Faith, there were three paths of retreat. The first was that taken by the Church of England into the secluded areas of 'Latitudinarianism', a viewpoint that may be described as 'broad convictions held with little emotion'. The Established Church became a haven for a quiet, unemotional theology, where orthodoxy was maintained as far as this was consistent with 'reason'. Horton Davies says that 'It was left to the Latitudinarians to conceive of a contradiction—Christianity without tears!' While there were some worthy churchmen who attempted to combat the advancing infidelity of the age, they could hardly be called heroes of the faith. Their tactics were exclusively intellectual rather than spiritual—a masterly use of words without the unction of the Holy Spirit.

Another escape route was taken by those Dissenters who were not too worried about capitulating to the enemy; they sacrificed much orthodoxy in order to appear rational, which meant a rejection of the evangelical Calvinism of the Puritans, a declension that became Arminianism and finally Unitarianism. The Presbyterians of the seventeenth century eventually became the Unitarians of the eighteenth century. Albeit at a late stage in our period, Joshua Toulmin (1740–1815) was a notorious example: he lapsed from Presbyterian via Baptist to Unitarian convictions. Despite the heavy artillery of the Westminster Confession of Faith, the gunners deserted their positions. The Presbyterian strategy of men like Manton, Watson and Flavel did not convince the junior officers of a later generation.

The third path of retreat was that made by those who claimed to be faithful to the Calvinism of the Puritans. The spectacle was a sad one indeed; men who had formerly been the crack troops of Puritan Independency under

---

1   *God's Concern for His Glory in the British Isles and The Security of Christ's Church from the Gates of Hell* (London: John Clark, 1715), 50.

Owen and Goodwin, retreated with Bibles in their hands, but with a weighty system of hyper-calvinism upon their backs. These stalwarts fled to the barren wastes of dead orthodoxy, where the watchword became 'survival'. The Independents were joined by the Particular Baptists, and they both agreed in this, that it was safest to rest their weary legs and take off their boots. Thus the liberalism of the Presbyterians and the ultra-orthodoxy of the Particular Baptists represented the early eighteenth-century extremes of traditional Calvinistic Dissent.

So, the general picture was far from encouraging. The Church of England appeared like a senile old man, still revealing traces of his former glory, but now quite impotent. The Presbyterians suggest the picture of a once respectable young lady now despising the virtues of orthodoxy, a courtship which issued in the bastard of heterodoxy, while the Independents and Particular Baptists remind one of a prudish old couple with stern, joyless countenances, denouncing all this theological permissiveness with pharisaical precision. For the common people, this apparent defeat for the Christian faith only provided an excuse to live without regard for right or wrong, salvation or damnation, heaven or hell. This was an age that required a man of God who could provide an anchor during a storm of uncertainty and confusion. This was the age in which Almighty God called Edmund Calamy to serve Him and His people. But before we look at his ministry, let us take a brief look at the man.

CALAMY'S LINEAGE

We dare not ignore Edmund Calamy's remarkable ancestry. He was the third Edmund in a line beginning with his grandfather (1600–66) whose own Norman French Huguenot father came to England via Guernsey following the St Bartholomew persecution of 1572. A graduate of Pembroke Hall, Cambridge and an eminent preacher among the Puritans, Edmund I played a prominent part in the Westminster Assembly (1643–9). Our Edmund's father—Edmund II (1634–85)—was born in Bury St Edmunds, Suffolk, his father having previously ministered in Swaffham, Norfolk. Edmund II became Rector of Moreton in Essex, losing his living—as did his father in London—at the time of the Great Ejection (1662). In these momentous times—the Plague of 1665 followed by the Great Fire of London in 1666—Edmund I died. The sight of the devastated city soon brought him to his grave. Our

Edmund was born in London in 1671. Then Edmund III's son Edmund IV (1697–1755) also became a minister of the Gospel. Not forgetting Calamy's significant Huguenot origins, he was conscious of his godly pedigree: 'I count it my honour to be descended on ye side both of Father & Mother from the Old Puritans'.[1] Accordingly, his early published sermons indicated that the author was 'E. F. & N.'—Edmundus Filius et Nepos (i.e. Edmund, son and grandson).

CALAMY'S LIFE

Knowing the grace of God early in his life, Edmund's education prepared him for future pastoral service. Robert Tatnal's school in Westminster, then Thomas Doolittle's Academy at Islington led via Thomas Walton's School in Bethnal Green to Merchant Taylors' School after his father's death in 1685. A year later he entered Samuel Cradock's Academy at Wickhambrook near Newmarket, Suffolk. Professing personal conversion at this time, he then 'went to the Lord's Table'. In every respect, he declared: 'I must freely own I can look back on the time spent at Mr Cradock's academy with comfort and pleasure, blessing God for the benefit I there received … it was no small encouragement to me, to have this good old gentleman, upon his hearing me preach, a good many years after, come and embrace me in his arms, thanking God for the hand he had in my education'.[2]

In 1688, on the advice of the eminent Puritan John Howe (1630–1705), Edmund travelled to the Netherlands with other ministerial students to study at Utrecht. Studying in foreign Reformed institutions was the only way to obtain a higher education, entry to Oxford and Cambridge then being only open to Anglicans. This was a critical year for the future of European Protestantism. In October, Calamy saw William of Orange embark on his enterprise to liberate England from the Catholic designs of James II.

As much as Calamy and his generation valued the rigours of academic training, they were aware of the danger of unsanctified intelligence. Just as Baxter, Howe and others were careful to promote piety as well as sound learning, young Calamy shared their concerns. Besides escaping from a near-

---

1 Cited by Wykes, Oxford DNB (2004).

2 *An Historical Account of My Own Life* (London: Henry Colburn and Richard Bentley, 1830), i. 145 (cited in A. H. Drysdale, 'Dr Edmund Calamy' in *Short Biographies for the People by Various Writers* (London: Religious Tract society, 1890), vii. No. 77, 6).

fatal accident on Dutch ice, he was aware of the threat of frozen orthodoxy. On leaving Holland for home in 1691, he expressed regret that though there were many English ministerial students at Utrecht,

> ... we had no meetings among ourselves for prayer and Christian converse. Had I not been provided with many good practical books of English divinity, which I read frequently with profit and pleasure, I doubt it would have been worse with me than it was. From my own experience I can heartily recommend all students of theology, while laying in a stock of divinity in speculative way, to read pious and devotional works, so as to have a warmer sense of the things of God on their minds and hearts.[1]

Calamy's concern probably explains why he appreciated worshipping among the Huguenot refugees:

> In the French Church at Utrecht ... there was ... M. Saurin ... a very grave man, and one of great depth of thought; who was for going to the bottom of a subject, and when he had doctrinally opened it, had a marvellous way of touching the passions.[2]

Returning to London, Edmund met the aged Richard Baxter. This was an important event in his life, as he makes clear:

> I particularly waited on Mr Baxter, who talked freely with me about my good old grandfather, for whom he declared a particular esteem.

Part of this esteem would have related to the 'Amyraldian' (or Davenantian!) convictions articulated by Edmund Calamy I during the sessions of the Westminster Assembly.[3] Edmund continued:

> I several times heard [Mr Baxter] preach, which remembered not to have done before. He talked in the pulpit with great freedom about another world, like one that had been there, and was come as a sort of an express from thence to make a report concerning it. He was well advanced in years, but delivered himself in public, as well as in private, with great vivacity and freedom, and his thoughts had a peculiar edge. I

---

1   Ibid. 188 (Drysdale, 7).

2   *Account of My Own Life,* i. 145.

3   See Alan C. Clifford, *Atonement and Justification: English Evangelical Theology 1640–1790—An Evaluation* (Oxford: Clarendon Press, 1990/2002), 75.

told him of my design of going to Oxford, and staying sometime there, in which he encouraged me: and towards the end of the year, (Dec. 8) when I was actually there, he died; so that I should never have had an opportunity of seeing, hearing, or conversing with him, had I not done it now.[1]

The chief purpose of Calamy's studies at this time was to settle the question: was he to serve in the Church of England or among the Protestant Dissenters? So, aided by a letter of recommendation from one of his Dutch professors, he availed himself of the facilities of the Bodleian Library, Oxford. Among other works, he read Richard Hooker's *The Laws of Ecclesiastical Polity* (1590). However, as his detailed and comprehensive critique makes clear, Calamy remained totally unimpressed by the author's case for classical Anglicanism.[2] Carefully studying his Bible, 'and particularly the New Testament', he concluded that 'the plain worship of the Dissenters' was 'more agreeable to that, than the pompous way of the Church of England'.[3] William Chillingworth's *The Religion of Protestants* (1638) persuaded him that the Bible alone, rather than man-made confessions of faith (however sound), must be the basis of faith and concord among Christians.[4] Lodging with the Oxford Presbyterian minister Joshua Oldfield, Calamy was encouraged to preach his first sermon. As yet unordained, he felt somewhat intimidated by the event. His hearers included a 'greater number of scholars than usual'. However, our young preacher says "I bless God, however, I was not dashed, but came off pretty well. I discoursed both parts of the day from Heb.2: 3, 'How shall we escape if we neglect so great salvation?' "" Speaking of 'the great salvation of the Gospel', he expounded 'the necessity' of 'the satisfaction that our blessed Saviour made for sin by offering up himself as a sacrifice ... according to the common way of our Protestant writers'.[5]

Returning to London in 1692, Calamy accepted a call from Matthew Sylvester's congregation at Meeting-House Court, Blackfriars. He and five other candidates were eventually ordained at Dr Samuel Annesley's Meeting House on 22 June 1694, Dr Daniel Williams—the eminent Presbyterian

---

1 Calamy, *An Historical Account*, i. 220–1.
2 Ibid. 235–46.
3 Ibid. 224–5.
4 Ibid. 227–34.
5 Ibid. 268.

leader—and five ejected ministers officiating. This was the first public ordination of the Dissenters since the Act of Uniformity (1662). Calamy's first published sermon appeared around this time: *A Practical Discourse concerning Vows: with a special reference to Baptism and the Lord's Supper* (1694). This work, indicates Drysdale, 'proved' a blessing to 'more than his hearers. "If ever any saving impressions have been made upon my soul," writes one, "the reading of your treatise on vows was the great instrument. May I never forget the strong and lively influence it had on me."'[1]

The following year, Edmund Calamy became assistant to Dr Daniel Williams at Hand Alley, Bishopsgate Street. In the same year (1695) he married Mary Watts, a marriage that proved happy and fruitful until Mary died in 1713. Their eldest son, Edmund IV (d. 1755) was born in 1698.

CALAMY'S LEGACY

Having recently commenced a regular and dedicated pastoral ministry in London lasting 38 years, Calamy also embarked on his career as an historian. So, in 1696, he aided Matthew Sylvester in publishing Richard Baxter's *Autobiography: the Reliquiae Baxterianae*. Thereafter, he amazingly found time to preserve and promote the memory of Baxter and the ejected ministers. Believing that Sylvesters's devoted yet defective work would be more effective in an edited form, Calamy published *An Abridgement of Mr Baxter's History of His Life and Times with An account of the Ministers ... who were Ejected after the Restoration of King Charles II* (1702). Integral with his ministry, Calamy clearly felt called of God to transmit the heroic faith of Baxter and his brethren: "To let the Memory of these Men Dye is injurious to Posterity".[2] His *Abridgement* involved great courage, and it provoked a storm. At a time of continuing Anglican-inspired hostility to the heirs of the Puritans, this inspiring material marked out Edmund Calamy as 'the Champion of Nonconformity'.[3]

In 1702, Calamy was chosen as one of the Tuesday lecturers at Salters' Hall. Dating from earlier times, these public merchants lectures played a vital role in promoting Christian edification. Calamy's first and highly-impressive contribution was *Divine Mercy Exalted: or Free Grace in its Glory*. It was

---

1   Drysdale, 11.
2   Wykes, *Oxford DNB*.
3   Ibid.

'Published at the Request of Many Encouragers of the Lecture' the following year. Being the chief focus of this paper, the significance and importance of this lecture will shortly be explored.

That same year, Calamy became the minister of Tothill Street, Westminster. As his influence in the public affairs of the Dissenters began to increase, he was concerned clearly to define the Dissenting Presbyterian position *vis-à-vis* the Anglican Establishment, but without rancour and extremism. Thus, in the manner of Calvin, the Westminster divines and Baxter, and to vindicate the ejected clergy, this English churchman preached and published his *Defence of Moderate Nonconformity* (in three parts, 1703–5). For all his 'moderation', he presents a cogent and comprehensive biblical demonstration 'that presbyters are by Divine Right the same as Bishops'[1] and that the apostolic meaning of 'bishop' is *not* 'the sense the Church of England gives that word'.[2] Far from ignoring that biblical pastoral order is designed to promote practical piety in the lives of God's people, Calamy published Richard Baxter's *Practical Works* in 1707.[3] This was a major publishing event where Calamy was concerned. In his preface, after highlighting the 'valuable treatises of practical divinity published in this country', Calamy states that 'there are no writings of that kind among us, that have more of a true Christian spirit, a greater mixture of judgement and affection, or a greater tendency to revive pure and undefiled religion that have been more esteemed abroad, or more blessed at home for the awakening the secure, instructing the ignorant, confirming the wavering, comforting the dejected, recovering the profane, or improving such as are truly serious, than the Practical Works of this author'.[4] Adept at citing 'opposition' support, Calamy says 'That great man Bishop Wilkins was used to say of Mr Baxter, that if he had lived in the Primitive times he had been One of the Fathers of the Church: what then more fit than a collection of his works, that posterity may be taught to do him justice?'[5]

Concerned as he was to promote vital and fervent piety, Calamy was aware of the danger of fanaticism. This became an issue with the arrival of certain 'French prophets' in London. Such had provided much of the inspiration in

---

1   *Defence of Moderate Nonconformity* (London: Thomas Parkhurst, 1703), 71.

2   Ibid. 72.

3   *The Practical Works of the Late Reverend and Pious Mr Richard Baxter*, in Four Volumes (London: Thomas Parkhurst, 1707).

4   Ibid. p. iii.

5   Ibid.

the Cevénnes region of France during the war of the Camisards (1702–10). These wild 'charismatic prophets' attracted a significant fringe following in this country, even influencing a member of Calamy's own congregation. Thus early in 1708 he preached and published two sermons entitled *A Caveat against the New Prophets*.[1] These very valuable sermons—appreciated by Queen Anne, no less—included a historical survey of fanaticism. Tracing its rise to the second-century 'impostor' Montanus, Calamy includes Roman Catholicism and Islam when he argues that 'the superstitious and idolatrous corruptions of the Church of Rome prevailed in the West, much about the same time as the Muhammadan fooleries spread far and near in the East. And in the Romish Church an enthusiastical spirit has remarkably prevailed ever since its first degeneracy. The histories of the lives of their saints are full of visions, extraordinary revelations and ecstasies. Whenever anything was to be undertaken for the advancement of the Church; and when any new doctrine or worship was to be established, a revelation has still been coined to direct it, and confirm it. Thus was the way paved for the settlement of image worship'.[2]

Concurrent with these concerns, Calamy preached an excellent series of sermons at Salters' Hall on *The Inspiration of the Old and New Testament* between 1704–6. Published in 1710, the author was anxious to rescue the Bible from any aspersions that might be cast on its Holy Spirit-inspired character. In his dedication to the Queen, in view of the recent fanatical disturbances, Calamy writes that 'Your gracious acceptance of my endeavours in opposition to a late pretended inspiration, has encouraged me with all humility to present to Your Majesty this defence of the ancient, but real inspiration of the Holy Writings of the Old and New Testament; which are the standard of our religion, and the foundation both of its certainty and authority'.[3]

This interesting dedication to the 'Chief support of the Reformed Interest' takes note of the recent military victories of Sir John Churchill, Duke of Marlborough (Blenheim, 1704; Ramillies, 1706; Oudenarde, 1708 and Malplaquet, 1709), the humbling of Louis XIV and the Act of Union:

Your Majesty's reign will be celebrated in future for the steadiness

---

1   *A Caveat Against the New Prophets* (London: Thomas Parkhurst, 1708).
2   Ibid. 42.
3   *The Inspiration of the Holy Writings of the Old and New Testament Considered and Improved* (London: Thomas Parkhurst, 1710), The Dedication.

of your counsels, and the glorious success of your Arms; for giving an effectual check to the aspiring designs of universal monarchy, and fixing the balance of Europe; for uniting your two British Kingdoms, and confirming your subjects of all persuasions, in a just esteem of the great blessing of MODERATION'.[1]

The year before these important sermons were published revealed Calamy's continuing concern with 'moderation'. Having witnessed first-hand in his youth the cruelties of religious persecution, he agreed with Baxter that both sides had been guilty during the Civil War. There had been oppressive Presbyterians (not to forget the Cromwellian Independents) as well as oppressive Episcopalians. He thus sought to combine well-founded, sincerely-held convictions with a 'catholic spirit' or at least a respectful toleration of those who differ—not an easy balance to maintain. He therefore shunned the 'spirit of imposition'. During his travels to 'North Britain' in 1709, Calamy detected such a spirit during the General Assembly of the Church of Scotland, where he was an honoured guest, seated next to the Moderator. During one session when a suspected minister was being cross-examined, he caused some amusement when he remarked, "We in England should reckon this way of proceeding the inquisition revived."[2] Calamy returned to London with more than an interesting glimpse of Scottish Presbyterianism. He was honoured with DDs from the Universities of Edinburgh, Aberdeen and Glasgow. Thus 'DD' replaced 'E. F. & N.' on the title pages of his books.

In the midst of all his pastoral, public and literary activities—a new edition of his *Account of the Ejected* appeared in 1713—Edmund Calamy knew personal sadness. His first wife, Mary died that year. Besides encouraging his brethren there, an extended preaching tour in the West of England allowed him to recover from his grief. However, he was troubled by the unhappy disturbances caused by advancing Unitarian ideas among some of the Dissenters in Exeter. A year later, his devoted mother died. Then, in the aftermath of the accession of Hanoverian Protestant King George I (1714–27), the first Jacobite rising indicated significant Roman Catholic opposition in the North of England and Scotland. To settle disturbed minds and hearts among loyal Protestants, Calamy preached and published three remarkable sermons in 1715 entitled *God's Concern for His Glory in the British Isles and The Security of Christ's Church*

---

1   Ibid.
2   *An Historical Account*, ii.156.

from the Gates of Hell.[1] These sermons include a masterly survey of the church history of the British Isles from the earliest times to the early eighteenth century, with suitable applications to assure believers that 'an Almighty Jesus has undertaken the conduct of His own Church, and engaged that it shall in the end be victorious over all the designs of its enemies'.[2] No less impressive than the scholarly erudition of our pastor-historian is the author's deeply-moving dedication to one grief-stricken 'Much Honoured the Lady Levet' who had cared for his mother in her last illness: 'Your Ladyship's constant tenderness' and 'endearing love accompanied her to the last hours of her life'. This remarkable lady had not only stood out against the prevailing immorality of high society 'in one of the most populous and flourishing cities in the Universe'.[3] She had also suffered a degree of social rejection on account of her Dissenting convictions. She was clearly a trophy of God's grace in Dr Calamy's ministry. She died at Bath in 1722.[4]

In 1716, Calamy married Mary Jones who proved an ideal helpmeet for God's servant. His responsibilities increased when, on the death of Dr Daniel Williams that same year, Calamy became the recognised leader among the Dissenters, often acting on behalf of the three denominations, Presbyterian, Congregational and Baptist. Young men often sought his counsel respecting their ministerial aspirations. One such in 1718 was sixteen-year old Philip Doddridge. 'The Doctor' was not that impressed, urging young Philip to pursue a law career. As if to indicate that godly men are not infallible, happily for others and ourselves, God's call to Philip Doddridge was too clear to be discouraged. The rest is history.[5]

As Calamy's autobiography makes very clear, the descendants of the Puritans had largely lost the spiritual zeal of their forebears. That power for righteousness and godliness that had been so positively displayed in earlier times was now assuming a more negative character. This fact is clearly confirmed in the theological debates that dominated the life of the Dissenting congregations around the year 1719.

---

1   *God's Concern for His Glory in the British Isles and The Security of Christ's Church from the Gates of Hell* (London: John Clark, 1715).

2   Ibid. 87.

3   Ibid. dedication.

4   'Oct. 15. Died my good friend, the Lady Levet, at Bath' (*An Historical Account*, ii.463).

5   See my *The Good Doctor: Philip Doddridge of Northampton, a Tercentenary Tribute* (Norwich: Charenton Reformed Publishing, 2002).

Theological decline chiefly began to make itself felt following the publication of works by such men as Emlyn, Clark and Whiston. These men rejected the orthodox understanding of the Trinity, expounding views that eventually issued in Unitarianism. The new liberal ideas of the age revived the ancient heresy of Arianism. In no place did Arianism obtain a firmer grip than among the Presbyterian congregations at Exeter which favoured the heterodox James Peirce. The managing committee of the churches in Exeter decided to refer the matter to the ministers of the London churches. A committee of the three main dissenting bodies—Presbyterian, Independent and Baptist—drew up a 'Paper of Advices' to be sent to Exeter, as a means of reconciling the contending parties. This document was discussed by an assembly of the London ministers at the famous Salters' Hall on February 19, 1719. A heated division of opinion soon followed between those advocating a more conciliatory position and those who argued for a strict prohibition of ministers advancing Arian views.

The Salters' Hall Conference is a landmark in the history of English Nonconformity. From this time, the congregations became largely introspective, and mutual suspicion permeated the ranks of the ministers. The Conference revealed a sad anomaly, such that, recalling his study of Chillingworth's *The Religion of Protestants* at Oxford, Dr Calamy complained of 'a spirit of imposition'.[1] This development was not characteristic of the Dissenters. In 1662, these men had suffered because the Act of Uniformity had been imposed on them. How could they now yield to a spirit of persecuting imposition? On the other hand, many of the Presbyterians like those at Exeter, were now claiming further liberties in rejecting their own doctrinal standards. Over-heated logic tends to push things to extremes, and what was a desire for liberty *under* the Gospel in 1662 was becoming liberty *without* the Gospel in 1719. Orthodox liberty became heterodox liberalism.

A further development following Salters' Hall was that those of the 'Subscribing' party naturally tended to question the orthodoxy of the 'Nonsubscribers', even when there were no just grounds to do so. An inquisitorial attitude was at large. Those who advocated 'charity' in disputes were automatically suspected of Arianism, while those who contended for truth were accused of bigotry. There were many cases of both liberalism and bigotry, but there were others who sought to achieve a biblical balance.

---

[1]   See his narrative and assessment in *An Historical Account*, ii.403–29.

This division of opinion did not reflect any differences on the doctrines of the Trinity and the Deity of Christ, but simply whether human articles of faith should be subscribed to. As one minister present said, "It was not from any doubts in our minds as to the generally received opinions upon that subject, but from our scrupling to subscribe to any human articles of faith."[1] Despite the amount of heat dissipated, two sets of advice were sent down to Exeter. From all this, for all their distaste for Arianism, Dr Calamy and others remained uninvolved.

Together with the Congregational leader, Dr Isaac Watts (1674–1748)— undoubtedly more well-known on account of his hymns—Dr Edmund Calamy was probably the most distinguished example of this anti-imposition outlook. Others who attended the unsavoury debates agreed that Calamy and Watts took the wisest course in not attending. Certainly, if anyone doubted his attachment to truth, contrary to Dr Watts' later dubious deviations, Dr Calamy demonstrated his sound Bible-based convictions in his magnificent *Thirteen Sermons Concerning the Doctrine of the Trinity*, preached at Salters' Hall in 1719. When they were published in 1722, they included four other sermons from 1720 vindicating the genuineness of 'that celebrated Text, 1 John 5: 7'. Never perhaps has such sound, sanctified scholarship appeared in relatively-popular dress in the defence of the authentic biblical Gospel than in these sermons. In the hope that 'it might bring more persons to read the discourses',[2] they were dedicated by permission to King George I, to whom Dr Calamy had presented a loyal address in the name of the Protestant Dissenters in 1717.[3] There were, of course, perfectly valid political expectations in all this, as Calamy makes clear:

> I humbly presented my book to His Majesty, who received me very graciously, took it into his hands, and looked on it; and then was pleased to tell me, he took us Dissenters for his hearty friends, and desired me to let my brethren in the city know, that in the approaching election of members of Parliament, he depended on them, to use their utmost influence, wherever they had any interest, in favour of such as were hearty for him and his family.[4]

---

1   Thomas Wright, *The Life of Isaac Watts* (London: Farncombe & Sons, 1914), 139.
2   See *An Historical Account*, ii. 444.
3   Ibid. ii. 366ff.
4   Ibid. 446–7.

While the Dr Calamy and others had grave concerns about the spiritual health of the Dissenters at this time, his own ministry knew the unmistakeable blessing of God. A growing congregation required a new building, as he joyfully explains:

> April 23. 1721 I entered on the new place of worship, erected at a considerable expense in Long Ditch, Westminster [in Princes Street]. It was near two years building. Soon after, the whole was paid for, which I thought I had reason to reckon among the considerable mercies of my life. The necessity we were under of erecting a new place of worship was great, and the difficulties we met with were very considerable; but we had our helps, the juncture was favourable, and a kind Providence carried us through all ... To God be the praise!'[1]

Regarding the 'living church' that filled the building, one observer wrote:

> [Dr Calamy] had many persons of considerable figure in his congregation, and continued to preach there till his death, discharging the duties of the Christian ministry with great constancy and diligence.[2]

By all accounts, if he seldom rose to the heights of Baxterian eloquence, Dr Calamy was a good, solid, warm and faithful preacher.[3] His large congregation obviously appreciated his pastoral emphases. His published sermons reveal a minister with the highest spiritual concerns. Promoting—as did Richard Baxter—'serious, practical Christianity' and discouraging 'party spirit' and censoriousness, he urged:

> Let it be your endeavour to get well furnished minds, warm hearts, governable spirits, tender consciences, and heavenly affections, and your stability and fruitfulness will be signal. Often reflect on the strength and sacredness of the divine vows you are under [especially regarding Baptism and the Lord's Supper], ... and take care to live faithfully up to them, if

---

1 Ibid. 441–2.

2 Cited in John Stoughton, *Religion in England under Queen Anne and the Georges 1702–1800* (London: Hodder and Stoughton, 1878), i. 185.

3 A visitor from Northampton (and clearly no friend of Presbyterianism) remarked on Calamy: 'He is a good preacher, but a zealous man for the Kirk, ...' (cited in Stoughton, *Religion in England,* i. 226). Another observed that 'He preached very well, but he has a stiff, affecting manner of delivery, though a good voice and the delivery pretty good' (*The Diary of Dudley Ryder, 1715–1716,* ed. W. Matthews (1939), 224, cited in Wykes, *Oxford DNB*).

you have any regard to the favour of God, the honour of Christ, your own present peace, or future happiness.[1]

As a pastor's pastor (in a brotherly not a pseudo-episcopal sense!), Calamy's ordination sermons clearly set forth the biblical ministerial model. Regarding doctrine, a pastor should avoid a man-made confessionalism:

Adhere firmly to [your doctrine] as it is delivered in the Holy Scriptures, which are the true standard which all creeds and confessions, systems and theological tracts and discourses are to be measured by: and be ready to maintain and defend it, and oppose them that teach any other doctrine.[2]

Regarding a pastor's personal piety, Calamy urges:

Aim at excelling in that love to God, that zeal for Christ, that compassion for the souls of men, that humility of mind, that mastery of your appetites, and that mortification and deadness to this world, that becomes the character and profession you have taken upon you.[3]

Regarding a pastor's public example, they should aim at a holy consistency between lip and life:

Men are so disposed, that they'll much more mind how you live, than what you say. And what can be more dreadful, than for ministers to pull down and destroy by their bad examples, what they seem to take pains to build up with the words of their mouths![4]

CALAMY'S LAST YEARS

Believing that posterity would be 'injured' without an awareness of its godly heritage, Calamy continued with his historical ministry. In 1724 he published the *Memoirs of John Howe*. Three years later—1727—he published *A continuation of the Account of the Ministers* (including further account of Baxter).

---

1   *A Practical Discourse concerning Vows: with a special reference to Baptism and the Lord's Supper* (London: Thomas Parkhurst, 1704), The Epistle Dedicatory.

2   *The Principles and Practice of Moderate Nonconformists with Respect to Ordination* (London: John Clark, 1717), 26.

3   Ibid. 28.

4   Ibid. 29.

Despite the national rejoicing at the accession of King George II that same year, Calamy's public involvement in presenting loyal addresses at Court on behalf of the Protestant Dissenters[1] and the magnificence of the Coronation (some of which he witnessed[2]), his heart was heavy. Many lapsed Dissenters were conforming to the Church of England and the health of the churches generally was not good. He longed for true spiritual revival:

> Let us beg a fresh effusion of the Divine Spirit from on high to revive the power and life of religion in our midst. Nothing can be more manifest than that the Church of Christ at this day is most sadly degenerated, has long been in a very languishing state, and is become too much like the rest of the world. Formality has eaten out the spirit of piety; and selfishness, covetousness, pride, wrathfulness, envy and malice have most shamefully abounded in the Christian Church, and sadly defaced, disquieted and infested it. And all parties have been such sharers in the common guilt that none must pretend an exemption. The great doctrines of the Christian religion have lost their force, and are professedly believed but for fashion's sake. ... And many that make great profession are lost in carnality and are crumbled into parties enflamed against each other, striving which shall get the better, which is much to be lamented.[3]

Calamy took note of widespread discussion in 1730 about 'the decay of the Dissenting interest'.[4] He read most of the pamphlets produced in response to *An Inquiry into the Causes of the Decay*, authored by a Dissenter who shortly after joined the Anglicans. Philip Doddridge's anonymous response[5] was noted, as is another by Isaac Watts.[6] In some respects he was puzzled by concern over numbers. In some areas growth was evident if decline occurred elsewhere. Certainly, his own congregation was flourishing, as were others

---

1 *An Historical Account*, ii. 496–500.

2 'Wednesday, Oct. 11, the King and Queen were crowned, in great pomp and state. The procession to and from the Abbey upon that occasion, of which I was a spectator, was very magnificent. Dr Potter, Bishop of Oxford, preached the coronation sermon from 2 *Chron. ix. 8*' (ibid. ii. 500).

3 *A Continuation of the Account of the Ministers*, cited in Drysdale, 16.

4 See *An Historical Account*, ii. 529–31.

5 *Free Thoughts on the most probable means of reviving the Dissenting Interest* (London: Richard Hett, 1730).

6 *An Humble Attempt towards the Revival of Practical Religion among Christians, and particularly the Protestant Dissenters* (London: 1731).

in London. However, he did not deny that 'at the same time, a real decay of serious religion, both in the Church and out of it, was very visible'.[1]

Calamy's health began to decline by 1729. That summer he spent ten weeks at Scarborough 'taking the waters'. Yet his faith remained bright and his focus unchanged. In 1731 he preached at Dr Williams's Library to the ministers of the three denominations (the first of such gatherings) on *Gospel Ministers, the Salt of the Earth*.[2] Planning another health visit to Bath in 1732 (though not expecting that his end was that close), Dr Calamy preached what proved to be his farewell sermon:

> Were I assured this was the last sermon I should ever preach to you, I know not any better text to fasten on than my text, 'The grace of our Lord Jesus Christ be with you all,' and to this I can heartily say Amen. For, brethren, my heart's desire and prayer for you is that you may be saved. And may you but have the grace of the Lord Jesus Christ with you, I shall not doubt of it. ... May it be on you and in you more and more. May you have it in your homes and in your attendance on God in His house. You will be much in my thoughts, and I trust I shall not be out of yours.[3]

Calamy returned to London where he died on 9 June. Daniel Mayo (Doddridge's former pastor at Kingston-upon-Thames) preached his funeral sermon. There we learn that:

> There was a constant calmness and easiness on his mind with respect to another world, a firm faith in the Gospel method of salvation, and good hope through grace. He was ever inclined to thankfulness, without distrust or complaint, and comforted several in distress that came to visit him. ... A few days before his death, he plainly apprehended that his end was near, and did in a particular manner pray for a blessing on his wife and children, that were about him, and then took his leave of them, and hardly ever had the use of his reason afterwards.[4]

We may surely say, 'The memory of the righteous is blessed' (*Proverbs 10: 7*).

---

1   *An Historical Account*, ii. 531.
2   This was never published and remains in MS at DWL.
3   Cited in Drysdale, 16.
4   Cited in *An Historical Account*, ii. 535.

CALAMY'S LECTURE

In a thoroughly dismissive manner, the Unitarian historian Alexander Gordon declared that 'no one reads Calamy's sermons'.[1] Neither does he bother to mention the important Salters' Hall lecture *Divine Mercy Exalted: or Free Grace in its Glory* (1703), to which we now turn. Even Dr David Wykes (also a Unitarian), while stating that 'Calamy was Baxterian in theology',[2] fails to mention this most important work wherein Calamy's Baxterian soteriology is evident. Far more sympathetically, Alexander Drysdale commends the sermon as 'entirely evangelical' even if it lacks 'the warmth and glow of utterance congenial to such a theme'.[3] But this 'sermonic lecture' was clearly intended not only to edify his hearers but to advertise the young minister's commitment to 'Baxterian Calvinism' *vis-à-vis* the prevailing extremes of Arminianism and Owenism. Judging by the title page, it met a widespread need for clarity over many of the most controversial issues of recent history. Indeed, this work is a well-structured, biblically-based and luminously-insightful exposition of the Gospel which repays careful study. The following inadequate overview is intended to indicate the main drift of Calamy's case.

In the preface to *Divine Mercy Exalted*, Calamy reveals his perspective on the subject in hand. In order to express his position, he appeals not to the over-refined orthodoxy of the Westminster Assembly (1643–9) but to the unexaggerated theology of the Synod of Dort (1618). While he often made respectful references to the WCF in later years, Calamy was evidently happier with the more moderate stances of Dort and of Bishop John Davenant who was one of the British delegates at the Synod:

> I have considered Divine grace as actually discovering itself to sinners, rather than as purposed in the Decree: but he that would see that discussed, and the doctrine of particular election maintained, consistently with a general love of God to the world, would do well to consult the learned and peaceable Bishop Davenant's *Animadversions upon Hoard's Treatise of God's Love to Mankind*; a book which is not valued according to its worth: though one would think it were therefore the more to be regarded in these points, because the worthy author was so considerable a member

---

1 See the article on Calamy in the *DNB* (Oxford: OUP, 1885–1900).
2 David L. Wykes, 'Calamy, Edmund (1671–1732)', *Oxford DNB* (Oxford University Press, 2004).
3 Drysdale, 'Dr Edmund Calamy', 11.

of the forementioned Synod, in which the controversy about grace and free-will was so distinctly debated.[1]

Without even a single reference to Richard Baxter, Calamy does what his hero also did—appeal to John Davenant's 'middle way' between 'free will' Arminianism and what became 'limited atonement' Owenism (and later hypercalvinst Gillism). In the context of these debates, Davenant's *Dissertation on the Death of Christ* is well known (even though the Banner of Truth Trust deleted it from their recent edition of Davenant's *Exposition of Colossians*, an omission remedied by Dr Digby James of the Quinta Press).[2] However, Calamy's citation of Davenant's lesser-known-work against the Arminian Anglican Samuel Hoard is important in dealing with the predestinarian background to the atoning work of Christ. Indeed, Davenant's *Animadversions* is probably the best, balanced albeit brief biblical exposition of predestination ever written. Besides resolving numerous knotty issues, it provides practical guidance to preachers on how and how not to preach on the subject. In the process of rescuing the Bible's teaching on this subject from Hoard's repeated misrepresentations, Davenant also rescues John Calvin from the unjust aspersions cast on him on account of the doctrine.[3] In short, Davenant's teaching was the perfect Bible-based antidote to a later extremism of the kind Baxter and later Calamy sought to oppose. This was a Gospel stance[4] which could not only claim support from Calvin and many other reformers. Above all, Calamy—like Baxter—believed such was the true teaching of the Holy Scriptures.

Calamy's text is 'So then it is not of him that willeth, nor of him that

---

1   *Divine Mercy Exalted: or Free Grace in its Glory* (London: 1703), pp. iii–iv.

2   See my Introduction to John Davenant, *A Dissertation on the Death of Christ* (Weston Rhyn: Quinta Press, 2006).

3   See John Davenant, *Animadversions Upon a Treatise Intitled God's Love to Mankind* (Cambridge: 1641), 26, 39, 42, 64, 96, 99, 135, 139–43, etc.

4   'Christ died for all and every singular person, who by repentance and faith in His blood may, according to the tenor of the Gospel, have eternal life given him through Jesus Christ our Lord. And Christ died thus for all, not only because His death was in regard of the worth a sufficient ransom for all and more than all, but because it is God's settled purpose, by Christ's bloodshed to save any man that shall believe truly in Him, and to save no man that continueth an unbeliever. Christ died not to save any few selected ones without their repentance and faith; and Christ died not with an exception or exclusion of any one man in the world from the benefit of salvation, performing the condition of faith and repentance' (ibid. 472–3).

runneth, but of God that sheweth mercy' (*Romans 9: 16*). He has no hesitation in affirming that 'the reason why the gentiles, and why particular sinners that are unworthy, are embraced and peculiarly favoured by God, while the Jews and other sinners are left in their chosen impenitency and infidelity, is not from any antecedent worthiness or disposedness, that God saw in the former above the latter, but from his free differencing grace and mercy'.[1] In short, salvation 'is not to be ultimately resolved into human pains and industry: the spring of it is to be searched for, not in man but in God'.[2] Indeed, God's mercy 'is exercised in a sovereign way'.[3]

Yet Calamy is quick to rescue the text from fatalistic hypercalvinist inertia when he says: 'Yet [the Apostle] is far from intimating that willing and running is needless; or that the mercy of God will act alone ... without a subservient agency on our part'.[4] Would we tell the farmer and the businessman that 'the blessing of the Lord that maketh rich' (*Prov. 10: 22*) does not require their 'diligence and industry'?[5] Developing his case from text after text, Calamy encourages (with a touch of Baxterian eloquence) the unassured seeker after God who desires but doubts God's mercy, thus:

He that waits to be gracious, and hath assured us with an oath, that He hath 'no pleasure in the death of the wicked, but that he turn from his way and live' (*Ezek. 33: 11*); He that seeks us so carefully as lost sheep while we are wandering from Him in the ways of vanity and folly, cannot certainly turn His back upon us, when our wills are fixed for Him; and we are bent upon running in the way of His commandments.[6]

Tracing our salvation to God's mercy, Calamy carefully explains what his text is *not* saying. In the case of those who are unsaved, the cause is our sin and unwillingness, not 'God that delighteth in severity'.[7]

The text keeps on the bright side, and states the case of those whom God treats and embraces as His own; and there it tells us we must fasten upon unaccountable mercy as the rise of all: but if we turn to the darker

---

1   *Divine Mercy Exalted*, 5–6.
2   Ibid. 7.
3   Ibid. 9.
4   Ibid. 9–10.
5   Ibid. 10.
6   Ibid. 13.
7   Ibid. 14.

side, and view the case of those who are cast off by God, we are not allowed to fasten upon unaccountable severity as the procuring cause. … Our saviour hath Himself sufficiently cleared that matter, when He in so many words tells those among whom He preached, and before whom He wrought His miracles, that this was their ruin: 'Ye will not come to me that ye might have life' (Jn. 5: 40).[1]

After explaining that sinners are lost from their own 'self-hardening', and that Romans 9: 22–3 only speaks of *'prior* preparation' in the case of the saved, Calamy concludes—and the Greek supports him—that God 'with much long-suffering and patience endured [the unsaved]. A clear evidence that He rather permitted them when left to themselves, to harden their own hearts, than positively concurred in it. And indeed, though Divine mercy is ever free, yet God's severity is always deserved'.[2]

Having refuted common ultra-Calvinist abuse of the doctrine of predestination, Calamy then proceeds in his first main proposition to present Christ's coming into the world:

> The providing a Mediator, and all overtures about reconciliation through Him, are 'of God that sheweth mercy'. Nothing but meer pity and compassion could move Him, when so affronted, to think of a Saviour for a lost world; whom He might have left to perish in their miserable state.[3]

In his second proposition, Calamy highlights the 'given' unmerited nature of God's grace. Thus we should simply be amazed at the Gospel, realising that had God withheld His mercy from humanity, no injustice would have been done. After showing how 'providential means' and 'ministerial helps' in the recovery of sinners combine to 'point out their Saviour to them, set Him in all His charms before them, and press them to accept His offered help',[4] Calamy reminds us of God's sovereign initiative in dealing with nations:

> Some that pretend to have made an exact calculation, do observe, that if the earth, as far as it is at this day known, were divided into 30 equal parts, 19 of them are pagan, 6 Muhammadan, and but 5 Christian. Who

---

1 Ibid. 14–15.
2 Ibid. 16–17.
3 Ibid. 17.
4 Ibid. 21.

that gives way to consideration, can forbear wondering that these five parts of the earth should be more favoured than the other 25![1]

In his third main proposition, Calamy is careful to show that when sinners seek God, their endeavours are 'not from themselves, but given and stirred up by God that sheweth mercy'.[2] In expounding our natural deadness and aversion regarding spiritual things from a range of biblical texts, Calamy is careful (in Amyraldian style) to distinguish between 'moral' and 'natural' impotency.[3] Indeed, 'dead' sinners are 'alive' and guilty with active hostility to God! It is our *wilful* opposition rather than any defect in psychological faculties that demonstrates 'our absolute dependence upon a powerful Divine operation, for anything in us that hath a saving tendency'.[4]

God's use of means—afflictions in the case of Manasseh (see 2 Chron. 33) and the Gospel Word preached as in the case of Lydia (see Acts 16: 14)—all indicate that salvation is not the fruit of free will initiative but of God's sovereign 'good pleasure'.[5] Yet this does not reduce sinners to being blocks of stone or mere puppets on a string. Therefore, a proper grasp of the 'grace vs. free-will' dispute is essential. At this point, Calamy cites the opinions of two eminent 'Amyraldians', James Ussher and Jean Daillé that the Council of Orange (AD 529) provided the best decision 'in all antiquity' on this issue, viz. 'that it is from special grace, and the influence of the [Holy] Spirit, that any inclination is produced in the will of a corrupt creature towards God'.[6]

This last emphasis is developed in Calamy's fourth and final proposition. Obviously reflecting the 'free offer' theology of Calvin, Davenant and Baxter, Calamy is anxious to avoid the extremes[7] of Hypercalvinism and Arminianism.

For though 'tis through special mercy, that any are recovered and saved, yet the mercy of God is so far exerted towards all, that He's ever before hand with them, and never stops the current of His favour towards them,

---

1   Ibid. 22.
2   Ibid. 26.
3   Ibid. 27.
4   Ibid. 28.
5   Ibid. 29–33.
6   Ibid. 34–5.
7   Ibid. 37.

till they obstinately reject the grace he offers, and wilfully abuse that common grace which had been afforded to them.[1]

For Calamy, this points the way to a proper balanced view of the Gospel:

> Let us put things together, and take notice, that general grace and special are very reconcilable; … The Scripture appears clear as to both; and where's the inconsistency? Why must we deny general grace to exalt that which is special [as John Gill did later]? Or deny and depress special grace, to advance that which is general [as John Wesley did later]? … *And is not this very consistent with our owning that 'God so loved the world' in general, as 'that He gave His only-begotten Son, that whosoever believeth in Him, might not perish, but might have everlasting life'?* And on the other side, is not general grace sufficiently secured by our maintaining God's love to the world, and His willing the salvation of all men, on condition they turn to Him? … and why then should we go about to dash these truths against each other which are fairly consistent, and agree well together? Let us beware of extremes: and stand upon our guard, lest for fear of one error, we fall into another.[2]

Indeed, together with their disciples, ancient and modern, it would have done Gill and Wesley both good to have studied this sermon by Calamy!

Applying his carefully balanced exposition, Calamy concludes by warning against hypercalvinist inertia: 'Let us never pretend to open a way for the greater honour to the mercy of God, by indulging [in] negligence and sloth. That would be a 'turning the grace of our God into lasciviousness' (Jude 5).[3] Likewise he warns against Arminian self-congratulation: 'Let all such as heartily do will and run, thankfully adore that God that hath shewn mercy. Let them do so more earnestly, because of their natural aversion, which they cannot but have found and felt. With what ardour should you love Him that hath made you special objects of His favour'.[4] In short, by citing Philippians 1: 6 and Psalm 115: 1, Calamy insists that God has the 'entire glory' in our salvation.[5]

---

1   Ibid. 40.
2   Ibid. 44–54 (emphasis and parenthetic comments mine).
3   Ibid. 45.
4   Ibid. 46.
5   Ibid.

Lastly, Calamy is not content that we posses only an accurate 'head knowledge' of all he's argued for in this impressive sermon: 'Let us endeavour to get our hearts impressed with as deep a sense as may be, of the riches and freeness of [Divine mercy]'.[1] For those who feel paralysed in unbelief, our preacher provides a final exhortation:

> And therefore as thou canst, complain of thy spiritual deadness, stupidity, and enmity, and beg of God that he would cure it by His victorious grace. ... God ... had much rather His mercy should triumph in thy effectual 'willing' and 'running', till thou reachest everlasting salvation; than that His justice should be displayed, upon thy persisting in incurable hardness, in thy final ruin and destruction'.[2]

Such was the character and quality, the faithfulness and compassion of Dr Edmund Calamy's Gospel preaching. In the noble tradition of Richard Baxter, such teaching directed his faithful London ministry, conducted during the depressing days of the early eighteenth century.

THE CALAMY LINK

We conclude with a significant and interesting aspect of Edmund Calamy's legacy. This concerns that young man whom he mistakenly discouraged from entering the Christian ministry, one Philip Doddridge. In his early days at Kibworth in Leicestershire, young pastor Philip received a gift of books (from a Mr Haldon) which had a dramatic impact on his development and future ministry. These were Dr Calamy's 4-volume 1707 edition of the *Practical Works of Richard Baxter*. Unimpressed by the works of those 'mysterious men', the over-orthodox John Owen and Thomas Goodwin, Doddridge had been drawn to the writings of Archbishop John Tillotson. However, in 1724, Calamy's *Baxter* changed everything. Writing to his brother-in-law, Doddridge revealed the Apostle of Kidderminster's impact upon him:

> Baxter is my particular favourite, and it is impossible to tell you how much I am charmed with the devotion, good sense, and pathos, which are everywhere to be found in that writer. I cannot indeed forbear looking upon him as one of the greatest orators that our nation ever produced,

---

1 Ibid. 47.
2 Ibid. 48.

... I have lately been reading his *Gildas Salvianus* [The Reformed Pastor], which has cut me out some work among my people, that will take me off from so close an application to my private studies as I would otherwise covet.[1]

Whether or not Dr Calamy ever knew about this, his influence in Doddridge's development would have delighted him. He would doubtless have been astonished to know that after his death in 1732, his Princes Street, Westminster congregation desired Philip Doddridge as Calamy's successor! During a visit to London in July, 1733, Philip wrote to his wife Mercy, "I have been strongly besieged by Dr Calamy's people."[2] However, Doddridge—who in the same letter also refers to a financial inducement to join the Anglicans—had no doubt that God had called him to serve as a Protestant Dissenter in Northampton.

Despite that early discouragement, Doddridge clearly came to admire Calamy's contribution. Over twenty years later, the Northampton pastor cited Calamy's views on church order in his *Family Expositor*. Commenting on Acts 20: 25–8 (where Paul calls all the Ephesian elders 'overseers' or 'bishops'), Doddridge remarked:

> The late learned, moderate and pious Dr Edmund Calamy observes, that, if the apostles had been used (as some assert) to ordain diocesan bishops in their last visitation, this had been a proper time to do it; or that, if Timothy had been already ordained bishop of Ephesus, Paul, instead of calling them all bishops, would have surely given some hint to enforce Timothy's authority among them, especially considering what is added, ver. 29, 30 (see Dr Calamy's *Defence*, Vol. 1, p. 78).[3]

A final example of the Calamy-Doddridge link concerns revival. As we have seen, the London minister longed and prayed for 'a fresh effusion of the Divine Spirit from on high to revive the power and life of religion in our midst'. Little did he know that it was commencing while he was praying. Indeed, something remarkable happened at Northampton in 1729. In that

---

1   See my *The Good Doctor: Philip Doddridge of Northampton*, 36.

2   Geoffrey F. Nuttall (ed.), *Calendar of the Correspondence of Philip Doddridge DD (1702–1751)*, Letter 385.

3   See Doddridge's *Works* (Leeds: E. Williams & E. Parsons, 1805), viii. 209. Doddridge cites Calamy's *Defence of Moderate Nonconformity* (London: Thomas Parkhurst, 1703).

year, soon after Doddridge's settlement at Castle Hill, he preached his sermon *Christ's Invitation to Thirsty Souls*. The preacher wrote of the occasion that 'something of a peculiar blessing seemed to attend the discourse, when delivered from the pulpit; and that to such a degree, as I do not know to have been equalled by any other sermon I ever preached'.[1] This was six years before Whitefield's conversion (1735) and nine before John Wesley's (1738)! This extraordinary sermon was eventually published in 1748, some years after the revival had become a nationwide phenomenon. When Whitefield obtained and read a copy, he wrote to Doddridge:

> ... dear Sir, I must thank you for your sermon. It contains the very life of preaching, I mean sweet invitations to close with Christ. I do not wonder you are dubbed a Methodist on account of it ...[2]

Recalling the unhappy division within the Methodist movement over Calvinism and Arminianism, is it too much to suggest that—by the grace of God—the revival began, not through the Owenite Whitefield or the Arminian Wesley but the Baxterian Philip Doddridge? Professor Alan Everitt expressed the opinion that 'If any event can be regarded as beginning the Evangelical Movement it is probably the appointment of the Independent Philip Doddridge to Castle Hill Chapel in 1729'.[3]

One final comment is in order. In the light of Calamy's 1703 sermon *Divine mercy Exalted*, one easily detects a distinct 'Calamynian' orthodoxy in Doddridge's *Christ's Invitation to Thirsty Souls*, delivered as it was with something close to Baxterian fervour.[4] In which case, Edmund Calamy made a distinct contribution to the great work of God known as the Great Evangelical Awakening of the eighteenth century. As we sample Philip Doddridge's sermon, let us learn and profit from these things. May God have mercy upon our desperately needy world, to His eternal glory. Amen!

---

1   *The Good Doctor*, 172–3.

2   Ibid. 172.

3   Ibid. 173.

4   For a recent discussion of Doddridge's theology, see Richard A. Muller, 'Philip Doddridge and the Formulation of Calvinistic Theology in an Era of Rationalism and Deconfessionalization' in R. D. Cornwall and W. Gibson (eds.), *Religion, Politics and Dissent, 1660–1832* (Aldershot: Ashgate, 2010), 65–84. While he recognises the Baxter-Doddridge link, Dr Muller's attempt to distance Doddridge from Amyraut's type of hypothetical conditionalism is unfounded (see Doddridge, *Works*, v. 240; x. 327).

In the history of the Evangelists ... we there find our blessed Redeemer publishing the free and unlimited offers of his grace, to all that were willing to accept it ... Do you thirst for the pardon of sin? ... Do you thirst for the favour of God? ... Do you thirst for the communications of the Spirit? The Lord Jesus Christ can abundantly relieve you ... Do you thirst for the joys and glories of the heavenly world? The Lord Jesus Christ is able to relieve you ... I know there is a great deal of difference between the common operations of the Spirit on the minds of those who continue obstinate and impenitent, and those special influences by which he sweetly but powerfully subdues the hearts of those who are chosen in Christ Jesus before the foundation of the world. Yet I am persuaded, that none to whom the Gospel comes are utterly neglected by that sacred agent ... Behold then the tears of a Redeemer over perishing souls, and judge by them of the compassions of His heart ... Surely nothing can be more melting, than such tears, falling from such eyes, and in such circumstances. And if our Lord could not give up the impenitent sinners of Jerusalem without weeping over them, surely He will not despise the humble and penitent soul, who is, perhaps with tears, seeking His favour, and flying to his grace as his only refuge ...

The tears of our blessed Redeemer must needs be convincing and affecting, if the mind be not sunk into an almost incredible stupidity; but his blood is still more so. View him, my brethren, not only in the previous scenes of his abasement, his descent from heaven, and his abode on earth; but view him on mount Calvary, extended on the cross, torn with thorns, wounded with nails, pierced with a spear; and then say, whether there be not a voice in each of these sacred wounds, which loudly proclaims the tenderness of his heart, and demonstrates, beyond all possibility of dispute or suspicion, his readiness to relieve the distressed soul, that cries to him for the blessings of the gospel. He died to purchase them, not for himself, but for us; and can it be thought he will be unwilling to bestow them? We may well conclude that he loved us, since he shed his blood to wash us from our sins (Rev. 1: 5): ... that while we were strangers and enemies he hath died for us. (Rom. 5: 8).

I hope, through grace, there are some such among you ... who are now thirsting for the blessings of the Gospel ... To you my friends, I would briefly say … Go directly, and plead the case with Him … for that soul will surely be relieved, and God in Christ be glorified and exalted.[1]

Until his early death in 1751, Doddridge became personally involved in the Methodist movement. Besides making his own unique contribution to the Great Awakening, he served as an occasional adviser to Whitefield and John Wesley. But the Dissenters remained his closest friends, and, to cap it all, during his various visits to London, he often enjoyed lunch and fellowship with Edmund Calamy IV.[2] They doubtless discussed often the enduring legacy of Dr Edmund Calamy, the 'Champion of Nonconformity'!

---

1 *The Good Doctor*, 171–2.
2 See Doddridge, *Calendar*, Letters 436, 1082, 1337, 1337, 1377.

12. The Gospel According
to Philip Doddridge[1]

Prologue

The reader will find several references to Richard Baxter in this paper. This serves to advertise the belief that Baxter was a major influence in Doddridge's teaching. This belief is also evident in my later biography of Doddridge.[2] However, in his recently published thesis,[3] Dr Robert Strivens—while documenting areas of doctrinal agreement between the two men—seems anxious to distance Doddridge from Baxter as far as possible. It was certainly never my concern to claim that Baxter was the only major influence in Doddridge's development, but an attempt to play down his influence indicates a nervous aversion for Baxter that Doddridge definitely did not share. When Dr Strivens concludes that Doddridge was 'in all the most important points, a Calvinist'[4] —an early statement from 1724 equally applicable to Baxter himself—he fails to appreciate the true significance of Doddridge's mature position. Indeed, in 1748, just three years before his death (the date only mentioned by Dr Strivens in a footnote[5]), Doddridge unambiguously declared that 'Baxterian Calvinist' was 'a very

---

1   *The Christian Mind of Philip Doddridge (1702–1751) or The Gospel According to an Evangelical Congregationalist*, A paper first given at the Congregational Studies Conference (EFCC) on 3 April 1982.

2   See Alan C. Clifford, *The Good Doctor: Philip Doddridge of Northampton—A Tercentenary Tribute* (Norwich: Charenton Reformed Publishing, 2002).

3   See Robert Strivens, *Philip Doddridge and the Shaping of Evangelical Dissent* (Farnham, Surrey: Ashgate, 2015) , p. 45.

4   Ibid. 45.

5   Ibid. 24.

321

proper expression'.[1] The point is not that Doddridge wasn't a Calvinist but that he wasn't an 'Owenian Calvinist'. Notwithstanding an appreciation for some of John Owen's books, this was obviously important to Doddridge regarding the nature and extent of the atonement and the nature of justifying faith (inclusive of obedience).

Philip Doddridge is usually remembered as a hymnwriter. For the majority of English speaking Christians, their knowledge of him stops there. This lecture is concerned to demonstrate that Doddridge represents all that is best and biblical in the 'evangelical congregationalist' tradition. His evangelicalism is conspicuous in his hymns, and his convictions regarding church order and baptism place him in that denomination of Protestant Dissenters known as 'Congregationalists'.

As a hymnwriter, Philip Doddridge needs no introduction. The hymn books of many denominations suggest that his name will not be forgotten. 'Hark the glad sound' and 'O happy day' still find a place in worship of God's people. It is no small commendation that 'O God of Bethel' was chosen for the Queen's Silver Jubilee service at St Paul's Cathedral in June 1977.

Yet Doddridge's hymns were just a fraction of his vast literary output[2] and an even smaller part of his many and widely creative activities. Apart from Doddridge's regular preaching ministry, the hymns might never have seen the light of day. They were written to supplement the sermon, and given out, line by line, after it had been preached. The hymns were used as a teaching aid, designed to reinforce and apply the preached word. This fact reminds us that Doddridge was primarily a minister of the Gospel of Jesus Christ, a calling which he considered 'the most desirable employment in the world'.[3]

From the time of his settlement in Northampton, in December 1729, to his death in October 1751, Philip Doddridge served the cause of Christ with

---

1   See *Calendar of the Correspondence of Philip Doddridge, DD* (1702–51) (London: HMSO, 1979), 287; see also my *Good Doctor*, 137, 169 and 254ff.

2   See Erik Routley, 'The Hymns of Philip Doddridge', in *Philip Doddridge, His Contribution to English Religion*, ed. Geoffrey F. Nuttall (London: Independent Press, 1951), 46ff. Hereinafter *Doddridge and English Religion*. Also Ernest Payne, 'The Hymns of Philip Doddridge', in *Philip Doddridge: Nonconformity and Northampton*, ed. R. L. Greenall (Leicester: University of Leicester, 1981), 15ff. Hereinafter Greenall.

3   Job Orton, *Memoir of the Life, Character and Writings of the late Rev. P Doddridge, DD of Northampton* (1766), in Doddridge, *Works*, ed. Williams and Parsons (Leeds: 1802–5), i. 260.

intense energy and total dedication. As Charles Stanford wrote in 1880, he 'seemed to live—so many lives at a time'.[1] In addition to being the pastor of Castle Hill Independent Church—his ordination took place on 19 March 1730—he was principal tutor of what was to become the most famous of all the Dissenting Academies.[2]

The dual role of pastor and tutor involved Doddridge in a wide range of interests and pursuits. As a tutor, he became an apologist (or defender of the faith), philosopher and a man of science, besides being a theologian, training young men for the ministry. What Doddridge managed to accomplish in 21 busy years was directed by a single preoccupation. In the words of Dr Geoffrey Nuttall, evangelism was 'the thread on which his multi-coloured life was strung. It was for this above all that he wrote, preached, corresponded and educated his students in the Academy'.[3]

Doddridge lived at a time when rationalism was gnawing at the roots of Christianity. Fierce theological controversy was commonplace, it was no easy thing for a young minister to be certain which opinion best reflected 'the mind of God in the Scriptures'. It was a day of extremes, and Doddridge believed with Richard Baxter before him that the Bible demanded a 'middle-way'. That meant avoiding the incipient fatalism of much High Calvinism on one hand, and the implicit humanism of Arian-Arminianism on the other.[4]

Agreeing with Baxter's theological eclecticism (seeking the best of all traditions), Doddridge was also deeply concerned with Protestant unity. He did all he could to root out bigotry and sectarianism, being a friend to all who 'Loved the Lord Jesus in sincerity and truth'. He had fraternal relations with Dissenters and Churchmen alike.[5]

In his Academy lectures[6] we see how rigorous was the intellectual training Doddridge provided for his students. In his teaching method he was 'liberal' rather than 'dogmatic'; in other words he encouraged free enquiry. He was

---

1   Charles Stanford, *Philip Doddridge* (London: Hodder & Stoughton, 1880), 41.

2   See Irene Parker, *The Dissenting Academics in England* (Cambridge: CUP, 1914), 101.

3   Introduction to *Calendar of the Correspondence of Philip Doddridge, DD (1702–51)* (London: HMSO, 1979), p. xxxv.

4   See Geoffrey F. Nuttall, *Richard Baxter and Philip Doddridge: A Study in Tradition* (London: Dr Williams's Library, 1951).

5   See Geoffrey F. Nuttall, 'Chandler, Doddridge and the Archbishop: A study in eighteenth-century ecumenism', *Journal of the URC History Society*, Vol. 1, No. 2 (1973), 42ff.

6   See 'Lectures on Pneumatology, Ethics and Divinity', in Doddridge, *Works*, iv–v.

impatient with any theological system which failed to observe the balance of Biblical truth. Scripture was to be the only ultimate authority. He was concerned that truth itself, rather than his or any man's opinion, should mould his students' minds.

Doddridge's essentially conservative outlook is best seen in his magnum opus, *The Family Expositor*,[1] and his *Dissertation on the Inspiration of the New Testament*.[2] His theological foundations being assured, Doddridge was an advocate of the 'good old evangelical way of preaching'.[3]

In acquainting his students with philosophy and scientific questions, Doddridge wanted them to be thoughtful preachers, who would be able to say *why,* as well as *what,* they believed. He believed Christianity was capable of a rational defence. He was therefore concerned with apologetics. Doddridge's reply to Dodwell's *Christianity not founded on argument* was his most ambitious intellectual piece of writing, in which he demonstrates that faith and reason do not necessarily conflict.[4]

Of equal importance to Doddridge was the practical impact of the gospel. He was no armchair theologian. As co-founder of the Northampton Infirmary and promoter of a charity school in the town, Doddridge demonstrated the power of Christian example. His patriotic activity in connection with the invasion of Bonnie Prince Charlie in 1745, when he urged his congregation to join the Northampton Militia and thus helped to decide the invaders to turn back at Derby, reveals his sense of Christian social responsibility.[5]

Nowhere is Doddridge's commitment to evangelism more clearly seen than in the welcome he extended to the infant Methodist movement.[6] His friendship with George Whitefield, John Wesley and others, was typical of his spirit. When older Dissenters, including Isaac Watts, viewed the revival with cool and suspicious detachment, Doddridge was ready to perceive the

---

1   Many editions were published. See Doddridge, *Works*, vi–x.

2   *Works*, iv. 168ff.

3   Orton, in Doddridge, *Works*, i. 153.

4   Ibid. 469ff.

5   See Malcolm Deacon, *Philip Doddridge of Northampton* (Northampton: Northamptonshire Libraries, 1980), 114ff, and also Victor A. Hatley, 'A Local Dimension: Philip Doddridge and Northampton Politics', in Greenall, 77ff.

6   See my 'Philip Doddridge and the Oxford Methodists' in *Proceedings of the Wesley Historical Society*, XLII. 3 (1979), 75–80. Also Alan Everitt, 'Philip Doddridge and the Evangelical Tradition' in Greenall, 31ff.

hand of God at work. He rejoiced that God had raised up such men, in such an ungodly age. The new Dissent turned to the old for guidance. Whitefield asked Doddridge to revise his *Journal* and John Wesley consulted him for a reading list for his preachers. Doddridge's own lasting contribution to the revival was his most popular book, *The Rise and Progress of Religion in the Soul*. It was to the reading of this book that William Wilberforce traced his own spiritual awakening.[1] As with Mozart in another context, one feels that Doddridge's life was cut short. He died and was buried in Lisbon, whither he had been sent by his congregation in the hope of restoring his health, at the age of 49. One cannot but be amazed at the consistent Christian dedication of a life all too brief. His life and example have bequeathed a rich and lasting legacy to the churches.

Whereas a certain amount of interest in Doddridge has been generated in recent years, more attention has been paid to the man than to his beliefs. This is understandable, since Doddridge was an attractive personality by any standard. However, it is also unfortunate, since for Doddridge personally, his faith and his life were of a piece: what he *was*, was due, in great measure, to what he *believed* and *thought*. At least two reasons can explain the deficiencies in current Doddridge interest. *Firstly,* Doddridge was not an original and profound thinker of the stature of Augustine, or Thomas Aquinas, of Luther, Calvin or Barth, although he was an independent one. *Secondly,* the late twentieth century is little interested in the kind of theological convictions shared by Doddridge and his generation. This was stated quite explicitly in the bicentenary celebrations of Doddridge's death in 1951, when Roger Thomas said, 'The important thing for us, however, is not Doddridge's theological opinions'.[2]

Renowned as Doddridge was for his gracious and charitable disposition, it has become necessary to dispel the myth that truth and conviction were unimportant to him. His daughter's oft quoted retort to a critic of her father's theological views, 'My father's orthodoxy is charity'[3] has reinforced the fact that, in his lifetime, Doddridge was accused of being indifferent to theological convictions. The truth, however, is otherwise, although in an ecumenical age, one is not surprised to find that the myth is preferred to the reality. Whilst

---

1   See R. I. and S. Wilberforce, *The Life of William Wilberforce* (London: John Murray, 1838), i. 760.

2   Roger Thomas, 'Doddridge and Liberalism' in *Doddridge and English Religion*, 134.

3   *Doddridge and English Religion*, 35.

Doddridge always lectured, preached and wrote according to the apostolic maxim of 'speaking the truth in love', it must never be forgotten that it was undiluted Biblical truth which he attempted to proclaim. We must not allow Doddridge's charm to seduce us into neglecting Doddridge's theology.

The task before us is to allow Doddridge the theologian to speak to us. It would have been much more *entertaining* to dwell upon the purely biographical and anecdotal details of this godly man's life, but we must be concerned, not so much with entertainment, as with instruction. My desire is to complete the picture, to correct any misconceptions, and to justify a continuing study of the life and work of Dr Philip Doddridge.

What we are doing needs little justification. Serious Christian people are aware that important issues demand our attention. Ours is the day of such books as *The Myth of God Incarnate*. It is also the day of the Ecumenical movement, the Nationwide Initiative on Evangelism, Liberation theology, the Charismatic movement and the Papal visit. The Christian Church is a restless institution, uncertain of its message, and doubtful of its relevance or place in the modern world.

Whilst Philip Doddridge is no infallible guide, he did at least address himself to issues very similar to those which face us today. Since these issues are of eternal significance, we are not being retrogressive in considering some of his views, although they were uttered 250 years ago.

Doddridge was, pre-eminently, a biblical theologian in the Reformed tradition. He believed in the full Divine Inspiration and authority of the Bible. For him, the Bible was the Word of God. In his *Dissertation on the Inspiration of the New Testament*, he tackles the issues which still trouble biblical scholars. His view of inspiration does not lead him to deny that the human instruments employed their own choice of words; he is not therefore committed to the crudely mechanical dictation theory of inspiration. Whilst denying that the original documents had any errors, he does not feel that the cause of truth is lost in admitting the possibility of minor errors in copies. Doddridge emphasises the relationship between *inspiration* and *authority:*

Nothing can be more evident, than that a firm and cordial belief of the inspiration of the sacred scripture is of the highest moment; not only to the edification and peace of the church, but in a great measure to its very existence. For if this be given up, the authority of the revelation is enervated (or weakened), and its use destroyed: The star which is to direct our course, is clouded; our compass is broke to pieces; and we are left to make the voyage of life in sad uncertainty, amidst a thousand rocks, and shelves, and quicksands.[1]

For Doddridge, the Bible itself is above theology. It tests and regulates our thinking:

Let us therefore always remember that we are indispensably obliged to receive with calm and reverend submission all the dictates of scripture; to make it our oracle; and, in this respect, to set it at a due distance from all other writings whatsoever; as it is certain, there is no other book in the world, that can pretend to equal authority, and produce equal or comparable proofs to support such a pretention. Let us measure the truth of our own sentiments, or those of others, in the great things which scripture teaches, by their conformity to it. And O that the powerful charm of this blessed book might prevail to draw all that do sincerely regard it, into this centre of unity.[2]

On so basic a doctrine as the Trinity, Doddridge honestly faced the problems we all have in making rational sense of our faith. He was afraid of giving the impression that there are three gods—a misunderstanding which the Athanasian creed might suggest—and equally he was at pains to avoid the idea that the names of the three persons are but mere names of *one* person—the Sabellian heresy. His statement of the Trinity in his *Divinity Lectures* is simple and straightforward:

The Scripture represents the Divine being as appearing in, and manifesting himself by the distinct persons of *Father*, *Son*, and *Holy Ghost*, each of which has his peculiar province in accomplishing the work of our redemption and salvation, and to each of which we owe an unlimited veneration, love and obedience.[3]

The fundamental difficulty reason poses for faith is met by a quotation from Jeremy Taylor, the famous seventeenth century bishop:

Dr Jeremiah Taylor says, 'that he who goes about to speak of the mystery

---

1 'Dissertation on the New Testament', *Works*, iv. 168.
2 Ibid. 193.
3 *Works*, v. 187.

of the trinity, and does it by words and names of man's invention, talking of essences and existences, hypostases and personalities, priorities in co-equalities, &c, and unity in pluralities, may amuse himself and build a tabernacle in his head, and talk something he knows not what; but the good man, that feels the power of the Father, And to whom the Son is become wisdom, sanctification and redemption, in whose heart the love of the Spirit of God is shed abroad, this man, though he understands nothing of what is unintelligible, yet he alone truly understands the Christian doctrine of the Trinity.'[1]

It is surely wise to settle the matter thus!

The early eighteenth century debates about the doctrine of the Trinity centred on the person of Christ. The most urgent question of the day was, 'What think ye of Christ; whose son is he?' Arianism denied the full deity of Christ, insisting that he was created rather than begotten, and, in his early years, Doddridge admits to leaning toward this view. By the time he commenced his ministry, his views were thoroughly orthodox. In the *Family Expositor* we read:

(I AM ALPHA AND OMEGA). That these titles should be repeated so soon, in a connection which demonstrates they are given to Christ, will appear very remarkable. And I cannot forbear recording it, that *this text* has done more than any other in the Bible, toward preventing us from giving in to *that scheme*, which would make our Lord Jesus Christ no more than a deified creature (Note on Rev. 1: 11).[2]

I am deeply sensible of the sublime and mysterious nature of the doctrine of Christ's deity, as here declared; but it would be quite foreign to my purpose to enter into a large discussion of that great foundation of our faith, it has often been done by much abler hands. It was, however, a matter of conscience with me, on the one hand, thus strongly to declare my belief of it; and, on the other, to leave it as far as I could in the simplicity of scripture expressions (Note on John 1: 1).[3]

Justly hath our Redeemer said, blessed is the man that is not offended

---

1   Ibid. 193.

2   *Works*, x. 431.

3   *Works*, vi. 24.

in me: and we may peculiarly apply the words to that great and glorious doctrine of the *deity of Christ,* which is here before us. A thousand high and curious thoughts will naturally arise in our corrupt hearts on this view of it; but may divine grace subdue them all to the obedience of an humble faith; so that, with Thomas, we may each of us fall down at his feet, and cry out with sincere and unreserved devotion, My Lord and my God! (Comment on John 1: 1–14).[1]

When such foundational truths of the Bible were discarded, it was common for many to preach a gospel of morality, rather than a gospel of Grace. When 'evangelical doctrines' were under threat, Doddridge made his unequivocal response in his two sermons on *Salvation by Grace.*

Salvation by grace is not a subject which grows out of date in a few months. This glorious doctrine has been the joy of the church in all ages on earth; and it will be the song of all that have received it in truth throughout the ages of eternity, and be pursued in the heavenly regions with evergrowing admiration and delight.[2]

At the very heart of the Gospel was the cross of our Lord Jesus Christ. For Doddridge, there was no salvation, but through the precious blood of Christ. It was a substitutionary atonement. In his sermon *Christ's Invitation to Thirsty Souls,* he declares:

The tears of our blessed Redeemer must needs be convincing and affecting, if the mind be not sunk into an almost incredible stupidity; but his blood is still more so. View him, my brethren, not only in the previous scenes of his abasement, his descent from heaven, and his abode on earth; but view him on mount Calvary, extended on the cross, born with thorns, wounded with nails, pierced with a spear; and then say, whether there be not a voice in each of these sacred wounds, which loudly proclaims the tenderness of his heart, and demonstrates, beyond all possibility of dispute or suspicion, his readiness to relieve the distressed soul, that cries to him for the blessings of the gospel. He died to purchase them, not for himself, but for us; and can it be thought he will be unwilling to bestow them? We may well conclude that he loved

1   Ibid. 29.
2   *Works,* ii. 553.

us, since he shed his blood to wash us from our sins (Rev. 1: 5): For greater love hath no man than this, that a man lay down his life for his friends (John 15: 13); but he hath commended his love toward us, hath set it off by this illustrious and surprising circumstance, that while we were strangers and enemies he hath died for us (Romans 5: 8).[1]

That our salvation was in the hands of God, and that the initiative of redemption was with him, led Doddridge to embrace two other great Bible truths which were under attack in his day—Predestination and Election. In the *Family Expositor* we read:

> Let us go back with unutterable pleasure to the gracious purpose which he was pleased to form in his own compassionate breast, when he chose us in Christ before the foundation of the world, when he predestinated us through him to the adoption of children. Let us acknowledge the freedom of his grace in it, that we are thus predestinated according to the purpose of him who, with proper regard to the nature of his intelligent and free creatures, worketh all things agreeably to the good pleasure of his will, and maketh us accepted in the beloved, that we may be to the praise of the glory of his grace (Comment on Eph. 1: 1–14).[2]

In short, grace was the saving work of a sovereign God. In his Divinity Lectures we read:

> From hence it will further appear, that the reason of God's predestinating some to everlasting life, was not fetched from a foresight of their faith and obedience, considered as independent upon any communication of grace from him, but that it is to be referred into his sovereign mercy and free grace; which is also the language of many other scriptures. Titus 3: 4,5: Ephesians 2: 8, 9.[3]

Therefore, as a concomitant to the natural unbelief of the human heart, Doddridge—with Calvin and Baxter—resolves the difference between the believer and unbeliever in terms of *Common and Special Grace*. In Christ's *Invitation to Thirsty Souls* he says:

---

1   Ibid. 601–2.
2   *Works*, ix. 328.
3   *Works*, v. 259.

I know, there is a great deal of difference between the common operations of the Spirit on the minds of those who continue obstinate and impenitent, and those special influences by which he sweetly but powerfully subdues the hearts of those, who are chosen in Christ Jesus before the foundation of the world. Yet I am persuaded, that none to whom the Gospel comes are utterly neglected by that sacred agent.[1]

As a theological tutor, Doddridge was aware of the danger of pushing logic too far: it must be kept under a tight rein. As with Richard Baxter before him, Doddridge resisted the temptation to deduce from election that Christ only died for the elect. There were too many 'alls' in Scripture. So, in his Divinity Lectures, Doddridge says:

It is plain that there is a sense, in which Christ may be said to have died 'for all', i.e. as he has procured an offer of pardon to all, provided they sincerely embrace the Gospel. Cf. John 3: 16, 6: 50,51, Romans 5: 18, 8: 32, 1 Corinthians 8: 11, 2 Corinthians 5: 14,15,19, 1 Timothy 2: 4, 6, Hebrews 2: 9, 1 John 2: 2.[2]

It is interesting to observe at this point, that Doddridge refers his students to John Calvin's views on the extent of the atonement. What Dr R. T. Kendall[3] has stunned the Reformed Evangelical world with in recent days was known to Baxter and Doddridge—that Calvin believed Christ died for all men.[4] The doctrine of limited atonement was an instance of logic going

---

1   *Works*, ii. 600.

2   *Works*, v. 214.

3   See *Calvin and English Calvinism* (Oxford: OUP, 1979), 13f.

4   Calvin on the extent of the Atonement: (a) It is incontestable that Christ came for the expiation of the sins of the whole world. Hence, we conclude that, though reconciliation is offered to all through him, yet the benefit is peculiar to the elect. God reconciles the world to himself, reaches to all, but that it is not sealed indiscriminately on the hearts of all to whom it comes so as to be effectual (*Concerning the Eternal Predestination of God*, tr. J. K. S. Reid (London: James Clarke, 1961), 148–9).

(b) Paul makes grace common to all men, not because it in fact extends to all but because it is offered to all. Although Christ suffered for the sins of the world, and is offered by the goodness of God without distinction to all men, yet not all receive him (*Commentary on Romans* (5: 18), tr. Ross Mackenzie (Edinburgh: Oliver & Boyd: 1961), 117–118).

(c) Christ suffered sufficiently for the whole world but effectively only for the elect. I allow the truth of this (*Commentary on St John and 1 John*, (1 Jn 2: 2) tr. T. H. L. Parker (Edinburgh: Oliver & Boyd, 1961), ii. 244).

beyond Scripture. Thus Dr John Owen, whose view Baxter opposed, was called the 'over-orthodox doctor',[1] because of his work on the atonement, *The Death of Death in the Death of Christ*. Owen's position was embryonic hyper-Calvinism—what Doddridge called 'High Calvinism'. He, like Baxter, was known as a 'moderate' (or 'true') Calvinist.

However, the efficacy of the atonement was guaranteed by election, and this was where 'moderate' Calvinism differed from the universalist view of the Arminians. So, with Baxter and Calvin, Doddridge says in his Lectures:

> There (is) a sense, in which Christ might be said to die for all; as all men partake of some benefit by his death, and such provision is made for their salvation, as lays the blame of their ruin, if they miscarry, entirely upon themselves: but it was in a very peculiar and much nobler sense, that he died for the elect, intending evidently to secure for them, and only for them, the everlasting blessings of his Gospel. John 10: 15,16,26; 17: 2,9,16.[2]

Doddridge had no inhibitions about being evangelistic as a result of the Bible's teaching about election. To say that God's sovereignty makes humans mere automatons, or that evangelism is unnecessary, and that strivings for holiness are pointless, is to abuse the doctrine of election and fly in the face of God's Word. Therefore, Doddridge shows us the biblical basis for human activity. In the *Family Expositor*, he says:

> (Will have all men to be saved) It is far from being my design, in any of these notes, to enter deep into controversy, but I must confess I have never been satisfied with that interpretation which explains all men here merely as signifying some of all sorts and ranks of men; since I fear it might also be said, on the principles of those who are fondest of this gloss that he also wills all men to be condemned On the other hand, if many are not saved, it is certain the words must be taken with some limitation, which the following clause, he wills their coming to the knowledge of the truth, must also prove. The meaning therefore seems to be, that God has made sufficient provision for the salvation of all, and that it is to be considered as the general declaration of his will, that all

---

1   See Nuttall, *Richard Baxter and Philip Doddridge*, 10.

2   *Works*, v. 263.

who know the truth themselves, should publish it to all around them, so far as their influence can extend (Note on 1 Tim. 2: 4).[1]

With the advent of the Methodist revival, attention became focused on the doctrine and work of the Holy Spirit. Doddridge made plain his view of the Holy Spirit's work in the new birth through his *Discourses on Regeneration*.[2] As regards what is known today as the 'Baptism in the Holy Spirit', Doddridge believed a distinction was to be drawn between the new birth and the baptism of the Spirit. In the *Family Expositor*, he comments on the outpouring of the Holy Spirit at Pentecost thus:

> Thus did the blessed Jesus accomplish what had been foretold concerning him (Matthew 3: 11), that he should baptize his disciples with the Holy Ghost and with fire. And surely the sacred flame did not only illuminate their minds with celestial brightness, but did also cause their whole hearts to glow with love to God and zeal for his gospel. To this purpose, may he still be imparted to us, whether we hold public or private stations in the church; and may our regards to him be ever most dutifully maintained. Especially may he be poured out upon the ministers of it, to direct them how they should speak the wonderful things of God; and may their hearers, under his gracious energy, gladly receive the word (Comment on Acts 2: 1–21).[3]

Doddridge understood the 'sealing' or 'witness' of the Holy Spirit in the context of the pentecostal blessing. He expounds Romans 8: 16 as 'some inward impression of God's Spirit upon the believer's mind, assuring them that they are Christians indeed'.[4] For this blessing Doddridge urges the doubting believer to 'Plead hard at the throne of grace. Lay hold on God by faith; and say, Lord, I will not let thee go till thou bless me.'[5] However, Doddridge also distinguished between the Baptism of the Spirit and the extraordinary gifts of the Spirit. Now that the Canon of Scripture was complete, the latter were not necessary. He was at one with the Reformers, Puritans and Methodists when he said that:

---

1   *Works*, ix. 581.
2   *Works*, ii. 371ff.
3   *Works*, vii. 514.
4   'The Witness of the Spirit' in *Sermons* (London: J. Hatchard & Son, 1826), ii. 381.
5   Ibid. iii. 15.

Many things may be said of the charismata, or the extraordinary gifts and powers of the Apostles and primitive (early) Christians, which were so peculiar to that age, that we have no personal concern in them at all.[1]

Doddridge also shared Baxter's passion for Christian Unity, what we would regard today as evangelical unity. He was grieved at the Christian 'fragmentation' of his day. In his comment on John 17: 21, he says:

(That the world may believe that thou hast sent me.) This plainly intimates that dissentions among Christians would not only be uncomfortable to themselves, but would be the means of bringing the truth and excellence of the Christian religion into question: and he must be a stranger to what hath passed, and is daily passing, in the world, who does not see what fatal advantage they have given to infidels to misrepresent it as a calamity, rather than to regard it as a blessing to mankind. May we be so wise as to take the warning, before we are quite destroyed one of another! (Galatians 5: 15) (Note on John 17: 21).[2]

Doddridge was impatient with denominationalism, which he called 'party spirit'. He did all he could to bring Christian people together, believing that what was agreed upon was much greater than what divided them. Listen to his rebuke of our divisions:

In the meanwhile, let us avoid, as much as possible, a party spirit, and not be fond of listing ourselves under the name of this, or that man, how wise, how good, how great soever, for surely, if the names of Peter and Paul were in this view to be declined, much more are those, which, in these latter days, have so unhappily crumbled the Christian and Protestant interest, and have given such sad occasion to our enemies to reproach us. Christ is not divided: nor were Luther, or Calvin, or even Peter, or Paul, crucified for us; nor were we baptised into any of their names (Comment on 1 Cor. 1: 10–17).[3]

Christian reunion did not mean the sinking of differences, or that our sincere convictions were to be suppressed. It was a case of 'speaking the truth in love', as he explained in a sermon:

---

1   *Works*, i. 554.
2   Note on John 17: 21 (*The Family Expositor*), *Works*, vii. 339.
3   *The Family Expositor, Works*, viii. 564.

Truth is indeed too sacred a thing ever to be denied on any consideration: and so far as we are in our own consciences persuaded that any particular truth is important, neither honour or charity will allow us to give it up, as a point of mere indifferent speculation. Let us therefore ever be ready, when properly called out to the service, to plead its cause in the name of the God of truth, but let it be in a manner worthy of him, a manner which may not offend him as the God of love. And let us be greatly upon our guard that we do not condemn our brethren, as having forfeited all title to the name of Christians, because their creeds or confessions of faith do not come up to the standard of our own.[1]

Doddridge possessed what was called a 'catholic' spirit. His concern for unity brought him a wide acquaintance. He had discussions with the Archbishop of Canterbury, Dr Herring, as well as Baptist Pastors; he was a friend of Methodist revivalists as well as more traditional Dissenters. However, it is obvious from his correspondence and writings that he was concerned with *Protestant* Unity, in days when no one doubted that the Church of England was a Protestant Church.

If he could not justify perpetual divisions between the Protestant bodies, he had no doubts about the duty of separation from the Roman Catholic Church. In his sermon on the *Iniquity of Persecution*, he starts with this forthright statement:

If Popery be considered in a religious view, it must appear the just object of our contempt, as well as our abhorrence.[2]

In another sermon, he explains his position very clearly:

My brethren, pardon the freedom of my speech. I should have thought it my duty to have separated from the Church of Rome, had she pretended only to determine those things which Christ has left indifferent: How much more when she requires a compliance with those, which he hath expressly forbid? You shall not only bow at the venerable name of our common Lord, but you shall worship an image: You shall not only kneel at the communion, but kneel in adoration of a piece of bread: You shall not only pronounce, or at least appear to pronounce, those accursed,

---

1   'Christian Candour and Unanimity', *Works*, iii. 267.

2   *Works*, iii. 119.

who do not believe what is acknowledged to be incomprehensible, but those who do not believe what is most contrary to our reason and senses. When these are the terms of our continued communion, the Lord judge between us and them! Had nothing but indifferent things been in dispute, we should have done, as we do by our brethren of the Church of England, taken our leave of them with decency and respect: We should have loved them as our brethren, while we could not have owned them as our Lords. But when they require us to purchase our peace, by violating our consciences and endangering our souls, it is no wonder that we escape as for our lives.[1]

For Doddridge, the position and power of the Pope, the doctrine of the Mass and transubstantiation, and worship of the Virgin Mary were major issues at stake. On papal power and influence, he says:

(Above all that is called God, &c.) The usurpation of the papacy in Divine things is so unequalled, that if these words are not applicable to it, it is difficult to say, who there ever has been, or can be to whom they should belong. The manner in which the Pope has exalted himself above magistrates (civil governments) is equally remarkable and detestable (Notes on 2 Thessalonians 2: 4).[2]

The scandalous and extravagant pretences which the followers of the papacy have made to miracles, exceeding in number, and some of them in marvellous circumstances, those of Christ and his apostles, plainly display the energy of Satan, that father of frauds, pious and impious. And the most incredible lies, which they have, by solemn and irrevocable acts, made essential to their faith, shew the strength of delusion (Comment on 2 Thessalonians 2: 1–12).[3]

For Doddridge, the doctrine of transubstantiation was as ridiculous as it is unbiblical:

(This is my body) When I consider that (as a thousand writers have observed) on the same foundation on which the papists argue for transubstantiation from these words, they might prove, from Ezekiel

---

1   'Lectures on Popery', quoted in 'Orton's Memoir', *Works*, i. 123.

2   *The Family Expositor*, *Works*, ix. 551

3   Ibid. 554.

5: 1–5, that the prophet's hair was the city of Jerusalem; from John 10: 9 and 15: 1 that Christ was literally a door and a vine; and from Matthew 26: 27,28, and from 1 Corinthians 11: 25, that the cup was his blood, and that Christ commanded his disciples to drink and swallow the cup; I cannot but be astonished at the inference they would deduce from hence (Note on Matt. 26: 26).[1]

Prayers to the Virgin Mary were a failure to grasp the nature of our Lord's authority as well as a denial of the direct access we have to the throne of grace:

> If his mother met with so just a rebuke for attempting to direct his ministrations in the days of his flesh, how absurd it is for any to address her as if she had a right to command him on the throne of his glory (Comment on John 2: 1–11).[2]

It is plainly true, therefore, after the survey we have made of some of Doddridge's convictions, that he was far from indifferent to doctrine. Indeed, it was clearly of the greatest importance to him.

However, Doddridge also made it clear that there was more to being a Christian than doctrinal exactness and precision. He makes this judicious observation in the *Rise and Progress of Religion in the Soul:*

> The exercise of our rational faculties upon the evidences of divine revelation, and upon the declaration of it as contained in Scripture, may furnish a very wicked man with a well-digested body of orthodox divinity in his head, when not one single doctrine of it has ever reached his heart.[3]

Doddridge's views on Roman Catholicism may cause disappointment to some who have viewed him as an ecumenical prophet, and yet reassurance for others. It must be said in all truth that he clearly drew a distinction between Roman Catholicism and Roman Catholics, between the system and its blind devotees. Nowhere is this more perfectly illustrated than in the 'Connell Affair'. One Bryan Connell was found guilty of murdering a man at Weedon, near Northampton. Doddridge befriended the poor man, who pleaded innocence, and Doddridge believed that he was not guilty. Despite an

---

1   Ibid. vii. 296.
2   Ibid. vi. 135.
3   *Works*, i. 422.

appeal, Connell was executed on 3 April 1741. Now Connell was a Roman
Catholic, and Doddridge's concern for him even led many to suggest that the
Reformed pastor had inclinations towards Roman Catholicism. In a letter to
Connell, written only two days before the execution took place, Doddridge
pleads with the condemned man to seek salvation in Christ. The letter also
tells us a great deal about Doddridge—the Protestant, the Evangelical, the
spiritual and truly Christian man that he was:

> I beseech you by the worth of your precious and immortal soul! that
> in these solemn moments, you guard against every false dependence.
> You well remember how frequently and how earnestly I have repeated
> this caution. I rejoice in finding you so often declare, that you put no
> confidence in the power of a Priest to forgive sin; nor in the efficacy
> of sacraments to save an impenitent sinner; nor in the intercession of
> saints and angels; nor in the value of your own blood, supposing it, in
> this respect innocent, to make satisfaction to God for the sins of your
> life; but that you desire to trust in the mercy of God, through the blood
> and intercession of our Lord Jesus Christ alone. Whatever your opinion
> of the church of Rome may be, which this is not a time to debate, you
> are in all these things a very good Protestant in your notions; but let me
> remind you, Sir, that we cannot be saved by the soundest notions, but
> must feel their power to change our hearts, and must act upon them. I
> do therefore again, that I may deliver your soul and my own, solemnly
> exhort you most earnestly to seek the renewing influences of Divine
> grace, to change your sinful heart, and to fit you for the presence of
> God. Pray that God may give you repentance unto life, not merely a
> grief for temporal ruin, and a dread of that future punishment which
> the worst of men must desire to escape, but a repentance arising from
> the love of God, attended with a filial ingenuous (or sincere) sorrow for
> the indignity and dishonour which your sins have offered to so excellent
> and so gracious a Being. Oh! while there is yet hope fly to the blood and
> the righteousness of Christ, and to the free grace of God in the Gospel
> which is manifested to the greatest of sinners, and shall be manifested
> in you, if you sincerely believe. I am glad I have seen no crucifix near
> you, but in a spiritual sense to lie at the foot of the cross, and to look
> by faith unto him that died upon it, is the safest and best thing you can
> do. Pardon and grace, help and happiness must be sought here, not only

by you, my friend, but by the most upright and virtuous man upon the earth, or he will appear a condemned sinner before God. God is my witness that this is my refuge: let it be yours, and we may have a happier meeting than we have known upon earth.[1]

For Doddridge, his Protestant, Reformed, and evangelical orthodoxy was no negative thing. For him, the truth of God should lead to the God of truth; the written word should lead us to the Incarnate Word, and Gospel of Christ should lead us to the Christ of the Gospel:

> Would to God that all the party-names, and unscriptural phrases and forms, which have divided the Christian world were forgot, and that we might agree to sit down together, as humble, loving disciples; at the feet of our common Master, to hear his word, to imbibe his spirit, and transcribe his life in our own.[2]

This was the main spring of Doddridge's Christianity—without which, it is impossible to arrive at a correct estimate of the man. He summed up the blessed secret of his life a secret all may share, in his own epigram on the family motto DUM VIVIMUS VIVAMUS (In living, LIVE), described by Dr Samuel Johnson as one of the finest in the English language:

> Live, while you live, the epicure would say,
> And seize the pleasures of the passing day,
> Live, while you live, the sacred preacher cries,
> And give to God each moment as it flies.
> Lord, in my life let both united be,
> I live in pleasure, when I live to thee.[3]

---

1 *Correspondence and Diary of Philip Doddridge, DD*, ed J. D. Humphreys (1829–30), iii. 556f; *Calendar*, ed. Nuttall, Letter 667). It seems that Connell was not converted (see Humphries, v. 425).

2 Preface to *The Family Expositor, Works*, vi. 13.

3 Nuttall, 'Doddridge's Life and Times', in *Doddridge and English Religion*, ed. Nuttall, 21 and other places.

13. JOHN CALVIN & JOHN WESLEY[1]

INTRODUCTION

Had Augustine of Hippo (354–430) been honoured with a quincentenary celebration somewhere in the Holy Roman Empire in 854, a 'positive' paper on the 'British heretic' Pelagius (ca. 350–420) would not have been welcomed by the hyper-Augustinian monk of Orbais, Gottschalk (d. ca. 869).[2] Just in case any suspicious conference delegates here in Geneva imagine a similar paper on the 'British Arminian heretic' John Wesley (1703–91) to be inappropriate during our Calvin celebration, let me assure them that my choice of subject is not an English attempt to undermine Calvin's legacy in any way. However, while I am neither Pelagian nor Arminian, I claim to be (the Servetus aspect apart) 'an authentic English Calvinist'. In which case, delegates might reasonably have expected a paper on 'Calvin and John Owen' or, more appropriate in 18th century terms, one on 'Calvin and (Wesley's antagonist) George Whitefield' (if not on John Gill).

WESLEY 'IN' GENEVA

That said, my subject was not only prompted by the anniversary of John Wesley's 'evangelical conversion' in 1738. Indeed, the 24 May—the very day our Calvin Congress commenced—continues to be a day of celebration in England and beyond. And why? Besides the gratitude for Wesley's ministry felt by English-speaking Christians unashamed still to be 'Evangelical' and 'Protestant', historians like Lecky and Halévy have justified the gratitude of those more interested in socio-political reforms than matters strictly

---

1 'John Calvin and John Wesley: An English Perspective', a paper originally given at the International Calvin Congress in Geneva on 26 May 2009.
2 See G. P. Fisher, *History of Christian Doctrine* (Edinburgh: T. & T. Clark, 1896), 206.

religious. Indeed, Wesley's life and labours made an epochal contribution to civilisation.[1] But for him and his Methodist brethren, England might well have faced a bloody revolution like that in France. For all their not-insignificant differences, even George Whitefield—the Calvinist who requested that John Wesley take his funeral service in 1770—would be happy in great measure to endorse a contribution on Wesley here in Geneva. These reasons apart, my choice is deliberately theological, believing as I have argued elsewhere that 'in several respects, John Wesley's theology is closer to John Calvin's than John Owen's is'.[2] By substituting 'Whitefield' for 'Owen', the same point is made in strictly eighteenth-century terms.

PREDESTINARIAN PERPLEXITIES

We need not be detained by Wesley's well-known yet predictable protest against Calvin's doctrine of predestination.[3] Without trivialising the very real and profound differences involved, the problems highlighted by Wesley are not in fact unique to Calvinism. Indeed, doesn't Arminianism share them too? True, the Calvinist doctrine of divine foreordination raises perplexing philosophical questions about the nature of evangelistic endeavour, but the Arminian doctrine of divine foreknowledge or prescience—the basis of conditional election—poses a similar one: 'if God knows beforehand who will accept and reject Christ, is it not merely academic to say that salvation is possible to all?' In other words, telling an unbeliever about Christ seems pointless if God already knows that their response will be negative. To say that we do not possess God's knowledge, and that such knowledge is not given for evangelistic enterprise is as much a Calvinist as an Arminian answer. The chief difference between us lies in the interaction between the divine and human wills. Calvinists say the final factor in conversion is the divine will whereas Arminians insist that it is the human will. Although 'foreknowledge' has no necessitarian connotations as such, yet if God's foreknowledge or prescience is certain—which it must be, irrespective of what makes it so—then it is

---

1   See J. Wesley Bready, *England: Before and After Wesley* (London: Hodder & Stoughton, 1939), 449, 451.

2   See my *Atonement and Justification: English Evangelical Theology 1640–1790—An Evaluation* (Oxford: OUP, 1990, 2002), 134.

3   See 'A Dialogue between a Predestinarian and His Friend' in *The Works of John Wesley*, ed. T. Jackson (London: J. Mason, 1841), x. 250–56.

as sure as if it were determined. So, do the contending parties not have to agree, in the final analysis, that in the mysterious divine-human interaction in salvation, God remains God, the just yet sovereign creator, and man remains man, the dependent yet accountable creature?

WESLEY ON CALVIN

For all his life-long opposition to Calvinism, Wesley had *something* good to say about Calvin, despite several criticisms on various issues including his repeated lamentations over the latter's 'persecution' of Servetus. In 1766, Wesley was careful to say 'I believe Calvin was a great instrument of God; and that he was a wise and pious man',[1] repeating four years later (while defending the memory and reputation of Arminius) that 'John Calvin was a pious, learned, sensible man'.[2] As for Calvinism itself, Wesley was not as antipathetic as his usual stance would seem to suggest. Dr J. I. Packer is right to remark that 'Wesley's teaching included so much Reformation truth about the nature of faith, the witness of the Spirit, and effectual calling. Wesley's Arminianism, we might say, contained a good deal of its own antidote'.[3]

AUTHENTIC CALVINISM

Realising that Dr Packer rescues much of Wesley's reputation from a strictly 'Owenite' or 'Whitefieldian' perspective, much more may be reclaimed from an 'authentic Calvinist' one (meaning thereby—to be open about my own perspective—an Amyraldian one). To clarify my stance, I present a summary of Calvin's balanced biblicism, which explains why Moïse Amyraut (1596–1664)[4] effectively rejected the *unbalanced* soteriologies of both Arminius *and* Beza. Rooted in a dualistic [double-intention] conception of the divine will (see *Deuteronomy 29: 29*), Calvin taught that Christ's atoning death was universal in scope, and that He was offered as the Redeemer of the whole world according to God's 'revealed' conditional will, albeit only received by

---

1 'Some Remarks on "A Defence of the Preface to the Edinburgh Edition of Aspasio Vindicated"', *Works* (1841), x. 337.

2 'The Question, "What is an Arminian?" Answered, by a Lover of Free Grace' in *Works*, x. 346.

3 See J. I. Packer, 'Arminianisms' in *The Manifold Grace of God* (Puritan Conference Report, London: 1968), 32.

4 See my *Amyraut Affirmed* (Norwich: Charenton Reformed Publishing, 2004).

elected believers according to God's 'hidden' absolute will. Notwithstanding the rationally-challenging paradox involved, Calvin maintained the doctrines of universal atonement and divine election side by side. Faced by clear biblical evidence for both, he refused to tamper with the scriptural texts. Logic was not allowed to dictate one emphasis at the expense of the other. Typical of his numerous statements on the extent of the atonement, Calvin commented thus on Romans 5: 18: 'Paul makes grace common to all, not because it in fact extends to all, but because it is offered to all. Although Christ suffered for the sins of the world, and is offered by the goodness of God without distinction to all men, yet not all receive him'.[1]

ON THE EDGE OF CALVINISM

Notwithstanding Wesley's standard Arminian response to Calvinism, none can doubt the Calvinistic elements in his thought. Not forgetting his life-long exposure to Puritan works in general, the special influence of Baxter's writings and the not entirely negative response to Whitefield in the 1740s probably

---

1   Calvin, *Comment on Romans 5: 18*. Significantly, Roger Nicole admits that Calvin's comment on Romans 5: 18 'comes perhaps closest to providing support for Amyraut's thesis' (*Moyse Amyraut (1596–1664) and the Controversy on Universal Grace* (Harvard University thesis, 1966), 83, n. 38). Richard Muller also states that 'Calvin's teaching was ... capable of being cited with significant effect by Moïse Amyraut against his Reformed opponents' (*The Unaccommodated Calvin* (Oxford: OUP, 2000), 62). For further extracts (90 in total), see my *Calvinus: Authentic Calvinism, A Clarification*, 2nd ed. (Norwich: Charenton Reformed Publishing, 2007). A particularly compelling example is the following: 'Yet I approve of the common reading, that He alone bore the punishment of many, because the guilt of the whole world was laid upon Him. It is evident from other passages ... that 'many' sometimes denotes 'all' ... That, then, is how our Lord Jesus bore the sins and iniquities of many. But in fact, this word 'many' is often as good as equivalent to 'all'. And indeed, our Lord Jesus was offered to all the world. For it is not speaking of three or four when it says: 'God so loved the world, that He spared not His only Son'. But yet we must notice what the Evangelist adds in this passage: 'That whosoever believes in Him shall not perish but obtain eternal life.' Our Lord Jesus suffered for all and there is neither great nor small who is not inexcusable today, for we can obtain salvation in Him. Unbelievers who turn away from Him and who deprive themselves of Him by their malice are today doubly culpable. For how will they excuse their ingratitude in not receiving the blessing in which they could share by faith? And let us realize that if we come flocking to our Lord Jesus Christ, we shall not hinder one another and prevent Him being sufficient for each of us ... Let us not fear to come to Him in great numbers, and each one of us bring his neighbours, seeing that He is sufficient to save us all' (*Sermons on Isaiah's Prophecy*, trans. T. H. L. Parker (London: James Clarke, 1956), 136, 141–4).

left some favourable impressions. However impatient he was with *High Calvinism*, he still retained the essential evangelical emphasis of Reformation Calvinism. At the 1745 Methodist Conference, it was admitted that 'the truth of the Gospel' lies 'very near' to Calvinism: 'Wherein may we come to the very edge of Calvinism? (1) In ascribing all good to the free grace of God. (2) In denying all natural free will, and all power antecedent to grace, and (3) In excluding all merit from man; even for what he has or does by the grace of God'.[1] Even after the publication of Wesley's main counter-blast against Calvinism, *Predestination Calmly Considered* (1752),[2] he continued to live 'on the edge of Calvinism' in his view of divine grace.

Of course, the *raison d'etre* of Wesley's mission was the doctrine of universal redemption. His famous sermon on *Free Grace* (1740)[3] reveals the preacher's dislike for Calvinism. As he saw it, the doctrines of election, reprobation, and especially limited atonement were a total negation of evangelistic enterprise. Aware of his views, Whitefield had discouraged Wesley from publishing the sermon in the interests of unity, but not long after Whitefield's departure for America, Wesley published it. In his reply, Whitefield argued that Wesley's theology was inconsistent with Article XVII of the Church of England, 'Of Predestination and Election'. He then proceeded to insist, as Dr John Owen had done a century before, that the atonement was limited to the elect: 'Our Lord knew for whom he died'.[4]

If Whitefield's arguments had a profound but temporary influence over Wesley, the latter's thinking was influenced from another source. In the wake of the 'Free Grace' controversy, Wesley published a small pamphlet which revealed his awareness of John Calvin's teaching on the extent of the atonement. His *Serious Considerations Concerning the Doctrines of Election and Reprobation* (1740)[5] consisted of extracts from Chapter 13 of Isaac Watts' *The Ruin and Recovery of Mankind* (1740).[6] A disciple of Richard Baxter

---

1 'Minutes of Some Late Conversations Between the Rev. Mr. Wesleys and Others', *Works*, viii.274.

2 See Wesley, *Works*, x. 197.

3 See Wesley, *Works*, vii. 356.

4 *George Whitefield's Journals*, ed. I . H. Murray (London: The Banner of Truth Trust, 1960), 587.

5 See listing in Wesley, *Works*, xiv. 202. For all its brevity, this penny pamphlet was reissued in 1752, 1769, 1773, 1778, 1782 and 1790. For some reason, Wesley withheld the author's name in every issue.

6 For examples of Calvin's universal atonement statements, see *The Works of The Revd and*

rather than John Owen, Watts (the well-known spokesman for Protestant Dissent) produced six quotations from Calvin on universal atonement. In his pamphlet, Wesley cited only four of these, also omitting Watts' summary: 'Thus it appears that Calvin himself thought that Christ and his salvation are offered to all, and that in some sense he died for all'. As the Wesleyan scholar Dr Herbert Boyd McGonigle points out, 'Watts offered a sixth consideration in defence of universal grace which Wesley's abridgement omitted altogether'.[1] What is interesting is that Wesley never seems to have used the Calvin evidence in his frequent debates with Calvinists, despite the reformer's belief in the universal love of God.[2] He evidently missed seeing any significant potential in the 'Calvin vs. the Calvinists' debate. Why is a mystery. Perhaps he thought Calvin's 'concessions' too insignificant in the context of the reformer's predestinarian thought. Perhaps he felt that enlisting Calvin's support against the Calvinists might have reduced the impact of his sharply-polarised polemic against Calvinism. Perhaps too, Wesley feared his enemies might use Calvin's authority to induce him to make even further shifts in their direction.

Later, in 1743, John Wesley wrote a brief and equally-fascinating memorandum entitled *Calvinistic Controversy*.[3] Anxious to avoid 'needless dispute' with Whitefield, Wesley declared his sentiments in a distinctly Calvinistic manner. But, in affirming unconditional election, irresistible grace and final perseverance, he significantly omits limited atonement. Although Wesley had been cautious about leaning 'too much towards Calvinism' in the 1744 Methodist Conference, he—as we have seen—was willing in his doctrine of grace to 'come to the very edge of Calvinism' at the 1745 Conference. It was probably the question of the extent of the atonement which turned the scales in favour of Arminianism, a fact confirmed by the subtitle of *The Arminian Magazine: consisting of Extracts and Original Treatises on Universal Redemption*, issued by Wesley from 1778–91. Wesley's 'moderately Calvinistic' phase was therefore temporary.

Learned Isaac Watts, DD, ed. D. Jennings and P. Doddridge (London: 1753), vi. 287–8.

1   H. B. McGonigle, *Sufficient Saving Grace: John Wesley's Evangelical Arminianism* (Carlisle: Paternoster Press, 2001), 122.

2   See my *Calvinus*, 30, 36.

3   Wesley, *Works*, xiii. 478–9.

ANGLICAN CALVINIST: WHITEFIELD OR WESLEY?

If Whitefield's appeal to the Thirty-Nine Articles was a source of embarrassment to Wesley (whose denial that this was the case is not entirely convincing[1]), Calvinist Whitefield was also involved in an anomaly which Wesley was not slow to exploit in a later exchange (in 1772) with Rowland Hill.[2] Indeed, as surely as Article XVII acknowledges personal predestination and election, Article XXXI states that the atonement was 'for all the sins of the whole world, both original and actual'. A year later, Wesley rightly appealed not only to the Articles, Homilies and Catechism of Church of England,[3] but also to the universalist statements of such Anglican reformers as Ridley, Hooper and Latimer to vindicate his position.[4] In this respect, Whitefield

---

1   See Wesley, *Works*, x. 313, 407.

2   See 'Some Remarks on Mr Hill's "Review of all the Doctrines Taught by Mr John Wesley" ', *Works*, x. 368.

3   He first did this in *The Doctrine of Salvation, Faith, and Good Works, Extracted from the Homilies of the Church of England* (London: 1738). Article XXXI explicitly affirms that 'The offering of Christ once made is that perfect redemption, propitiation, and satisfaction, for all the sins of the whole world, both original and actual; ...' Consistent with this, the *BCP* prayer of consecration from the service of Holy Communion states that Christ made 'a full, perfect and sufficient sacrifice, oblation, and satisfaction, for the sins of the whole world'. The *Catechism* teaches the catechumen to believe that God the Son 'hath redeemed me, and all mankind' while it hastens to add, in Calvinist rather than Arminian fashion, that God the Holy Ghost 'sanctifieth me, and all the elect people of God'. The *Homily for Good Friday* is equally clear: 'So pleasant was this sacrifice and oblation of His Son's death, which he so obediently and innocently suffered, that he would take it for the only and full amends for all the sins of the world' (*Sermons or Homilies* (London: Prayer-Book and Homily Society, 1833), 287). See my *Atonement and Justification*, 79.

4   See 'Some Remarks on Mr Hill's "Farrago Double-Distilled" ', *Works*, x. 409. Archbishop *Thomas Cranmer* stated that Christ 'by His own oblation ... satisfied His Father for all men's sins and reconciled mankind unto His grace and favour'. Bishop *John Hooper* affirmed that Christ died 'for the love of us poor and miserable sinners, whose place he occupied upon the cross, as a pledge, or one that represented the person of all the sinners that ever were, be now, or shall be unto the world's end'. Bishop *Nicholas Ridley* declared that the sacrifice of Christ 'was, is, and shall be forever the propitiation for the sins of the whole world'. Bishop *Hugh Latimer* preached that 'Christ shed as much blood for Judas, as he did for Peter: Peter believed it, and therefore he was saved; Judas would not believe, and therefore he was condemned'. Even particularist *John Bradford* admitted that 'Christ's death is sufficient for all, but effectual for the elect only'. The Elizabethan Anglicans were no different in their understanding. Bishop *John Jewel* wrote that, on the cross, Christ declared "It is finished" to signify 'that the price and ransom was now full paid for the sin of all mankind'. Elsewhere, he made clear that 'The death of Christ is available for the redemption of all the world'. *Richard Hooker* stated an identical view when he said that Christ's 'precious and

was simply out of order. However, nowhere does Wesley augment his appeals by citing the views of John Calvin, as he might well have done. The simple fact remains that, in view of the consistency of the reformer's ubiquitous universal atonement statements with the Anglican formularies, Calvin would have endorsed Wesley against Whitefield.

It is important to remember that John Wesley claimed an English precedent for his thinking in the works of the Arminian Puritan John (not to be confused with Calvinist Thomas) Goodwin (1594?–1665). Again, this is important in relation to Calvin, since Goodwin's ample treatises on universal redemption[1] and justification by faith[2] include substantial quotations from Calvin, not to mention several other reformers. Unlike Wesley, Goodwin clearly saw potential in Calvin to bolster the Arminian view of the atonement. Clearly valuing Goodwin's treatise *vis-à-vis* the high Calvinist John Owen,[3] Wesley did not seemingly make much use of Goodwin's appeal to Calvin.

However, the picture is decidedly different where the doctrine of justification is concerned. In this respect, aided by Goodwin, Wesley was justly at odds with Whitefield's views on the imputation of Christ's righteousness, not least on account of the dangers of antinomianism. According to biblical exegesis and in line with the Anglican formularies, Wesley argued that 'The plain scriptural notion of justification is pardon, the forgiveness of sins'[4] and that 'Christ by his death alone (so our Church teaches) fully satisfied for the sins of the whole world'.[5] However, in his sermon, *The Lord our Righteousness*, Whitefield—teaching that justification is more than pardon—argued that 'the word righteousness ... implies the active as well as passive obedience of the Lord Jesus Christ. We generally, when talking of the merits of Christ, only mention the latter, his death; whereas the former, his life and active

---

propitiatory sacrifice' was 'offered for the sins of all the world' and that he 'hath thereby once reconciled us to God, purchased his general free pardon, and turned away divine indignation from mankind' (for bibliographical details, see my *Atonement and Justification*, 79).

1   *Redemption Redeemed* (London: 1651).

2   *Imputatio Fidei, or a Treatise of Justification* (London: 1642).

3   In a letter to Walter Sellon in 1768, Wesley wrote: 'I am glad you have undertaken the "Redemption Redeemed." But you must in no wise forget Dr Owen's Answer to it: otherwise you will leave a loop-hole for all the Calvinists to creep out. The Doctor's evasions you must needs cut in pieces, ...' (*The Letters of the Revd John Wesley, AM,* ed. J. Telford (London: Epworth Press, 1931), v. 96).

4   See Wesley, 'Justification by Faith', *Works,* v. 52, and my *Atonement and Justification,* 169ff.

5   'Preface to a Treatise on Justification', *Works,* x. 313.

obedience, is equally necessary'.[1] On the other hand, Goodwin argued that 'he that is completely justified by having his sins forgiven, is justified without the imputation of this active obedience or righteousness of Christ'.[2] Strikingly, Goodwin justifies his argument by launching into several pages of Calvin citations, a fact highlighted by Wesley![3] In short, Whitefield's view reflects not Calvin's but Beza's over-developed orthodoxy, the type later expounded by John Owen.[4] In his writings on the subject, Wesley not only published an edition of Goodwin's *Imputatio Fidei*; he explicitly appeals to Calvin himself. In his preface to Goodwin's treatise on justification, Wesley insists that he employs the expression 'imputed righteousness' just as Calvin did.[5] In his own sermon, *The Lord our Righteousness* (1765), Wesley quotes from Calvin's *Institutes*.[6] In the same year, Wesley insisted that 'I think on justification just as I have done any time these seven-and-twenty years (i.e. since 1738); and just

---

1   *Select Sermons of George Whitefield* (London: The Banner of Truth Trust, 1959), 74.

2   *Imputatio Fidei*, 118.

3   Wesley, *Works*, x. 304. John Calvin's statements are thoroughly explicit on this matter. 'Justification by faith is reconciliation with God and ... this consists solely in the remission of sins' (*Inst.* III. xi. 21); 'God justifies by pardoning' (ibid); '... this justification may be termed in one word the remission of sins' (ibid); 'Thus the Apostle connects forgiveness of sins with justification in such a way as to show that they are altogether the same ...' (ibid). It is obvious that Calvin's position has been something of an embarrassment to later Reformed theologians who, like Owen, wish to argue that justification is more than pardon. Although Calvin did speak of 'the imputation of the righteousness of Christ' (*Inst.* III. xi. 2) he plainly regarded 'justification', 'imputation' and 'remission of sins' as synonymous terms (see *Inst.* III. xi. 4; *Comm. Gal.* 3: 6; Luke 1: 77). Furthermore, it is precisely because justification is no more than forgiveness that Calvin never suggested the imputation of Christ's active obedience: 'Our righteousness has been procured by the obedience of Christ which he displayed in His death' (*Comm.* Rom. 4: 25); '... Christ has attained righteousness for sinners by His death, ...' (*Comm.* Rom. 5: 9). It was Theodore Beza who insisted that justification was more than pardon. Mere forgiveness was deemed insufficient; the believer needed a more 'positive' righteousness before God. Hence Christ's passive obedience in death *and* his active obedience to the law form the basis of that righteousness imputed to the believer (see T. Beza, *Tractationes theologiae* (Geneva: 1570–82), iii. 248, 256). While Calvin clearly grounds Christ's saving work in the whole of his obedience, he suggests that his 'active' [the term is post-Calvin] obedience was intended to demonstrate his qualification to be the guiltless sin-bearer. His own obedience was thus immediately relevant to himself, and only to the believer's justification indirectly (*Inst.* II. xvi. 5). For further discussion, see my *Atonement and Justification*, 169ff.

4   See my *Atonement and Justification*, 169ff.

5   Wesley, *Works*, x. 326.

6   Wesley, *Works*, v. 226.

as Mr Calvin does. In this respect, I do not differ from him a hair's breadth'.[1] As late as 1770, the year the second Calvinistic controversy commenced, Wesley argued in his tract *What is an Arminian?* that Calvin never asserted justification by faith more strongly than Arminius and the Methodists had done.[2] The inescapable conclusion is obvious, that regarding the doctrines of the atonement and justification, Arminian Wesley is the Calvinist!

DR DODDRIDGE AND THE *VIA MEDIA*

In the eighteenth-century English context, one may say—in view of the above portrayal of Calvin's 'authentic Calvinism'—that neither Wesley *nor* Whitefield can validly lay claim to the *full* title 'Calvinist'. The only real contender of note is their fellow labourer, the godly pastor and Dissenting tutor Dr Philip Doddridge of Northampton (1702–51).[3] Known and respected by the two Methodists, who had both sought his advice, Doddridge's early death deprived the polarised preachers of his ongoing personal influence. Indeed, his wise and insightful biblical scholarship would have facilitated greater personal, theological and organisational harmony. Amounting to a *via media* between Bezaism and Arminianism, the Northampton pastor's position had potential to attract both Whitefield and Wesley to a biblical middle ground.

Whitefield's particularism and Wesley's universalism are alike one-sided accounts of the Gospel. At their biblical best, *both* men may be regarded as semi-Calvinists, albeit from opposing perspectives. They both stress different sides of the same coin, paradoxical truths Calvin held in tension. Alternatively, agreeing with Richard Baxter (and one may include Isaac Watts), Doddridge was concerned to expound the textual data in an integrated manner, without suppressing either the general or the particular aspects of the Gospel. Like Calvin and Baxter, Doddridge—*data-driven* rather than *dogma-driven*—accepted the fact of paradox, urging the need to restrict theological activity to the confines of the evidence. Thus he adopted a dualistic hermeneutic in his theology of grace. The atonement is to be seen in a two-sided manner: it

---

1   *The Journal of the Revd John Wesley, AM,* ed. N. Curnock (London: Epworth Press, 1909–16), v. 116.

2   See Wesley, *Works,* x. 345.

3   See my *The Good Doctor: Philip Doddridge of Northampton—A Tercentenary Tribute* (Norwich: Charenton Reformed Publishing, 2002).

is general in provision, though particular in application, both aspects being part of the divine intention. While Doddridge (and Baxter before him) was accused of compromise, his concern was not merely dictated by the demands of an ecumenical vision. His was a convinced theological evaluation of the issues. He was not therefore 'diluting' truth, but restoring what had become a 'super-concentrate' to its proper biblical 'strength'. In this latter respect, both Baxter and Doddridge had a clear precedent in John Calvin. Indeed, Doddridge's Baxterianism (give or take one or two details) was the eighteenth century expression of authentic Calvinism. Of course, judged by the criteria of *High* Calvinism, it was bound to look like a compromise with Arminianism. Like Amyraut (who still remains Calvin's most accurate exponent overall)[1] and Baxter, Doddridge considered that, at their biblical best, both High Calvinists and Arminians expressed features that were united in Calvin's theological and pastoral thought. He saw that as the Arminian was not all wrong, so the High Calvinist was not all right, and *vice versa*.

CONCLUSION

Returning to Wesley, it remains to be repeated that, the *metaphysics* of grace apart, John Wesley was at least a partial disciple of John Calvin, an assessment he might have accepted with some degree of equanimity, especially where the doctrine of justification is concerned. Without exceeding the scope of this paper, it is not inappropriate to indicate that in their justifiably-negative views of Rome[2] and Islam,[3] Calvin and Wesley also saw eye to eye. Even

---

1   See my *Amyraut Affirmed* (Norwich: Charenton Reformed Publishing, 2004) and 'Justification: the Calvin-Saumur Perspective', *The Evangelical Quarterly*, 79. 4 (2007), 331–48.

2   See O. A. Beckerlegge, *John Wesley's Writings on Roman Catholicism* (London: Protestant Truth Society, n.d.).

3   (1) *Wesley on Islam*: 'Ever since the religion of Islam appeared in the world, the espousers of it ... have been as wolves and tigers to all other nations, rending and tearing all that fell into their merciless paws, and grinding them with their iron teeth; that numberless cities are raised from the foundation, and only their name remaining; that many countries, which were once as the garden of God, are now a desolate wilderness; and that so many once numerous and powerful nations are vanished from the earth! Such was, and is at this day, the rage, the fury, the revenge, of these destroyers of human kind' ('The Doctrine of Original Sin', *Works*, ix. 205); 'How far and wide has this miserable delusion spread over the face of the earth! Insomuch that [Muslims] are considerably more in number (as six to five) than Christians. And by all accounts, ... these are also, in general, as utter strangers to all true religion as their four-footed brethren; as void of

on matters of church order, despite the Genevan reformer's lack of episcopal ordination, quasi-presbyterian Wesley defended the 'great work' of Calvin's Genevan ministry.[1] Had they 'met' here (through the diplomatic efforts of Philip Doddridge and Jean-Alphonse Turretin[2]), they doubtless would have embraced one another, as they certainly do now in heaven, the divine light having long dispersed all disagreements and discord forever!

---

mercy as lions and tigers; as much given up to brutal lusts as bulls or goats: so that they are in truth a disgrace to human nature' ('The General Spread of the Gospel', *Works*, vi. 261). (2) *Calvin on Islam and Rome*: 'Muhammad and the Pope have this religious principle in common, that Scripture does not contain the perfection of doctrine, but that something higher has been revealed by the Spirit. The Anabaptists and Libertines have in our own day drawn their madness from the same ditch' *(Comment on John 14: 25); '*This error [of additional revelation beyond Christ] is followed by another, no less intolerable; that having said goodbye to Christ's law, as if His reign were ended, and He now nothing at all, they substitute the Spirit in His place. From this source have flowed the sacrileges of the Papacy and Muhammadanism. For although those antichrists are dissimilar in many respects they have a common starting point: that in the Gospel we are initiated into the true faith, but that the perfection of doctrine must be sought elsewhere, to perfect us completely. If Scripture is brought against the Pope, he denies that we should keep to it, since the Spirit has also now come and has lifted us above it by many additions. Muhammad proclaims that without his *Qur'an* men always remain children. Thus, by a false claim to the Spirit, the world has been bewitched to leave the simple purity of Christ. For as soon as the Spirit is severed from Christ's Word the door is open to all sorts of craziness and impostures. Many fanatics have tried a similar method of deception in our own age. The written teaching seems to them to be of the letter. Therefore they were pleased to make up a new theology consisting of revelations' *(Comment on John 16: 14).*

1   'A Farther Appeal to Men of Reason and Religion', II, *Works*, viii. 214.

2   The outlooks and concerns of Doddridge and Turretin were very similar. Opposed to the anti-Amyraldian *Formula Consensus Helvetica* (1675), 'The younger Turretin was reacting against what he considered to be the overly defined nature of Reformed, scholastic theology because of its divisiveness and lack of concern for personal piety. He preferred to return to Calvin's pastoral emphasis, as well as that on the salvific nature of Scripture' (See M. I. Klauber, *Between Reformed Scholasticism and Pan-Protestantism: Jean-Alphonse Turretin (1671–1737) and Enlightened Orthodoxy at the Academy of Geneva* (Selinsgrove: Susquehanna University Press/London and Toronto: Associated University Presses, 1994), 14). For a recent survey, see Paul T. Nimmo & David A. S. Ferguson, *Reformed Theology* (Cambridge: CUP, 2016), 217–20.

14. THE GOSPEL ACCORDING TO JOHN JONES TALSARN[1]

INTRODUCTION

Since some kind of connection may be demonstrated between Daniel Rowland and all the other subjects of our conference, what link is there to justify the special 'coupling' implied by my title? After all, Daniel Rowland (1713–90) died six years before John Jones, Talsarn (1796–1857) was born. It may be claimed that these two Welsh servants of Christ were the greatest gospel preachers of their respective centuries. One difference is obvious. While thousands travelled from all parts of Wales to hear Daniel Rowland at Llangeitho for about five decades, John Jones, Talsarn travelled thousands of miles all over Wales for over thirty years in much-blest evangelistic endeavour. Among other things, and driven by the love of Christ, the two men shared an extraordinary degree of 'hiraeth' for the salvation of the Welsh people. Consistent with this, and in tune with the perspective of this conference, it might surprise some to know that this pair of Calvinistic Methodists expressed 'Amyraldian features' in their gospel theology.

To clarify terminology used in this paper, 'High Calvinism' is properly defined as the theology of Theodore Beza, the *Westminster Confession* and John Owen, as distinct from the original teaching of John Calvin which Amyraut claimed to reaffirm as 'authentic Calvinism'. Losing Calvin's biblical balance, 'High Calvinism' was the prelude to the antinomian hypercalvinism which blighted Wales for a while, as it did England and elsewhere. In short, the Owenite 'limited atonement' teaching created evangelistic and pastoral havoc, as it still does.

---

1 *A Refuge for the Guilty Race—Amyraldian Features in Welsh Calvinism: Daniel Rowland & John Jones Talsarn*, a paper first given at the 9th Amyraldian Association Conference on Friday 12 April 2013.

I begin my case for linking the two preachers by citing the testimony of a preacher and historian from Caernarfonshire, one Robert Jones, Rhoslan (1745–1829).[1] He had heard the seraphic Daniel Rowland during several visits to Llangeitho. An old man in his seventies when he first heard John Jones, Talsarn, he remarked: "Well, indeed, here is a preacher like old Rowland, with a voice much more melodious, and, possibly, talents more bright."[2]

Whatever might be true of Wales in general, Daniel Rowland is undoubtedly better-known today than John Jones, at least in Reformed and Nonconformist circles. What better way is there of refreshing our memories of Daniel Rowland than to quote the dust-jacket blurb of Dr Eifion Evans's superb biography?[3]

Daniel Rowland (1711–90) has been described by J. C. Ryle as 'one of the spiritual giants of the eighteenth century'. Lady Huntingdon considered him to be 'second only to Whitefield'. Howel Harris wrote of him, 'In his pulpit he is a second St Paul', while others acclaimed him as 'the greatest preacher in Europe'. Yet he has been one of the least known leaders of that age. The loss of manuscripts shortly after his death, the Welsh language barrier, the remoteness of the scenes of his ministry, and the fact that all his closest friends were also preachers rather than authors, all contributed to leave only a shadowy impression of his greatness. Now, after many years of work, Dr Eifion Evans has succeeded in breaking through a multitude of difficulties and in presenting for the first time a full-scale biography.

Here is a record of revivals, of friendships with other leaders, of persecutions and divisions, and the birth of a new age for Wales. Amidst it all, Dr Evans excels in showing what made Rowland the preacher and the humble Christian that he was.

Rowland was a man of abounding energy. He walked to London for ordination, ran beside his native River Aeron when turned 70, and travelled nearly 3,000 miles a year on foot or on one of his 'little nags'

---

1   See Owen Thomas, Owen, trans. John Aaron, *The Atonement Controversy in Welsh Theological Literature and debate, 1707–1841* (Edinburgh: The Banner of Truth Trust, 2002), 375. Hereinafter *Atonement Controversy*.

2   Owen Jones, *Some the Great Preachers of Wales* (London: Passmore & Alabaster, 1885), 474. Hereinafter *Great Preachers*.

3   Eifion Evans, *Daniel Rowland and the Great Evangelical Awakening in Wales* (Edinburgh: The Banner of Truth Trust, 1985). Hereinafter *Daniel Rowland*.

for more than 50 years. At death, when reminded that he had been instrumental in the conversion of thousands to Christ, he protested, 'It is nothing. I die as a poor sinner, depending fully and entirely on the merits of a crucified Saviour'.

J. C. Ryle writes of Rowland: 'Never, perhaps, did any preacher exalt Christ more ... No British preacher of the 18th century kept together in one district such enormous congregations of souls for fifty years as Rowland did'. And Dr D. M. Lloyd-Jones asks, 'Has there been preaching which has had anything like the effect of his preaching since those days?'

Who then was John Jones, the preacher with 'a voice much more melodious' than Rowland's and possibly more talented? Unfortunately for English readers, no one has done for John Jones what Eifion Evans has done for Daniel Rowland. The chief source for John Jones remains the scholarly Dr Owen Thomas's impressive 1,000-page *Cofiant Y Parchedig John Jones, Talsarn,* a work 'unhappily, never translated from Welsh into English', wrote Iain Murray in 1990.[1] First published in 1874, the work is considered to be 'the best biography ever written in Welsh. ... No Welshman can consider himself to be cultured unless he has read it'.[2] However, Owen Jones's *Some of the Great Preachers of Wales,* published in 1885, provides in English a substantial final chapter on John Jones, Talsarn. Using Dr Thomas's biography and other sources, the author thus provides a fairly full and vivid account of John Jones.

Born on 1 March 1796 at Tan-y-Castell near Dolwyddelan (5 miles west of Betws-y-Coed), John Jones experienced the power of God's grace around the time of the famous Beddgelert Revival (1817–22). Coming from a family remarkably blest by God, John became an extraordinary preacher. Greatly admired by the illustrious veteran preacher John Elias,[3] the late Dr R. Tudur Jones also described him as one of the princes of the period.[4] These appraisals are reflected in the impressive monument to the Jones family at Tan-y-Castell. The column for John Jones reminds us that he was a composer of hymn tunes (and a few hymns) as well as an eloquent preacher. Of course, John

---

1   Iain H. Murray, *D. Martyn Lloyd-Jones: The Fight of Faith 1939–1981* (Edinburgh: The Banner of Truth Trust, 1990), 711.

2   *Atonement Controversy,* p. ix.

3   *Great Preachers,* 470.

4   Eryl Davies, *The Beddgelert Revival* (Bridgend: Bryntirion Press, 2004), 163.

Jones is famously remembered as 'John Jones, Talsarn'[1] (or more correctly
Talysarn, about 10 miles south of Caernarfon, his home from 1823 until his
death in 1857). He is buried in the churchyard at Llanllyfni (the name given
to one of his tunes), where a fine and moving epitaph records the amazing
impact of his ministry. Close communion with God was the source of his
pulpit power. Indeed, writing thirty years after the death of John Jones,
Owen Jones wrote that 'not far from his house there was a copse of wood,
silent and lonely, except for the chirping of the birds. Here he used to go
[and pray], and remain for hours. There is a path in it to this day made by
his own feet, where he used to walk backwards and forwards'.[2]

John Jones's nationwide ministry—from Bangor to Swansea, from Mold to
Carmarthen (not to forget preaching in London)—helped lay the foundations
of the glorious events of 1859. Significantly, his preaching after 1835 was marked
by a personal directness often lacking among his brethren. Revealing the
influence of Dr Edward Williams, Rotherham on his thinking, he identified
the growing dangers of antinomian hypercalvinism. In short, he criticised a
tendency among some Calvinists to stress the exposition of God's sovereign
grace at the expense of application and human responsibility. Coupled with
deeply felt conviction, John Jones's 'practical' sermons possessed a compelling
immediacy few could resist. Not surprisingly, wrote John Aaron, 'many
thousands [ascribed] their conversions to the influence of his preaching'.[3]

When he died at Talysarn on Sunday, 16 August 1857, John Jones proved
the blessedness of all he'd preached to others. Despite advancing weakness,
his spirit was filled with rapture as he was heard to whisper, "O dear Jesus!
O beloved Jesus! Blessed be Thy name forever!"

As depicted by Owen Jones, John Jones's funeral indicated the impact of
his ministry:

> On Friday, 21 August, the day he was buried at Llanllyfni, the shops were
> closed in Talysarn and all the country around; and even in Caernarfon,
> which is several miles away; and the work in the slate quarries was at a
> stand that day. And in the eyes of some, great Snowdon seemed to wear
> a pall … Before leaving the house in Talysarn, Henry Rees spoke to the
> large crowd of mourners: "It is not becoming to say much now. Silence is

---

1 Thus distinguished since there were numerous John Joneses in Caernarfonshire at that time!
2 *Great Preachers*, 528.
3 *Atonement* Controversy, p. xiv.

the most eloquent. If you desire to have a real sermon today, look at the coffin, the funeral car, and the grave, and think of your sweet-mouthed preacher, who is now silent forever. His name was well known throughout the Principality for thirty or thirty-five years, and his eloquence roused and charmed the minds of Welshmen. But today there is no John Jones, Talsarn, in Wales. Far be it from us, however, to weep for him as men which have no hope. 'For if we believe that Jesus died and rose again, even so, them also which sleep in Jesus will God bring with Him!' " In the funeral procession there were eight medical men, sixty-five ministers and preachers, three abreast; seventy deacons four abreast; two hundred singers, six abreast; six thousand men and women, six abreast, trending slowly on the road from Talysarn to Llanllyfni, singing on the way some of the old Welsh tunes, 'Yn y dyfroedd mawr a'r tonau', 'Ymado wnaf a'r babell', the hills around and Snowdon in the distance echoing the sound. That day and for many a day after a great gloom rested upon Wales.[1]

Such sadness simply reflected the widespread hiraeth for one who radiated the love of Christ. While others—such as Henry Rees—laboured on faithfully and effectively, the loss of John Jones, Talsarn was relieved in measure by the remarkable if less spectacular ministry of his son David Lloyd Jones (1843–1905).[2]

Dr Owen Thomas wrote that 'We are disposed to think that he, during those years (from 1821 to 1857), made for himself a deeper home in the affections of his fellow-countrymen than perhaps any of his mighty predecessors or contemporaries—so deep a home, indeed, that the longing that is still felt for him in the breasts of his hearers is as keen and strong as if he had died yesterday'.[3]

Owen Jones himself wrote that John Jones 'consecrated all the powers of his soul for the Gospel of Christ. Preaching absorbed all the energies of his life … He became the most efficient and most popular preacher of the age in Wales. The epithet is applied to him to this day, "The preacher of the people."

---

1 *Great Preachers*, 520–1.

2 See Elias Jones, John Williams, T. Charles Williams, *Cofiant a Phregethau Y Diweddar Barch. David Lloyd Jones, MA Llandinam* (Gwrecsam: Hughes A'i Fab, 1908); R. Hughes (ed), *Memoir and Sermons of the Late Rev. David Lloyd Jones, MA, Llandinam* (Wrexham: Hughes and Son, 1912).

3 Cited in *Great Preachers*, 462.

And no one since his time has arrived at anything like his popularity'.[1] Of course, this author was not to know that, less than fifteen years later (1899), a boy named David Martyn Lloyd-Jones was born in Cardiff whose influence, by the grace of God, was possibly to demand a revised assessment?

From a strictly theological perspective, English readers are indebted to translator John Aaron and the Banner of Truth Trust for providing a window on the views of John Jones, Talsarn. Published in 2002, *The Atonement Controversy in Welsh Theological Literature and Debate, 1701–1841*[2] is simply Chapter 11 of Owen Thomas's original biography, comprising about a third of the entire work! This substantial section provided a comprehensive historical and theological background to the author's subject. Covering a period of nearly two centuries, the chapter's very existence indicates the problematic and vexed nature of continual controversies over the atonement. Following his very illuminating but highly-critical introduction, the translator follows the author's division of the subject matter thus: Part 1 charts the debates between Calvinists and Arminians, 1707–1831. Part 2 covers debates among the Calvinists of all denominations, 1811–41. Part 3—with which we are chiefly concerned—focuses on internal debates among the Calvinistic Methodists (later known as the Presbyterian Church of Wales), 1814–41.

This book has an intriguing feature. Judging by his highly-biased introduction, the translator is largely at odds with the material he translates. Anxious to alert us to the 'weaknesses' of the author's own standpoint, his 'Word of Caution' is in effect a 'health warning' against the author's so-called 'moderate Calvinism'![3] Concerned to expose the governmental theory of the atonement, he totally ignores the flawed commercial or mercantile 'price for price' view rightly rejected by many who otherwise subscribe to Dr John Owen's doctrine of limited atonement.[4] For a while, even the veteran Welsh colossus John Elias embraced this erroneous and 'unscriptural position'.[5] Revealing his strongly-Owenite bias, Aaron laments that 'Owen Thomas's

---

1   Ibid. 532.

2   See my review in Evangelical Quarterly, Vol. 77.2 (2005), 187–90.

3   *Atonement Controversy*, p. xxv.

4   For a discussion of competing theories of the atonement, see my *Atonement and Justification: English Evangelical Theology 1640–1790* (Oxford: The Clarendon Press, 1990/2002), 125ff. Hereinafter *Atonement and Justification*.

5   R. Tudur Jones, *John Elias—Prince Amongst Preachers* (Bridgend: The Evangelical Library of Wales, 1975), 28.

heart is with John Jones ... He wishes the 'New System' [of Dr Edward Williams, Rotherham] to prevail'.[1] Among other things, he is accused of lacking 'objectivity in his arguments' in thinking that heroes such as John Elias and Henry Rees—both opponents of hypercalvinism—sympathised with the need to 'modify' the older Calvinism.[2]

John Aaron's dubious analysis tends to deflect the reader from the heart of the problem being addressed by Owen Thomas. The author and many of his brethren were convinced that the High-Calvinist 'Owenite' doctrine of limited atonement involved an 'unscriptural limitation'[3] which, besides its faulty biblical exegesis, discouraged active and compassionate evangelism.

Thomas and his friends were persuaded that by stating that '[Christ's] Person [stood] in the stead of those persons (and those only) who had been given him to redeem', Article 18 of the Calvinistic Methodist *Confession of Faith* (1823)[4] was 'wise above what is written'.[5] Indeed, no biblical text supports such an explicit view. Indeed, this article *Of Redemption* is arguably more 'particular' than the *Westminster Confession of Faith* equivalent. These arguments had significant effect. In 1874, the year Thomas's biography was published, the General Assembly of the denomination (Carmarthen, 1874; Portmadoc, 1875) amended the interpretation of the article with an appendix stressing the infinite sufficiency of the atonement.[6] In this way, a long-standing problem was in great measure (but not entirely[7]) resolved. That said, it is hardly right to say this 'sufficiency' is an 'opposite' truth; 'complimentary' is surely better.

In short, the whole controversy concerned a right understanding of the Gospel and the true character of Calvinism. Aaron's assumption that 'Calvinism' really means 'limited atonement Owenism' prevents him from appreciating this. Despite the translator's criticisms, Owen Thomas had done his homework well in an extensive and highly-accomplished historical-

---

1   *Atonement Controversy,* p. xxvi.

2   Ibid. p. xxx.

3   Ibid. 323.

4   *Confession of Faith of the Calvinistic Methodists or the Presbyterians of Wales* (Caernarfon: D. O. Owen, 1900), 74.

5   *Atonement Controversy,* 323.

6   Ibid. 324.

7   'universality' was implied but not specifically mentioned. Dr J. Cynddylan Jones (1840–1930) was later to argue for this, in line with the emphasis evident in Calvin, Edward Williams, arguably Thomas Jones and John Jones, Talsarn (see ibid. pp. xxxviif.).

theological survey. For instance, he was thoroughly aware that John Calvin and many other reformers both Continental and British did not teach the doctrine of limited atonement and that the Canons of Dort maintain a universal dimension in the atonement. In his highly-biased critique (conditioned by an uncritical reliance on Paul Helm[1] and others), the translator fails to perceive the integrity and accuracy of the author's case. As we shall see, by blaming 'moderate Calvinism' as 'Calvinism in decay',[2] Aaron is effectively saying that 'Calvin's Calvinism' is dangerous!

As a not-insignificant aside, there is a surprising omission in Dr Owen Thomas's survey. I have in my possession his personal copy of Thomas Chalmers's *Institutes of Theology* (1849). It is worth noting that Thomas had studied under Chalmers in Edinburgh. As John Aaron indicates, the two men corresponded and continued to be very close.[3] Now, in the course of his historical survey of the atonement controversy, before he looked—very sympathetically—at France and Amyraut, Owen Thomas does not quote Thomas Chalmers in the section dealing with Scotland. Yet under his nose— in Chalmers's *Institutes*—was a statement which supports John Jones, Owen Thomas and other brethren in Wales who sought to express a more biblical and non-Owenite Calvinism. The Scottish colossus stated:

> I cannot but think that the doctrine of Particular Redemption has been expounded by many of its defenders in such a way as to give an unfortunate aspect to the Christian dispensation. As often treated, we hold it to be a most unpractical and useless theory, and not easy to be vindicated, without the infliction of an unnatural violence on many passages of Scripture ... Its ministers are made to feel the chilling influence of a limitation upon their warrant. If Christ died only for the elect, and not for all, they are puzzled to understand how they should proceed with the calls and invitations of the gospel. ... Now for the specific end of conversion, the available scripture is not that Christ laid down His life for the sheep, but that Christ is set forth a propitiation for the sins of the world. It is not because I know myself to be one of the sheep, or one of

---

1   Ibid. 123.
2   Ibid. p. xxxii.
3   Ibid. p. xii.

the elect, but because I know myself to be one of the world, that I take to myself the calls and promises of the New Testament.[1]

Doubtless, Owen Thomas heard statements like this from Chalmers's own lips. This one undoubtedly justifies his assessment and verdict on the entire controversy. Interestingly, the Free Church leader was never seemingly-challenged for exceeding the soteriological limits of the *Westminster Confession of Faith*! Chalmers and Thomas clearly believed that Christian evangelism would be more biblical and healthy if it avoided the distortions of both Arminianism and Owenism. In addition, was Owen Thomas ever aware that, on his death-bed, Chalmers expressed considerable sympathy with the views of Richard Baxter[2] whose undeniably-important stance he also omitted in his survey? Baxter's name nowhere appears in the index of Dr Owen Thomas's *Cofiant John Jones, Talsarn*. A possible reason for this is that Baxter was ignorantly dismissed as an Arminian by William Williams, Pantycelyn.[3] Hence he wouldn't have been regarded as a sympathetic supporting authority. Whether or not he ever read his works, John Jones was one with the seraphic 17th-century English Puritan Richard Baxter.[4]

The simple fact is that Owen Thomas and his friends saw the need to 'moderate' not Calvin's teaching but the 'ultra-Calvinism' of the day in order to return to a Bible-based 'Authentic Calvinism'. One may say that they sought to rescue the denomination from 'Owenistic Methodism' and to be true to correctly-defined 'Calvinistic Methodism'. In this respect, contrary to the standpoint of both translator and publisher, the author—despite ignoring Chalmers and Baxter—produced a persuasive, praise-worthy and illuminating study in historical theology.

Another intriguing feature of this book is a dust-jacket appeal to Dr D. Martyn Lloyd-Jones's enthusiasm for it. One can only conclude that Dr Lloyd-

---

1   Thomas Chalmers, *Institutes of Theology* (Edinburgh: Sutherland and Knox, 1849), ii. 403–6.

2   See William Hanna, *Memoirs of Thomas Chalmers, DD, LlD* (Edinburgh: Thomas Constable and Co., 1854), ii. 512.

3   Ibid. 150. This might well explain why Owen Thomas did not present Baxter's views in his historical survey. His whole case would have been reinforced had he known Baxter's agreement with Amyraut whom he did cite. Of a kind Dr Thomas would have approved, Baxter's views on the atonement are clearly evident in the *Call to the Unconverted*.

4   However, several of Baxter's works were translated into Welsh, including the famous *Call to the Unconverted;* see Eifion Evans, 'Richard Baxter's Influence in Wales' in *The National Library of Wales Journal*, XXXIII. 2, Winter 2003, 149ff.

Jones preaching was indeed influenced by Owen Thomas's monumental work, but not in the manner assumed either by the translator or the publisher.[1] While I share Mr Aaron's concerns over several liberal theological developments in the post-Thomas era, my enthusiasm for *The Atonement Controversy* does not extend to the translator's over-reactionary introduction.

This brings us to John Jones and the 'New System' of Dr Edward Williams, Rotherham, first introduced into Wales in 1814 by one of his students at Oswestry, John Roberts, Llanbryn-mair. Wrongly accused by Aaron of forging a compromise between Calvinistic and Arminian views,[2] Roberts's and Williams's position may be styled as a *via media* between Owenism and Arminianism. Owen Thomas expresses surprise at the strong opposition to John Roberts and his broadly biblical views compared with the 'strange, narrow and unscriptural' mercantile or commercial view of the Atonement advanced by the Baptist preacher Christmas Evans in 1811. He concludes that 'the land' had been 'to a significant degree leavened with very High Calvinist ideas'.[3] As we have noted already, such was the stance eventually taken by John Jones, Talsarn. Owen Thomas provides a vivid and highly-significant account of young John Jones's studies with other youths led by an educated young man named Evan Evans [Ieuan Glan Geirionydd], a member of the Calvinistic Methodist church at Trefriw in the Vale of Conwy:

> In the meetings, to which we referred, they went over much of the work of Dr Edward Williams, *On the Equity of Divine Government and the Sovereignty of Divine Grace,* and also his *Defence of Modern Calvinism,* being his answer to *Refutation to Calvinism,* that was published by Bishop Tomline. Mr Evans read part of Dr Williams to them in Welsh. Then great research was done into the meaning of that area, when they had decided on that standpoint as a topic for conversation, and commonly as a text for discussion, some taking the opinion of the Doctor and the remainder opposing. If it contained a topic of great importance that stood as a topic of discussion in the Christian world, they would spend several meetings on it. And great would be the searching and meditation on it by the next meeting. The two main books of Dr Williams, would be under the same detailed investigation by them, tortuously setting them

---

1 See my *My Debt to the Doctor* (Norwich: Charenton Reformed Publishing, 2009), 51–2.
2 See *Atonement Controversy,* 379.
3 Ibid. 161.

sentence by sentence, some pulling one way and others the other to test the power of the assertions that were taught them. These meetings, as can be easily thought, and as he himself acknowledged with gratitude to the end of his life, were of immense advantage to Revd John Jones, not only because he didn't understand the English himself, but also, at that time, he only had very few Welsh books. A new field opened wide in the forefront of his mind at this time, and after that he meditated diligently on it for many years. *He couldn't bear anyone say anything derogatory about Doctor Williams's work. He would be particularly surprised to hear men of Calvinistic ideas doing that; and always judged that they had not read the writings themselves, or had done so prejudicially or else inappropriately by virtue of their mental disability to place fair judgement on such writings.*[1]

What was it about the so-called 'New System' of Edward Williams that so impressed John Jones, Talsarn? Two things stand out. *First*, as a Bible man first and foremost, he was persuaded that Williams was faithful to the Scriptures, and *second*, he was persuaded that Williams taught nothing contrary to properly-defined Calvinism. On the first point, Edward Williams's affirmation of the Gospel reflects biblically-rooted 'Amyraldian features', viz. that the Gospel makes a universal provision of mercy for the entire human race, notwithstanding the sovereign purposes of God to save the elect, and that such an understanding facilitates evangelistic enterprise:

We conclude, therefore, that the rectoral design of the death of Christ (whatever higher speciality there is in it) extends to all the human race; not merely to those who have been, or actually shall be, but also such as may be evangelised or discipled—that is, all the nations, past, present, and future; and with St John we may affirm, without either trembling for the cause of orthodoxy, or throwing dust in the eyes of its enemies by far-fetched criticisms: 'He is the propitiation for our sins, and not for ours only, but also for the sins of the whole world' (1 *Jn* 2: 2). And with St Paul: 'We thus judge, that if one died for all then were all dead; and' (we further judge) 'that he died for all', with the same rectoral intention by which He gives His promises and Himself to all, to the end that they may have the means of being obedient and happy; and with

---

the higher and more specific end, 'that they who live' (as justified by sovereign grace, and made alive by virtue derived from Christ) 'should not henceforth live unto themselves, but unto Him who died for them and rose again' (*2 Cor 5: 14–15*). Thus, in a word, Jesus Christ is, in the plan of DIVINE GOVERNMENT, the appointed and intended 'Saviour of all men, but, especially', with a decretive infallible speciality, 'of those that', through gracious influence, 'believe' (*1 Tim 4: 10*). 'There is one mediator between God and men, the man Christ Jesus, who gave Himself a ransom for all, to be testified in due time' (*1 Tim 2: 5–6*).[1]

On the second point, Edward Williams was confident that his theology was in tune with John Calvin's actual views, whatever so-called Calvinists of later generations have thought. Indeed, his admiration for Calvin is emphatic and unambiguous:

That illustrious reformer and admirable writer, Calvin, has treated much of predestination and the doctrines of special grace; but though his works consist of nine volumes folio, I do not think that there is one sentence in them all that militates against the above representation; and in many places he expresses himself in a manner that abundantly justifies it, particularly his comments on several passages of the New Testament. To instance only the following: 'The word 'many' does not mean a part of the world only, but the whole human race' (*Comm. Mark 14: 24*).—'Although Christ suffered for the sins of the world, and is offered by the goodness of God without distinction to all men, yet not all receive him' *(Comm. Rom 5: 18)*.[2]

Edward Williams was concerned to demonstrate that authentic Calvinism did not commit its advocates to the doctrine of limited atonement. He made this clear in the second treatise studied by John Jones, Talsarn. In response to an attempted refutation of Calvinism by the Bishop of Lincoln, Edward Williams appeals to Calvin against the bishop's assumption that all Calvinists teach the doctrine of limited atonement:

---

1   Edward Williams, *An Essay on the Equity of Divine Government, and the Sovereignty of Divine Grace* (London: J. Burditt, 1809), 106–111. Hereinafter, *Essay on Equity.*

2   Ibid. 106 (Calvin's Latin quotes given in English from modern editions). For more examples of Calvin's statements, see my *Calvinus—Authentic Calvinism, A Clarification* (Norwich: Charenton Reformed Publishing, 1995, 2nd ed. 2007).

His Lordship I hope will excuse me for asserting, in return, that this eminent reformer did not 'directly' oppose the doctrine of universal redemption, in the sense now explained, as far as I have been able to collect by a frequent search into his voluminous writings. He admitted a universal price of redemption; but he had reasons innumerable against the notion of an actual redemption of all men from sin and misery. He maintained that the remedy was universal, and that it was universally proposed to mankind, according to God's rectoral design; but not that it was the sovereign design of God by it to make mankind universally and indiscriminately submissive, and compliant with the terms on which the blessings resulting from it were to be enjoyed.[1]

While Williams's views on double predestination are thought to be at variance with Calvin's, the discrepancy is more between a caricature of Calvin's views than the reformer's correctly-perceived teaching. For all that he has been charged with 'double predestination', Calvin requires a carefully nuanced interpretation, in line with Williams's general endorsement plus minor qualifications about some of Calvin's ill-digested expressions.[2] While seeking to be a faithful servant of the Word of God, Calvin still acknowledges the decree of reprobation to be 'dreadful', clearly taking no improper delight in teaching it, as Williams is careful to point out.[3] Calvin's unequivocal affirmation of it was blended with humility and caution. He plainly taught—while affirming an ultimate agnosticism over the advent of sin—that while God providentially arranges all the factors behind human choices, *without being the author of sin*, the 'cause and matter' of reprobation is foreknown human guilt rather than a naked supralapsarian decree. Williams clearly agrees with such an interpretation of Calvin.[4]

Despite 'High-Calvinist' Geoffrey Thomas's rather negative portrayal of Edward Williams,[5] there can be no doubt that the latter had a high regard for 'that illustrious writer' John Calvin.[6] Furthermore, despite other literary influences, and feeling 'uneasy' at the excesses of some Methodist revivalists,

1   Edward Williams, *A Defence of Modern Calvinism* (London: James Black, 1812), 192.

2   Ibid. 373.

3   Ibid. 374; *Institutes* 3: 23: 7.

4   Ibid.; *Institutes* 3: 23: 7–9.

5   See articles by Geoffrey Thomas, 'Edward Williams and the Rise of 'Modern Calvinism' ', *The Banner of Truth* (London: January, 1971, pp. 43–8; March, 1971, pp. 29–35).

6   *Essay on Equity*, 374.

John Jones's 'mentor' was perfectly 'at home' with the evangelical authors of the seventeenth and eighteenth centuries including George Whitefield, John Newton[1] and others. Warmly commending 'honest' Richard Baxter's 'glowing heart',[2] Williams especially admired Philip Doddridge and Jonathan Edwards, even producing editions of their works in 1802–5 and 1806 respectively. It is worthy of note that one of Doddridge's favourite Northampton pupils, Benjamin Fawcett of Kidderminster (where Baxter had laboured gloriously in the previous century) preached at Williams's ordination at Ross-on-Wye in 1776. Williams's early enthusiasm for John Owen's *Exposition of Hebrews* (an edition of which he published in 1790) evidently did not extend to the Puritan's 'limited atonement' treatise *The Death of Death*. Williams quotes at length another Puritan whose understanding was obviously permeated with 'Amyraldian features':

The great Mr Charnock, who for depth of penetration and accuracy of judgement was equalled by few, expresses himself, in his *Discourse of*

---

1   In the *Banner of Truth* special issue JOHN NEWTON (August/September, 2007), 16, Iain Murray cites Newton's 'dread of high Calvinism' (without realising that such was Owen's standpoint), also giving a footnote impression that there was nothing amiss in Newton's sermon on John 1: 29! Yet in this sermon on the atonement, Newton rejects the commercial theory of the atonement, on which Owen's entire thesis rests (see *The Works of John Newton,* (1820; fac. Edinburgh: Banner of Truth Trust, 1985), iv. 188ff). He also refuses to reduce 'world' to 'the world of the elect' and he accepts the distinction between natural and moral inability. Murray is incorrect to side with A. A. Hodge that this distinction 'has no warrant in Scripture' ('Pink on the Sovereignty of God' in *The Banner of Truth* (January 2013), 9. On this issue, see J. C. Ryle in *Expository Thoughts on the Gospels*, St John, Vol. 2 (Edinburgh: The Banner of Truth Trust, 1987), 132. See also Calvin on John 8: 43, very probably part of the inspiration for Amyraut's teaching, also shared by Jonathan Edwards. See my 'The Case for Amyraldianism' in ed. Alan C. Clifford, *Christ for the World: Affirming Amyraldianism* (Norwich: Charenton Reformed Publishing, 2007), 15. Thus (as I have demonstrated in my *Atonement and Justification*, Oxford, 1990), Iain Murray's assessment of Newton's theology is simply deceptive and misleading to say the least. In short, between the polarised positions of Wesley and Whitefield, the earlier 'Anglican Calvinist' tradition [e.g. Davenant] re-emerged in the wake of the Methodist revival. While shunning Arminianism, John Newton (1725–1807) still shared Wesley's aversion for High Calvinism: 'That there is an election of grace, we are plainly taught; yet it is not said, 'that Jesus Christ came into the world to save 'the elect', but that he came to save 'sinners', to 'seek and save them that are lost' ... And therefore the command to repent implies a warrant to believe in the name of Jesus, as taking away the sin of the world' (see *Atonement and Justification*, 80–1).

2   See W. T. Owen, *Edward Williams, DD—His Life, Thought and Influence* (Cardiff: University of Wales Press, 1963), 15. Hereinafter *Edward Williams*.

the acceptableness of Christ's death, thus: ... The blood of Christ is a stream, whereof all men may drink; an ocean, wherein all men may bathe. It wants not value to remove our sins, if we want not faith to embrace and plead it' (Charnock's *Works*, ii. 564 (London, 1699).[1]

Such were the influences on young John Jones, Talsarn. Williams's theology became his theology. Only ignorance could smear Edward Williams's theology as some defective 'New System', a kind of liberal departure from the 'Old System' of John Owen and his 'High Orthodox' friends—'Calvinism in decay'.[2] If anything—as Dr R. Tudur Jones agreed[3]—it was largely a return to an 'older system'—that of John Calvin's 'authentic Calvinism' and, more importantly, the Bible! Thus it is entirely incorrect for John Aaron to argue that this stance was a 'compromise' between Calvinism and Arminianism,[4] and to repeat[5] W. T. Owen's restatement of R. W. Dale's criticism of Edward Williams that his so-called 'Moderate Calvinism' was a failure to 'begin and end with Calvin!'[6] On the contrary, he 'started' and 'ended' with Calvin without going beyond him as his High Calvinist critics did! The reality is that 'authentic Calvinism' is the biblical middle ground between Owenism and Arminianism.

Just as Edward Williams was a leading light in mission and evangelism in England, so his theology directed and animated John Jones, Talsarn's mission in Wales. W. T. Owen is right to conclude that 'Among the Methodists no one did more to free his denomination from the grip of hypercalvinism than John Jones of Talsarn.[7] That said, as noted earlier, the *Confession of Faith* was adopted in the same year his sermon was preached. Sadly, the confession bore the stamp of John Elias's 'High Calvinism'. Matters become clear when we scrutinize the standpoints of both John Jones and John Elias whose views represent the polarized positions among the Calvinistic Methodists of the period. While both preachers rejected Arminianism, John Jones may be

---

1 *An Essay on Equity*, 106.

2 R. W. Dale, cited in W. T. Owen, *Edward Williams, DD—His Life, Thought and Influence* (Cardiff: University of Wales Press, 1963), 149.

3 'Although R. W. Dale was to castigate that as 'Calvinism in decay', it may well be that in some of its emphases it was a reversion to Calvin's Calvinism' (tutor's personal letter, 17 January 1983).

4 *Atonement Controversy*, 379.

5 Ibid. p. xxxii.

6 *Edward Williams*, 149.

7 *Edward Williams*, 136.

called a *biblical* 'authentic Calvinistic Methodist' whereas John Elias was a *confessional* 'Owenistic Methodist'. Whereas for the former, 'The Bible was the chief book of his life',[1] the latter was governed by an undue attachment to the objectionable phrase (limiting Christ's atoning death to the elect) 'and those only' ('a hwy yn unig') in Article 18 of the 1823 *Confession of Faith*. His extreme reaction to Robert Roberts, Rhosllannerchrugog's objection was, "I would prefer to lose my right arm than to lose these words from our Confession of Faith."[2] Such a reaction to an unscriptural, man-made phrase is appalling for a Protestant. Calvin would never say such a thing, although Beza might.[3] Well might John Jones have said concerning the universal wording of John 1: 29, 3: 16, 1 Timothy 2: 6 and 1 John 2: 2, etc, 'I would prefer to lose my right arm than to lose these words from the Holy Bible'. There is a precedent for such a thought, since Dr John Davenant, one of the English delegates at the Synod of Dordt said as much.[4]

Although he was strongly-opposed to hypercalvinism and was wonderfully and fruitfully evangelistic, Elias and his brethren would have been wiser in following the stance of Thomas Jones of Denbigh who argued for the 'moderate orthodoxy' of the Anglican formularies.. Dr Eifion Evans is right to remark that the North Wales Methodist leader's 'great contribution lay in steering the Methodism of the [19th] century safely between the rocks of Arminianism and High Calvinism ... both Thomas Jones and Thomas Charles [Bala] were following in the tradition of Rowland and Williams'.[5] However, despite the concerns of Thomas Jones of Denbigh and the similar parallel teaching of Edward Williams, their biblical stance was not reflected in the 1823 *Confession of Faith*. Sadly, although there was little *practical* difference between Elias and John Jones, Article 18 provided a seed-bed for fatalistic hypercalvinism, against which both men and others rightly protested. Tensions would have been eased had John Elias been consistent with his agreement with John Newton, that 'election' (like Calvinism) 'is to be preached, not on its own, but as permeating though our whole ministry, ... just as sugar

---

1   *Great Preachers*, 528.

2   *Atonement Controversy*, 324.

3   Ibid. 123.

4   See my Introduction to John Davenant, *Dissertation on the Death of Christ* (Western Rhyn: Quinta Press, 2006), p. xiii; also Dr Owen Thomas's accurate depiction of Davenant's contribution at Dordt in *Atonement Controversy*, 124–5.

5   *Daniel Rowland*, 339.

sweetens tea'.[1] Was Elias aware that John Newton rejected the very Owenite particularism insisted on by the Welsh veteran?[2]

Sadly, John Elias was a divided man. He was torn between confessionalism and biblicism.[3] So, after a passionate and ground-breaking sermon by John Jones which brought blessing to thousands present, John Elias was not at all happy.[4] How sad that he should disapprove of that wonderful Gospel sermon. Hence John Jones and others who shared his stance became objects of suspicion, as Dr Owen Thomas made clear:

> John Jones, in particular, was one; especially after his sermon in the Bala Association of 1835. His ministry at this time was in evident opposition to the narrow and extreme views held by some on the atonement of Christ, and he would lay particular emphasis on the sufficiency of the provision in Jesus Christ for sinners, as sinners, and indiscriminately; and would impress specifically upon the consciences of all his hearers that if they were lost at the last, the fault for that would be theirs alone, and that their blood could never be required at the hand of Almighty God.[5]

Let us sample the anointed heavenly oratory of the hero from Talsarn. The text of *Coming to Christ* was 'No man can come to Me except the Father which hath sent Me draw him: and I will raise him up at the last day' *(John vi. 44)*:

> If the Government of England were to send an order to the British Admiral to bring the Fleet home from the Mediterranean Sea, you would not suppose that the Government intended that the Admiral and his men should carry the ships home? Nothing of the kind. We all know full well that the meaning of the order would simply be that the Admiral should make the proper preparations; that they should employ the proper means in order to bring the ships home—weigh the

---

1 *Atonement Controversy*, 342. John Newton's statement is: 'Calvinism should be diffused through our ministry as sugar is in tea; it should be tasted everywhere, though prominent nowhere'; see John H. Pratt (ed), *The Thought of the Evangelical Leaders* (Edinburgh: The Banner of Truth Trust, 1978), 281.

2 See n. 41.

3 See Edward Morgan, *John Elias: Life, Letters and Essays* (Edinburgh: The Banner of Truth Trust, 1973), 142.

4 John Morgan Jones & William Morgan, tr. John Aaron, *The Calvinistic Methodist Fathers of Wales* (Edinburgh: The Banner of Truth Trust, 2008), ii. 745. Hereinafter *Methodist Fathers*.

5 *Atonement Controversy*, 334.

anchors, turn their prows towards the deep, that they should put them in the way of the great forces of nature: spread the sails, and steer the vessels home; let the winds play upon them, and the waves and the tides carry them. Meanwhile, the men on deck might take it easy; they could enjoy themselves, and sing their native songs, while the mighty elements co-operated to bring them home.

In the same manner, God in the Gospel calls upon you to repent, to believe, and to lead a pious and godly life. But He does not mean that you should do all this of your own individual resources. No; He intends that you should put yourselves as you are under the operation of the mighty forces of the Gospel; that you should faithfully employ the means which He has commanded. Turn the prow of thy little vessel to the deep; let it sail upon the wide ocean of Christ's Atonement; spread the sails, and steer it on by the guidance of the Word of God. The winds will blow, the mighty forces of redemption will play upon thy vessel; the tides will carry it, and thou shalt find thy little bark one day in the haven of eternal rest.

You have, my friends, something yourselves to do, and it is of no use at all to expect the operations of the Spirit of God, while we ourselves neglect our duty. 'But what can I do?' Canst thou not read? Open thy Bible; look at it, read it bring thy mind into contact with the great saving forces, and wait for help from above. 'But I cannot pray.' Canst thou not try? Canst thou not bend thy knee, and put it down on the ground? 'But I must pray from the heart, and this I cannot do.' Wouldst thou give Him thy heart? Give Him thy body, give Him thy tongue; and if thou canst not say a word, there is One up there who can open His lips to intercede for thee. Try fairly; do your best for your own salvation. Do not, at least, rush headlong into perdition. I, indeed, have made up my mind long ago that I shall not go there so. If I must go to hell at all, I shall not go there straight along. No; I shall loiter a good deal about the Garden of Gethsemane; I shall go many a round about the hill of Calvary; I shall bend my knees daily at the throne of grace. I shall be good enough for hell, if I have to go there, after all these efforts. But, blessed be the name of God, we have every reason to believe that this is the high road to heaven, and that no one ever went to hell in that way, and that no one ever will.[1]

While most of John Jones's material is locked away in Welsh, we are indebted to John Aaron for translating an important letter from Owen Thomas's biography,[2] written just before decades of damaging debate were happily ended at a Calvinistic Methodist conference in Mold, Flintshire in March 1841. It was a lengthy plea to Thomas Richard of Fishguard to attend the conference, since John Jones believed his very presence would help restrain John Elias and his ilk from imposing their oppressive opinions on others. Bearing on the issues of hypercalvinism, this letter reveals John Jones's deeply-felt, pastorally-driven theological concerns. After complaining about an ill-digested and excessive prominence given to predestination, and a preoccupation with an over-refined orthodoxy, he exposes the causes of widespread barren evangelism:

In a word, for some years they have been preaching in a polemic, controversial way, and not in the most appropriate way for convincing a sinner of his danger and of exhorting him to flee from the wrath to come. If the wickedness and misery of man is under consideration, the sermon tends not to stress that the fault is completely due to man, but rather shows *how it is he became* a sinner and then refers to the covenant of works. If the atonement is the subject, the tendency will be to stress the particularity of its appointments rather than the fact that it is the only refuge for life for the sinner and he be urged to flee to it; if the work of the Spirit is preached, the emphasis will not be on the encouragement to seek him and the directions given as to how to find him in the means by which he works, but rather that everything attempted or sought is in vain until the Spirit come; etc., etc.

John Jones believed that many of the problems he identified were due to an over-reactionary response to Wesleyan Arminianism in North-eastern Wales in the early 19th century resulting in something akin to Islamic fatalism:

Our fathers made such an attack upon Arminianism here in north Wales that the common people were led to harmful extremes on the

---

1   *Great Preachers*, 487–9.
2   *Atonement Controversy*, 350–54.

contrary side. They are full of Antinomian views which have as disastrous an effect upon them as Mahometanism has upon the Egyptians. What is most necessary therefore, in my view, before such an attitude of mind and judgement, is to drive them out of their false hiding places, to tear away their excuses, and to press them in the most importunate way to give themselves to the Saviour.

Assured of his theological foundations, John Jones felt liberated to preach in a 'practical' rather than a polemical and excessively-doctrinal manner:

We do not choose to preach practically in order to oppose our brethren or from a contentious spirit, but, before my Judge, I can testify that it is from the demands of conscience and from seeing the good effects produced that I have so purposed.

John Jones also believed the content of preaching has a vital bearing on fruitfulness, that a close biblical correlation exists between style and success:

Know, dear brother, and I mention it with tears, that many of our older brethren in the ministry preach many of their sermons with the purpose of persuading their listeners to believe in things that are not necessary to salvation. It is as clear to me as that the sun is in the sky that they are not producing any good effect. In contrast, I can declare with confidence, and prove it by many evident facts from at large, that practical, convincing and exhortative preaching has been, under the blessing and unction of the Holy Spirit, the means of returning many hundreds in Caernarvonshire this last year. It is believed that between 1800 and 2000 have been added to our churches in the area during the year, and it is acknowledged that it is the change in the style of ministry, with less topical sermons and a more practical, persuasive emphasis, that was instrumental in this. But such is the jealousy of these for preaching their own narrow views that they cannot acknowledge these conversions as being the work of God's Spirit and they then declare boldly in the Associations that they suspect the genuineness of the work. How it grates upon my ear to hear such words and in such a place, more or less blaspheming the work of God's Spirit in the souls of sinners. At Rhosllannerchrugog there was the addition of some hundreds to the church last year. It is well known that the labours of our faithful friend, Mr Robert Roberts, were the means of bringing forward this revival—his warnings and encouragements to the church to pray for revival and to maintain frequent meetings for prayer amongst themselves, pleading for a visitation from the Lord. Gradually the church was brought to a state of deep longing for such a visitation, and they did not have to wait long after that.

In the providence of God, John Elias was too ill to attend the conference. In fact, it proved to be his last illness. While John Jones and his brethren deeply lamented the loss of the mighty preacher, events proved propitious for a biblically-balanced view of the Gospel. In short, the complementary twin 'Amyraldian features' of the atonement's universality and particularity were widely embraced. As we noted earlier, such an understanding found eventual confessional expression in 1874, the very year Owen Thomas's biography of John Jones, Talsarn was published.

Owen Thomas's claims that John Elias and Henry Rees diluted their High Calvinist views in their later days are dismissed as 'wishful thinking' by John Aaron.[1] However, besides the evidence of his lovely hymn 'And was it for my sin that Jesus suffered so',[2] it is certain at least that Elias repudiated his attachment to the commercial theory of the atonement after a heated discussion with Thomas Jones of Denbigh in 1814.[3] As we have seen, such a view had been advocated by Christmas Evans in 1811.[4] Yet John Aaron fails to engage with this detail[5] (albeit identified in Owen Thomas's account[6]). Sadly, despite Elias's repudiation of the commercialistic error, it made no difference to his limited atonement thinking. He continued to insist that our Saviour's death 'was appointed for the Church alone'.[7] As for Henry Rees, whose essay *Christ Suffering the Punishment of His People* (1831) is undeniably Owenite, there is some evidence that by the 1860s his emphasis had shifted to embrace a wider sufficiency in the atonement. As Owen Thomas indicates, this was probably due to Rees's acquaintance with works by Richard Baxter's

---

1   Ibid. p. xxx.

2   Translated from Welsh by Noel Gibbard, this appears in *Christian Hymns* (Bridgend: Evangelical Movement of Wales, 1977), hymn 199. John Jones would have been happy to sing this hymn, and it can be sung to one of his tunes.

3   See Edward Morgan, *John Elias: Life, Letters and Essays* (Edinburgh: The Banner of Truth Trust, 1973), 141; *Methodist Fathers*, ii. 607–8, 628, 682.

4   See *Atonement Controversy*, 152ff.

5   Ibid., pp. xvi–xvii.

6   Ibid. 293–6.

7   Ibid. 296.

Amyraldian friend John Howe, Andrew Fuller and others.[1] In a sermon preached at Mold in 1864 and repeated at Bala in 1867, ideas of Owenite limitation are absent:

> It was God that appointed Christ as Saviour … And as the authority of God was with him, there was infinite value and merit in what He did. So that now, by that perfect obedience which Christ gave, the greatest sinner can safely venture to believe … The Spirit of God can give us [all riches of the full assurance of understanding], and may He give unto us some degree of it before we die. The language of such a man would be this: 'Whatever God and holiness may be; whatever the law and its demands may be, I am perfectly sure that there is infinite value in Christ's death in my behalf.[2]

This tends to confirm a statement by Robert Ellis, Llanddeiniolen that 'the Mr Rees of 1841 was very different from the Mr Rees of 1861'.[3]

By way of conclusion, let us return to the fascinating similarities between John Jones and Daniel Rowland detected by Robert Jones, Rhoslan. Indeed, we may ask, what would the preacher of Llangeitho think of the preacher of Talysarn? While the former would humbly rejoice that the latter possessed 'a voice much more melodious, and, possibly, talents more bright', are there any grounds to suggest that Rowland would approve of John Jones's theological stance?

As Eifion Evans makes clear in his excellent biography, Daniel Rowland was undoubtedly a Calvinist: 'Rowland followed Calvin in his understanding of grace'.[4] While Calvinistic Methodism 'had its own distinctives' of 'fervent spirituality' and 'lively proclamation', it 'bore unmistakable resemblance to the teaching and piety of Augustine and Calvin'.[5] Indeed, Rowland's sermon on our Saviour's words to the dying thief, *Free Grace indeed*,[6] confirms such claims. His acceptance of the doctrine of election is unmistakable: 'By saving one thief, and leaving the other to receive the due reward of his deeds, is

1   Ibid. 363.

2   *Great Preachers*, 424–6.

3   *Atonement Controversy*, 362.

4   *Daniel Rowland*, 130.

5   Ibid. 137.

6   Daniel Rowland, *Eight sermons upon practical subjects* (London: 1774), 47–72. Hereinafter *Eight Sermons*.

signified to us, that the election prevailed ...'[1] The fact that Rowland's sermons are 'practical' rather than polemically-doctrinal is important. In this respect, he anticipated the concerns of John Jones, Talsarn in the next century. In short, an 'unmistakable resemblance' is evident in this respect too. Indeed, Rowland deliberately shuns a controversial discussion of election, since 'God's judgements are very secret, and unsearchable. It is our duty to honour, and reverence them, rather than to dispute about them'.[2] Dr Evans rightly highlights this feature thus: 'In Rowland's view, these deep truths were for the eye of faith to admire, rather than for the skill of reason to judge'.[3]

However, another question is: does Rowland's understanding of grace bear an 'unmistakable resemblance' to the High Calvinism of John Owen? On this issue, Dr Evans sheds no light. That said, judging by the only available published sermons of Rowland—the translated *Eight Sermons* of 1774 and the *Three Sermons* of 1778, the answer seems to be 'no'. While Rowland states in the later sermons that Christ 'was the Lamb intentionally slain for his people before the world was made',[4] there is no Owenite qualification that He was slain *only* for 'his elect people'. Indeed, later in the same evangelistic sermon, Rowland affirms *generally*: 'Though you are lost and wandering sheep, yet here is a good shepherd, who laid down his life for you, that he might save you from perishing'.[5]

What is striking about this sermon is the assurance given to 'encourage every poor sinner to repent and come to Jesus Christ' because the good shepherd's 'shoulders imply strength—and in this parable they represent the all-sufficiency of grace and merit that there is in Christ Jesus to justify the guilty and uphold the weak'.[6] In a sermon concerned to challenge both Arminians and Antinomian High Calvinists alike,[7] Rowland stresses *particularly* that Christ 'hath often snatched his chosen ones' from the mouth of the devil, yet He is *generally* 'the Saviour of the lost and perishing'.[8] The emphasis on Christ's general provision of all-sufficient grace is ubiquitous

1 Ibid. 54.
2 Ibid.
3 *Daniel Rowland*, 134.
4 *Three Sermons upon practical subjects* (London: 1778), 15.
5 Ibid. 17.
6 Ibid. 27–8.
7 Ibid. 33–34.
8 Ibid. 31.

in Rowland.[1] For this reason he feels free to make his evangelistic appeals: 'Here are strong shoulders which can carry us *all* to heaven. O that many of us may be laid on them this day'.[2] Clearly these sermons exhibit 'Amyraldian/ Baxterian features'.

What is at least hinted in the *Three Sermons* is even clearer in the *Eight Sermons*. In fact, while Dr Evans rightly appealed to the second sermon *Free Grace indeed* for Rowland's teaching on election, what might he have said about the first entitled *The Redeemer's Voice*? Based on the text 'Behold! I stand at the door and knock' (*Revelation 3: 20*), Rowland's sermon is remarkable for at least three reasons. *First*, because he obviously attached great importance to what was a widely-appreciated publication. According to the editor Thomas Davies, 'The first sermon was published ten years ago, and met with great reception; it has lately been enlarged by the Author'.[3] *Second*, this truly-gripping sermon is remarkable for an important theological clarification. While it is intended as a 'practical' evangelistic message rather than a theological essay, yet something akin to a single footnote appears towards the end. Probably a late addition inspired by concerns over hypercalvinist tendencies among Calvinists, it speaks for itself:

> Every faithful ambassador of Christ will preach the gospel unto every creature, and spread forth as far as he can, the infinite compassion and excellencies of the Lamb. He will declare the richness of his atoning blood, and in a pointing manner, show the sinner his danger and remedy, will invite the indigent to become rich, and the guilty to accept pardon, and with the Apostle beseech and intreat sinners to be reconciled to God—without this how can Gospel ministers be free from the blood of all men, if they warn them not? ... If salvation by Jesus Christ is not to be offered—how can sinners be said to refuse and reject? Yet God says, 'because I have called and ye have refused' again—'Ye have put away the word of eternal life'. How can a thing be refused if not offered?—If it is not the duty of a sinner to believe—how can unbelief be a sin? That mankind are dead in trespasses and sins is no objection, because the Spirit

---

1   See ibid. 36, 62.
2   Ibid. 17 (emphasis mine).
3   *Eight Sermons*, 11.

of God is Almighty to quicken—and 'tis his usual method to work in the way above mentioned.[1]

Third, the sermon is remarkable because of the preacher's exegesis of his text. Judging by the context, Revelation 3: 20 has more to do with a 'back-slidden' congregation of professing Christians than an audience of unbelievers. Yet Rowland uses the text in a totally evangelistic way. Whatever the character of his hearers, he proclaimed God-in-Christ as a 'pleader', much in the manner of the Old Testament (see Ezekiel 33: 11, the text of Richard Baxter's famous *Call to the Unconverted*). While there are Calvinistic precedents for this,[2] Reformed commentators are generally agreed that such a use of Rowland's text is inadmissible.[3] Some would say Rowland's approach is thoroughly Arminian! Indeed, how can Rowland defend himself from such a charge in view of the climax of his sermon? Since he has no inhibitions about telling his hearers that Christ died for them, his rousing conclusion seems to break every 'Reformed' rule:

> Consider in whose stead, and to whom it is that I beseech you to open your hearts. It is to him who gave and preserves your lives—to him who shed his blood for you, and is kind to you every moment—even 'to the Lamb of God who taketh away the sins of the world' [*Jn. 1: 29*] ... Lamb of God! patient, spotless Lamb of God! set up thy throne in our hearts and enable us to cry before thee 'Hosannah to the King of saints' ... To this happy state may God of his infinite mercy bring us *all* through Jesus Christ, Amen.[4]

---

1   Ibid. 44.

2   For a puritan precedent, see John Flavel's sermons on this text in *The Works of John Flavel* (London: The Banner of Truth Trust, 1968), iv. 1–268.

3   For a recent criticism, see Lee Gatiss, *For Us and For Our Salvation—'Limited Atonement' in the Bible, Doctrine, History and Ministry* (London: The Latimer Trust, 2012), 118. Hereinafter *For our Salvation*.

4   *Eight Sermons*, 45–6. Even in the second sermon *Free Grace indeed*, Rowland is happy to use biblical language without qualification. Christ is 'the Saviour of the world' (47) and 'greater is the Lord's mercy than the sins of the whole world' (59). The fourth sermon, *The Superiority of the Lowly over the Proud*, concludes with 'Remember the prayer of the Saviour of the world, "Father forgive them for they know not what they do"' (130). In the sixth sermon, *Good News to the Gentiles*, we read that 'the atoning sacrifice admitted of neither increase nor diminution. It was always the same to all persons: and it prefigured that 'Lamb of God, which taketh away the sins of the world' John 1: 29' (161). In the seventh sermon, *Christ is all, and in all*, the preacher describes Christ as 'the

In reply to Lee Gatiss's criticism of R. T. Kendall,[1] does Rowland's language need defending? Since the Saviour of the world declared that God loves the world, how dare we *not* say 'God loves you and Christ died for you'? As Calvin, Baxter and many others have made clear, God's special love for His elect does not exclude His general love for all.[2] If Rowland is out of order on this issue, what would Gatiss[3] and Aaron say about a 'whiff' of the Governmental theory in Rowland?[4]

All this evidence points in one direction. In steering a course between Arminianism and High Calvinism, Daniel Rowland's gospel grasp fits the contours of the Amyraldian/Baxterian *via media*. Of the three most eminent preachers of the Methodist revival, this makes Daniel Rowland sounder than the 'sub-orthodox' Arminian Wesley and sounder than the 'ultra-orthodox' High Calvinist Whitefield. The Welshman had an edge over the two Englishmen! His understanding of the biblical message possessed a balance missing in his two brethren. It is surprising that, in his essay on Rowland, 'Amyraldian' J. C. Ryle[5] never highlighted the 'Amyraldian features' in Rowland's sermons. However he relevantly quotes our friend Robert Jones, Rhoslan's amazing response to Rowland's equally-remarkable preaching of John 3: 16:

Fervent and deep feeling was the last characteristic which I mark in Rowland. He never did anything by halves. Whether preaching or praying, whether in church or in the open air, he seems to have done all he did with heart and soul, and mind and strength. "He possessed as much animal spirits," says one witness, "as were sufficient for half-a. dozen men." This energy seems to have had an inspiring effect about it,

---

Son of man, and the redeemer of a lost world' (196), adding that He was anointed by God 'for us men, and for our salvation' (196) and that 'the Lord Jesus, as mediator, [was] predestined by the "determinate council and foreknowledge of God" [Acts 2: 23] to the weighty business of redeeming and saving sinful man' (197). While Jesus was 'anointed that he might be the priest of his people' (207) and that He 'furthers the salvation of his chosen' (213), Rowland is at ease employing broader phraseology that Christ's 'work was to make atonement for sin, and to reconcile God to man ... So great is his tenderness, compassion, and long-suffering towards our fallen race' (208, 212).

1   See *For Our Salvation*, 114.
2   See my *Atonement and Justification*, 152ff.
3   See *For Our Salvation*, 11.
4   See *Eight Sermons*, 217.
5   See my *Atonement and Justification*, 81.

and to have swept everything before it like a fire. One who went to hear him every month from Carnarvonshire, gives a striking account of his singular fervour when Rowland was preaching on John 3: 16. He says, "He dwelt with such overwhelming, extraordinary thoughts on the love of God, and the vastness of his gift to man, that I was swallowed up in amazement. I did not know that my feet were on the ground; yea, I had no idea where I was, whether on earth or in heaven. But presently he cried out with a most powerful voice, 'Praised be God for keeping the Jews in ignorance respecting the greatness of the Person in their hands! Had they known who he was, they would never have presumed to touch him, much less to drive nails through his blessed hands and feet, and to put a crown of thorns on his holy head. For had they known, they would not have crucified the Lord of glory.'"[1]

All this surely confirms a summary provided by the authors of *The Calvinistic Methodist Fathers of Wales*:

> The Methodist Fathers were never, at first, Hyper-Calvinists, ... The doctrine that was undoubtedly believed among them was that of the Articles of the Established Church, and in agreement with these they preached Jesus Christ as a sufficient Saviour for the whole world, inviting all to him. One need only read the journal of Howell Harris, the sermons of Daniel Rowland, and the hymns of William Williams, to see that they laid down no limits to the value of the Saviour's sacrifice. But just as one extreme always produces the opposite, many of the Calvinists, in the warmth of their zeal against the Wesleyans, claimed that there was no universal aspect to the call of the gospel; that the elect alone were to be called ...[2]

So Robert Jones, Rhoslan was right to compare Daniel Rowland and John Jones, Talsarn in the way he did. One is surely entitled to add that the two preachers, separated by a period of theological exaggeration and inevitable strife, shared the same theological emphases and compassionate concern.

---

1 J. C. Ryle, *Christian Leaders of the Eighteenth Century* (Edinburgh: The Banner of Truth Trust, 1978), 214–5. Besides the *Great Preachers* version, 59–60, see a slightly differently-worded account in *Daniel Rowland*, 294.

2 *Methodist Fathers*, ii. 605.

Hence what Owen Jones said of the hero from Talysarn also applies to the hero of Llangeitho:

His discourses brought the love of God, the death of Christ, heaven with all its bliss and glory within the reach of every man, and made every individual man responsible for the loss of them.[1]

God grant that in our respective spheres and callings we might in some measure do likewise! Amen!

---

1   *Great Preachers*, 486.

Appendix 1: Review Article:
From Heaven He Came and Sought Her:

Definite Atonement in Historical, Biblical,
Theological and Pastoral Perspective

Edited by David Gibson & Jonathan Gibson
(Wheaton, Illinois: Crossway, 2013).
ISBN 978-1-4335-1276-6 (hardcover) £32.99

This heavy-weight 1 kg tome of 703 pages must rank as the most impressive defence of the doctrine of 'definite atonement' to date. Twenty-three in-depth scholarly contributions provide a comprehensive demonstration of the classical doctrine of 'limited atonement', now commonly known in the literature as 'definite atonement'. In view of the fact that at one time, the only serious contestants over the 'Doctrines of Grace' were 'Calvinists' and 'Arminians', one wonders whether the sheer size of this publication reflects a growing concern over a certain resurgence of Amyraldian 'middle-ground' thinking in recent years.

Besides a vintage foreword by Dr J. I. Packer (who seeks to rescue the doctrine from the 'menacing' negativity of 'limited atonement'), the editors set out the book's agenda with a comprehensive introduction entitled 'Sacred Theology and the Reading of the Divine Word'. The book's thesis appears in the opening paragraph thus: 'The death of Christ was intended to win the salvation of God's people *alone*' (33, my emphasis). Interestingly—from the outset—the Preface raises questions by the editors' disclaimer: '... we do not refer to our position as "Calvinist"' (18). Is this because Calvin might question the exclusive '*alone*'? For reasons to be explained, the reviewer claims—from the outset—that this review/response is decidedly "Calvinist".

One notices that the book derives its title not from a biblical text but from a hymn. Applauded by Dr Packer, the notion of 'winning' the salvation of 'God's people' is related to Samuel John Stone's beautiful hymn, 'The church's one foundation'. This was chosen to 'elucidate' the contributors' understanding of the *exclusive* purpose of our Saviour's sacrifice upon the cross. Highlighting Christ's love for His own, the second half of the first verse inspires the book's title:

> From heaven He came and sought her
> To be His holy bride;
> With His own blood He bought her,
> And for her life He died.

One notes that the hymn actually avoids an *exclusive* qualification. The poetry is not exhaustive. Not everything is said, and neither Calvin nor Amyraut would have any difficulty singing it! However, reflecting the *duality* of Scripture,[1] their words indicate that Christ came with a 'dual intent'. He came to 'woo the world' in general as well as 'win the church' in particular'. Thus Calvary's cross displays universal provision as well as particular application:

> First, we must understand that as long as Christ remains outside of us, and we are separated from him, all that he has suffered and done for the salvation of the human race remains useless and of no value for us.[2]

> ... Our Lord made effective for [the pardoned thief on the cross] His death and passion which He suffered and endured for all mankind ...[3]

> Christ is in a general view the Redeemer of the world, yet his death and passion are of no advantage to any but such as receive that which St Paul shows here. And so we see that when we once know the benefits brought to us by Christ, and which he daily offers us by his gospel, we must also be joined to him by faith.[4]

---

1   See Matthew 22: 14; John 6: 33, 37, 51; 1 Timothy 4: 10, this being the model for Christian generosity in Galatians 6: 10.

2   *Institutes of the Christian Religion,* trans. H. Beveridge (Edinburgh: Calvin Translation Society, 1845—), III. i. 1.

3   *Sermons on the Saving Work of Christ,* trans. L. Nixon (Grand Rapids: Baker Book House (1980 rep.), 151.

4   *Sermons on Ephesians* (Edinburgh: Banner of Truth Trust, 1973), 55.

The same points were repeated in the next century by Calvin's fellow Frenchman, Moïse Amyraut:

The nature of men being such, *if God had had no other intention in ordaining to send his Son to the world than to present him as Redeemer equally and universally to all*, as great as the love is from which this council proceeded, it would have been useless to the human race and the sending and the sufferings of his Son entirely frustrated.[1]

Back to the book, its subtitle indicates the categories in which the subject is explored and expounded. Scanning the Contents, the sheer range of topics and the assembled expertise shows that no stone has been left unturned in tackling the most fundamental, profound yet controversial feature of the Reformed Faith. Section I, 'Definite Atonement in Church History' includes 'We Trust in the Saving Blood' (*Michael Haykin*), 'Sufficient for All, Efficient for Some' (*David Hogg*), 'Calvin, Indefinite Language, and Definite Atonement' (*Paul Helm*), 'Blaming Beza' (*Raymond Blacketer*), 'The Synod of Dort and Definite Atonement' (*Lee Gatiss*), 'Controversy on Universal Grace' (*Amar Djaballah*) and 'Atonement and the Covenant of Redemption' (*Carl Trueman*).

Section II, 'Definite atonement in the Bible' embraces 'Because He Loved Your Forefathers' (*Paul Williamson*), 'Stricken for the Transgression of My People' (*Alec Motyer*), 'For the Glory of the Father and the Salvation of His People' (*Matthew Harmon*), 'For Whom Did Christ Die?' (*Jonathan Gibson*), 'The Glorious, Indivisible, Trinitarian Work of God in Christ' (*ditto*) and 'Problematic Texts for Definite Atonement in the Pastoral and General Epistles' (*Thomas Schreiner*).

Section III, 'Definite atonement in Theological Perspective' examines 'Definite Atonement and the Divine Decree' (*Donald Macleod*), 'The Triune God, Incarnation and Definite Atonement' (*Robert Letham*), 'The Definite Intent of Penal Substitutionary Atonement' (*Garry Williams*), 'Punishment God Cannot Twice Inflict' (*ditto*), 'The New Covenant Work of Christ' (*Stephen Wellum*) and 'Jesus Christ *the* Man' (*Henri Blocher*).

The final category, Section IV, 'Definite Atonement in Pastoral Practice' deals with the evangelistic and pastoral practicalities of the doctrine: 'Slain for the World?' (*Daniel Strange*), 'Blessed Assurance, Jesus is Mine?' (*Sinclair*

---

1 *Brief Traitté de la Predestination* (Saumur: Isaac Desbordes, 1634), 102, trans. R. Lum (1985).

Ferguson) and, last of all, 'My Glory I Will Not Give to Another' (*John Piper*). As one would expect in such a work, there is a Select Bibliography and three indexes—Biblical References, Names and Subjects.

Undoubtedly, this book will establish itself as a major resource for students for years to come. Thus acknowledged, the scale and depth of the erudition surely requires at least a small paperback-length review to do it justice. So, to avoid being excessively tiresome, one is grateful to the two editors for giving advice not only to readers but also to reviewers? During an interview for *Evangelicals Now* by Paul Levy, they were asked: '... it's a big book, and most folk are unlikely to read all of it, so where should they start?' The Gibsons helpfully replied: 'With the Preface, as it sets the tone for the book. After that, the Introduction, Garry Williams' two chapters on the intent of penal substitutionary atonement and the problem of double payment for an unlimited atonement. Henri Blocher's chapter is a very helpful overview of the whole doctrine—it sort of encapsulates the argument of the book as a whole. Finally, John Piper's chapter will stir the affections as well as the mind'.[1]

One may sharpen one's focus even more. Indeed, what is striking about the contributions of Williams (at 480, 515), Blocher (at 570–1) and Piper (at 648–9) is the close attention they all give to the so-called 'double-payment' objection to any form of universal atonement (Arminian or Amyraldian). A. M. Toplady's oft-quoted poetry (incorrectly cited by Blocher from Packer's defective source at 571) makes the point well:

> And will the righteous judge of men
> Condemn me for that debt of sin,
> Which, Lord, was charged on Thee?
> Payment God cannot twice demand,
> First from my bleeding Surety's hand,
> And then again at mine.[2]

Before this reviewer proceeds any further, it would be disingenuous not to declare an interest, despite every endeavour to provide a fair review. Indeed, one's own contributions are occasionally cited in the pages of this book, my views summed up as an undisguised 'Authentic Calvinist' perspective on Augustine, Calvin, Amyraut, Baxter, *et al.* However, none of the contributors

---

1 'Definite Atonement', *Evangelicals Now*, March 2014, p. 15.

2 *Diary and Selection of Hymns* (London: Gospel Standard Baptist Trust, 1969), 193.

engage with the *fundamental feature* of my major criticism of the book's agenda anticipated in my publications.[1] This criticism directly concerns the 'double-payment' objection.

This brings us face-to-face with the iconic Dr John Owen whose towering and seemingly-decisive presence—famously promoted by Dr Packer (whose 'Owenite' orthodoxy fellow 'Authentic Anglicans' John Davenant[2] and J. C. Ryle[3] would rightly question)—may be said to dominate the Crossway book page after page, especially with regard to the 'double-payment' objection. For the benefit of the uninitiated as well as those more familiar with the debates, I summarise the issues at stake.

John Owen insisted that the satisfaction of Divine justice or payment made in the death of Christ concerned the sins of the elect alone. Invoking the terminology of medieval scholasticism, Owen affirms that the suffering Saviour paid in His death the *identical* punishment threatening the elect. If the atonement satisfied for the sins of all, including those of the damned in hell, then sin was being punished twice over. Enter Richard Baxter, who argued that Christ paid not the *identical* punishment but a *substituted equivalent*.[4] Since

---

1   See especially *Atonement and Justification: English Evangelical Theology 1640–1790 —An Evaluation* (Oxford: Clarendon Press, 1990/2002); *Calvinus: Authentic Calvinism, A Clarification* (Norwich: Charenton Reformed Publishing, 1995/2007) and *Amyraut Affirmed, or 'Owenism, a Caricature of Calvinism'* (Norwich: Charenton Reformed Publishing, 2004).

2   Contrary to the conclusions of Lee Gatiss (163), see my Introduction to John Davenant, *Dissertation on the Death of Christ* (Weston Rhyn: Quinta Press, 2006); also at: http://www.nrchurch. co.uk/pdf/davenantintroduction.pdf

3   See *Ryle on Redemption: The Gospel According to John Charles Ryle* (Norwich: Charenton Reformed Publishing, 2014).

4   Owen insisted that God's justice was only satisfied by Christ's payment of the same penalty or debt owed by the elect to God on account of their sins—the *solutio eiusdem*. Richard Baxter argued that, in virtue of the differences (in detail and duration) between Christ's sufferings and the actual sufferings of the lost, Christ only paid an equivalent debt—the *solutio tantidem*. Since the penalty of the law threatens eternal punishment to impenitent offenders, Christ clearly did not suffer the identical punishment, for his resurrection terminated his banishment. God therefore relaxed the law both with regard to the persons who should suffer (a fact Owen obviously agreed with) and the penalty suffered. Clearly, there was not the 'sameness' Owen pleads for. The *idem-tantundem* distinction automatically answers Owen's objection that if any suffer eternally for whom Christ died, then 'double-payment' is being demanded. But there is no duplication of payment. Those who reject the gospel do not suffer again what Christ has suffered for them. He 'paid' the *tantundem* or equivalent penalty; they will 'pay' the *idem* or exact price. Baxter was surely correct to state that both Christ *and* his sufferings were inseparably substituted for the law's strict demands. Had the

our sins are threatened with eternal punishment, Christ would be in hell if He paid the same satisfaction. In short, a proper biblical doctrine of penal substitution means that *both* Christ *and* His sufferings were 'in the place' of all we deserve. Contrary to Carl Trueman's discussion (210–11), reputable commentators have always made clear that 'the wages of sin' (Rom. 6: 23) involve *eternal* death, and not only *temporal physical* death.[1] Baxter's case is luminously clear: had Christ paid the precise punishment due, He would be in the place of the damned, but His resurrection terminated His banishment. Undeniably, the saved still die, so Christ's death delivers them from *eternal* death (and physical death eventually through resurrection).

At this point, Owen admits the differences between Christ's limited sufferings and those threatening the damned, insisting still that they are 'essentially' the same. Such a verbal device is used by those who try to argue that things obviously different are really the same! At this key moment in the debate, Owen utilises Aristotle's metaphysical 'essence/accidents' (or substance/attributes) distinction,[2] without which it is impossible to establish his case for limited atonement.

In harmony with Henri Blocher, John Piper, and also Carl Trueman (203ff), Garry Williams defends Owen, insisting that the *exact* penal nature

---

law not been relaxed with regard to the offender, none would be saved; had it not been relaxed with regard to the penalty, Christ himself would have suffered 'the everlasting torments of hell' (*Catholick Theologie* (London, 1675), I. ii. 40) Baxter's argument is irrefutable when he observes that the law did not permit the punishment of a substitute in the place of an offender: 'For the law made it due to the sinner himself. And another's suffering for him fulfilleth not the law (which never said, Either thou or another for thee shalt die) But [Christ's death] satisfied the Law-giver as he is above his own law, and could dispense with it, his justice being satisfied and saved' (ibid. 50). In other words, coupled with the infinite dignity of the suffering Saviour, his sufferings were accepted as a satisfactory equivalent for all that is deserved by mankind.

1   See Robert Haldane, *Exposition of the Epistle to the Romans* (London: The Banner of Truth Trust, 1958 facs.), 265.

2   Owen clearly saw that his doctrine of limited atonement hung on the 'sameness' between Christ's sufferings and those deserved by the elect. However, he could only argue his case with the aid of Aristotle's metaphysics. His very language betrays him: 'When I say the same, I mean *essentially* the same in weight and pressure, though not in all the *accidents* of duration and the like; for it was impossible that he should be detained by death' (*Death of Death, The Works of John Owen*, ed. W. H. Goold (London: Johnstone and Hunter (1850–55), x. 269–70). Owen therefore resorts to Aristotle's dubious essence/accidents theory to prove his point. In Baxter's view, even this statement 'yieldeth the cause' (Appendix to *Aphorismes of Justification* (London: 1649; Hague *alias* Cambridge, 1655), 138).

of the atonement necessarily points to a limited or 'definite' atonement. He (at 497) and Trueman (at 210–11) fail to detect the flaw in Owen's reliance on Aristotelian metaphysics. Since a 'thing' is what its 'accidents' or 'attendancies' are, they miss Owen's self-refuting concession.[1] No exact 'sameness' between Christ's sufferings and those threatening sinners exists.

Furthermore, even if there is no necessary connection between Owen's strictly-commercial view of the atonement and his exact payment idea, Garry Williams also fails (at 482) to see how Owen's commercial theory actually negates the idea of the atonement's universal sufficiency. The 'over-orthodox doctor' (as Baxter called him)[2] really paid little more than lip-service to the time-honoured 'sufficient for all-efficient for the elect' distinction.[3] In other words, if the atonement is strictly limited, then the 'credit facilities' of the gospel are only sufficient for the elect. In short, it is only sufficient for whom it is efficient, a conclusion at odds with Peter Lombard and Thomas Aquinas (despite David Hogg's unconvincing attempt to 'tighten' their position at 75–95).

---

1 After learning of Baxter's criticism, Owen granted that 'There is a sameness in Christ's sufferings with that in the obligation in respect of essence, and equivalency in respect of attendancies' (*Of the Death of Christ, the Price He Paid, Works*, x. 448). But Owen's employment of this philosophical distinction simply obscures the fact that there is a real difference between Christ's temporary sufferings and the eternal sufferings deserved by the elect. He cannot establish his concept of 'sameness' without philosophical double-talk. If he is prepared to grant an equivalence in either respect, then he is forced to concede that there is only a similarity, and not a sameness at all. Clearly, Aristotle's metaphysical formula (see *Metaphysics*, tr. J. Warrington (London: J. M. Dent (1956), 173, 46) only serves to permit unreal and meaningless distinctions. Despite Dr Carl Truman's unconvincing attempt to laugh off the point, philosopher Bertrand Russell was correct to describe this as a 'muddle-headed notion, incapable of precision' (*History of Western Philosophy* (London: George Allen & Unwin (1961), 177). For Truman, see *The Claims of Truth: John Owen's Trinitarian Theology* (Carlisle: Paternoster Press (1998), 216.

2 Richard Baxter, *Reliquiae Baxterianae* (London: 1696), ii. 199.

3 Making the sufferings of Christ commensurate with the sins of the elect in a quantitative, commercialistic sense explains why Owen modified the sufficiency/efficiency distinction. His deliberate redefinition of it means that the atonement is only sufficient for whom it is efficient: '... it is denied that the blood of Christ was a sufficient price and ransom for all and everyone ...' (*Death of Death*, 296). Christ's sacrifice would have been a sufficient ransom 'if it had pleased the Lord to employ it to that purpose; ...' (ibid. 295). Baxter writes: '... they cannot without absurdity be interpreted to mean, that his death is sufficient for all if it had been a price for them; and not a sufficient price for them; For that were to contradict themselves ...' (*Universal Redemption of Mankind* (London: 1694), 59.

In Williams' elaborate discussion of the 'specificity' of atonement (471ff), the model of the Day of Atonement is surely the most appropriate one (see Leviticus 16). (As an aside, one cannot argue a strict 'sameness' between the death of the sacrificial victims and the penalty threatening the guilty.) One notes the 'nationwide' reach of atoning grace in the chapter (vs. 16–17, 24, 30, 33–4). Clearly, within the context of 'national Israel', the provision of atonement is 'universal', even though many might not avail themselves of it. Contrary to Motyer's unconvincing case (at 254–5) but in line with Calvin's uncluttered exposition,[1] this makes sense of the 'all' of Isaiah 53: 6. While only penitent believers—the spiritual elect within the elect nation, or the 'many'—enjoy the blessing of actual pardon (see Isa. 53: 11), it is offered to all (see Isa. 55: 1–7). The global New Testament Gospel is simply an internationalisation of the 'provision/application' distinction (see John 1: 29; 3: 16; 12: 47 and John Calvin's comments on these passages).

These things apart, Dr Williams is surely correct to rescue Grotius *vis-à-vis* Socinus from the charge that his 'Governmental' theory of the atonement excludes the idea of God's retribution for sin (490–2). Clearly, Baxter was aware of the Dutchman's exact teaching: 'Yet did [Christ] in the person of a mediator ... suffer the penalty, *nostro loco*, in our stead ... to satisfy God's wisdom, truth and justice, and to procure pardon and life for sinners ... The perfection of Christ's satisfaction consisteth not in its being instead of all the

---

[1] 'Yet I approve of the common reading, that He alone bore the punishment of many, because the guilt of the whole world was laid upon Him. It is evident from other passages ... that 'many' sometimes denotes 'all' ... That, then, is how our Lord Jesus bore the sins and iniquities of many. But in fact, this word 'many' is often as good as equivalent to 'all'. And indeed, our Lord Jesus was offered to all the world. For it is not speaking of three or four when it says: 'God so loved the world, that He spared not His only Son.' But yet we must notice what the Evangelist adds in this passage: 'That whosoever believes in Him shall not perish but obtain eternal life.' Our Lord Jesus suffered for all and there is neither great nor small who is not inexcusable today, for we can obtain salvation in Him. Unbelievers who turn away from Him and who deprive themselves of Him by their malice are today doubly culpable. For how will they excuse their ingratitude in not receiving the blessing in which they could share by faith? And let us realize that if we come flocking to our Lord Jesus Christ, we shall not hinder one another and prevent Him being sufficient for each of us ... Let us not fear to come to Him in great numbers, and each one of us bring his neighbours, seeing that He is sufficient to save us all' (*Sermons on Isaiah's Prophecy*, trans. T. H. L. Parker (London: James Clarke, 1956), 136, 141–4).

sufferings due to all for whom he died, but … in its full sufficiency to those ends for which it was designed by the Father and Son …'[1]

The above issue is truly the 'Achilles heel' of the Owenite thesis, and therefore of this book. Other matters may be touched on briefly. For instance Paul Helm's acutely ambiguous case that Calvin 'was not'/'was' committed to 'the doctrine of definite atonement' (98) is simply implausible, once the sheer ubiquity of Calvin's universal atonement statements is acknowledged.[2] Helm and others are simply 'in denial' where the Calvin evidence is concerned. I argued this with Helm in private correspondence thirty years ago. The same case may be made against Richard Muller (cited by Helm at 112) whose attempt to drive a wedge between Calvin and Amyraut over Ezekiel 18: 32 lacks credibility.[3] The Saumur professor actually shared Calvin's view that the will of God was 'one' despite its apparent duality. Both men held to what may be defined as the 'double-aspect' divine will, not 'two wills'.

Regarding Muller's monumental *Post Reformation Reformed Dogmatics* 2003),[4] he refuses exclusively to associate scholasticism with post-Calvinian high orthodoxy. His overall case is that all Reformed theologians of the period 1520–1725 (including Calvin to a degree, and Amyraut) were in the same scholastic soup, so to speak (my words). He insists that, rather than view the term 'scholasticism' in a pejorative, anti-biblical sense, it simply relates to 'a method and not a particular content'[5] when used in the Reformed theology of the period. This highly questionable evaluation fails to distinguish between 'scholastic' and 'scholarly'. The former—in Owen's hands—permits deductions not favoured by proper exegesis of the biblical text, whereas 'scholarly' discussion remains within the boundaries of the textual data. In this respect, Dr Muller's defence of Owen is frankly complacent to say the least.[6] The fact remains that significant differences in 'content' exists. Hence

---

1   *Catholick Theologie*, I. ii. 39.

2   See the accumulated data in my *Calvinus: Authentic Calvinism, A Clarification* (Norwich: Charenton Reformed Publishing, 1995/2007).

3   See my 'Mulling over Muller' at http://www.nrchurch.co.uk/pdf/Mulling%20over%20Muller.pdf.

4   Richard A. Muller, *Post Reformation Reformed Dogmatics: ca. 1520 to ca. 1725*, 4 Vols., 2nd ed. (Grand Rapids: Baker Book House, 2003). Hereinafter *PRRD*.

5   *PRRD*, i. 35, 132.

6   *PRRD*, i. 214.

John W. Tweeddale's enthusiastic endorsement is highly questionable,[1] not least his claim that Muller's output has made the 'Calvin vs. the Calvinists' debate obsolete. Repeating a mistake made by Paul Helm,[2] Tweeddale's initial assertion that Muller demonstrates the 'development' of Reformed orthodoxy is arguably flawed. Isn't this the darling claim of the Church of Rome contested by the Protestant reformers, that the Faith of Christ and the Apostles *developed* into her later unbiblical dogmas? In short, while the New Testament reveals the planting of an acorn, Rome developed something very different from an oak tree. This, albeit on a smaller scale, is the Amyraldian case against Reformed 'ultra' orthodoxy: 'dogma' takes priority over 'data'. For instance, the rediscovery of the biblical 'acorn' by the reformers produced (through the excessive systematising activity of some of their successors) 'genetic modifications', especially regarding the doctrines of the atonement and justification. In short, conclusions were drawn *beyond* the perspicuous biblical textual data.

Typical of Calvin's numerous statements is his comment on Romans 5: 18: 'Paul makes grace common to all, not because it in fact extends to all, but because it is offered to all. Although Christ suffered for the sins of the world, and is offered by the goodness of God without distinction to all men, yet not all receive him'.[3] Even John Owen (Thrussington) concludes from 'this sentence that Calvin held general redemption'.[4] Roger Nicole admits that Calvin's comment on Romans 5: 18 'comes perhaps closest to providing support for Amyraut's thesis'.[5] Even Richard Muller admits that 'Calvin's teaching was ... capable of being cited with significant effect by Moïse Amyraut against his Reformed opponents'.[6]

Contrary to Amar Djaballah's welcome acknowledgement of my efforts (at

---

1   See his review of *PRRD* on the 'Monergism' website (www.monergism.com/0801026180_reformed_dogmatics.php).

2   P. Helm, 'Calvin, English Calvinism and the Logic of Doctrinal Development', *The Scottish Journal of Theology*, 34. 2 (1981), 179–85.

3   Calvin, *Comment on Romans 5: 18* (Edinburgh: Oliver & Boyd edition, 1959–63).

4   See Owen's note in Calvin's *Commentary on Romans* (Edinburgh: Calvin Translation Society, 1845—), 212.

5   Dr Nicole flies in the face of the obvious when he adds: 'it may well refer simply to the relevance of the sacrifice of Christ to a universal offer, without actually asserting a substitutionary suffering for all mankind' (*Moyse Amyraut (1596–1664) and the Controversy on Universal Grace* (Harvard University thesis, 1966), 83, n. 38).

6   *The Unaccommodated Calvin* (Oxford: OUP, 2000), 62

197–8), Raymond Blacketer's dismissive footnote (at 123, n. 11) is inaccurate at best. I am charged with a failure to 'distinguish' my own 'theological agenda' from my 'analysis of the historical record' and that my arguments have been 'refuted'. I can assure him that after prolonged study I was compelled by the data to change my 'agenda' from an 'Owenite' one to what I define as 'Authentic Calvinism'. Speaking very personally, I know where he's coming from since, theologically speaking, I once stood where he stands. We even called our first son 'John Owen'![1] Regarding the second charge, I have replied to my critics in a work Blacketer failed to consult.[2]

While—like Muller—Blacketer seeks to demonstrate continuity between Calvin and Beza, he does admit that the latter's teachings 'are clearer and more refined than those of Calvin' (140), a rationalising detail missed by one over-enthusiastic reviewer.[3] Indeed, in view of the significant differences between Calvin and Beza, even Muller—for all his pleas that doctrinal and scholastic continuity existed—early acknowledged that the latter was 'more rationalistic' than the former.[4] Whether or not Calvin gave unqualified approval to Beza's 'rationalising' Tabula praedestinationis (1555), he evidently did not share his successor's aversion to 'a two-fold counsel of God' and its consequent 'errors'. What is undeniable is that Calvin—with clear implications for his doctrine of universal redemption—continued to adopt the two-fold will of God distinction in A Harmony of the Gospels (1555), Sermons on Ephesians (1558) and the final edition of the Institutes (1559). While Beza tampered with the text of Calvin's Eternal Predestination (1552),[5] presumably in the interests of 'tightening up' the latter's teaching and eliminating his 'errors', Calvin continued to use the distinction between the absolute and conditional wills of God in his uncompleted 1564 lectures on Ezekiel (see Comment on 18: 23). Perpetuating Calvin's theological programme, the Amyraldians rightly resisted Bezan rationalism and the 'limited atonement' mentality it produced.

---

1   I have revised the rationale behind our son's name: 'John' is now derived from the Amyraldian Welsh Calvinistic Methodist preacher John Jones, Talsarn (1796–1857) and 'Owen' from the preacher's biographer Dr Owen Thomas (1812–91) (see note 3 on page 399).

2   See 'Calvin and Calvinism: Amyraut et al' in John Calvin 500: A Reformation Affirmation (Norwich: Charenton Reformed Publishing, 2011) for my replies to J. I. Packer, Paul Helm, Iain Murray, Carl Trueman, Ian Hamilton, Richard Muller, David Gay, Joel Beeke and Pieter Rouwendal.

3   See Ewan W. Wilson's review in the British Church Newspaper (13 June 2014).

4   R. A. Muller, Christ and the Decree (Grand Rapids: Baker Book House, 1988), 12.

5   See J. K. S. Reid edition (London: James Clarke, 1961), 105, n. 2.

For all his attempts to close the gap between Calvin and Beza, Muller fails to do so with regard to the extent of the atonement.[1] He actually agrees that Calvin's use of 'satisfaction' and 'expiation' connotes 'unlimited atonement', but that the reformer uses 'reconciliation' and 'redemption' in respect of 'limited atonement'.[2] There is confusion here. Calvin clearly uses *all* these terms to express 'benefits' available to all but only 'actually' enjoyed by the elect. Surprisingly, Muller fails to document his claims. The simple fact is that Calvin clearly used 'reconciliation' and 'redemption' in a universal sense, as a few brief specimens will show:

When the Father calls Him the Beloved ... He declares that He is the Mediator in whom He reconciles the world to Himself.[3]

For [by Christ's death] we know that by the expiation of sins the world has been reconciled to God.[4]

Moreover, we offer up our prayers unto Thee, O most Gracious God and most merciful Father, for all men in general ... as Thou art pleased to be acknowledged the Saviour of the whole human race by the redemption accomplished by Jesus Christ.[5]

The draught appointed to Christ was to suffer the death of the cross for the reconciliation of the world.[6]

We have been reconciled to God by the death of Christ, Paul holds, because His was an expiatory sacrifice by which the world was reconciled to God.[7]

God was in Christ and ... by this intervention He was reconciling the world to Himself. ... [Paul] says again that a commission to offer this reconciliation to us has been given to ministers of the Gospel ... He says that as He once suffered, so now every day He offers the fruit of His

---

1   For an accurate brief assessment of Beza's scholastic rationalism, see Michael Jinkins, 'Theodore Beza: Continuity and Regression in the Reformed Tradition', *The Evangelical Quarterly* (64. 2) 1992.

2   *Christ and the Decree*, 34.

3   J. Calvin, *Comment on Matthew 17: 5* (Edinburgh: St Andrew Press, 1972).

4   J. Calvin, *Comment on John 17: 1* (Edinburgh: Oliver & Boyd edition, 1959–63).

5   J. Calvin, *Forms of Prayer for the Church* (Edinburgh: Calvin Translation Society, 1849).

6   J. Calvin, *Comment on John 18: 11* (Edinburgh: Oliver & Boyd edition, 1959–63).

7   J. Calvin, *Comment on Romans 5: 6–10* (Edinburgh: Oliver & Boyd edition, 1959–63).

sufferings to us through the Gospel which He has given to the world as a sure and certain record of His completed work of reconciliation.[1]

Whereas it is said that the Son of God was crucified, we must not only think that the same was done for the redemption of the world: but also every of us must on his own behalf join himself to our Lord Jesus Christ, and conclude, It is for me that he hath suffered. ... But when we once know that the thing was done for the redemption of the whole world, pertaineth to every of us severally: it behoveth every of us to say also on his own behalf, The Son of God hath loved me so dearly, that he hath given himself to death for me.[2]

A highly-important piece of Calvin evidence concerns Blacketer's discussion (at 133) of Beza's tussle with the Lutheran Jacobus Andreae at the Colloquy of Montbéliard, also highlighted by Williams (at 512–13). When Beza declared, 'Christ did not die for the sins of the damned', he clearly went beyond Calvin's unambiguous view

True it is that the effect of [Christ's] death comes not to the whole world. Nevertheless, forasmuch as it is not in us to discern between the righteous and the sinners that go to destruction, but that Jesus Christ has suffered his death and passion as well for them as for us, therefore it behoves us to labour to bring every man to salvation, that the grace of our Lord Jesus Christ may be available to them.[3]

Before I make some observations on the Gibson brothers' 'Introduction', I allude again to their reluctance to refer to their position as "Calvinist" (18). In view of the perspicuous Calvin data, one wonders whether the reformer's statements on the extent of the atonement are something of an embarrassment to those who only feel comfortable with the 'ultra-orthodoxy' of Beza, Owen and the Westminster Confession of Faith. Besides a tendency to 're-invent' Calvin, or to 'explain away' his stance on the subject, the book provides too many instances of authors citing writers whose stance does not favour Owen's position. Even on page 18, the admirable quotation from John Newton regarding spiritual humility in the midst of controversy

---

1   J. Calvin, *Comment on 2 Corinthians 5: 19* (Edinburgh: Oliver & Boyd edition, 1959–63)..

2   J. Calvin, *Sermons on Galatians,* tr. Arthur Golding (London, 1574), 106–7.

3   *Sermons on Job,* (facs: Edinburgh: Banner of Truth Trust, 1993), 548 (later interpolation deleted, as per CO, 34: 696 *(Ioannis Calvini opera quae supersunt omnia (Corpus Reformatorum))*.

ignores the fact that Newton never favoured Owen's type of orthodoxy.[1] Another example from the Introduction (33) is Andrew Fuller, who decisively rejected Owen's 'commercial' theory of the atonement.[2] The same may be said of 'proto-Amyraldian' Augustine[3] (cited at 70) and 'quasi-Amyraldian' Jonathan Edwards[4] (cited at 36, 634) who firmly endorsed his avowedly

---

[1]   In this 'Messiah' sermon on the atonement (based on John 1: 29), Newton rejects the commercial theory of the atonement. He also refuses to reduce 'world' to 'the world of the elect' and he accepts the Amyraldian distinction between natural and moral inability (see *The Works of John Newton* (1820; fac. Edinburgh: Banner of Truth Trust, 1985), iv. 188ff).

[2]   See *The Gospel Worthy of All Acceptation* in *The Works of Andrew Fuller*, ed. A. G. Fuller (Edinburgh: The Banner of Truth Trust, 2007 facs.), 170.

[3]   On the atonement, Augustine wrote: 'For it is good for all men to hear [Christ's] voice and live, by passing to the life of godliness from the death of ungodliness. Of this death the Apostle Paul says, "Therefore all are dead, and He died for all, that they which live should not henceforth live unto themselves, but unto Him which died for them and rose again." (2 Cor. 5: 14–15). Thus all, without one exception, were dead in sins, whether original or voluntary sins, sins of ignorance, or sins committed against knowledge; and for all the dead there died the only one person who lived, that is, who had no sin whatever, in order that they who live by the remission of their sins should live, not to themselves, but to Him who died for all, for our sins, and rose again for our justification ...' (*The City of God*, Works, ed. M. Dods (1872), ii. 354).Richard Baxter's comment on Augustine is relevant here: 'As for Augustine and some Protestants, they oft deny that Christ redeemeth any but the faithful, because the word redemption is ambiguous, and sometimes taken for the price or ransom paid, and often for the very liberation of the captive sinner. And when Austin denieth common redemption, he taketh redemption in this last sense, for actual deliverance. But he asserteth it in the first sense, that Christ died for all. Yea, he thought his death is actually applied to the true justification and sanctification of some reprobates that fall away and perish, though the elect only are so redeemed and saved. Read yourself Augustine ... and you will see this with your own eyes' (*Catholick Theologie*, 1675, II. 57–8; quoted in my *Atonement and Justification*, 91).

[4]   'UNIVERSAL REDEMPTION. Atonement Is Sufficient. Christ did die for all in this sense: that all by his death have an opportunity of being saved. He had that design in dying that they should have that opportunity by it, for it is a thing that God designed that all men should have such an opportunity, or they would not have it, and they have it by the death of Christ' (*The Works of Jonathan Edwards*, ed. Thomas A. Schafer (New Haven, CT: Yale University Press, 1994), Vol. 13, *Miscellanies*, Entry Nos: a–z, aa–zz, 1–500, #424). Edwards clearly thinks that 'all men' are offered the opportunity of salvation in gospel preaching. Thus unbelievers are guilty for rejecting Christ's provision: 'For your refusals of the gospel, and your rejections of this way of salvation, are so much the oftener repeated. Every time you hear the gospel preached, you are guilty of a renewed rejection of it, the guilt of which therefore you will have lying upon you' ('The Wisdom of God, Displayed in the Way of Salvation' in Edwards, *Works* (1834), Vol. 2, p. 155). In what sense then did Edwards say 'Christ did not die for the damned' ('Sermon VII' in *Selections*, ed. A. B. Grosart, p.204)? Here, he resembles Beza's identical statement to the Lutheran Andreae at the Colloquy of Montbéliard. It is impossible to square Edwards statement with plain Scripture (see *Rom. 14: 15;*

Amyraldian pupil Joseph Bellamy.[1] A glaring example is Sinclair Ferguson's misrepresentation of Thomas Chalmers (at 613, n. 23) who doubtless would not endorse the book's exclusive agenda. True, Chalmers held to the 'universal offer of the gospel'. He also firmly rejected Owen's type of commercialistic particularism,[2] even endorsing Richard Baxter shortly before his death.[3] In view of the book's affirmation of the 'free offer of the gospel' (664), one is somewhat surprised to find so much credence given by both Packer (at 14) and especially Haykin (at 57ff)—but not by Blocher (at 547, n.28)—to John Gill, an enemy of the 'free offer' and regarded by Spurgeon as 'the Coryphaeus of hypercalvinism'.[4] Furthermore, regarding Gill's credentials as an interpreter of the Fathers, Dr Curt Daniel demonstrated how dubious they are.[5]

---

1 Cor. 8: 11), unless it is explained in Baxter's manner: 'Christ did not die for [the damned in hell] as such, but as in their antecedent, recoverable, pardonable sin and misery' (*Catholick Theologie* (London: 1675), II. p. 72).

  1   See my 'Jonathan Edwards—Amyraldian?' at http://www.nrchurch.co.uk/pdf/Jonathan%20 Edwards%20Amyraldian.pdf

  2   After dismissing the usual 'doctrine of particular redemption' and its associated 'arithmetical style', as well as lamenting 'an unnatural violence on many passages of Scripture', Chalmers added: 'If Christ died only for the elect, and not for all', then ministers 'are puzzled to understand how they should proceed with the calls and invitations of the gospel. ... Now for the specific end of conversion, the available scripture is not that Christ laid down His life for the sheep, but that Christ is set forth a propitiation for the sins of the world. It is not because I know myself to be one of the sheep, or one of the elect, but because I know myself to be one of the world, that I take to myself the calls and promises of the New Testament' Testament' (*Institutes of Theology* (Edinburgh: Sutherland & Knox, 1849), ii. 403, 406).

  3   '"Yes, Baxter holds that Christ died for all men; but I cannot say that I am quite at one with what some of our friends have written on the subject of the atonement. I do not, for example, entirely agree with what Mr. Haldane says on the subject. I think that the word *world*, as applied in Scripture to the sacrifice of Christ, has been unnecessarily restricted; the common way of explaining it is, that it simply includes Gentiles as well as Jews. I do not like that explanation; and I think that there is one text that puts that interpretation entirely aside. The text to which I allude is, that "God commandeth *all men, everywhere*, to repent [Acts 17: 30b]."' Here the Doctor spoke of the connexion between the election of God, the sacrifice of Christ, and the freeness of the offer of the Gospel. He spoke with great eloquence, and I felt that he was in the pulpit, as some of his finest bursts rolled from his lips. 'In the offer of the Gospel,' said he, we must make no limitations whatever. I compare the world to a multitude of iron filings in a vessel, and the Gospel to a magnet. The minister of the Gospel must bring the magnet into contact with them all: the secret agency of God is to produce the attraction'" (W. Hanna, *Memoirs of Thomas Chalmers* (Edinburgh: Thomas Constable, 1854), ii. 773).

  4   C. H. Spurgeon, *Commenting & Commentaries* (London: The Banner of Truth Trust, 1969), 9.

  5   'Gill quotes extensively from these writers but his proof is strained. His own presuppositions

Coming to the Introduction, one welcomes an acknowledgement of 'the sufficiency of Christ's death for all' (34, 51), in parallel with the claim for its definite intent. However, since Owen's commercial theory effectively evacuates the universal sufficiency of significance,[1] the book's view of definite atonement really has no place for any sufficiency beyond the salvation of the elect. Regarding the 'hijacked' use of 'definite' to re-present the doctrine of limited atonement, an alternative model does justice to the concept of sufficiency no less 'definitely'. One may say that, according to the 'double-aspect' will of God, there is a 'definite', all-sufficient provision for the world as well as a 'definite' efficacious application for the elect. This is the 'definite' Amyraldian doctrine of the atonement. Such a model insists that the atonement should be viewed from two perspectives: whereas the 'efficacy' of the atonement may be viewed 'through the lens of election' (34), the sufficiency should be viewed via the lens of the universal gospel, to be preached to 'every creature' (Mark 16: 15). In short, good news for all necessarily assumes a provision for all.

Such a hermeneutic rescues the universal texts from fallacious text-tampering particularisation. D. Broughton Knox's claim that the properly-named doctrine of 'limited atonement' is 'a textless doctrine' (35) may be strengthened: it is simply 'an untexted untruth'. As R. T. Kendall rightly indicated (35), there are *no* biblical texts stating that Christ died for the elect *alone*. Rather than spurn an appeal to perspicuous texts as 'biblicism', making them say something different with the aid of some 'biblico-systematic web' involves the most undisguised rationalism.[2] It gives dubious priority to systematic theology over biblical theology, although the Introduction seems nervous to acknowledge (40, n. 21) that theory must be the servant of the data, not *vice-versa*. This is why Calvin and Amyraut were able to recognise and accept 'tension' within the biblical revelation. Against the background of the double-aspect divine will (Deut. 29: 29), they embraced the 'secret' and the 'revealed', the 'absolute' and the 'conditional', the 'particular' and the 'universal' features of

---

greatly govern his interpretation of them. Often he argues that such-and-such was Particularist because he said that Christ died for the Church, even though the writer does *not* say that Christ died only for the Church and that He did not die for the non-elect. This is usually how Particularists exegete the relevant portions of scripture. Most of Gill's evidence is irrelevant to the whole enquiry' (Curt Daniel, unpublished Ph.D. thesis, 'John Gill and Hypercalvinism' (Edinburgh, 1983), 495.

1   See my *Atonement and Justification*, 112, 127.

2   For a recent example of this mistake, see David Silversides, 'The Biblical Doctrine of the Atonement' in *English Churchman* (7927, 10 July 2015), 10.

the gospel. In view of Michael Thomas' criticism of the 'instability' of the arrangement (100), (also noted by Richard Snoddy[1]), it is only 'unstable' to academics whose theorising forbids an allowance of any trace of 'incoherent' antinomy in the biblical revelation (see Macleod at 434). In this respect, unlike John Owen, Calvin was the purest and humblest of theologians. He never manipulated texts in his *Institutes* according to a rationalising 'map'. Like Luther—whose view of the atonement he shared[2]—Calvin's conscience was 'captive to the Word of God'. Helm is surely (half) correct: 'Calvin did not commit himself to any version of the doctrine of definite atonement' (98). Only by 'manipulation' can his ubiquitous universalism be made consistent with 'limited atonement'. As suggested earlier, the 'unmanipulated' Calvin data is plainly an embarrassment to the advocates of 'Owenism'. Hence, as the editors admit, 'Calvinist' is 'largely absent from' this book (42). How extraordinary, that the greatest theologian of the Reformation is virtually air-brushed out of the picture. How convenient is the revisionism that 'suggests that the term "Calvinism" is of no real use to intellectual history' (Trueman, 43, n.29). How embarrassing is the gap between Packer's view (cited at 48) that the saving power of the cross does not 'depend on faith being added to it' and Calvin's:

> To bear the sins means to free those who have sinned from their guilt by his satisfaction. He says many meaning all, as in Rom. 5: 15. It is of course certain that not all enjoy the fruits of Christ's death, but this happens because their unbelief hinders them.[3]

Since Calvin's legacy has been manipulated, it is hardly surprising to find his 'disciple' Amyraut receiving similar treatment. While even Muller denies that Amyraldianism should be regarded as a 'heresy',[4] this book also granting

---

1   See Richard Snoddy, *The Soteriology of James Ussher: The Act and Object of Saving Faith* (Oxford: OUP, 2014), 41.

2   'Although many Calvinists consider the total pattern of Calvin's theology, especially considering his doctrine of predestination, to fit better within a limited conception of atonement, Calvin himself certainly does not recognise these implications ... Certainly, Luther and Calvin, who both strongly adhere to the biblical doctrine of predestination, find no contradiction between their universalistic design of redemption and the eternal election of mankind' (Stephen Alan Strehle, *The Extent of the Atonement Within the Theological Systems of the Sixteenth and seventeenth Centuries* (Unpublished Ph.D. dissertation, Dallas Theological seminary (1980), 93–4).

3   J. Calvin, *Comment on Hebrews 9: 27* (Edinburgh: Oliver & Boyd edition, 1959–63).

4   R. A. Muller, 'Beyond Hypothetical Universalism: Moïse Amyraut (1596–1664) on Faith,

Hypothetical Universalists and Amyraldians a place 'under the umbrella of the Reformed community', yet they are regarded as 'the awkward cousins in the family' (Blacketer, 43, n.30). This raises the question: does not Calvin's teaching also make him 'awkward'? While Amyraldianism and Arminianism are often conflated by Amyraut's critics, those who are acquainted with his writings[1] (and not just second-hand verdicts) know that he does *not* disconnect 'Christ's redemptive work' from 'the election of his people' (46), nor does he create Trinitarian incoherence (50),[2] or suggest that the decree to save the elect is an 'afterthought' (47). In his 'heresy' trial during the Synod of Alençon in 1637, Amyraut was careful to connect the efficacy of the atonement with election:

> That Jesus Christ died for all men sufficiently, but for the elect only effectually: and that consequentially his intention was to die for all men in respect of the sufficiency of his satisfaction, but for the elect only in respect of its quickening and saving virtue and efficacy; which is to say, that Christ's will was that the sacrifice of his cross should be of an infinite price and value, and most abundantly sufficient to expiate the sins of the whole world; yet nevertheless the efficacy of his death appertains only unto the elect; ... for this was the most free counsel and gracious purpose both of God the Father, in giving his Son for the salvation of mankind, and of the Lord Jesus Christ, in suffering the pains of death, that the efficacy thereof should particularly belong unto all the elect, and to them only ...'

Neither does Amyraut allow any temporal order within the Divine decree, a fact at least recognised by Macleod (at 427–8):

> ... though they [Amyraut and Testard] considered [the divine] Decree as diverse, yet it was formed in God in one and the self-same moment, without any succession of thought, or order of priority and posteriority. The will of this most supreme and incomprehensible Lord, being but

---

Reason and Ethics' in Martin I. Klauber (ed), *The Theology of the French Reformed Churches from Henri IV to the Revocation of the Edict of Nantes* (Grand Rapids, Michigan: Reformation Heritage Books (2014), 216.

1   See my *Amyraut Affirmed, or 'Owenism, a Caricature of Calvinism'* (Norwich: Charenton Reformed Publishing, 2004).

2   Ibid. 49–50.

one only eternal act in him; so that could we but conceive of things as they be in him from all eternity, we should comprehend these [absolute and conditional] decrees of God by one only act of our understanding, as in truth they be but one only act of his eternal and unchangeable will.[1]

In conclusion, I believe this book—at worst—involves a deletion of truth, and—at best—a presentation of only half the picture. Packer's maxim from his famous 1959 'Introductory Essay' to John Owen's *Death of Death* applies to himself and the Crossway tome: 'a half-truth masquerading as a whole truth becomes a complete untruth'.[2] In short, to insist that the biblical Gospel is *only* about its efficacy in redeeming the elect, is to present *partial* (though undeniable) truth. This is not the emphasis of the New Testament, and certainly not the dynamic of 'the Great Commission'. The Church's preaching priority must always be evangelism based on the *divinely-intended* universal sufficiency of the Atonement, assured that ultimate success is guaranteed by its *divinely-intended* sovereign efficacy. As painful controversy within nineteenth-century Welsh Calvinistic Methodism demonstrated,[3] both aspects must be properly maintained. In terms of practical impact, whether or not the book will lead to a new explosion of global evangelism remains to be seen. I am personally very doubtful. I suspect it will inspire a growing number of 'cerebral readers' rather than a host of 'compassionate pleaders'.

While academic rationalism and 'confessional correctness' prevail (as evidenced in Kevin Bidwell's review),[4] it is unlikely that the polarisation of Arminianism and Owenism will ever be resolved. In the final analysis, a biblically-balanced *sola scriptura* solution shorn of dubious exegesis must commend itself to all parties. Having demonstrated the cogency of Richard Baxter's scholastic case against the 'double payment' objection, the reviewer suggests we conclude with a brief exploration of his direct engagement with Holy Scripture. This will commend itself to those who (like ignored Ryle[5]

---

1 John Quick, *Synodicon in Gallia Reformata* (London: 1692), ii. 354–5.

2 Introductory Essay to John Owen's *Death Of Death In The Death Of Christ* (London: The Banner of Truth Trust, 1959), 2.

3 See my *John Jones Talsarn, Pregethwr Y Bobl/The People's Preacher* (Norwich: Charenton Reformed Publishing, 2013).

4 'After reading these many pages, I sought refuge in the distilled sentences of the *Westminster Confession* ...' (*Evangelical Times* (September, 2014), Reviews).

5 The reference to Ryle (at 42) has nothing to do with his teaching on the atonement.

and Lloyd-Jones[1]) wish to 'preach the word' rather than 'teach the system'. In line with the editors' desire that sound doctrine should 'stir the affections',[2] we will end with a specimen of Baxter's warm pastoral concern. Before this is done, in view of the oft-cited misrepresentation of his position, we confirm his credentials by remembering his allegiance to John Calvin (whose views on the atonement he cited[3]) and the Canons of Dort (without ignoring his positive assessment of the Westminster Assembly):[4]

Baxter on Calvin:

I know no man, since the Apostles' days, whom I value and honour more than Calvin, and whose judgement in all things, one with another, I more esteem and come nearer to.[5]

Baxter on Dort:

In the article of the extent of redemption, wherein I am most suspected and accused, I do subscribe to the Synod of Dort, without any exception, limitation, or exposition, of any word, as doubtful and obscure.[6]

1　See J. E. Hazlett Lynch, *Lamb Of God—Saviour Of The World: The Soteriology Of Rev. Dr David Martyn Lloyd-Jones* (Bloomington: WestBow Press, 2015).

2　'Definite Atonement', *Evangelicals Now*, March 2014, 15.

3　See *Richard Baxter's Catholick Theologie* (London: 1675), II. 51.

4　With reference to the Westminster Confession itself (Chapter VIII), Baxter emphatically denies that it opposes 'Amyraldus' method'. On the contrary, he asserts that the Confession was deliberately framed so as not to exclude the Amyraldian view. He was assured of this by 'an eminent divine, yet living, that was of the Assembly' that 'they purposely avoided determining that controversy' (Preface to *Certain Disputations of Right to Sacraments* (London: 1658). While it would appear from the detailed statements of the Confession (Chapters III. vi; VIII. v, viii) that Baxter's 'middle way' was rejected, at least by implication, he himself understood matters otherwise. His unqualified commendation of the Assembly is famous: 'The Divines there congregate were men of eminent godliness and learning ... the Christian world ... had never a Synod of more excellent divines (taking one thing with another) than this Synod and the Synod of Dort were' (*Reliquiae Baxterianae* (ed. Matthew Sylvester (London, 1696), i. 73).

5　*The Saints' Everlasting Rest* (London: 1658), 435.

6　William Orme (ed), *The Practical Works of the Revd. Richard Baxter* (London: James Duncan, 1830), i. 456.

FOR WHOM DID CHRIST DIE?

BAXTER'S BIBLICAL BALANCE

The Extent of the Atonement and Gospel Preaching
in the Writings of Richard Baxter

INTRODUCTION

According to the 'Limited Atonement' teaching of Theodore Beza, John Owen and others, Christ died for the elect ALONE. According to the 'Universal Atonement' teaching of Jakob Arminius, John Wesley and others, Christ died for ALL (yet salvation is uncertain for anyone). Richard Baxter— agreeing with Augustine, Martin Luther, Thomas Cranmer and John Calvin et al, and urging an avoidance of extremist exegesis—maintained that the Bible demands a balanced view of 'universality' and 'particularity', as follows:

RICHARD BAXTER'S BASIC VIEW OF THE GOSPEL TO BE PREACHED UNIVERSALLY (SEE MARK 16: 15):

For God, who is Love itself, so far loved lapsed and lost mankind, as that he gave his only begotten Son to be incarnate, and to be their Redeemer, by his meritorious Life, and Death, and Resurrection, and to make them this promise, covenant and offer, that whoever truly believeth in him, should have his sin forgiven; and should not perish, but have everlasting blessed life.[1]

II
His refusal to 'explain away' the 'universal' texts of the Bible:
When God saith so expressly that Christ died for all [2 Cor. 5: 14–15], and tasted death for every man [Heb. 2: 9], and is the ransom for all [1 Tim. 2: 6], and the propitiation for the sins of the whole world [1 Jn. 2: 2], it beseems every Christian rather to explain in what sense Christ died for all, than flatly to deny it.[2]

---

1   *A Paraphrase on the New Testament* (London: 1685), Comment on John 3: 16. Hereinafter, *Paraphrase*.

2   *The Universal Redemption of Mankind* (London: 1694), 286.

III

His explanation of the four texts cited above:

(1) 2 Corinthians 5: 14–15: For we have cause to judge, that they are great things, which our Redemption intimateth, even that Christ, who died for all, found all men dead in Sin and Misery; and that he therefore redeemed them by his Death, that they who are recovered by him should not hereafter live to themselves, but to him that died for them and rose again.[1]

(2) Hebrews 2: 9: [Christ's] death was suffered in the common nature of Man, and the sins of all men had a causal hand in it, and it was by God's Grace the purchasing cause of the conditional Covenant of Grace, and of all the good that men receive, so he died to bring Man to Glory with himself.[2]

(3) 1 Timothy 2: 6: For it must move us to pray for all, in compliance with this Will of God, that would have all Men saved; because there is One God who is good to all, and One Mediator between God and Mankind, who took on him the Common Nature of all men, and gave himself a Ransom for all ...[3]

(4) 1 John. 2: 2: For he is the Propitiation for our sins by virtue of his Sacrifice, now interceding for us in heaven: And he is a propitiation sufficient for the sins of the whole World (so far as that none of them shall be damned for want of a sufficient Sacrifice, but only for want of accepting his Grace) and actually effecting the Pardon of all in the world, who believingly trust and accept him and his Grace.[4]

IV

His view of the Atonement-based provision of the universal Gospel offer:

[We see] the wonderful love and mercy that God hath manifested in giving his Son to be the Redeemer of the world, and which the Son hath manifested in redeeming them by his blood; for all his full preparation by being *a sufficient sacrifice for the sins of all*; for all his personal excellencies, and that full and glorious salvation that he hath procured; and for all his free offers of these, and frequent and earnest invitation of sinners ... [He] declareth his person and nature, and the great things that he hath done and suffered for man; his redeeming him from the wrath of God by his blood, and procuring a grant

---

1   *Paraphrase*, Comment on 2 Corinthians 5: 14–15.
2   *Paraphrase*, Comment on Hebrews 2: 9.
3   *Paraphrase*, Comment on 1 Timothy 2: 5–6.
4   *Paraphrase*, Comment on 1 John 2: 1–2.

of salvation with himself. Furthermore, the same gospel maketh an offer of Christ to sinners, that if they will accept him on his easy and reasonable terms, he will be their Saviour, the Physician of their souls, their Husband, and their Head.[1]

V
His distinction between the 'general' and 'special' aspects
of the atonement in relation to predestination:

[God's people] are a small part of lost mankind, whom God hath from eternity predestined to [everlasting] rest, for the glory of his mercy, and given to his Son, to be by him in a *special manner* redeemed, and fully recovered from their lost estate, and advanced to this higher glory; all which Christ doth, in due time, accomplish accordingly by himself for them, and by his Spirit upon them.[2]

... Christ is, in *some sense, a ransom for all*, yet not in that *special manner* as for his people. He hath brought others under the Conditional Gospel-Covenant; but them under the absolute. He hath, according to the tenor of his covenant, *procured salvation for all*, if they will believe; but he hath *procured for his chosen even this condition of believing*.[3]

Christ's blood hath purchased the Church in a *fuller sense* than he is said to *die for all*.[4]

Husbands, imitate Christ, in loving your wives, as Christ did his Church, for which (in a *special sense*) he gave himself by death, ...[5]

VI
His view of God's provision and man's responsibility:

Whoever is damned, it is not because no ransom was made for him, or because it was not sufficient for him ... God hath made an Universal Act of Grace or Oblivion, giving pardon of all sin, and right to life in Christ, to all men, without exception, on condition of believing acceptance, and hath commissioned his Ministers to offer this gift to all men, to the utmost of their power, and entreat them to accept it; ... Few Christians have the

---

1   *Making Light of Christ and Salvation* (London: 1656), 4–5, emphasis mine.
2   *The Saints Everlasting Rest* (London: 1658), 125, emphasis mine. Hereinafter *Saints' Rest.*
3   *Saints Rest*, 126, emphasis mine.
4   *Paraphrase*, Comment on Acts 20: 28, emphasis mine.
5   *Paraphrase*, Comment on Ephesians 5: 25, emphasis mine.

face to affirm, that this universal Conditional Pardon and Gift (or Law of Grace) is no fruit of the Death of Christ.[1]

VII

Affirming the biblical teaching on predestination and election, Baxter makes plain that evangelistic preaching is to be motivated not by God's secret eternal decrees and absolute purposes but His revealed conditional purposes, desires and promises (see Deuteronomy 29: 29):

It is further proved by the sufferings of his Son, that God takes no pleasure in the death of the wicked. Would he have ransomed them from death at so dear a rate? Would he have astonished angels and men by his condescension; would God have dwelt in flesh, and have come in the form of a servant, and have assumed humanity into one person with the Godhead? Would Christ have lived a life of suffering, and died a cursed death for sinners, if he had rather taken pleasure in their death?

Suppose you saw him but so busy in preaching and healing of them, as you find him in Mark 3: 21, or so long in fasting, as in Matt. 4, or all night in prayer, as in Luke 6: 12, or praying with the drops of blood trickling from him instead of sweat, as Luke 22: 44, or suffering a cursed death upon the cross, and pouring out his soul as a sacrifice for our sins,—would you have thought these the signs of one that delights in the death of the wicked?

Think not to extenuate it by saying, that it was only for his elect. For it was thy sin, and the sin of all the world, that lay upon our redeemer; and his sacrifice and satisfaction is sufficient for all, and the fruits of it are offered to one as well as to another; but it is true, that it was never the intent of his mind, to pardon and save any that would not by faith and repentance be converted.

If you had seen him weeping and bemoaning the state of disobedient impenitent people, Luke 19: 41, 42, or complaining of their stubbornness, as Matt. 23: 37, 'O Jerusalem, Jerusalem, how oft would I have gathered thy children together, even as a hen gathereth her chickens under her wings, and ye would not!' Or if you had seen and heard him on the cross, praying for his persecutors, 'Father, forgive them, for they know not what they do' [Luke 23: 34]; would you have suspected that he had delighted in the death of the wicked, even of those that perish by their wilful unbelief?

When God hath so loved (not only loved, but so loved) the world as to give his only-begotten Son, that whosoever believeth in him (by an effectual

---

1   *Paraphrase*, Note on 1 Tim. 2: 5–6.

faith) should not perish, but have everlasting life', [John 3: 16], I think he hath hereby proved, against the malice of men and angels, that he takes no pleasure in the death of the wicked, but had rather that they would turn and live .[1]

BAXTER'S PASTORAL HEART

The persons for whom 'eternal rest' is designed—the 'people of God'—are 'the chosen of God from eternity' (John 17: 2). That they are but a small part of mankind is too apparent in scripture and experience. They are the 'little flock', to whom 'it is their Father's good pleasure to give the kingdom' (Luke 12: 32). Fewer they are than the world imagines; yet not so few as some drooping spirits think, who are suspicious that God is unwilling to be their God, when they know themselves willing to be His people.[2]

---

1   *A Call to the Unconverted* (London: 1658), 98–100 (paragraphing and emphasis mine).
2   *Saints Rest* (ed. London: The Religious Tract Society, 1833), 68.

406

APPENDIX 2: CRITICS CRITIQUED

J. C. RYLE, J. I. PACKER AND IAIN H. MURRAY

I

Some critics have balanced their criticisms with varying degrees of approval, while others have written with pronounced negativity. From an Anglican perspective, J. C. Ryle's warm and semi-popular treatment has much to commend it despite some questionable critical observations. Indeed, his essay features some serious anomalies. Applauding Baxter to the skies as 'a real man—a true spiritual hero',[1] Ryle laments what the Act of Uniformity did to Baxter and his ejected brethren. Yet Baxter is criticized for not conforming.[2] Ryle further chides our hero thus: 'I regard his refusal of a bishopric as a huge mistake'.[3] However, this 'establishment' view is a total failure to grasp Baxter's oft-argued biblical case for rejecting inflexible Anglicanism and its unbiblical episcopal structure. Baxter and his brethren regarded the terms of the Act of Uniformity as intolerable and contrary to Scripture. They considered the Oath of Canonical Obedience to be 'especially evil and against the Word of God'.[4] Comparing Baxter's devastating critique of the 1662 *Book of Common Prayer* with Ryle's utterly-unpersuasive defence (not least over the concept of 'baptismal regeneration)[5] does not speak well of one noted for being a faithful, Bible-believing Protestant. His rejection of Baxter's 'scruples'[6] can

---

1   J. C. Ryle, 'Richard Baxter' in *Light from Old Times,* 335.
2   Ibid. 318.
3   Ibid. 335.
4   Baxter, *Reliquiae Baxterianiae* (London: 1696), II. 425.
5   Compare Ibid. II. 313 with J. C. Ryle, *Knots Untied* (London: James Clarke, 1964), 103ff.
6   J. C. Ryle, 'Richard Baxter', 318.

only testify to a cherry-picking appeal to biblical authority, typical of the culture of compromise for which Anglicanism has been infamous.

Another anomaly concerns Ryle's assessment of Baxter's theology. After generously stating that Baxter 'held no heresy'[1] (a point several would contest!), one who is rightly well-known for dismissing John Owen's dogma of 'limited atonement' strangely (and incorrectly) insists that, compared with Owen's, 'you will not find such a clear, full gospel in [Baxter's] writings'.[2] Yet, certain 'systematized' details apart, it was Baxter's view of the atonement that Ryle passionately taught and preached. Indeed, it was the Puritan's 'clear and full gospel'—permeated by his view of the atonement—that drove his wonderfully-successful ministry. On this issue, current discussion is not helped by Iain H. Murray's omission of Ryle's explicitly-stated and perspicuous views in his new biography,[3] and which I challenged in an e-mail.[4] *On this fundamental Gospel point,* one is happy to endorse Ryle whose conformity to the XXXIX Articles and the Prayer Book is totally and biblically valid, as Baxter would have undoubtedly said. Indeed, in view of the clarity of his soteriology, one may pardon the defects of his ecclesiology.

II

Then, half a century ago, Dr J. I. Packer (who shared Ryle's Anglican churchmanship but not his soteriological position) expressed an acute ambivalence towards the subject of his highly-acclaimed 1954 DPhil thesis.[5] In his 1969 Puritan Conference paper[6] and his 'Introduction' to the 1974 Banner

---

1   Ibid. 331.

2   Ibid. 335.

3   Iain H. Murray, *J. C. Ryle: Prepared to Stand Alone* (Edinburgh: The Banner of Truth Trust, 2016).

4   "You obviously refuse to comment on this. What you have done is to re-create Ryle in your own image. This will naturally please the Anglican Owenites. You should have acknowledged he held to universal atonement while announcing your dissent from him at that point, rather than simply ignore the issue. That would have had integrity. Instead, you have suppressed his view, thus misrepresenting him on a truth which was obviously of fundamental importance to him, and deceiving your readers in the process. This is defective handling of history."

5   See J. I. Packer, 'The Redemption and Restoration of Man in the Thought of Richard Baxter', D. Phil. thesis (Oxford, 1954); pub. *The Redemption and Restoration of Man in the Thought of Richard Baxter* (Vancouver, BC: Regent College Publishing, 2003).

6   See J. I. Packer, 'The Doctrine of Justification in Development and Decline among the

of Truth Trust edition of *The Reformed Pastor*,[1] Packer effectively 'prosecutes' Baxter before he 'praises him'. More recently, in his 'Foreword' to the 2004 Regent College edition of Baxter's *Saints' Everlasting Rest*,[2] Packer fails to avoid a 'dig' at Baxter's alleged doctrinal defects. While commending his personal and pastoral accomplishments, he judged that Baxter's theology of atonement and justification was 'something of a disaster'.[3] As I demonstrated in *Atonement and Justification*, it is strangely incoherent that Packer can lament Baxter's theological activity, yet praise his pastoral accomplishments. After all, many of the ideas objected to in the theological treatises can be found (albeit with reduced intensity) in the very devotional and practical writings Packer praises so highly. Baxter's theological and pastoral activities were all of a piece: the conclusions of his 'polemical' works drove the teaching evident in his 'practical' works. He was a thoroughly integrated 'pastor-theologian'. In short, there is no valid basis for Packer's dichotomy.

Packer also went for the 'man' rather than the 'ball'! Criticism of Baxter's alleged 'poor performance in public life'[4] reveals more about Packer's Anglican and Owenite bias than Baxter's alleged failures. Had Baxter been charmingly diplomatic, are we to imagine he'd have been successful at the Savoy Conference (1661) in winning over intransigent clerics like Bishop Morley; and, in pursuit of Presbyterian-Independent unity (1669), stubborn 'over-orthodox' Puritans like John Owen? No, Baxter's lack of 'success' arguably reflects the reluctance of those who, unlike Baxter's numerous nationwide friends and supporters, were too entrenched in their ways meekly to appreciate the wisdom of his persuasive anti-sectarian Bible-based proposals.

Neither does Packer's dubious psycho-analysis of Baxter stand up to scrutiny. To attribute Baxter's 'plain' outspokenness to 'compensation for an inferiority complex'[5] hardly fits with Packer's own acknowledgement that Baxter was 'a brilliant cross-bencher, widely learned, with an astounding capacity for instant analysis, argument and appeal', and one who 'could

---

Puritans' in *By Schisms Rent Asunder* (Puritan and Reformed Studies Conference, 1969).

1 See Richard Baxter, *The Reformed Pastor* (Edinburgh: The Banner of Truth Trust, 1974).

2 See Richard Baxter, *The Saints' Everlasting Rest*, ed. John T. Wilkinson (Vancouver, BC: Regent College Publishing, 2004).

3 'The Doctrine of Justification', *By Schisms Rent Asunder*, 27.

4 Introduction, *Reformed Pastor*, 10.

5 Ibid. 11.

run rings round anyone in debate'.[1] Clever and correct statements, yes, but their significance not-so-cleverly missed. Indeed, no man in England had less cause to feel inferior to anyone than Richard Baxter! It seems evident that his opponents were simply irritated by his over-matching intellectual brilliance and irresistible eloquence. Unlike the 'politically-correct', Baxter always told it 'as it was'. He was not in the business of obfuscation, especially in the presence of those determined to destroy his God-honouring legacy.

The same applies to Packer's charge that 'Baxter's interventions regularly deepened division, as when in 1690 he published *The Scripture Gospel Defended* to stop Crisp's sermons from causing trouble and thereby wrecked the 'Happy Union' between Presbyterians and Independents almost before it had begun'.[2] This assessment simply fails to grasp the gravity of Tobias Crisp's blasphemous antinomianism. For Baxter, to tolerate a gross perversion of Christianity would have led to a most 'unhappy' and ungodly union. It would also have added fuel to social and political suspicions regarding the morals of Protestant Dissenters and reinforced Roman Catholic detestation of Protestantism in general. For him, it was that fundamental, and he was right to speak up.

Looking back at my assessment of Packer in *Atonement and Justification*, I think I was too lenient with Packer and perhaps too critical of Baxter. One wonders too whether Packer's negativity towards Baxter was due to his awareness of the great Puritan's irrefutable criticisms of unbiblical Anglican church order. Having affirmed—contrary to the Anglican Articles and Prayer Book—John Owen's view of limited atonement in 1959, he was also involved a decade later—at the very time he was publically demolishing Baxterianism (1969)—with non-evangelical high churchmen in the highly-dubious ecumenical proposals outlined in *Growing into Union* (1970).[3] This publication precipitated a division within the growing Reformed constituency. It led to a cancellation of the Puritan conference that year, the gathering re-emerging as the Westminster Conference in 1971.

While Geoffrey Nuttall's 1965 biography had reminded the Christian world that Richard Baxter was an ecumenical pioneer, nothing of his contribution appears in *Growing into Union*. Baxter would have every reason not to be amused! One may say that Packer's anomalous public behaviour raises questions

---

1   Ibid. 9.

2   Ibid. 11.

3   See C. O. Buchanan, E. L. Mascall, J. I. Packer, The Bishop of Willesdon, *Growing into Union* (London: SPCK, 1970).

about his own 'psychology'. Puzzled as I was at the time that Packer could appear as a stalwart pro-Owen Puritan one year, then as a compromised anti-puritan ecumenist the next, I asked an Anglican friend to explain the anomaly. The reply was striking: 'When Dr Packer sits around the fire with those of contrary views, his convictions begin to melt in the heat.' This propensity became even more evident in the 'Evangelicals and Roman Catholics Together' era when Packer took part in a public discussion in Belfast with a Roman Catholic priest.[1] How extraordinary all this is! Baxter, who wrote several hard-hitting books against Rome, is still pilloried for flirting with Rome, while Packer can retain his standing within the Reformed constituency despite his own highly-publicized flirtations!

Judging by his Foreword to the big 2013 Crossway tome on the atonement, *From Heaven He Came and Sought Her*,[2] and a recent issue of *The Banner of Truth* magazine (May 2015), it is unfortunate to see Packer's ongoing unquestioning propagation of 'Owenism'.[3] More recently, sympathetic admirers such as Joel Beeke have not been able to avoid highlighting Baxter's alleged defects over justification and his 'Arminian tendencies'.[4] Then, in late 2015, American 'pro-Owen' scholar R. Scott Clark decried Baxter's doctrine of justification as 'theological arsenic'.[5] We are told that Baxter 'effectively scuttled the Reformation doctrine of justification'. The question for such critics is simply stated: from a strictly Christian perspective, how could Baxter be so successful if he was so unsound?

Having critiqued Packer's view of Baxter in my *Atonement and Justification*, I now supply examples of his disregard of the actual evidence. Indeed, Packer—aided by Robert Traill[6]—flies in the face of Baxter's unambiguous teaching. His detailed criticisms[7] of Baxter are highly misleading at best.

---

1   Listen to the cassette recording: *Evangelicals and Roman Catholics in Relationship: Issues for the 21st Century* (Belfast: ECTI, c/o 66 North Road, Belfast BT5 5NJ, 2003).

2   See *From Heaven He came and Sought Her: Definite Atonement in Historical, Biblical, Theological and Pastoral Perspective,* ed. David and Jonathan Gibson (Wheaton, Illinois: Crossway, 2013).

3   See J. I. Packer, 'John Owen on Spiritual-Mindedness' in *The Banner of Truth*, 620 (May 2015). See also Packer's contributions in issues 629 (February 2016) and 635–6 (August-September 2016).

4   See Joel Beeke, https://www.uniontheology.org/resources/historical/reading-the-puritans

5   See R. Scott Clark, *Burying The Lead On Baxter: Baxter's doctrine of justification* http://theaquilareport.com/burying-the-lead-on-baxter/#.Vknkzb6LqnE.facebook

6   See Robert Traill, *Justification Vindicated* (Edinburgh: The Banner of Truth Trust, 2002), p. ix, 12ff.

7   See J. I. Packer, 'The Doctrine of Justification in Development and Decline among the

Packer. 'Baxter's scheme ... fails to come to terms with the representative headship of Christ, the second Adam, as this is set forth in Romans 5: 12ff.'

Baxter: 'That as we are told that Adam was the natural root or parent of mankind; so also that Christ was the Federal root of all the saved ...'[1]

Packer accuses Baxter of directing the distressed sinner to his faith rather than to 'the cross of Christ.'

Baxter: 'Christ's sacrifice for sin, and his perfect holiness, are so far satisfactory and meritorious for all men, as that they render Christ a meet object for that faith in him which is commanded men ...'[2] '[There is] no question but the faith that we talk of, is *faith in Christ*, even the believing receiving of a Saviour and his Grace freely given to us ... And there is no doubt but Christ is the soul's riches which faith receiveth.[3]

Packer also implies that by adopting his 'political method', Baxter 'externalises sin' as if it were 'crime', understressing its personal and 'demonic corporate influence.'

Baxter: 'All ministers, tutors, parents, Christians; yea, persons find how woefully hard it proveth to cure one sin; to cure the ignorant, the unbelieving, the hard-hearted, the proud, the lustful, the covetous, the passionate; much more the malignant enemies of God and holiness. What need of the sanctification of the Spirit, or the medicinal grace of Christ, if the very depraved will can do all in a moment of itself, and depose its enmity?'[4]

Packer criticises Baxter for seeing 'Christ as the Head of God's government rather than of His people.'

Baxter: 'Christ is first filled with his Spirit personally himself, that he may be a fit Head of vital influence to all his members, who by the previous operations of his Spirit are drawn and united to him.'[5]

Packer also suggests that Baxter viewed the death of Christ as 'one presupposition of our sins being remitted rather than the procuring cause of it ...'

Baxter: 'Christ's righteousness, merit and satisfaction may be said to be

---

Puritans' in *By Schisms Rent Asunder* (Puritan and Reformed Studies Conference, 1969), 26–8.

1   *Catholick Theologie* (London: 1675), I. ii. 77–8; see also *A Paraphrase on the New Testament* (London: 1685) on Romans 5: 12ff.

2   Ibid. I. ii. 51.

3   *The Scripture Gospel Defended* (London: 1690), 34.

4   *Catholick Theology*, II. 84.

5   Ibid. II. 178.

imputed to us, ... God reputeth or judgeth us righteous ... which indeed is done for Christ's meritorious righteousness procuring it.'[1]

Packer also charges Baxter for viewing the remission of sins 'as public pardon rather than personal forgiveness', making Christ 'remote' and 'more like a judge than a Saviour.'

Packer seems to fly in the face of 2 Corinthians 5: 10, 'we must all appear before the judgement seat of Christ.'

Baxter: 'All our past sins are pardoned at our first faith or conversion' while justification is completed at the day of judgement 'which ... is done by Christ as Judge, and so is an act of his kingly office.'[2]

As for Christ seeming 'remote', even in a somewhat technical treatise like *Catholick Theologie*, Baxter is still able to write of Christ's mediatorial work as 'the way to the Father, to bring man home to his creator,' and that the Holy Spirit's work is to apply what is 'given by Christ' by 'giving us the love of God, and other graces' and 'by giving us the comfort of all.'[3]

Packer strangely laments Baxter's theological activity, yet praises his pastoral accomplishments. After all, many of the ideas objected to in the theological treatises can be found in the very devotional and practical writings Packer praises so highly. Baxter's theological and pastoral activities were all of a piece. It is true, the 'political' terminology is much less prominent in Baxter's more popular works, but there is no solid basis for Packer's dichotomy.

Lastly, it is simply incorrect to accuse Baxter for having 'a streak of legalism' in his 'theological system'. Merely to stress that Christ's kingdom involves the believer in duties and obligations is bound to appear legalistic from an antinomian perspective. Living under Christ's kingship is proper legality not improper legalism.

Baxter recognises that Christ is both Saviour and Lord, and that saving faith has passive *and* active features. That said, he carefully distinguishes between means and motive. One does not observe the requirements of Christ the king in a mercenary manner. 'Other service is undertaken for the love of the wages, but this is undertaken for the love of the Master and the work, and is wages itself to them that go through with it.'[4]

---

1 Ibid. I. ii. 64.

2 Ibid. I. ii. 85.

3 Ibid. I. ii. 88–90.

4 *Directions to a Sound Conversion* in *The Practical Works of Richard Baxter: Select Treatises* (1863; rep. Grand Rapids, MI: Baker Book House, 1981), 584.

III

Returning to Iain H. Murray, his 1991 critique of Baxter,[1] besides being a piously-presented character assassination, is seriously adrift at several points. As well as generally endorsing Packer's anomalous stance,[2] he failed to take account of my defence of Baxter published in the previous year.[3] In fact, having relied on Paul Helm to provide a hopelessly subjective and negative review in his organization's magazine,[4] he dismissed the book to my face at the Banner of Truth Ministers' Conference in 1991, having permitted me to advertise it at the previous year's conference: 'Had I known what was in it, I wouldn't have allowed you to.'

Among other things, Murray is entrenched in the seventeenth-century caricature of Calvinism properly identified as 'Owenism'. Such 'confessional correctness' rendered him incapable of understanding Baxter's theological concerns. As I have demonstrated, this mistaken perspective is productive of a chain of errors. When we are told that 'Baxter declined to regard himself as a Calvinist',[5] clarity of definition is vital. Murray ignores Baxter's unqualified admiration for the reformer: 'I know no man, since the Apostles' days, whom I value and honour more than Calvin, *and whose judgement in all things, one with another, I more esteem and come nearer to'*.[6] In short, Baxter had problems with John Owen not with John Calvin. In fact, regarding the righteousness of believers, Baxter specifically appeals to Calvin's extensive comment on Luke 1: 6 in his *Aphorismes*.[7] Had Murray examined my case, he would have seen that Owen's unbiblical dogmas of the imputed *active* obedience of Christ, a once-for-all justification and limited atonement—never taught by Calvin—were the root cause of the problems Baxter felt compelled to challenge throughout his life. These very points (among others) were

---

1   See 'Richard Baxter—the Reluctant Puritan?' (Thornton Heath, Surrey: Westminster Conference report, 1991). Hereinafter 'Reluctant Puritan'.

2   Ibid. 19.

3   See *Atonement and Justification: English Evangelical Theology 1640–1790—An Evaluation* (Oxford: Clarendon Press, 1990).

4   *The Banner of Truth* (October 1990), 29–31.

5   'Reluctant Puritan', 8.

6   *Saints Everlasting Rest* (1650), 526; (1658), 559 (emphasis mine).

7   See *Aphorismes of Justification* (Hague alias Cambridge: 1655), 213. Calvin's comments on Luke 1: 77 regarding justification also express views later held by Baxter.

highlighted by his early-nineteenth century admirer T. W. Jenkyn[1] (whom Murray selectively quotes[2]). In short, Baxter may be called a 'Calvinist' but not a '*High* Calvinist', a distinction he rightly considered had enormous evangelistic and pastoral implications.

It is evidently too painful for Owenite critics like Murray to admit that Calvin was on Baxter's side. Evaluating the Puritan from such a perspective would make it clear that *they* are 'out of step', not Baxter. They are the 'eccentrics', not Baxter.[3] He was 'tenacious' for truth not error.[4] Sadly, Murray's readiness to charge Baxter with 'errors' and 'mistakes' simply indicates the gap between the Reformation and Puritan 'High orthodox' agendas. For instance, challenging Baxter's *Aphorismes of Justification* involved Murray's complete failure to grasp the author's main point.[5] Yes (in line with the *Westminster Confession*), Baxter said he did not 'quarrel' with the idea that 'the Gospel declareth and offereth [Christ's legal righteousness] … because it is a way to justification, which only the Gospel revealeth'.[6] What Baxter rejected was the idea that the believer's justification does not involve 'conditions' on his part. In short, in complete harmony with Calvin[7] (and not the *Westminster Confession?*[8] but certainly the Bible!), he insists that Christ does not believe for us:

> To affirm therefore that our evangelical or new covenant righteousness is in Christ, and not in ourselves, or performed by Christ, and not by ourselves, is such a monstrous piece of antinomian doctrine, that no

---

1 T. W. Jenkyn, 'Essay on His Life, Ministry and Theology' in Richard Baxter, *Making Light of Christ,* etc. (New York: Wiley & Putnam, 1846), pp. li–lv.

2 'Reluctant Puritan', 24.

3 Ibid. 13.

4 Ibid.

5 Ibid. 8.

6 *Aphorismes,* 71–2.

7 'Repentance and faith must needs go together … God receiveth us to mercy, and daily pardoneth our faults through his free goodness: and that we be justified because Jesus Christ hath reconciled him unto us, inasmuch as he accepteth us for righteous though we be wretched sinners: in preaching this, it behoveth us to add, how *it is upon condition that we return unto God*: as was spoken of heretofore by the prophets' (John Calvin, *Sermons on Timothy and Titus,* tr. L. T. [sic] (1579; fac. Edinburgh, 1983), 1181–2).

8 *The Westminster Confession of Faith,* Chapter XV 'Of Repentance unto Life', III.

man who knows the nature and difference of the Covenant can possibly entertain, and which every Christian should abhor as unsufferable.[1]

And did Baxter imagine that we perform the 'conditions' in our own strength?

> Christ hath done all his part, but he hath appointed us a necessary part which must be done by ourselves; and though without him we can do nothing [Jn. 15: 5], yet by him we must believe and be new creatures, and by him that strengtheneth us we can do something [Phil. 4: 13]; and must work out our salvation, while he worketh in us to will and to do [Phil. 2: 12–13].[2]

Murray totally misjudges Baxter's theological motivation when he dismisses the latter's declared concern to be *biblically* correct in the Preface to his *Catholick Theologie*. Assuming an equivalence between his '*Westminster Confession-*Owenite' mindset and the Bible, Murray says 'Baxter, however, did not go only to Scripture. He also went to the writings of the innovative Scotsman, John Cameron, and to Cameron's French successors, Moïse Amyraut and Jean Daillé, from whom he learned what has been called 'hypothetical universalism'.[3] Yes, he eventually endorsed their teaching because he believed it possessed biblical integrity. However, at that stage in his 1640s development, it was Dr William Twisse, the first prolocutor of the Westminster Assembly (whom Murray acknowledges Baxter had read) who helped him grasp a more biblical view of the Gospel:

> I had ... engaged myself as a disputer against Universal Redemption ... but [when] new notions called me to new thoughts ... I went to the Scripture, where its whole current, but especially Matth. 25 did quickly satisfy me in the doctrine of Justification: and I remembered two or three things in Dr Twisse (whom I most esteemed) ... [who] ... every where professeth, that Christ so far died for all, as to purchase them Justification and Salvation, if they believe.[4]

---

1   *Aphorismes*, 72.

2   *The Scripture Gospel Defended* (1690), 35. I have added the Bible references to indicate the biblical basis of Baxter's words.

3   'Reluctant Puritan', 14.

4   *Richard Baxter's Catholick Theologie* (London: 1675), Preface.

Contrary to Murray's account of Baxter's Shropshire origins,[1] his distance from Cambridge and Oxford proved to be an advantage. Yes, he had access to books, but free from the ultra-orthodox influences of the academic community, he was less likely to be drawn away from perspicuous 'Scripture sufficiency'. Indeed, judging by Baxter's commendation of the universal/ particular soteriology of Calvin (and many others) in his *Catholick Theologie*,[2] and his own exegetical comments in his *Paraphrase on the New Testament*, it is clear that Baxter's 'conscience' (like Luther's) was 'captive to the Word of God'. On this basis alone did he endorse the Amyraldian teaching. However embarrassing to the Owenites (then and now), it was an obvious bonus that Amyraut and his brethren could claim Calvin's support for their distinctive teaching. Yet the Bible was 'king' and not even Calvin. Such an observation demands only one conclusion. Contrary to Murray's blinkered stance, Baxter 'attacked' not '*biblical* doctrine'[3] but the 'over-orthodox' *unbiblical* 'spin' of the 'confessionally correct'. On the subject of justification, Murray's mistaken *WCF*-inspired assumption that the Bible teaches 'a once-for-all justification'[4] is really his undoing. This among a cluster of associated ideas is found wanting once—yes, with Calvin's help!—careful biblical exegesis is undertaken.

Murray's charge that Baxter's 'controversial writings were not founded upon close scriptural exegesis'[5] is scandalously false. No one was more wedded to the text of Holy Scripture than our maligned Puritan. This was very evident from the start in his *Aphorismes of Justification* (1649). Even an intricate work like *Catholick Theologie* (1675) is often peppered with biblical references in margins as well as the main text. Baxter's opening 'intreaty' to 'the wrathful, contentious, zealous dogmatists' urges them 'conscientiously to study' three full folio pages of extensively-quoted Bible passages. Such was the basis of all his subsequent 'close' reasoning. There's no denying that Baxter's extended intense discussions are often intellectually challenging if not cerebrally excessive, but even when engaging with scholastic and other authors, the Bible is his unerring compass. In defence of his sometimes confusing but oft-misunderstood teaching on Justification, Baxter appeals to the Bible thus in his *Catholick Theologie*:

---

1 'Reluctant Puritan', 10–11.
2 *Catholick Theologie,* II. 51.
3 'Reluctant Puritan', 15.
4 Ibid. 8 and 15.
5 Ibid. 20.

Christ's sermons, *Matth.* 5. & 6. 7. & 10. & 13. & 18. & 21. and *Luk.* 5 & 11. & 12. & 16. & 18. & 19. and *Joh.* 1. & 3. & 5. & 6., etc. with all the sermons in the *Acts*, and all the Catholick Epistles of *Peter, James, Jude* and *John*, and *Paul's* Epist. to the *Rom.* Chap. 1. 2. 4. 6. 7. 8. 12, etc. *Gal.* 5. & 6. and a great part of the rest of his Epistles, are made up of this Doctrine of Grace which I have asserted; And the *reading* of them will better instruct you in the true sense of *Remission* and *Justification*, than most Treatises written on that Subject which I have seen.[1]

On the subject of the atonement, if Murray means by 'close scriptural exegesis' the kind of 'explaining away' of the universal texts John Owen indulged in, Baxter's treatise on *Universal Redemption* leaves one in no doubt what he thought of such textual tampering:

When God saith so expressly that Christ died for all [2 Cor. 5: 14–15], and tasted death for every man [Heb. 2: 9], and is the ransom for all [1 Tim. 2: 6], and the propitiation for the sins of the whole world [1 Jn. 2: 2], it beseems every Christian rather to explain in what sense Christ died for all, than flatly to deny it.[2]

Murray simply perpetuates the traditional misperception of Baxter's theological agenda. No less opposed to Arminian errors, Baxter aimed to establish a *via media, not* between Arminianism and Calvinism, but between Arminianism and Owenism. Murray and his school miss this key point.[3] Also, to charge him with 'undermining the atonement'[4] and virtually inspiring a tradition that 'became Unitarian'[5] is—as I've demonstrated in this book—absurd, malicious and prejudiced nonsense. Murray's own rather deplorable 'Packerian' demolition job on God's faithful servant Richard Baxter reveals how pernicious a false perspective can be. So the question I put to Packer must be put to Murray. Even allowing for the fact that God only ever uses and blesses fallible men, if Baxter was so unsound, how could he be so successful? To concede that 'Baxter did immense good' and that 'His books

1   *Catholick Theologie*, II. 123.
2   *The Universal Redemption of Mankind* (London: 1694), 286.
3   'Reluctant Puritan', 15–16.
4   Ibid. 15.
5   Ibid. 19.

have pointed untold thousands to heaven and helped them there'[1] while castigating his theology as 'disastrous'[2] is arguably a highly-flawed opinion. How can 'disastrous theology' do 'immense good'? Isn't 'immense good' a fruit of 'good theology'?

Finally, to further state that 'Hold fast the form of sound words' is not 'a Baxterian emphasis' and then charge Baxter with emphasising charity at the expense of truth[3] is too ridiculous for words if not utterly outrageous. Concerned with the biblical emphasis on 'speaking the truth in love' (Eph. 4: 15), Baxter's own paraphrase on the text cited by Murray [2 Tim. 1: 13] is a perfect riposte:

> Keep before thee the Form, or Summary of Sound Doctrine which thou heardest of me, which consisteth of the Articles of Faith, and the Precepts of Love, of both which Christ is the Object and Sum, or which form of Sound Doctrine thou must hold fast by a Firm Belief, and Practical Love of Christ and his cause.[4]

This is quintessential Baxter. It is a summary which repays repeated meditation. Thus it is time to stop blaming him for the abuses of those (Arminians, Owenites and Unitarians) who, in later generations, failed to observe his biblical balance.

Returning finally to Calvin, doubtless buoyed up by Paul Helm's *Calvin and the Calvinists* (1982),[5] Murray is evidently unwilling to allow the possibility that seventeenth-century so-called 'Calvinism' is at odds with Calvin's actual teaching. For that reason, when I demonstrated the differences in my *Calvinus: Authentic Calvinism, A Clarification* (1996), an impatient and incoherent review appeared in *The Banner of Truth* magazine.[6] I consequently 'reviewed the review' in the second edition of *Calvinus*.[7]

---

1 Ibid. 17.
2 Ibid. 19.
3 Ibid. 20.
4 *Paraphrase on the New Testament* (London: 1685).
5 I reviewed this publication in the *Evangelical Times* (see this book, Part III, chapter 1, postcript).
6 Iain H. Murray, 'Calvin and the Atonement' in *The Banner of Truth* (November 1996), 17–20.
7 *Calvinus: Authentic Calvinism, A Clarification* (Norwich: Charenton Reformed Publishing, 2007).

THE REVIEW REVIEWED

*See Iain H. Murray, 'Calvin and the Atonement' (*The
Banner of Truth, *November 1996, pp. 17–20).*

Committed to the high orthodoxy of John Owen, the Revd Iain Murray's review of *Calvinus* was predictable. It merely recycles conventional anti-Amyraldian propaganda. Indeed, it shows only a superficial attempt to evaluate the Calvin evidence on which Amyraut's case was based. Since I anticipated and answered all Mr Murray's criticisms, those who take the trouble to study the evidence objectively will rapidly perceive how flawed and inadequate his response is. His disclaimer that the definition of 'authentic Calvinism' is 'a question of little consequence' (p. 20) is not very convincing, since he insists on rescuing Calvin from the imputation of Amyraldianism (pp. 18, 19). Of course, Mr Murray is a victim of the high-orthodox Owenite neurosis that Amyraldianism involves compromise with Arminian error. Thus when he compares the Arminian and Amyraldian versions of the universal and particular features of the gospel, he cannot avoid aligning Amyraldianism with the Arminian view of universal expiation (p. 17). The fact remains that Amyraut derived his distinctives from Calvin and—more importantly—the Bible.

Mr Murray's failure to consider the historical case made by *Calvinus* is not impressive—especially for one who claims to be a historian. His appeal to what he calls 'traditional reformed theology' ignores the fact that Amyraut's position had a precedent in the early Reformed confessions (including the Canons of Dordt) as well as in Calvin. On the subject of the atonement, the *Heidelberg Catechism* (1563), Q. 37, was expounded by its author Dr Zacharias Ursinus using the very 'combination of the universal with the particular' Murray attributes to Amyraut (p. 18). From this historical perspective, Murray's so-called 'traditional reformed theology' was a novelty of the post-Dordt era. His statement that 'God has not chosen to explain how salvation is offered to those for whom it has not been obtained' (p. 18) would have been dismissed as ludicrous by late sixteenth-century Reformed theologians. Even Dr William Twisse, the first prolocutor of the Westminster Assembly could write that 'everyone who hears the gospel (without distinction between elect and reprobate) is bound to believe that Christ has died for him, so far as to procure both the pardon of his sins and the salvation of his soul, in case he believes and repents'. Such is the obvious drift of the New Testament rightly recognised by first and second generation Calvinists. Murray's difficulties derive from erroneous scholastic departures from an earlier and more biblically balanced Calvinism. One wonders what more Calvin should have said to persuade Murray that he taught (besides its certain efficacy for the elect) 'a conditional, hypothetical redemption' for all. The conclusion is obvious: the *Calvinus* evidence has been largely dismissed.

One is encouraged that Mr Murray grants some concessions, a fact which might not please his Owenite friends. Indeed, regarding the view that God still desires the salvation of those whom he decrees finally not to save, Amyraut is a disciple of Calvin (p. 18). Now, if Murray can see this in Calvin, how can he miss the correlative truth that Calvin also taught 'an atonement for all conditionally' (p. 19)? How can he also deny that Calvin taught 'the idea of an atonement decreed for those to whom it is never applied' (p. 19)? The simple truth is that he is unwilling to admit the evidence. At the risk of being tedious, I quote Calvin again: 'The sacrifice [of Christ] was ordained by the eternal decree of God, to expiate the sins of the world' (#31). 'God commends to us the salvation of all men without exception, even as Christ suffered for the sins of the whole world' (#65). 'Although Christ suffered for the sins of the world, and is offered by the goodness of God without distinction to all men, yet not all receive him' (#58). 'God receiveth us to mercy ... upon condition that we return unto God' (#74). 'It is of course certain that not all enjoy the fruits of Christ's death, but this happens because their unbelief hinders them' (#77). What could be clearer?

Anxious to distance Calvin from Amyraut, Mr Murray seeks to refute the latter's view of the divine decree without implicating the former. But clearly, Amyraut derived his 'double decree' doctrine from Calvin (see *Calvinus*, #21, 22, 27, 71–3, 83). Instead of honestly criticising Calvin as well, Murray targets Amyraut by appealing to George Smeaton's criticism of the Amyraldian position (p. 19). We are told that the general and special aspects of the decree are 'conflicting', 'discordant' and 'incoherent' (p. 19), and that Amyraldianism arises from 'confused thought' (p. 20). Such language reveals the incipient rationalism of Smeaton, Murray and others of the Owenite school. Now, unlike Calvin and Amyraut, their rationalist critics are unhappy with paradox. But the conditional and absolute elements in the decree are at worst paradoxical and at best complementary rather than contradictory. The latter would only apply if the two elements involved two absolute divine purposes. Just as Calvin views the divine will (or decree) in a two-fold manner, so does Amyraut. However, exactly like Calvin, Amyraut is anxious to argue that this two-fold will is 'one only act of [God's] eternal and unchangeable will' (*Calvinus*, p. 29). Had Mr Murray read this, he would not have cited John Murray's perfectly acceptable view of the divine will as a futile device to separate Calvin from Amyraut (p. 19).

Mr Murray's unscholarly refusal to discuss the details of the debate is his undoing. His attempt to denigrate my supposed 'mastery of Calvin' (p. 19) unhappily backfires. I am accused of citing Calvin's Commentary on 1 Timothy 2: 4–6 to the neglect of the Reformer's Sermons on the same passage, as if the two expositions conflict. However, the sermons in question are amply quoted in *Calvinus* (#73). Contrary to Murray's rather careless observation, they make the identical point to the Commentary that, in Calvin's view, Paul is not discussing the elective, efficacious will of God as Owen was to maintain. While I do not claim an omniscient mastery of Calvin's writings, I do understand him accurately in this instance, as any careful reader may verify. As for Mr Murray, a slightly more scholarly approach would have been less embarrassing for him; his misinformation does him no credit. Indeed, his patronizing review lacks integrity.

I emphatically do believe 'that a man cannot be a true Calvinist if he fails to believe with Amyraut in a redemption which is both universal and particular' (p. 20). According to authentic Calvinism, the entire Bible presents God's dealings with mankind in both conditional and absolute terms. There clearly is potentiality and actuality in the death of Christ. By itself, it saves no one without the application of the Holy Spirit. Even the elect are not actually saved until the benefits of the atonement are applied to them, notwithstanding God's eternal purpose to do so. Contrary to men of Mr Murray's stamp, Calvin was quite clear about this (see *Calvinus*, #7). As for the oft-lamented dangers of Amyraldianism, it no more inclines towards Arminianism than Owenism does towards hypercalvinism. It is an ungracious and fallacious slur to imply that the gospel is less safe with Amyraldians than with Mr Murray and his friends. Only a combination of arrogance and ignorance can deny that 'the Puritans and their successors' included 'authentic' as well as 'pseudo-Calvinists' like the Revd Iain Murray.

BIBLIOGRAPHY

ALLISON, C. F., *The Rise of Moralism: The Proclamation of the Gospel from Hooker to Baxter* (London: SPCK, 1966).

AMYRAUT, M., *Apologie pour ceux de la Religion Reformeé* (Saumur: Isaac Desbordes, 1647).

—— *Brief Traitté de la predestination et de ses principales dependences* (Saumur: Isaac Desbordes, 1634).

—— *Brief Treatise on Predestination*, trans. Richard Lum (Norwich: Charenton Reformed Pubishing, 2000).

—— *Cinq sermons prononcez a Charenton* (Charenton: A. Cellier, 1658).

—— *Defensio doctrinae J. Calvini de absoluto reprobationis decreto* (Saumur: Isaac Desbordes, 1641).

—— *Defense de la doctrine de Calvin* (Saumur: Isaac Desbordes, 1644).

—— *Discours chrestien sur les eaux de Bourbon* (Charenton: A. Cellier, 1658).

—— *Discours de l'estat des fideles apres la mort* (Saumur: Jean Lesnier, 1646); tr: *The Evidence of things not seen, or Diverse ... Discourses Concerning the State of Good and Holy Men after Death* (London, n. d.).

—— *Discours sur la souveraineté des rois* (Charenton: L. Vendosme, 1650).

—— *Du gouvernement de l'eglise contre ceux qui veulent abolir l'usage & l'autorité des synodes* (Saumur: Isaac Desbordes, 1653; 2nd ed. 1658, *Avec un appendice au livre du gouvernement de l'eglise où il est traité de la puissance des consistoires.*

—— *Traitté des religions contre ceux qui les estiment toutes indifferentes* (Saumur: Girard & de Lerpiniere, 1631); English translation full title: *A Treatise Concerning Religions, in Refutation of the Opinion which accounts all indifferent, wherein is also evinced the necessity of a Particular Revelation, And the Verity and preeminence of the Christian Religion above the Pagan, Mahometan, and Jewish rationally Demonstrated* (London: 1660).

ARISTOTLE, *Metaphysics*, trans. J. Warrington (London: J. M. Dent, 1956).

ARMSTRONG, B. G., *Calvinism and the Amyraut Heresy* (Madison: University of Wisconsin Press, 1969).

Articles of Faith and Rules (Gospel Standard Trust Publications: Harpenden, 2008).

AUGUSTINE, *The City of God* in *Works*, ed. M. Dods (Edinburgh: T & T Clark, 1872), ii.

BAIRD, H., *History of the Rise of the Huguenots* (2 vols.; London: Hodder & Stoughton, 1880).

—— *The Huguenots and Henry of Narvarre* (2 vols.; London: Hodder & Stoughton, 1886).

—— *The Huguenots and the Revocation of the Edict of Nantes* (2 vols.; London: Hodder & Stoughton, 1895).

BARNES, A., *A Popular Family Commentary on the New Testament* (London: Blackie & Son, 1850).

BATES, W., *A Funeral Sermon for the Reverend, Holy and Excellent Divine, Mr Richard Baxter* (London: 1692).

—— *The Whole Works of the Rev. W. Bates, DD*, ed. W. Farmer (4 vols., London: 1815).

BAYLE, P., *The Dictionary Historical and Critical of Mr Peter Bayle* (London: 1734).

BAXTER, R., *A Call to the Unconverted* (London: 1658).

—— *A Defence of Christ and Free Grace* (London: 1690).

—— *A Holy Commonwealth*, ed. W. Lamont (Cambridge: CUP, 1994.

—— *A Paraphrase on the New Testament* (London: 1685).

—— *A Third Defence of the Cause of Peace* (London: 1681).

—— *A Treatise of Justifying Righteousness* (London: 1676)

—— *Aphorismes of Justification* (London: 1649).

—— *An End of Doctrinal Controversies* (London: 1691)

—— *Calendar of the Correspondence of Richard Baxter*, ed. N. H. Keeble and G. F. Nuttall (Oxford: Clarendon Press, 1991), 2 vols.

—— *Catholick Communion Defended* (London: 1684).

—— *Certain Disputations of Right to Sacraments* (London: 1658).

—— *Directions and Persuasions to a Sound Conversion* (London: 1658).

—— *Five Disputations of Church Government* (London: 1659).

—— *Making Light of Christ and Salvation* (London, 1656).

—— *Methodus Theologiae Christianae* (London: 1681)

—— *Reliquiae Baxterianiae* (London: 1696).

—— *Richard Baxter's Catholick Theologie* (London: 1675)

—— *Richard Baxter's Confession of His Faith* (London: 1655),

—— *Sermon on Judgement* (London, 1658).

—— *The Autobiography of Richard Baxter*, ed. J. M. Lloyd Thomas (London: J. M. Dent, 1931).

—— *The Autobiography of Richard Baxter*, ed. N. H. Keeble (London: J. M. Dent, 1985).

—— ed. A. B. Grosart, *The Grand Question Resolved: What We Must Do to be Saved* (Liverpool: 1868).

—— *The Life of Faith* (London: 1660)

—— *The Practical Works of the Rev. Richard Baxter,* ed. W. Orme (London: James Duncan, 1830), i.

—— *The Practical Works of Richard Baxter: Select Treatises* (1863; rep. Grand Rapids, MI: Baker Book House, 1981).

—— *The Protestant Religion Truely Stated and Justified* (London: 1692).

—— *The Reformed Pastor* (Edinburgh: The Banner of Truth Trust, 1974).

—— *The Reasons of the Christian Religion* (London: 1667).

—— *The Saints Everlasting Rest* (London: 1650).

—— *The Saints Everlasting Rest* (London: 7th edn. 1658).

—— *The Saints' Everlasting Rest* (London: Religious Tract Society, 1833).

—— *The Saints' Everlasting Rest*, ed. John T. Wilkinson (Vancouver, BC: Regent College Publishing, 2004).

—— *The Scripture-Gospel Defended* (London: 1690).

—— *The Universal Redemption of Mankind* (London: 1694).

—— Universal Redemption at http://quintapress.macmate.me/PDF_Books/Universal_Redemption.pdf

—— *Two Disputations of Original Sin* (London: 1675)

BECKERLEGGE, O. A., *John Wesley's Writings on Roman Catholicism* (London: Protestant Truth Society, n.d.).

BEEKE, J. R., and JONES, M., *A Puritan Theology: Doctrine for Life* (Grand Rapids, MI: Reformation Heritage Books, 2012).

—— *Reading the Puritans* at https://www.uniontheology.org/resources/historical/reading-the-puritans

BELLAMY, J., *True Religion Delineated* (Edinburgh, 1788).

BENEDICT, P., *The Faith and Fortunes of France's Huguenots, 1600–85* (Aldershot: Ashgate, 2001).

BERKHOF, L., *Systematic Theology* (London: The Banner of Truth Trust, 1958).

BEZA, T., *Tractationes theologiae* (Geneva: 1570–82), iii.

BIERMA, L. D., trans. and ed., *A Firm Foundation: An Aid to Interpreting the*

Heidelberg Catechism (Grand Rapids/Carlisle: Baker Books/Paternoster Press 1995).

BLACKETER, R., 'Definite Atonement in Historical Perspective' in *The Glory of the Atonement*, ed. Charles Hill & Frank James (Downers Grove, Illinois: Inter Varsity Press, 2004).

BOERSMA, H., *A Hot Pepper Corn: Richard Baxter's Doctrine of Justification in Its Seventeenth-Century Context of Controversy* (Zoetermeer: Uitgeverij Boekencentrum, 1993).

BOLAM, C.G., GORING J., SHORT, H. L., and THOMAS R., *The English Presbyterians: From Elizabethan Puritanism to Modern Unitarianism* (London: G. Allen and Unwin, 1968).

BOND, David. F, 'Amyraldianism and Assurance' in *Christ for the World*, 2006 Amyraldian Association Conference Report, ed. Alan C. Clifford (Norwich: Charenton Reformed Publishing, 2007).

BOSWELL, J., *Boswell's Life of Johnson* (2 vols., 1791; London: Heron Books, 1960).

BREADY, J. W., *England: Before and After Wesley* (London: Hodder & Stoughton, 1939).

BUCHANAN, C. O., MASCALL, E. L., PACKER, J. I., The Bishop of Willesdon, *Growing into Union* (London: SPCK, 1970).

BUICK-KNOX, R., 'John Calvin—An Elusive Churchman' in *The Scottish Journal of Theology*, Vol. 34, (1981).

CALAMY, E., *A Caveat Against the New Prophets* (London: 1708).

—— *A Defence of Moderate Nonconformity* (London: 1703).

—— *A Practical Discourse concerning Vows: with a special reference to Baptism and the Lord's Supper* (London: 1704).

—— *An Abridgement of Mr Baxter's History of His Life and Times with An account of the Ministers ... who were Ejected after the Restoration of King Charles II* (London: 1702).

—— *An Abridgement Mr Baxter's History of his Life and Times*, first edition, 1702 at http://quintapress.macmate.me/PDF_Books/Calamy_1702_Text.pdf

—— *An Abridgement of Mr Baxter's History of His Life and Times*, (London: 2nd edn. 1713).

—— *An Abridgement Mr Baxter's History of his Life and Times*, second edition, Volume 1, 1713 at http://quintapress.macmate.me/PDF_Books/Calamy_1713_Volume_1_Text_v2.pdf

—— *An Historical Account of My Own Life* (London: Henry Colburn and Richard Bentley, 1830), i.

—— *Divine Mercy Exalted: or Free Grace in its Glory* (London: 1703).

—— *God's Concern for His Glory in the British Isles and The Security of Christ's Church from the Gates of Hell* (London: 1715).

—— *The Inspiration of the Holy Writings of the Old and New Testament* (London: 1710).

—— *The Practical Works of the Late Reverend and Pious Mr Richard Baxter* (4 vols.; London: 1707).

—— *The Principles and Practice of Moderate Nonconformists with Respect to Ordination* (London: 1717).

Calamy Revised, ed. A.G. Matthews (Oxford: Clarendon Press, 1934).

CALVIN, J., *Commentaries on the First Twenty Chapters of the Book of the Prophet Ezekiel*, trans. T. Myers (2 vols. Edinburgh: The Calvin translation Society, 1850).

—— *Concerning the Eternal Predestination of God*, trans. J. K. S. Reid (London: James Clarke, 1961).

—— *Institutes of the Christian Religion*, trans. H. Beveridge (2 vols.; London: James Clarke, 1962).

—— *Tracts and Treatises* (3 vols; Edinburgh: Calvin Translation Society, 1851).

—— *Sermons on Isaiah's Prophecy*, trans. T. H. L. Parker (London: James Clarke, 1956).

—— *Sermons on Job* (facs: Edinburgh: Banner of Truth Trust, 1993).

—— *Calvin's Commentaries*, ed. D. W. and T. F. Torrance (12 vols; Edinburgh: Oliver & Boyd, 1959–72).

—— *Sermons on the Epistle to the Ephesians*, trans. A. Golding, rev. L. Rawlinson and S. M. Houghton (Edinburgh: The Banner of Truth Trust, 1973).

—— *Sermons on the Saving Work of Christ*, trans. L. Nixon (Grand Rapids: Baker Book House, 1950).

—— *Sermons on Timothy and Titus*, tr. L. T. [sic] (1579; fac. Edinburgh, 1983).

CAPILL, M. A., *Preaching With Spiritual Vigour, Including Lessons from the Life and Practice of Richard Baxter* (Fearn, Ross-shire: Mentor, Christian focus Publications, 2003).

CHALMERS, T., *Institutes of Theology* (Edinburgh: Sutherland & Knox, 1849), ii.

CLARK, R. S., *Burying The Lead On Baxter: Baxter's doctrine of justification* at http://theaquilareport.com/burying-the-lead-on-baxter/#.Vknkzb6LqnE. facebook

CLIFFORD, A., *Methodus Evangelica; or, the Gospel Method of God's Saving Sinners by Jesus Christ* (London: 1676).

CLIFFORD, A. C., *Amyraut Affirmed, or Owenism, a caricature of Calvinism* (Norwich: Charenton Reformed Publishing, 2004).

—— *Atonement and Justification: English Evangelical Theology 1640–1790—An Evaluation* (Oxford: Clarendon Press, 1990).

—— 'Calvin & Calvinism: Amyraut et al', in *John Calvin 500: A Reformation Affirmation*, ed. A. C. Clifford (Norwich: Charenton Reformed Publishing, 2011).

—— *Calvin Celebrated: The Genevan Reformer & His Huguenot Sons* (Norwich: Charenton Reformed Publishing, 2009).

—— *CALVINUS: Authentic Calvinism—A Clarification* (Norwich: Charenton Reformed Publishing, 1996; 2nd ed. 2009.

—— ed. *Christ for the World*, Amyraldian Association Conference Report (Norwich: Charenton Reformed Publishing, 2007).

—— 'Geneva Revisited or Calvinism Revised', in *Churchman* 100. 4 (London: Church Society, 1986).

—— *John Jones Talsarn—Pregethwr Y Bobl/The People's Preacher* (Norwich: Charenton Reformed Publishing, 2013).

—— 'Jonathan Edwards—Amyraldian?' at http://www.nrchurch.co.uk/pdf/Jonathan%20Edwards%20Amyraldian.pdf.

—— 'Justification: the Calvin-Saumur Perspective', *The Evangelical Quarterly*, 79. 4 (2007).

—— *My Debt to the Doctor* (Norwich: Charenton Reformed Publishing, 2009).

—— 'Mulling over Muller' (2015) at http://www.nrchurch.co.uk/pdf/Mulling%20over%20Muller.pdf.

—— *Not in Word only—the Forgotten Doddridge* (Westminster Conference, 1972).

—— 'Philip Doddridge and the Oxford Methodists' in *Proceedings of the Wesley Historical Society*, XLII. 3 (1979).

—— Review of Owen Thomas, trans. John Aaron, *The Atonement Controversy in Welsh Theological Literature and Debate, 1701–1841* (Edinburgh: The Banner of Truth Trust, 2002) in *The Evangelical Quarterly*, Vol. 77.2 (2005).

—— 'The Christian Mind of Philip Doddridge (1702–1751) or The Gospel According to an Evangelical Congregationalist', *The Evangelical Quarterly* 56.4 (1984).

—— *The Good Doctor: Philip Doddridge of Northampton—A Tercentenary Tribute* (Norwich: Charenton Reformed Publishing, 2002).

—— 'The Gospel and Justification' (Norwich: 2016 at at http://www.nrchurch.co.uk/

CLIFFORD, S., *An Account of the Judgement of the Late Reverend Mr. Baxter* (London: 1701).

Christian Hymns (Bridgend: Evangelical Movement of Wales, 1977).

Confession of Faith of the Calvinistic Methodists or the Presbyterians of Wales (Caernarfon: D. O. Owen, 1900).

COOPER, T., *John Owen, Richard Baxter and the Formation of Nonconformity* (Farnham, Surrey: Ashgate, 2011).

—— 'Why Did Richard Baxter and John Owen Diverge? The Impact of The First Civil War' in *The Journal of Ecclesiastical History*, 61.3 (Cambridge: CUP, 2010).

CRISP, T., *Christ Alone Exalted* (London: 1643; rep. 1690).

CUNNINGHAM, W., *Historical Theology* (2 vols; 1862, rep. London: The Banner of Truth Trust, 1960).

—— *The Reformers and the Theology of the Reformation* (1862; fac. Edinburgh: The Banner of Truth Trust, 1967).

DABNEY, R. L., *Discussions: Evangelical and Theological* (London: The Banner of Truth Trust, 1967 rep.) ii.

DANIEL, C., 'John Gill and Hypercalvinism' (Unpublished Ph.D. thesis, Edinburgh, 1983).

DAVENANT, J., *Animadversions written by the Right Rev. Father in God, John, Lord Bishop of Salisbury, upon a treatise intituled, God's Love to Mankind* (Cambridge, 1641).

—— *Dissertationes Duae; prima, de Morte Christi; altera, De Praedestinatione et Electione, &c* (Cambridge, 1650) in *An Exposition of the Epistle of St Paul to the Colossians*, tr. J. Allport (London: Hamilton, Adams & Co., 1831), 2 vols.

—— *Dissertation on the Death of Christ* (Weston Rhyn, Oswestry, Shropshire: Quinta Press, 2006).

DAVIES, E., *The Beddgelert Revival* (Bridgend: Bryntirion Press, 2004).

DEACON, M., *Philip Doddridge of Northampton* (Northampton: Northamptonshire Libraries, 1980).

Dictionary of National Biography (1885–).

DE WITT, J. R., 'The Arminian Conflict and the Synod of Dort' in *The Manifold Grace of God* (Puritan Conference Report, 1968).

DODDRIDGE, P., *Calendar of the Correspondence of Philip Doddridge, DD (1702–1751)*, ed. G. F. Nuttall (London: HMSO, 1979).

—— *Correspondence and Diary of Philip Doddridge, DD*, ed J. D. Humphreys (5 vols.; London: H. Colburn and R. Bentley, 1829–30).

—— *Free Thoughts on the most probable means of reviving the Dissenting Interest* (London: 1730).

—— *Sermons on Various Subjects* (4 vols.; London: J. Hatchard & Son, 1826).

—— *The Works of the Rev. P. Doddridge, D. D.* ed. E. Williams and E. Parsons (Leeds: 1804).

DONNELLY, E., 'Richard Baxter—A Corrective for Reformed Preachers' in *The Banner of Truth Magazine*, 166–7 (July-August 1977).

DRYSDALE, A. H., 'Dr Edmund Calamy' in *Short Biographies for the People by Various Writers* (London: Religious Tract society, 1890).

—— *History of the Presbyterians in England* (London: Pubication Committee of the Presbyterian Church of England, 1889).

EVANS, E., *Daniel Rowland and the Great Evangelical Awakening in Wales* (Edinburgh: The Banner of Truth Trust, 1985).

—— 'Richard Baxter's Influence in Wales' in *The National Library of Wales Journal/Cylchgrawn Llyfrgell Genedlaethol Cymru*, XXXIII. 2 (2003).

EVERITT, A., 'Philip Doddridge and the Evangelical Tradition' in *Philip Doddridge: Nonconformity and Northampton*, ed. R. L. Greenall (Leicester: University of Leicester, 1981).

EVESON, P. H., *The Great Exchange: Justification by faith alone in the light of recent discussion* (Bromley, Kent: Day One Publications, 1996).

—— P. H., *Matthew Henry* (Darlington: EP Books, 2012).

FIELD, D. P., *Rigide Calvinisme in a Softer Dresse: The Moderate Presbyterianism of John Howe (1630–1705)* (Edinburgh: Rutherford House, 2004).

FISHER, G. P., *History of Christian Doctrine* (Edinburgh: T. & T. Clark, 1896).

—— *The History of the Christian Church* (London: Hodder and Stoughton, 1904).

—— 'The Writings of Richard Baxter' in *Bibliotheca sacra*, 9 (London, 1851).

FLAVEL, J., *The Works of John Flavel* (London: The Banner of Truth Trust, 1968), iv.

FULLER, A., *The Gospel Worthy of All Acceptation* in *Works,* ed. A. G. Fuller (London: Holdsworth & Ball, 1824), i.

—— *Works,* ed. A. G. Fuller (1841, rep. Edinburgh: The Banner of Truth Trust, 2007).

FULLER, M., *The Life, Letters & Writings of John Davenant, DD* (London: Methuen, 1897).

GATISS, L., *For Us and For Our Salvation—'Limited Atonement' in the Bible, Doctrine, History and Ministry* (London: The Latimer Trust, 2012).

GAY, D. H. J., *Four Antinomians Tried and Vindicated* (NP: Brachus, 2013).

GIBSON, J., 'Definite atonement' in *Evangelicals Now* (March 2014).

GIBSON, D., GIBSON J. (eds.), *From Heaven He came and Sought Her: Definite Atonement in Historical, Biblical, Theological and Pastoral Perspective* (Wheaton, Illinois: Crossway, 2013).

GOODWIN, J., *Imputatio Fidei, or a Treatise of Justification* (London: 1642).

—— *Redemption Redeemed* (London: 1651).

GRANT, A. J., *The Huguenots* (London: Thornton Butterworth/Oxford: OUP, 1934).

GREENALL, R. L. (ed.), *Philip Doddridge: Nonconformity and Northampton* (Leicester: University of Leicester, 1981).

GROSART, A. B., 'Baxter, Richard' in *The Dictionary of National Biography* (Oxford: Clarendon Press, 1885–1900), iii.

—— *Annotated List of the Writings of Richard Baxter* (Liverpool: 1868).

GWYN, R. D., *Huguenot Heritage: The history and contribution of the Huguenots in Britain* (London: Routledge, 1985).

HALDANE, R., *Exposition of the Epistle to the Romans* (London: The Banner of Truth Trust, 1958).

HAMILTON, I., *Amyraldianism—is it modified Calvinism?* (Worcester: Evangelical Presbyterian Church in England and Wales, 2003).

HANNA, W., *Memoirs of Thomas Chalmers, DD, LlD* (Edinburgh: Thomas Constable and Co., 1854), ii.

HARDING, M. S., *A critical analysis of Moïse Amyraut's atonement theory based on a new and critical translation of a Brief Treatise on Predestination* (Unpublished Ph.D. thesis, South–Western Baptist Theological Seminary, 2014).

HARMAN, A. M., *Matthew Henry: His Life and Influence* (Fearn, Tain, Ross-shire: Christian Focus Publications, 2012).

—— *Matthew Henry's Unpublished Sermons on the Covenant of Grace*, ed. Allan Harman (Fearn, Tain, Ross-shire: Christian Focus Publications, 2002).

HEATH, R., *The Reformation in France* (2 vols.; London: The Religious Tract Society, 1886).

HELM, P., *Calvin and the Calvinists* (Edinburgh: The Banner of Truth Trust, 1982).

—— 'Calvin, English Calvinism and the Logic of Doctrinal Development', *The Scottish Journal of Theology*, 34. 2 (1981).

HENRY, M., *Exposition of the Old and New Testaments* (9 vols.; London: James Nisbet, 1886).

—— *The Complete Works of Matthew Henry—Treatises, Sermons, and Tracts* (2 vols.; Grand Rapids: Michigan: Baker Books, 1997).

HILL, C., *The Century of Revolution, 1603–1714* (London: Nelson, 1961).

HOARD, S., *God's Love to Mankind, manifested by disproving his absolute Decree for their Damnation* (London: 1633).

HODGE, C., *Systematic Theology* (London: J. Clarke, 1960 rep.), ii.

HOLT, M. P., (ed.), *Renaissance and Reformation in France* (Oxford: OUP, 2002).

HOOKER, R., *Laws of Ecclesiastical Polity* in *Works*, ed. J. Keble (Oxford: Clarendon Press, 1836), iii.

HOOPER, J., *Later Writings of Bishop Hooper* (Cambridge: Parker Society, 1852).

HOWE, J., 'Man's Enmity to God and Reconciliation between God and Man' in *Works of the English Puritan Divines: John Howe* (London: Thomas Nelson, 1846).

HUGHES, R. (ed.), *Memoir and Sermons of the Late Rev. David Lloyd Jones, MA, Llandinam* (Wrexham: Hughes and Son, 1912).

HUME, D., *A Treatise of Human Nature*, 2 vols. (London: J. M. Dent, 1962).

JAMES, D., 'Richard Baxter 1615–1691', The Evangelical Library Lecture 2015 in *in writing*, The Evangelical Library (London: 2016).

JENKINS, D. Ll., 'Amyraut on other Religions' in *Christ for the World*, 2006 Amyraldian Association Conference Report (Norwich: Charenton Reformed Publishing, 2007).

—— *Saumur Redux: Josué de la Place & the Question of Adam's Sin* (Harleston, Norfolk: Leaping Cat Press, 2008).

JENKYN, T. W., 'Essay on His Life, Ministry and Theology' in *Richard Baxter, Making Light of Christ*, etc. (New York: Wiley & Putnam, 1846).

JEWEL, J., *Apologia Ecclesiae Anglicanae* in *Works* (Cambridge: Parker Society, 1848).

JINKINS, M., 'Theodore Beza: Continuity and Regression in the Reformed Tradition', *The Evangelical Quarterly* (64. 2) 1992.

JONES, E., WILLIAMS, J., WILLIAMS, T. C., *Cofiant a Phregethau Y Diweddar Barch. David Lloyd Jones, MA Llandinam* (Gwrecsam: Hughes A'i Fab, 1908).

JONES, H. R., 'The Death of Presbyterianism' in *By Schisms Rent Asunder* (London: Puritan and Reformed Studies Conference, 1969).

JONES, J. M., & MORGAN W., trans. John Aaron, *The Calvinistic Methodist Fathers of Wales* (Edinburgh: The Banner of Truth Trust, 2008), ii.

JONES, O., *Some the Great Preachers of Wales* (London: Passmore & Alabaster, 1885).

JONES, R. T., *John Elias—Prince Amongst Preachers* (Bridgend: The Evangelical Library of Wales, 1975).

KEEBLE, N. H., *Richard Baxter: Puritan Man of Letters* (Oxford: Clarendon Press, 1982).

KENDALL, R. T., *Calvin and English Calvinism to 1649* (Oxford: OUP, 1979).

KLAUBER, M. I., *Between Reformed Scholasticism and Pan-Protestantism: Jean-Alphonse Turretin (1671–1737) and Enlightened Orthodoxy at the Academy of Geneva* (Selinsgrove: Susquehanna University Press/London and Toronto: Associated University Presses, 1994).

—— *The Theology of the French Reformed Churches from Henri IV to the Revocation of the Edict of Nantes* (Grand Rapids, Michigan: Reformation Heritage Books, 2014).

LABROUSSE, E., *Bayle* (Oxford: OUP, 1983).

LADELL, A. R., *Richard Baxter: Puritan and Mystic* (London: SPCK, 1925).

LATIMER, H., *Sermons* (Cambridge: Parker Society, 1844).

LARROQUE, M., *The Conformity of the Ecclesiastical Discipline of the Reformed Churches of France with that of the Primitive Christians* (London: 1691).

LLOYD-JONES, D. M., *The Puritans: Their Origins and Successors* (Edinburgh: The Banner of Truth Trust, 1987).

LYNCH, J. E. H., 'Evangelistic Preaching—Amyraldian Style!' in *Christ for the World*, 2006 Amyraldian Association Conference Report, ed. Alan C. Clifford (Norwich: Charenton Reformed Publishing, 2007).

—— *Lamb Of God—Saviour Of The World: The Soteriology Of Rev. Dr David Martyn Lloyd-Jones* (Bloomington: WestBow Press, 2015).

MACAULAY, Lord, *History of England,* intr. A. G. Dickens (London: Heron Books, 1967), i.

MCGONIGLE, H. B., *Sufficient Saving Grace: John Wesley's Evangelical Arminianism* (Carlisle: Paternoster Press, 2001).

MARCHANT, J., *Dr. John Clifford, CH—Life, Letters and Reminiscences* (London: Cassell and Company, 1924).

MARTIN, H., *Puritanism and Richard Baxter* (London: SCM, 1954).

Methodist Hymn Book (London: Methodist Conference, 1933).

MITCHELL, A. F., STRUTHERS, J., eds., *Minutes of the Sessions of the Westminster Assembly of Divines* (Edinburgh: Blackwood, 1874).

MOORE, J. D., 'Theodore Beza (1519–1605)' in *Evangelical Times* (November, 2005).

—— *English hypothetical Universalism: John Preston and the Softening of Reformed Theology* (Grand Rapids, Michingan/Cambridge, UK: William B. Eerdmans Publishing Company, 2007).

MORGAN, E., *John Elias: Life, Letters and Essays* (Edinburgh: The Banner of Truth Trust, 1973).

MULLER, R. A., *Christ and the Decree* (Grand Rapids: Baker Book House, 1988).

—— *Post Reformation Reformed Dogmatics: ca. 1520 to ca. 1725*, 2nd ed. (4 vols.; Grand Rapids: Baker Book House, 2003).

—— 'Philip Doddridge and the Formulation of Calvinistic Theology in an Era of Rationalism and Deconfessionalization' in R. D. Cornwall and W. Gibson (eds.), *Religion, Politics and Dissent, 1660–1832* (Aldershot: Ashgate, 2010).

—— *The Unaccommodated Calvin* (Oxford: OUP, 2000).

MURRAY, I. H., *D. Martyn Lloyd-Jones: The Fight of Faith 1939–1981* (Edinburgh: Banner of Truth Trust, 1990).

—— *'Richard Baxter—the Reluctant Puritan?'* (Thornton Heath, Surrey: Westminster Conference report, 1991).

—— *J. C. Ryle: Prepared to Stand Alone* (Edinburgh: The Banner of Truth Trust, 2016).

—— 'Pink on the Sovereignty of God' in *The Banner of Truth* (January 2013).

—— *The Forgotten Spurgeon* (Edinburgh: The Banner of Truth Trust (1966 repr. 1994).

NEWTON, J., 'The Lamb of God, the Great Atonement' in *The Works of John Newton*, (1820; fac. Edinburgh: Banner of Truth Trust, 1985), iv.

NICOLE, R., 'John Calvin's view of the Extent of the Atonement' in *The Westminster Theological Journal*, Vol. 47 (1985).

NICOLE, R., *'Moyse Amyraut (1596–1664) and the Controversy on Universal Grace, First Phase (1634–1637)'* (Ph.D. Dissertation, Harvard University, 1966).

NIMMO, P. T. & D. A. S. FERGUSON, *Reformed Theology* (Cambridge: CUP, 2016).

NUTTALL, G. F., 'Chandler, Doddridge and the Archbishop: A study in eighteenth-century ecumenism', *Journal of the URC History Society*, Vol. 1, No. 2 (1973).

—— 'Doddridge's Life and Times', in *Philip Doddridge, His Contribution to English Religion*, ed. Geoffrey F. Nuttall (London: Independent Press, 1951).

—— and O. Chadwick (eds.), *From Uniformity to Unity* (London: SPCK, 1962).

—— *Richard Baxter and Philip Doddridge: a Study in a Tradition* (London: Dr Williams's Library, 1954).

—— *Richard Baxter* (London: Nelson, 1965).

—— 'The Personality of Richard Baxter' in *The Puritan Spirit: Essays and Addresses* (London: Epworth Press, 1967).

ORTON, J., *Memoir of the Life, Character and Writings of the late Rev. P Doddridge, DD of Northampton* (1766), in Doddridge, *Works*, ed. Williams and Parsons (Leeds: 1802–5), i.

OWEN, J., The *Works of John Owen, DD*, ed. W. H. Goold (Edinburgh: Johnstone & Hunter, 1850).

OWEN, W. T., *Edward Williams, DD—His Life, Thought and Influence* (Cardiff: University of Wales Press, 1963).

PACKER, J. I., 'A Letter from 1958' in *The Banner of Truth*, 629 (February 2016).

—— 'Arminianisms' in *The Manifold Grace of God* (Puritan and Reformed Studies Conference, 1968)

—— 'Calvin the Theologian' in *John Calvin*, ed. G. Duffield (Abingdon: Sutton Courtenay Press, 1966).

—— *'Fundamentalism' and the Word of God* (London: Inter-Varsity Fellowship, 1958).

—— *Evangelism and the Sovereignty of God* (London: Inter-Varsity Fellowship, 1961).

—— 'James Buchanan and the Doctrine of Justification' in *The Banner of Truth*, 635–6 (August–September 2016).

—— 'Introductory Essay' to John Owen, *The Death of Death in the Death of Christ* (London: The Banner of Truth Trust, 1959).

—— 'John Owen on Spiritual-Mindedness' in *The Banner of Truth*, 620 (May 2015).

—— 'The Doctrine of Justification in Development and Decline among the Puritans' in *By Schisms Rent Asunder* (Puritan and Reformed Studies Conference, 1969).

—— 'The Redemption and Restoration of Man in the Thought of Richard Baxter', D. Phil. thesis (Oxford, 1954).

—— *The Redemption and Restoration of Man in the Thought of Richard Baxter* (Vancouver, BC: Regent College Publishing, 2003).

PARKER, I., *The Dissenting Academics in England* (Cambridge: CUP, 1914).

PAYNE, E., 'The Hymns of Philip Doddridge' in *Philip Doddridge: Nonconformity and Northampton*, ed. R. L. Greenall (Leicester: University of Leicester, 1981).

PITTION, J.-P., 'Intellectual life in the Académie of Saumur, 1633–1685 (Unpublished Ph.D. thesis, Trinity College, Dublin, 1970).

POWICKE, F. J., *A Life of the Reverend Richard Baxter 1615–1691* (London: Jonathan Cape, 1924).

—— *Richard Baxter Under the Cross* (London: Jonathan Cape Ltd, 1927).

—— The Life of the Reverend Richard Baxter (1662–1691) at http://quintapress.macmate.me/PDF_Books/Life_of_Baxter.pdf

—— The Reverend Richard Baxter Under the Cross (1662–1691) at http://quintapress.macmate.me/PDF_Books/Under_the_Cross.pdf

PRATT, J. (ed.), *The Thought of the Evangelical Leaders* (Edinburgh: The Banner of Truth Trust, 1978).

PRESTWICH, M., 'The Huguenots under Richelieu and Mazarin, 1629–61: A Golden Age?' in Irene Scouloudi, ed., *Huguenots in Britain and their French Background, 1550–1800* (London: Macmillan Press, 1987).

QUICK, J., *Icones Sacrae Galllicanae* (on deposit at London: Dr Williams's Library, 1700).

—— *Synodicon in Gallia Reformata* (2 vols.; London: 1692).

—— *The Triumph of Faith* (London: 1698).

QUINTON, S. M., 'The Object of Faith in the Theology of John Owen and Richard Baxter' in *Christ for the World*, 2006 Amyraldian Association Conference Report, ed. Alan C. Clifford (Norwich: Charenton Reformed Publishing, 2007).

REYMOND, R. L., *New Systematic Theology of the Christian Faith* (Nashville: Thomas Nelson, 1998).

ROBERTS, M., 'Richard Baxter and His Gospel' in *The Banner of Truth Magazine*, 339 (December 1991).

ROUTLEY, E., 'The Hymns of Philip Doddridge' in *Philip Doddridge, His Contribution to English Religion*, ed. Geoffrey F. Nuttall (London: Independent Press, 1951).

ROWLAND, D., *Three Sermons upon practical subjects* (London: 1778).

—— *Eight sermons upon practical subjects* (London: 1774).

RUSSELL, B., *History of Western Philosophy* (London: George Allen & Unwin, 1961).

RYLE, J. C., *Christian Leaders of the Eighteenth Century* (Edinburgh: The Banner of Truth Trust, 1978).

—— *Expository Thoughts on the Gospels: St John* (London: W. Hunt & Co., 1865), i.

—— *Knots Untied* (London: James Clarke, 1964).

—— 'Richard Baxter' in *Light from Old Times* (London: Chas. J. Thynne, 1902).

—— *Ryle on Redemption: The Gospel According to John Charles Ryle*, ed. Alan C. Clifford (Norwich: Charenton Reformed Publishing, 2014).

SAMUEL, D. N., *'Christ Alone Exalted': Themes in the preaching of Tobias Crisp, D.D.* (Ramsgate: The Harrison Trust, 2008).

SCHAFF, P., *The History of the Christian Church* (Edinburgh: T. & T. Clark, 1883), viii.

SCOTT, T., *Theological Works* (London: 1839).

SELL, A. P. F., *The Great Debate* (Worthing: Walter, 1982).

Sermons or Homilies (London: Prayer-Book and Homily Society, 1833).

SILVERSIDES, D., 'The Biblical Doctrine of the Atonement' in *English Churchman* (7927, 10 July 2015).

SMILES, S., *The Huguenots in France after the Revocation of the Edict of Nantes* (London: Daldy, Isbister & Co., 1875).

—— *The Huguenots—their settlements, churches, and industries in England and Ireland* (London: John Murray, 1880).

SMITH, H. B., and SCHAFF, P., *The Creeds of the Evangelical Protestant Churches*, (London: Hodder & Stoughton, 1877).

SNODDY, R., *The Soteriology of James Ussher: The Act and Object of Saving Faith* (Oxford: OUP, 2014).

SPURGEON, C. H., *Commenting & Commentaries* (London: The Banner of Truth Trust, 1969).

STANFORD, C., *Philip Doddridge* (London: Hodder & Stoughton, 1880).

STOUGHTON, J., *Religion in England under Queen Anne and the Georges 1702–1800* (London: Hodder and Stoughton, 1878).

STREHLE, S. A., *The Extent of the Atonement Within the Theological Systems of the Sixteenth and seventeenth Centuries* (Unpublished Ph.D. dissertation, Dallas Theological seminary (1980).

STRIVENS, R., *Philip Doddridge and the Shaping of Evangelical Dissent* (Farnham, Surrey: Ashgate, 2015).

—— 'Richard Baxter and his Legacy' in *Authentic Calvinism?* (Dewsbury: Westminster Conference Report, 2014).

STRONG, A. H., *Systematic Theology* (New York: A. C. Armstrong, 1891).

SYLVESTER, M., *Elisha's Cry after Elijah's God* (London, 1696).

THOMAS, G., 'Edward Williams and the Rise of "Modern Calvinism"', *The Banner of Truth* (January, 1971; March, 1971).

THOMAS, G. M., *The Extent of the Atonement: A Dilemma for Reformed Theology from Calvin to the Consensus* (Carlisle: Paternoster Press, 1997).

THOMAS, O., trans. John Aaron, *The Atonement Controversy in Welsh Theological Literature and Debate, 1701–1841* (Edinburgh: The Banner of Truth Trust, 2002).

THOMAS, R., 'Doddridge and Liberalism' in *Philip Doddridge, His Contribution to English Religion*, ed. Geoffrey F. Nuttall (London: Independent Press, 1951).

TOPLADY, A. M., *Diary and Hymns of Augustus Toplady* (London: Gospel Standard Baptist Trust, 1969).

TORRANCE, J. B., 'The Incarnation and Limited Atonement' in *The Evangelical Quarterly*, Vol. 55 (April 1983).

TRAILL, R., *Justification Vindicated* (Edinburgh: The Banner of Truth Trust, 2002),

TREASURE, G., *The Huguenots* (New Haven and London: Yale University Press, 2013).

TRUEMAN, C. R., *The Claims of Truth: John Owen's Trinitarian Theology* (Carlisle: Paternoster Press, 1998).

TYACKE, N., *Anti-Calvinists: The Rise of English Arminianism c. 1590–1640* (Oxford: Clarendon Press, 1987).

URSINUS, Z., *The Commentary of Dr Zacharias Ursinus on the Heidelberg Catechism*, ed. G. W. Williard (Columbus, Ohio, 1852; fac. Phillipsburg, NJ: Presbyterian and Reformed Publishing Company, 1985).

VAN STAM, F. P., *The Controversy over the Theology of Saumur, 1635–1650: Disrupting Debates among the Huguenots in Complicated Circumstances* (Amsterdam & Maarsen: APA–Holland University Press, 1988).

WAKEMAN, H. O., *The Ascendancy of France, 1598–1715* (London: Rivingtons, 1959).

WARDLAW, R., *Discourses on the Nature and Extent of the Atonement of Christ* (Glasgow: Blackie, 1854).

WATKINS, O. C., *The Puritan Experience* (London: Routledge & Kegan Paul, 1972).

WATTS, I., *An Humble Attempt towards the Revival of Practical Religion among Christians, and particularly the Protestant Dissenters* (London: 1731).

—— *The Works of The Revd and Learned Isaac Watts, DD*, ed. D. Jennings and P. Doddridge (London: 1753), vi.

WESLEY, J., *Works of the Rev. John Wesley* (14 vols.; London: John Mason, 1842).

—— *The Doctrine of Salvation, Faith, and Good Works, Extracted from the Homilies of the Church of England* (London: 1738).

—— *The Journal of the Revd John Wesley, AM*, ed. N. Curnock (8 vols.; London: Epworth Press, 1909–16), v.

—— *The Letters of the Revd John Wesley, AM*, ed. J. Telford (8 vols.; London: Epworth Press, 1931), v.

WHITEFIELD, G., *George Whitefield's Journals*, ed. I. H. Murray (London: The Banner of Truth Trust, 1960).

—— *Select Sermons of George Whitefield* (London: The Banner of Truth Trust, 1959).

WILBERFORCE, R. I. and S., *The Life of William Wilberforce* (London: John Murray, 1838), i.

WILLIAMS, E., *A Defence of Modern Calvinism* (London: James Black, 1812).

—— *An Essay on the Equity of Divine Government, and the Sovereignty of Divine Grace* (London: J. Burditt, 1809).

WILLIAMS, G. J., 'The Definite Intent of Penal Substitutionary Atonement' and 'Punishment God Cannot Twice Inflict' in *From Heaven He Came and Sought Her: Definite Atonement in Historical, Biblical, Theological and Pastoral Perspective*, ed. David & Jonathan Gibson (Wheaton, Illinois: Crossway, 2013).

WILLIAMS, J. B., *Memoir of the Life, Character and Writings of the Revd Matthew Henry* ([1828] repr. Edinburgh: The Banner of Truth Trust, 1974).

WRIGHT, T., *The Life of Isaac Watts* (London: Farncombe & Sons, 1914).

WYKES, D. L., 'Calamy, Edmund (1671–1732)', *Oxford Dictionary of National Biography* (Oxford University Press, 2004).

INDEX OF SCRIPTURE

INDEX OF NAMES

A

B

M

N

O

P

Q

R

Rees, Henry   356, 359, 373
Reid, J. K. S.   231
Richard, Thomas   371
Richelieu, Cardinal   256, 258, 263, 264
Ridley, Nicholas   347
Roberts, John (Llanbryn-mair)   362
Roberts, Maurice   27
Roberts, Robert (Rhosllannerchrugog)   368, 372
Robinson, B. (Hungerford)   91
Rouse, Sir Thomas   10
Rouwendal, Pieter   391
Rowland, Daniel   353, 354, 368, 374, 376, 378, 379
Russell, Bertrand   283, 387
Russell, William   253
Ryle, J. C.   26, 220, 246, 247, 284, 285, 354, 355, 378, 385, 399, 407–422

S

Saurin, Jacques   63, 296
Schreiner, Thomas   383
Sell, Alan   216
Servetus, Michael   343
Sibbes, Richard   9
Smeaton, George   234, 421
Smiles, Samuel   251
Snoddy, Richard   397
Socinus, Faustus   283
Spurgeon, C. H.   7, 276, 284, 285, 395
Stam, Frans Pieter van   253, 257
Stanford, Charles   323
Stillingfleet, Edward   76
Stone, Samuel John   382
Strange, Daniel   383

Strivens, Robert   27, 321
Strong, A. H.   225
Sylvester, Matthew   20, 28, 33, 77, 78, 85, 297, 298

T

Tarente, Prince of   273–440
Tarente, Princess of   268
Tatnal, Robert   62, 295
Taylor, Jeremy   327
Testard, Paul   258, 398
Thomas, Geoffrey   365
Thomas, J. M. Lloyd   20, 27, 36, 80
Thomas, Michael G.   233, 397
Thomas, Owen   246, 247, 248, 355, 357, 358, 359, 360, 361, 362, 368, 369, 373
Thomas, Roger   102, 325
Tillotson, John   42, 76, 77, 113, 315
Tomline, Bishop   362
Toon, Peter   26
Toplady, A. M.   219, 384
Torrance, J. B.   220
Toulmin, Joshua   293
Traill, Robert   411
Trueman, Carl   242, 383, 386, 387, 391
Tully   254
Turretin, Francis   352
Turretin, Jean-Alphonse   352
Tweeddale, John W.   390
Twisse, William   10, 13, 101, 247, 416, 420

U

Ursinus, Zacharias   111, 420
Ussher, James   72, 81, 241, 313

THE AUTHOR

Dr Alan Clifford (b. 1941) hails from Farnborough, Hampshire. Reared in Methodism and converted in Anglicanism (1958), he embraced Puritanism through the influence of Dr D. Martyn Lloyd-Jones (1963). A career in mechanical and electrical engineering at the Royal Aircraft Establishment and the RAF Institute of Aviation Medicine, Farnborough (1958–66) was terminated after God's call to pastoral ministry. This led to university study (University of Wales, Bangor, 1966–69) and eventual ordination to the Congregational ministry (1969). Alan has pursued pastoral ministry in Northampton, Gateshead, Great Ellingham, Norfolk and is currently Pastor of Norwich Reformed Church. He remains (since 1988) a minister-without-charge of the Presbyterian Church of Wales. Academic attainments include B.A. (philosophy) 1969; M.Litt. (philosophy of religion) 1978; Ph.D. (historical theology) 1984. An in-depth study of Arminianism and Calvinism, Dr Clifford's doctoral thesis *Atonement and Justification* was published by Oxford University Press in 1990. Author of several books, articles and papers (and a few hymns) on this and related themes (including Philip Doddridge, John Calvin & the Huguenots, and the Welsh Calvinistic Methodist preacher John Jones, Talsarn), Dr Clifford has been absorbed in Baxter studies in recent years. He is married to Marian whom he met at Bangor in 1966. They have four grown-up children—three sons and a daughter—and four granddaughters and a grandson. His interests include aviation, railways, soccer (Newcastle United) and classical music (especially Buxtehude and Hummel).

www.ingramcontent.com/pod-product-compliance
Lightning Source LLC
Chambersburg PA
CBHW022111080426
42734CB00006B/92